LIVING THE DRAMA

LIVING THE DRAMA

Community, Conflict,
and Culture
among Inner-City Boys

DAVID J. HARDING

The University of Chicago Press Chicago and London

David J. Harding is assistant professor of sociology and research assistant professor in the Population Studies Center at the University of Michigan.

The University of Chicago Press, Chicago 60637
The University of Chicago Press, Ltd., London
© 2010 by The University of Chicago
All rights reserved. Published 2010
Printed in the United States of America

20 19 18 17 16 15 14 13 12 11 10   1 2 3 4 5

ISBN-13: 978-0-226-31664-2 (cloth)
ISBN-13: 978-0-226-31665-9 (paper)
ISBN-10: 0-226-31664-5 (cloth)
ISBN-10: 0-226-31665-3 (paper)

Library of Congress Cataloging-in-Publication Data

Harding, David J., 1976–
  Living the drama : community, conflict, and culture among inner-city boys / David J. Harding.
      p.   cm.
  Includes bibliographical references and index.
  ISBN-13: 978-0-226-31664-2 (cloth : alk. paper)
  ISBN-13: 978-0-226-31665-9 (pbk. : alk. paper)
  ISBN-10: 0-226-31664-5 (cloth : alk. paper)
  ISBN-10: 0-226-31665-3 (pbk. : alk. paper)   1. Boys—Massachusetts—Boston—Social conditions—Case studies.   2. African American boys—Massachusetts—Boston—Social conditions—Case studies.   3. Hispanic American boys—Massachusetts—Boston—Social conditions—Case studies.   4. City children—Massachusetts—Boston—Social conditions—Case studies.   5. Urban youth—Massachusetts—Boston—Social conditions—Case studies. 6. Urban poor—Massachusetts—Boston—Social conditions—Case studies.   7. Sociology, Urban—Massachusetts—Boston—Case studies.   I. Title.
   HT206.H273   2010
   307.3'3640974461—dc22

                                                                                     2009022516

⊗ The paper used in this publication meets the minimum requirements of the American National Standard for Information Sciences—Permanence of Paper for Printed Library Materials, ANSI Z39.48–1992.

FOR ALL THOSE WHO LIVE THE DRAMA EVERY DAY

CONTENTS

This book is about sixty black and Latino adolescent boys and the Boston communities where they live, particularly how those communities affect their experiences, their views, and the decisions they make about schooling, work, relationships, and childbearing. Two-thirds of the boys reside in poor, inner-city neighborhoods in two areas of Boston, which I call Roxbury Crossing and Franklin. The remaining third live in the type of community that gets considerably less attention but is the implicit comparison we often have in mind when we wonder how poor communities might be different—working-class black neighborhoods (in a section of Boston known as Lower Mills). I compare the experiences of the boys in the poor neighborhoods with those in the working-class neighborhoods. The goal is to understand how their daily experiences and cultural perspectives differ across neighborhood context and to thereby uncover some of the processes by which neighborhoods affect adolescent boys. By focusing on the lives of these sixty boys, I hope to begin to answer a much broader question: what is it about poor neighborhoods that matters for the individual adolescents who grow up in them?

The role of social context in individuals' lives is an enduring sociological question. It is only a slight exaggeration to say that sociologists who study inequality and poverty have focused on poor neighborhoods and their residents for at least a century, starting with W. E. B. Du Bois's *Philadelphia Negro* and the Chicago school studies of the early- to mid-twentieth century by Park and Burgess, Shaw and McKay, and Drake and Cayton. Many of the classic studies are investigations of the social and cultural properties of disadvantaged or segregated urban communities, from William Whyte's *Street Corner Society* to Gerald Suttles's *Social Order of the Slum*, Herbert Gans's *Urban Villagers*, Lee Rainwater's *Behind Ghetto Walls*, and Ulf Hannerz's *Soulside*. Our contemporary favorites, like Elijah Anderson's *Streetwise*, Sudhir Venkatesh's *American Project*, and Mario Small's *Villa Victoria*, also delve deeply into these matters. For those who endeavor to understand the conditions and consequences of urban poverty, neighborhoods still represent critical social spaces and enduring forms of social organization, even as our postmodern world has made local communities seemingly less and less relevant to the lives of the middle class and affluent. Rather than supplanting these giants, I see this book as standing on their shoulders. In my efforts to understand the experiences of my subjects, I found myself drawing upon (and in some cases resurrecting) and reformulating the arguments of these classics, adapting them to contemporary problems and to contemporary theoretical perspectives in the discipline of sociology more broadly.

One domain in which some of these classics were particularly illuminating was the cultural context of the neighborhoods I studied. For many years, culture was something of a third rail of scholarship on urban poverty. A theoretical orientation that posed structural constraints and cultural values as competing explanations meant that invoking culture quickly led to accusations of blaming the victim. Further consideration of culture would have to wait until scholars could come to terms with both the interdependency of culture and structure and the blurring of the stark line between them. With the publication of Wilson's *The Truly Disadvantaged* and Massey and Denton's *American Apartheid*, culture was on the table again, in a form in which cultural norms followed from the experiences of structural positions and as reactions to structural constraints. Thereafter, the dominant model was one in which racial segregation and economic marginalization led to the social and cultural isolation of residents of urban neighborhoods beset by concentrated poverty. In perhaps its most well-known form, this theory suggested that a deviant subculture developed in poor, segregated neighborhoods, a culture with unique social norms and values that led many young people to school dropout, unemployment, participation in the underground economy, sexual promiscuity, and unwed parenthood.

As I began to delve into these debates in my early years of graduate school, the notion that the inner-city poor were socially and culturally isolated from something called "mainstream" (or middle-class) society did not accord with my own prior experiences as a community organizer in Boston, Jersey City, and Springfield, Massachusetts. The vast majority of the individuals in the communities where I had briefly worked seemed to be just about as committed to "mainstream" values as those living in the white middle-class communities where I had grown up. A closer reading of the urban ethnographic literature, such as Newman's *No Shame in My Game* or Anderson's *Code of the Streets*, suggested that poor neighborhoods are actually sites of intense cultural conflict rather than dominant deviant sub-

cultures. It was this hypothesis and its implications that I set out to inves-
tigate in my own research, and it was the vagueness of the "mainstream"
comparison that motivated my comparative research design. The second
half of this book is about the cultural context of poor neighborhoods and
how it affects individual adolescents like those I interviewed. By drawing
upon new theoretical concepts developed by cultural sociologists, such as
frames, scripts, and repertoires, we can develop a more accurate description of the cultural context of poor neighborhoods, one that emphasizes
the cultural heterogeneity of such neighborhoods. In doing so, we can also
better understand the social and cultural processes by which poor neighborhoods affect their adolescent residents.

As frequently happens in field research, however, my interviews quickly
uncovered something unexpected, the importance of violence and fear of
victimization, which I now believe to be a second critical aspect of life in
poor urban communities, particularly for adolescent boys. I had initially
made a conscious decision not to focus on crime and violence, as much
recent research had explained why disadvantaged neighborhoods experienced higher rates of crime and violence than more advantaged communities. I wanted to understand the lives of boys beyond the identities
as predators that so plague them in popular culture. Yet as we discussed
their social networks and daily routines, violence and strategies for avoiding victimization loomed large in the lives of the boys in the poor neighborhoods. Whether it was where to go to school and how to get there,
whom to befriend and whom to avoid, or how to interpret the behavior of
the adults they encountered, many decisions could not be made without
reference to the violence that casts a constant shadow over their lives. I
realized that while the causes of violence in poor neighborhoods were
the subject of much research, the consequences of growing up in a violent neighborhood were less well understood, particularly the social and
cultural consequences. To understand those consequences, one needed to
comprehend not just the frequency of violence but how it was socially
organized. I found that neighborhood identities and rivalries structured
much of the most serious violence and that although only a tiny fraction
of neighborhood residents generated and sustained this violence, all the
boys felt its effects. The first half of this book focuses on the social organization of violence in Boston's poor neighborhoods and the consequences
of that violence for the boys who must cope with it on a daily basis. That
violence also plays an important role in cultural heterogeneity, as it determines in part who is socializing adolescent boys and shapes the lenses
through which they interpret their everyday experiences.

I examine the roles of neighborhood violence and neighborhood cultural context in the lives of the sixty adolescent boys by focusing primarily on two domains: schooling and romantic relationships, particularly how those relationships do or do not lead to early childbearing. In doing so, this book necessarily confronts popular and scholarly conceptions of young minority males that too often emphasize irresponsibility, shortsightedness, and self-destructive decisions. Young minority males like those featured in this book play a peculiar role in our contemporary culture. The celebrity of black musicians and athletes, and to a lesser extent actors and comedians, gives young black males a prominent role in our popular culture. Their accomplishments and their communities are regularly featured in our entertainment, whether across our airwaves, on our screens, or in our sports arenas. Their heroes are the nation's heroes. Yet at the same time, cultural prominence beyond this role is limited, and the cultural lens through which the average young minority male is viewed is dominated by notions of threat and promiscuity. These two halves of our collective understanding are integrally bound together, linked by common threads of physicality and aggression. These flawed yet mutually reinforcing images provide advantage in some domains but powerful constraints in most others.

When it comes to understanding young minority males, and the poor inner-city neighborhoods where many poor minorities live, our most common images portray them either as damaged and angry predators or as individuals floating like feathers buffeted by winds produced by economic and social forces beyond their control. While their experiences and perspectives are certainly structured by the constraints of social position and social identity, I aim also to portray the boys as active decision makers navigating their own courses through both the familiar trials of adolescence and the unique challenges they face as a result of their family backgrounds, racial identities, and neighborhoods. The strategies they construct to meet these trials and challenges can have unintended and long-term implications. A critical first step in understanding high school dropout, teenage pregnancy, and other problems of urban poverty is to recognize that such problems endure, not because of the absence of high goals or intentions toward responsibility, but in spite of their presence.

ACKNOWLEDGMENTS

This book would not exist without the generosity of the sixty boys and their families who participated in this research, graciously enduring my questions and teaching me about what it is like to live in their neighborhoods. Promises of anonymity prevent me from thanking them by name, but their contributions to this volume are beyond measure. I also thank the community leaders, social workers, youth workers, and neighborhood adults who helped me prepare for my interviews with the boys and their parents by telling me about their views and experiences. While I do not quote any such leaders directly, I hope they will recognize the issues they raised in the pages that follow. Many also helped me locate boys to interview; for that I am grateful.

This research project began in the Sociology and Social Policy Program at Harvard University, where I had the privilege of working with Katherine Newman, Christopher Winship, Christopher Jencks, and Robert Sampson, all invaluable advisers. Katherine Newman was a strong mentor and advised me at every stage of this research, from the initial design to drafting the manuscript, providing guidance on matters great and small. I'm sure I'm not the first to say she is a model mentor, applying the right combination of sharp and insightful criticism, unflagging enthusiasm, and practical advice. I strive to follow her example with the students who are just now starting to knock on my office door. Chris Winship, though perhaps most well-known for his methodological expertise (from which I benefited immensely), is also a dazzlingly creative social analyst who is fluent in a wide range of perspectives and literatures. He pushed me to see the larger issues and challenges in my work. This research benefited immensely from our conversations along the way, and I continue to draw much from our current collaborations. Sandy Jencks gave me my first research assistant position at Harvard, and in working with him I came to appreciate his hard-nosed empiricism, constant skepticism, and passion for simple, clear, and elegant prose. Rob Sampson pushed me to see the connections between this project and the earlier Chicago school literature, and his insightful comments pressed me to refine and elaborate the theoretical perspectives I employ. I am indebted as well to my undergraduate mentors from Princeton, Sara McLanahan, Julien Teitler, Bruce Western, Frank Dobbin, Howard Taylor, and Walter Wallace, who introduced me to the craft of sociological research and inspired me to pursue it as a career.

I also thank my colleagues and friends from the graduate program at the Harvard Sociology Department and Kennedy School of Government, particularly Jal Mehta, Andrew Clarkwest, Cybelle Fox, Wendy Roth, Jay Gabler, and Ali Marin. Their companionship, good spirits, and intellectual and emotional support over the years sustained me during the early stages of this project.

I am grateful for funding from the National Science Foundation (SES-0326727), the William T. Grant Foundation, the American Educational Research Association/Institute of Education Sciences, the MacArthur Foundation Network on Inequality and Economic Performance, and the Harvard Multidisciplinary Program on Inequality and Social Policy, which is funded by an NSF Integrative Graduate Education and Research Traineeship grant. I wrote the first draft of this book while funded by a Eunice Kennedy Shriver National Institute of Child Health and Human Development postdoctoral fellowship at the Population Studies Center at the University of Michigan, which also provided additional support.

Katherine Newman, Christopher Winship, Robert Sampson, Christopher Jencks, Jeff Morenoff, Al Young Jr., Renee Anspach, Andrew Clarkwest, Arland Thornton, Jal Mehta, Brian Goesling, Jennifer Barber, Yu Xie, Barbara Anderson, Tony Chen, Elizabeth Bruch, Sarah Burgard, and Fred Wherry provided thoughtful comments on this research at various stages in the process. Two reviewers for the University of Chicago Press provided critical but encouraging comments on the first version of the manuscript. Claude Fischer in particular deserves much credit for going above and beyond the responsibilities of a reviewer, providing detailed comments and suggestions that helped me strengthen the writing and the arguments in this book. I also thank Bill Axinn, Jennifer Barber, Renee Anspach, Howard Kimeldorf, Barbara Anderson, Jeff Morenoff, Yu Xie, Silvia Pedraza, Arland Thornton, Pam Smock, and Mark Mizruchi for their support and guidance during my first years as an assistant professor at the University of Michigan. At two different critical junctures in this research, Michèle Lamont and Kathy Edin each provided unsolicited but encouraging comments that helped me to see the larger importance of this project.

I was blessed with the assistance of excellent students who helped me on various aspects of this project. Johnathan Smith and Stephen Rose conducted some of the interviews with the adolescent boys and their parents. Shutsu Chai assisted with community outreach in the early phases of the fieldwork, assembled data on Boston public schools and students' neighborhoods, and implemented the first coding scheme for the interview transcripts. Alix Nyberg toiled many hours on preparation and analysis of the quantitative data. Shutsu Chai, Stephen Rose, Kai Jenkins, Lauren Galarza, Aghogho Edevbie, Meaghan Cotter, Amanda Braun, and Randall Monger worked tirelessly to code the interview transcripts.

I also thank Anthony Braga of Harvard University and Carl Walter of the Boston Police Department's Boston Regional Intelligence Center for providing the incident data presented in chapter 2. N. E. Barr provided excellent editing and assisted with the maps in the appendix, as did Diego Torres. Doug Mitchell was an early and enthusiastic supporter of the book from our first meeting and expertly shepherded the book through the review and production process. His eloquent e-mails always brought a smile.

Finally and most importantly, I thank my family for their enduring support and encouragement. Hopefully in this work my mother—a social worker—will recognize her passion for social issues, and my father—a biologist—will recognize his passion for scientific inquiry. And I thank my wife, whose own work inspires and whose companionship lifts my spirits every day.

In a *Boston Globe* photo, a police officer strong-arms a young black man, bleary-eyed in the early morning light, through the open doors of a paddy wagon. The boy is dressed in an oversized white T-shirt and baggy shorts, his head is bowed, and his arms are handcuffed behind him. In the background, white police officers dressed in windbreakers and bulletproof vests mill about outside Roxbury's newly renovated Orchard Gardens public housing development.[1] The accompanying headline declares, "Raid hits '24-hour' drug ring; 15 in Roxbury arrested," and heralds a multiagency effort to crack down on gang violence in Boston's inner city. Police sources say the fifteen young men and five others arrested a few days earlier are the remnants of the once fearsome and highly organized Orchard Park Trailblazers,[2] who "terrorized Boston in the late 1980's and early 1990's." Terrified by the violence, the article reports, some Orchard Gardens residents are trying to leave the neighborhood.[3]

"Daniel," a seventeen-year-old African American Roxbury resident, normally gregarious, soberly regards the photo and accompanying story. An unemployed high school dropout and the son of a poor single mother, Daniel has never been involved in drug dealing. Nevertheless, he is troubled by the newspaper account, especially the image of the young man. As he passes the newspaper back to me across the kitchen table in his mother's third-floor apartment, he notes:

> It's kinda sad because you don't know if he has a family or not. [They are] just taking him off because he had drugs or something . . . I'm not the police or anything, or I'm not none of the people that was there. So I don't know what happened. But it looks pretty awful though . . . He could have

been a good guy. Like he could have gave the drug money to kids. You don't know what he did with the money. You don't know if they're investing it back in the community, or did they try to go get a house somewhere to try to get out of the drug game.

Only a few weeks later another story of violence hits the pages of the *Boston Globe*. White teenagers, dressed in their Sunday best, hold up their hockey sticks to form an arch as the casket of a young white man is carried out of a suburban church in Somerville. The headline proclaims, "Teen died as he lived—helping others; Sullivan fatally stabbed aiding friend in fight." Ryan Sullivan, a sixteen-year-old from an inner-ring suburb, was stabbed as he and a nineteen-year-old friend, recently released from prison, fought with two men.[4] Apparently Ryan had sacrificed himself to save his friend.

The sharp contrast between these two newspaper accounts is telling. In comparison to young men from working-class communities, inner-city black men are often viewed and portrayed as little more than social categories: drug dealers, gangsters, rappers, or athletes. Although young men like Daniel are in fact a diverse lot, the popular media often promulgates more monolithic images—and these are often accepted at face value by a public that misunderstands or fears poor black men. Young men like Daniel feel the effects of these monolithic images in their day-to-day lives. When an older person crosses the street to avoid them or a teacher assumes they are great athletes but not great scholars, they know they have been pigeon-holed. Sadly, academics often fare no better than the public at large in understanding the lives of inner-city minority males. Even the literature on teenage childbearing focuses almost exclusively on the decision making of young women (for exceptions, see Anderson 1990, 1999).[5]

This book puts the focus back on adolescents like Daniel—black and Latino boys growing up in inner-city communities beset by poverty and violence. I examine the role of neighborhoods in their lives because these community contexts matter, shaping the social resources available to them and the cultural landscapes they inhabit during the risk-filled years of adolescence. What features of disadvantaged neighborhoods have important consequences for adolescent boys, and which boys are most susceptible to these influences? How do the social and cultural characteristics of disadvantaged neighborhoods influence outcomes such as teenage pregnancy and education? What are the social processes in disadvantaged neighborhoods that create neighborhood effects? These are the key questions I address.

While sociologists have been concerned with urban residents and their neighborhoods since the birth of the discipline (e.g., Du Bois 1899; Park and Burgess 1925; Shaw 1929), scholarship on the effect of neighborhood context on individuals was reignited by William Julius Wilson's *The Truly Disadvantaged* (1987). With this work, Wilson directly linked urban sociology to socioeconomic stratification, residential mobility, and race. In theoretical terms, neighborhoods became an important context in which the social processes driving stratification and racial inequality played out, and neighborhood context became a causal force in the lives of youth and adults. In brief, Wilson argued that the decline of manufacturing employment and the movement of middle-class blacks out of the central city led to a concentration of poverty and social isolation among inner-city minorities left behind. These changes exacerbated social problems in these communities, including single-parent families, male joblessness, crime, and the underground economy, and weakened support structures and institutions—all of which negatively affected the life chances of individuals living in poor urban communities.[6]

This new focus on urban neighborhoods and spatial segregation set off a sustained effort to understand the effects of neighborhood context on fertility, health, education, labor market, and delinquency outcomes, particularly for children and adolescents. Although some disagreement remains about how and why concentrated poverty increased between 1970 and 1990, most scholars agree that it has had detrimental consequences for the residents of affected neighborhoods (see Harding 2003 for a review of and evidence on this issue). Yet social scientists have only begun to uncover the mechanisms that translate neighborhood characteristics into long-term outcomes for individual residents. The task at hand is to understand how structural conditions, such as concentrated poverty, joblessness, and residential instability, lead to social processes that are harmful or helpful to young men like Daniel.

This book argues that two features of poor neighborhoods are critical mechanisms underlying neighborhood effects on adolescent boys: *neighborhood violence* and *cultural heterogeneity*. These characteristics both distinguish poor neighborhoods from other neighborhoods and have pronounced effects on the decision making and behavior of adolescent boys. Omnipresent in the daily lives of boys growing up in poor neighborhoods, violence plays a powerful role in structuring social relations, identity and hierarchy, use of space, perceptions, and cultural frameworks. While much social science research has focused on neighborhood differences in rates of violence and other crimes, scholars have paid less attention to the social and cultural implications of living in an environment where the threat of violent victimization is significant.

The ways in which violence is socially organized (as opposed to just its frequency) is critical to understanding the effect of violence in other domains. In Boston's poor neighborhoods, much of the violence experienced and perpetrated by youth is organized by cross-neighborhood rivalries. These rivalries, which both fuel and are fueled by neighborhood identities, mean that even those youth who do not participate in violence are subject to victimization through revenge and recrimination. Local neighborhoods, very small in geographic size, become safe spaces for residents—and those venturing into other neighborhoods or neutral territories risk confrontation. The result is that the neighborhood becomes an important social space, particularly with regard to participation in organizations and same-sex friendships.

The strategies that adolescent boys use to adapt to these realities have implications for the structure and strength of peer networks. For protection and status, younger adolescents seek out the older adolescents and young men who sit atop neighborhood status hierarchies that prize the ability to navigate dangerous streets. The result is greater cross-age social interaction in poor neighborhoods, facilitating *cross-cohort socialization*. In addition, boys form strong bonds of mutual protection with friends, heightening the importance and strength of same-sex friendships. These cross-age interactions and strong peer ties provide conduits for local socialization, imparting alternative scripts (ways of achieving goals) and frames (interpretive lenses) in domains such as romantic relationships and schooling.

Neighborhood violence and crime also have direct cultural consequences. In such an environment, those who perpetrate or are the victims of violence and crime become negative role models. Comparisons to such individuals serve to level expectations among both parents and youth and focus attention on keeping boys physically safe, away from dangerous peers, and off the streets, often at the expense of attention to other domains such as school or teenage pregnancy. Youth who live in violent or crime-prone neighborhoods also have greater contact with the criminal justice system, particularly police, even if they themselves are not involved in violence or crime. These contacts, often their first sustained interaction with a major social institution, are overwhelmingly negative, leaving youth feeling disrespected and mistreated. Coupled with the failure of police and other institutions to safeguard their neighborhoods, these negative personal contacts lead youth to develop a broader institutional distrust that can spill over into their interactions with other institutions, such as schools.

For many years, the study of culture was the "third rail" of scholarship on urban poverty. To propose an explanation that invoked culture seemed to blame the poor themselves for their predicament. Yet in the last two decades, cultural concepts have inched back into debates about poverty and inequality. Today the canonical account of the cultural context of poor neighborhoods, social isolation theory, holds that socially isolated neighborhoods where residents are overwhelmingly socially disadvantaged and opportunities are few develop a separate subculture that leads to nonmainstream attitudes and behaviors that reinforce social isolation. Cut off from the rest of society and faced with bleak educational and economic prospects, individuals in such neighborhoods are thought to develop "ghetto-specific" or "oppositional" cultural norms and values that, for example, reject schooling and work and valorize early childbearing.

I will argue that this description of the cultural context of poor neighborhoods is empirically inaccurate. Instead, adolescents in poor neighborhoods experience a cultural environment in which both mainstream and alternative cultural models are present and socially supported. A focus on cultural values is unhelpful, as the urban poor value education and marriage just about as much as other Americans. Instead, the context of poor neighborhoods is better described as culturally heterogeneous, with a mix of competing and conflicting cultural frames and scripts. Indeed, poor neighborhoods are especially heterogeneous in that they encompass a wide array of lifestyles and behaviors, and—as social organization theory suggests—because residents of poor neighborhoods have less capacity to regulate public behavior. Yet local and nonlocal institutions such as churches, schools, and the media transmit mainstream cultural messages that are taken to heart in even the poorest neighborhoods. I posit that individuals in poor neighborhoods experience the negative effects of cultural heterogeneity through three processes: model shifting, dilution, and simultaneity. *Model shifting* occurs when adolescents switch among competing cultural models because alternative models are readily available and socially supported. *Dilution* occurs when information about the detailed workings of any particular cultural model is diluted by the presence of many models, leaving an adolescent without the information necessary to construct effective pathways to achieve his goals. *Simultaneity* occurs when multiple competing models are mixed unsuccessfully, resulting in ineffective strategies for accomplishing the desired ends.

I first apply the concept of cultural heterogeneity to adolescent boys' romantic and sexual behaviors. In poor neighborhoods, adolescent boys have available to them an array of frames and scripts regarding girls, relationships, and responsible fatherhood. The multiplicity of frames regarding girls and relationships, from the good girl who is focused on school and career to the "stunt" who will toss a man aside once she has had her way with him, contributes to gender distrust and establishes the standards by which boys judge the strength of their own relationships and their risks of contracting a sexually transmitted disease. In this cultural context, condom use becomes fraught with meanings relating to love and trust, influencing decisions boys make about their contraceptive use. Multiple frames regarding responsible fatherhood, from the "player" who sleeps with as many girls as possible to the responsible family man who asserts his masculinity by supporting a family and "raising his kids up right," dilute messages about what is actually involved in being a father and allow boys to switch between fatherhood frames depending on the situation.

The concept of cultural heterogeneity also helps us understand boys' educational decision making. Adolescent boys in poor neighborhoods face an array of frames and scripts regarding school and the relationship between education and career trajectories. Multiple frames make it difficult for boys to construct effective pathways for educational and career success. Boys may jump from one pathway to another, or may find that each path is obscured or diluted by competing models for future success. This heterogeneity puts boys at a significant disadvantage as they navigate educational institutions.

Though neighborhood violence and cultural heterogeneity may seem at first blush to be disconnected, they are linked as mechanisms underlying neighborhood effects. Given strong support for conventional or mainstream cultural models among residents of poor neighborhoods, we face an important question for a theory of cultural heterogeneity: What is the source of alternative, local, or "ghetto-specific" cultural models? The consequences of neighborhood violence can help us understand this question. Cross-age interactions on the street provide conduits for the transfer of alternative cultural models across cohorts, and strong friendship ties among neighborhood youth further transmit these ideas among adolescents of the same age. Because the older adolescents and young men who are available in this capacity often are not engaged in mainstream pursuits such as work, school, and long-term relationships, they represent and may espouse cultural models at odds with mainstream or middle-class models, or with other cultural models in disadvantaged neighborhoods. Especially for younger adolescents, these older adolescents introduce young people to behavioral models that the wider society views as age inappropriate. Institutional distrust and the leveling of expectations further reinforce alternative cultural models.

Though this book emphasizes the importance of both violence and cultural context for understanding the experiences and decisions of adolescent boys in inner-city neighborhoods, I am not arguing that boys in poor neighborhoods are embedded in a "culture of violence." Though media accounts of inner-city neighborhoods often portray them as places where guns are the tool of first resort for dealing with conflict and where any sign of disrespect is met with swift violent retribution, the story is more complicated than the acceptability of violence or a short-term time horizon. As chapters 2 and 3 discuss, violence in poor communities is highly socially organized, and only a tiny fraction of young men who live in poor neighborhoods engage in deadly violence.

Scope of the Problem: Neighborhood Poverty in the United States

Between 1970 and 1990, the number of high-poverty census tracts—those in which 40 percent or more of families had incomes below the poverty line—doubled, and the number of individuals living in them increased from 4.1 million to about 8 million. African Americans were particularly hard hit by these trends, with the number living in high-poverty neighborhoods increasing by 75 percent, from 2.4 million to 4.2 million.[7] By 1990 about one-third of poor African Americans lived in high-poverty neighborhoods. In addition, growth in Latino populations resulted in a 171 percent increase in the number of Latinos living in high-poverty neighborhoods during this period, from 729,000 to 2.0 million (Jargowsky 1997). In 1990 about one in five poor Latinos lived in a high-poverty neighborhood.[8]

As the economy boomed in the 1990s and unemployment declined, the total number of residents living in high-poverty neighborhoods fell significantly in both central city and rural areas.[9] However, this overall decline in concentrated poverty, documented at the height of the economic boom, has almost certainly eroded somewhat since then. Even if it has not, concentrated poverty is still more prevalent today than in 1970, and racial and ethnic minorities still bear the brunt of its burdens.[10]

Because children in the United States, particularly minority children, are disproportionately poor, young people are even more likely than adults to live in high-poverty neighborhoods. Exposure to poor neighborhoods is especially high among African American and Latino children. Estimates from children born in the mid-1990s suggest that the typical African American or Latino child living in an urban or suburban area spends approximately half of his or her childhood living in a neighborhood in which 20 percent or more of families have incomes below the poverty line. More than half of African American and Latino children are born into such neighborhoods. Black children in particular are most likely to spend a significant portion of their childhood in neighborhoods where poverty rates are even higher, above 40 percent (Timberlake 2007).

Consequences of Growing Up in a Poor Neighborhood

Young men like Daniel are significantly disadvantaged by the racial and economic segregation that generates concentrated poverty in America's urban areas. The primary purpose of this book is to identify some of the social and cultural processes in poor neighborhoods that generate neighborhood effects. Researchers have found that, net of their individual and family backgrounds, young people growing up in poor neighborhoods tend to fare worse in terms of education, health, early childbearing, and employment than their counterparts in more advantaged neighborhoods.[11] This book focuses on understanding these neighborhood effects in two areas: educational outcomes, such as high school dropout and college enrollment; and romantic and sexual behaviors, particularly those that are key for understanding early pregnancy. In these domains the consequences of growing up in a poor neighborhood are substantial. For example, adolescents growing up in high-poverty neighborhoods (those with poverty rates above 20 percent) have twice the odds of dropping out of high school and more than twice the odds of teenage pregnancy than similar adolescents in low-poverty neighborhoods (those with poverty rates below 10 percent; Harding 2003).

Estimates such as these are frequently questioned on the grounds that neighborhood differences may be overstated because of unobserved individual or family differences among adolescents growing up in various types of neighborhoods. The concern is that observed differences in adolescent outcomes between families living in high-poverty neighborhoods and those living in low-poverty neighborhoods may be due to characteristics of individuals and families rather than to neighborhoods. Even estimates that statistically control for many observed individual and family characteristics may overlook an important characteristic, resulting in an overstatement of neighborhood effects. However, evidence shows that neighborhood effects on high school dropout and teenage pregnancy are actually quite robust (Harding 2003), and that any hypothetical unobserved individual or family characteristic, controlling for those individual and family factors that we do observe, would have to be extremely powerful to reduce estimates of neighborhood effects to zero.[12] The implication is that, while neighborhood effects could be smaller than those cited above, the effects of growing up in a high-poverty neighborhood on high school dropout and teenage pregnancy are real causal effects.

Skeptics of neighborhood effects point to results from the Moving to Opportunity (MTO) housing mobility experiment as evidence of small or nonexistent neighborhood effects on individuals. MTO randomly assigned public housing residents in five cities to a control group and two treatment groups, one that received rent vouchers that had to be used in low-poverty neighborhoods and one that received unrestricted rent vouchers. The researchers examined effects of the rent vouchers both in terms of the neighborhoods into which families in the treatment groups may have moved and outcomes such as health, employment, education, and criminal behavior.[13] At the evaluation conducted five to seven years after the treatment groups received the vouchers, few differences between the treatment group and control group were detected. What differences emerged had mainly to do with mental health, stress, and safety rather than physical health, education, or economic self-sufficiency, and among boys, those in the treatment group actually seemed to be doing worse on some outcomes (Kling, Ludwig, and Katz 2005; Kling, Liebman, and Katz 2007; Sanbonmatsu et al. 2006).[14] These results—from an experiment that seemed to account for all possible individual and family factors—suggest that prior nonexperimental studies finding neighborhood effects had merely failed to measure and hold constant important characteristics.

But do the MTO results really show that neighborhood effects are small or nonexistent? Researchers did in-depth interviews with subsets of MTO participants who had moved, to better understand their experiences. The qualitative results indicated that, although women and girls benefited from the greater safety of their new neighborhoods, many families that moved had a hard time being separated from friends and family, leading many to move again, and that new neighborhoods did not necessarily lead to better schools or more job opportunities (Comey, Briggs, and Weismann 2008; Popkin, Leventhal, and Weismann 2008; Ferryman et al. 2008; Cove at al. 2008). It seems that using a rent voucher to move into a better neighborhood did not always confer all of the neighborhood's social and economic benefits, at least not to the same degree that these benefits were available to "native" families. Similar results emerged from further analyses of the interim evaluation data.[15] While MTO was perfectly designed to evaluate the policy question of whether rent vouchers (coupled with housing counseling) would improve the neighborhoods and the long-term social and economic well-being of recipients, it did not produce enough variation in neighborhood context to provide a good test of neighborhood effects.[16] As Clampet-Lundquist and Massey (2008) and Sampson (2008) have pointed out, the very social and economic processes that sort families into advantaged and disadvantaged neighborhoods may have undone the changes that the experiment was expected to produce.

Conceptualizing Neighborhood Effects

At its core, the idea underlying neighborhood effects is relatively simple: there are consequences of living in a high-poverty neighborhood where, in addition to facing the hardships of personal family poverty, residents live with and are influenced by many other families in similarly desperate straits. One Boston mother explained the challenges of raising a fifteen-year-old son in a neighborhood in which the poverty rate is close to 40 percent:

> Most of the kids have something going on with them. No one has a mother and father in the household and living a so-called normal life. There's chaos in every household around here. All the people that visit my house have some shit with them. Their mother's a junkie or they're a foster kid or they're growing up in a single-parent home.

Yet the mere physical proximity of many poor families does not by itself produce neighborhood effects. We must understand the "emergent" properties of high-poverty neighborhoods, the social and cultural conditions that result from the geographic concentration of poverty. For researchers trying to understand these properties, the analytical challenges are immense. They include (1) separating individual- and family-level effects from contextual effects (discussed above), (2) understanding the relationships between neighborhood context and other social contexts such as schools, and (3) determining which neighborhood characteristics actually shape behavior and which are merely ancillary. Up to this point, research has largely focused on determining the presence and magnitude of neighborhood effects, without examining how these effects come about. In fact, most analysts do not make a conceptual distinction between identifying the social and cultural characteristics of poor neighborhoods and gauging the effects of those characteristics on the individuals living in poor neighborhoods.

In other words, studying neighborhood effects is not the same as studying neighborhood dynamics or neighborhood organization, though the three topics are closely linked. While knowledge of neighborhood organization and dynamics is essential to understanding neighborhood effects, the effect of local context on individuals presents a distinct research problem. In studies of organization and dynamics, the unit of analysis is the neighborhood, and the focus is on understanding neighborhood-level outcomes, such as the amount of violence or crime a neighborhood experiences or how and whether the residents of a neighborhood are able to act collectively for the common good. In neighborhood effects research, the unit of analysis is the individual, and the primary goal is to understand how an individual's life might have been different had he or she grown up in a different neighborhood environment.[17] Understanding neighborhood effects requires identifying and understanding not just the neighborhood-level processes, but also how those processes are experienced by individuals and how they shape their actions.

Recent empirical research on neighborhood effects has suffered from important methodological and theoretical limitations. Many studies rely on "compositional" models of neighborhood effects (one exception is Sampson, Raudenbush, and Earls 1997), in which the social, economic, or racial composition of a neighborhood is related to a particular outcome among youth who grow up in that neighborhood, such as years of education. As Cook, Shagle, and Degirmencioglu (1997) note, these compositional measures are usually meant to proxy for some social or cultural process that is actually responsible for neighborhood effects, such as the character and availability of role models. However, without direct measures of those processes, it is impossible to draw firm conclusions about their importance. The task at hand is to move from compositional measures to models that explicitly consider the social and cultural processes that emerge as a result of concentrated poverty. Understanding why youth from disadvantaged neighborhoods fare worse than their counterparts in more advantaged neighborhoods requires understanding how the social and cultural processes of daily life differ across neighborhoods.

A second important limitation is the failure to consider heterogeneity within neighborhoods.[18] In other words, most studies implicitly posit a single average neighborhood effect and ignore differences among individuals in their experiences in the same or similar neighborhoods. The classic ethnographies tell us that multiple forms of social organization exist within any single community, whether they be Whyte's corner boys and college boys (1943), Gans's sex- and age-differentiated peer groups (1962),

Suttles's ordered segmentation (1968), or Hannerz's lifestyle groups (1969). This was true before fair housing encouraged desegregation—leading to middle-class out-migration—and it remains true today.

Census data tell us that poor neighborhoods are diverse. In 1990, when concentrated poverty was near its peak in the United States, the average neighborhood in which the poverty rate was 40 percent or higher was one in which 46 percent of men and 36 percent of women were employed, 15 percent of workers were managers or professionals, 63 percent of households received some income from work, 43 percent of families were headed by men, 48 percent of those twenty-five and older had graduated from high school, and 12 percent of individuals age twenty-five and older had at least an associate's degree (Jargowsky 1997). Clearly, even residents in the highest-poverty neighborhoods are not 100 percent poor, and poor neighborhoods are not dominated by ways of life that are entirely divorced from mainstream society (Newman 1999).[19]

Theories that posit a relationship between the structural or compositional characteristics of neighborhoods and adolescent behavior should be able to account for the fact that many if not most adolescents in disadvantaged neighborhoods avoid negative outcomes such as high school dropout and teenage pregnancy. And certainly any investigation of the social processes in disadvantaged neighborhoods must provide an explanation of why adolescents in the same neighborhood experience those processes differently. The heterogeneity of poor neighborhoods means that a purely structural approach cannot suffice—it does not predict the variation in outcomes that we observe. Individual agency and culture matter.

Research Methodology

Qualitative studies of neighborhood effects often fail to compare neighborhoods that differ in the characteristic of interest. For example, a study that examines social processes in high-poverty neighborhoods cannot tell us what is unique about high-poverty neighborhoods without including more affluent neighborhoods for comparison. This problem can be partly overcome by in-depth knowledge acquired through qualitative research, which allows the researcher to see how the structural characteristics of the neighborhood affect individual lives, but the results would be far more convincing with cross-neighborhood comparisons. Thus the central challenge for qualitative research on neighborhood social processes is to create a research design that yields in-depth data on the experiences of similar residents in different types of neighborhoods. The research in this book does so by including adolescents from neighborhoods with both high and low poverty rates.

This study is based primarily on in-depth, unstructured interviews with sixty adolescent boys, ages thirteen to eighteen, living in three predominantly black areas in Boston, with twenty boys per area. The appendix provides a more detailed description of the fieldwork and analysis, including subject and neighborhood characteristics, subject recruitment, interview content, data interpretation and cross-checking, analysis procedures, and challenges in conducting fieldwork with this population, including issues of race and social distance. It also includes neighborhood maps and census data for the three study areas.

The teenage boys in this study were African American, Latino, or of mixed race, with Latinos being primarily of Puerto Rican or Dominican descent. Each boy was interviewed multiple times, with at least two and as many as four sessions per subject. Multiple interview sessions were required to cover all the material in detail, but they also provided the benefit of repeated interactions with the subjects, which can serve to build trust and rapport (Eder and Fingerson 2003). These interviews are supplemented by interviews with the boys' parents and with other neighborhood adults, community leaders, local officials, and social service workers. The parent interviews provided a caretaker's perspective on a boy's experiences and a check on the accounts offered by the adolescent boys. Each interview session lasted from sixty to ninety minutes. Prior to the interviews with the boys and their caretakers, I interviewed fifty community leaders, ministers, youth workers, social workers, and school officials who were knowledgeable about the study neighborhoods or about youth issues in the Boston area. These "neighborhood informant" interviews provided background information on and entrée into the fieldwork neighborhoods, as well as an additional check on the boys' accounts and descriptions of their neighborhoods. In addition, many neighborhood informants assisted with recruiting the participating boys and their parents.

The three geographic areas I selected allow for explicit comparisons among similar youth in areas that vary on a key structural characteristic: the family poverty rate. Two of the areas (Roxbury Crossing and Franklin) have high rates of family poverty (between 35 and 40 percent in the 2000 census). The third (Lower Mills) has a low poverty rate (below 10 percent).[20] Each area consists of two contiguous census tracts. As I have defined them, Roxbury Crossing, Franklin, and Lower Mills are geographic areas of the city rather than social neighborhoods. Each area encompasses multiple locales that more closely approximate neighborhoods, as recognized by local residents. Although the neighborhoods within each area share broadly parallel histories, demographic and structural characteristics, and relations to the larger Boston metropolitan area, when the boys and their parents describe their neighborhoods, they are referring to much smaller spaces, often only a few blocks in any direction (see chapter 4). The terms "Roxbury Crossing," "Franklin," and "Lower Mills" serve as shorthand to delineate the three comparison study areas and to provide anonymity for the research subjects by broadening the geographic scope of reference.

Because of the need to work in multiple neighborhoods, I conducted "surgical" fieldwork—that is, focused on particular theoretical questions. Hence this study is not a neighborhood ethnography in the tradition of Hannerz (1969), Gans (1962), and Suttles (1968). Rather, my fieldwork was designed to generate theoretically motivated comparisons across neighborhoods, comparisons that will illuminate the pathways that lead some boys to negative outcomes and some to positive outcomes with regard to schooling and romantic and sexual behavior.

My interviews with the boys explored the scripts, frames, and knowledge that adolescent boys employ when they think about sex, relationships, pregnancy, education, and work, and how these understandings relate to their neighborhood context, peer networks, and perceptions of opportunity structures. Only by engaging in conversations, interacting, and observing was I able to gain insights into how boys like Daniel see their world, process and employ cultural symbols, and make decisions. We spent most of our time together talking about three general topics. First, we discussed the relationship between the young man's geographic neighborhood and "social" neighborhood, including peer networks, use of neighborhood and nonneighborhood institutions and organizations, time use, and nuclear and extended family. Second, we explored the young man's experience with school and work, including plans for the future. Third, we talked about the young man's experience with girls, romantic and sexual relationships, contraception, and fatherhood, including plans for the future and views of marriage and child rearing. I also talked extensively with an adult—usually the mother—in most boys' families. Here we focused on developing a brief life history, talked about the neighborhood, discussed parenting attitudes and strategies, and explored the boy's educational, work, and relationship experiences as well as his prospects for the future in those domains.

It was especially important to compare boys from similar family backgrounds across the different areas. I selected subjects to achieve an economically diverse group of boys in each area. In the low-poverty area, this meant taking particular care to locate youth from more disadvantaged family backgrounds. In the high-poverty areas, this meant identifying youth from more advantaged family backgrounds. While the mean characteristics of the boys in the three areas are not identical, there is sufficient overlap in the boys' background characteristics across areas to allow for individual-level comparisons of similar boys in low-poverty and high-poverty areas. In addition, I wanted to include boys of diverse ages, interests, and behaviors. Age was important because I wanted to capture perceptions and understandings both before and after key decisions are made or outcomes are realized. Adolescence is a period in which the brain is developing, social identities and interests are forming, and behaviors are changing. Including subjects with diverse interests and behaviors was important to investigating the full range of experiences in the neighborhood. Too often, neighborhood studies focus on individuals with the greatest influence or on adolescents with the most severe problems.

I used a variety of procedures to recruit the teenage boys who participated in this study. First, subjects were recruited through the social networks of the neighborhood informants. Since this was a diverse group, ranging from ministers to street workers to ex-convicts, the young people recruited in this way were also a diverse group. Second, I posted flyers around the neighborhoods, which also generated a diverse set of subjects. It was primarily parents and other guardians who responded to these flyers, but they varied considerably. On one extreme were parents who regularly grabbed any opportunity for their son and saw the chance to talk to a university researcher as yet another potentially positive experience. On the other extreme were parents at the end of their wits in trying to control their son's behavior and who were hoping the interview experience would serve as a positive shock. Third, a few youth were recruited via meetings on the street. Finally, I also recruited subjects through snowball sampling—tapping the friends of other subjects. Neighborhood informants were recruited through letters to heads of key institutions and organizations and through meetings at community events.

All research methodologies have strengths and weaknesses. Compared to quantitative studies, which usually rely on representative survey data and allow for statistical control of competing influences, qualitative studies such as this one provide greater depth of information on a smaller number of subjects. They are better at uncovering individuals' perceptions and cultural frameworks and at capturing the details of social processes as they unfold. As such, qualitative studies can provide the data required to study the mechanisms, both social and cultural, that link neighborhood environments to individual outcomes, particularly when those mechanisms are not known in advance. But they cannot answer questions about how individual and neighborhood characteristics relate to one another in the wider population. For that we need nationally representative survey data with a large number of cases. For this reason, this book also draws upon my statistical analyses of survey data from the National Longitudinal Study of Adolescent Health (Add Health), which followed thousands of children from adolescence to young adulthood and contains information on their neighborhoods, schools, and families, as well as their frames, scripts, goals, and outcomes in a number of domains. The details of these statistical analyses are in previously published academic journal articles and research reports that are referenced throughout this volume. Interested readers can consult these papers for further information.

Finally, given Boston's history of racial strife, it is important to understand how race did—and did not—play a role in this research. Race and ethnicity were far more salient in the parent interviews than in the interviews with the adolescent boys. Black parents discussed, and lamented, racial changes in the neighborhood as Latinos moved into Boston's public housing, and Latino parents often blamed blacks for violence and other neighborhood problems. Some black parents also expressed considerable distrust of whites—particularly the working-class whites associated with South Boston and past racial conflicts over school integration—and white-controlled institutions such as city hall and the police. Notable in this study, and as has been reported elsewhere (e.g., Carter 2005), race was far less salient to adolescents. Many reported having friends of other racial or ethnic groups, and because large-scale Latino immigration is relatively new in Boston, there is less history of conflict between black and Latino gangs than in other cities such as Chicago and Los Angeles.[21] Boston is a relatively small city, and racial isolation is less severe. In contrast to what one might expect from neighborhoods on the South Side of Chicago, for example, most residents of the study areas regularly see whites in their neighborhoods and interact with whites in stores, schools, or other institutional settings. Other than the challenges in overcoming the "social distance" between myself and the subjects (see the appendix), I experienced no racial hostility. I may have been helped in this regard by my affiliation with Harvard University, which has a positive reputation in many of Boston's poor communities as a result of community service projects (summer camps, after-school programs, mentoring programs) that Harvard undergraduates run with university and community support.[22]

Because this study compares neighborhoods of different socioeconomic status but of similar racial/ethnic and immigrant composition (all three areas studied are majority black), features of neighborhoods that may vary by ethnicity or immigrant composition cannot be investigated. The study design certainly does not imply a belief that race is unimportant for understanding neighborhood poverty. A long line of research documents the importance of race, discrimination, and racialized institutions in the creation and perpetuation of racially segregated, concentrated poverty neighborhoods (e.g., Massey and Denton 1993). Indeed, few whites experience the levels of neighborhood poverty experienced by African Americans, and to a lesser extent by Latinos, in the United States (Sampson and Wilson 1995; Jargowsky 1997). In Boston in 2000, for example, there were no majority white census tracts with poverty rates anywhere near as high as those of Franklin and Roxbury Crossing, making it impossible for me to compare high-poverty white and black neighborhoods.

The decision to focus on three majority African American neighborhoods also means that the sample of boys from these neighborhoods is largely African American with some Latinos or mixed-race boys included. As a result, the sample lacks the racial/ethnic variation needed to profitably conduct comparisons across groups, and I do not attempt to do so. However, I do not wish to convey that race is unimportant for understanding the lives of the boys who participated in this study. As will become clear in later chapters, the racial landscape in Boston—and in the United States more broadly—informs their understandings of teachers, police, social workers, and others they come into contact with regularly. However, because most have yet to enter the labor market or integrated institutions of higher education, their perceptions of opportunity are largely unstructured by race. As Young (2004) describes, those least exposed to white-dominated institutions can be the most optimistic about equal opportunity.

Living the Drama

A secondary intent of this book is to shed more light on the lives of African American and Latino adolescent boys growing up in the inner city. Often misunderstood by the general public and academics alike, this group is at highest risk for incarceration, poor schooling, victimization by violence, low wages, and high unemployment as they mature into adulthood. In 1999—near the peak of the last economic boom—23 percent of all African American men and 13 percent of Latino men age sixteen to twenty-four were idle (neither enrolled in school nor employed), compared to 9 percent for young white men (Edelman, Holzer, and Offner 2005). When incarcerated individuals are included in these estimates, the proportion that is idle increases to 29 percent for African Americans and 15 percent for Latinos, compared to 10 percent for whites. Today, at any given time, about one-third of all young African American men are under the supervision of the criminal justice system, with about one-third of these in prison or jail and the rest on probation or parole (Edelman, Holzer, and Offner 2005). These problems are undoubtedly even more severe in urban neighborhoods beset by poverty. Young men from poor neighborhoods are at greater risk than any other demographic group for unemployment, low education, and involvement in violence and crime. However, these figures tell only part of their story. By presenting their perspectives and experiences in this book, I hope to shed light on the sources of these problems and ways to bring these young men closer to full participation in American society.

The title of this book, *Living the Drama*, derives from the way residents of Boston's poor neighborhoods often talk about violence, particularly those episodes of violence and confrontation that result from long-standing neighborhood rivalries. When groups of boys from rival neighborhoods begin feuding, residents say these boys "have drama." At stake, at least for the boys who are involved, is respect, status, and protection of their home turf. For other neighborhood residents, these feuds "bring drama," including the potential for violent victimization. This kind of conflict, coupled with other forms of violence and crime that are endemic to many high-poverty areas, has subtle but detrimental consequences for everyone in the afflicted neighborhoods. Moreover, it is especially damaging for young people because of the way it influences schooling and fertility. Using nationally representative survey data, I find that among boys in high-poverty areas, neighborhood violence explains about one-fifth of the neighborhood effect on teenage pregnancy and almost half of the neighborhood effect on high school dropout (Harding 2009a). The chapters that follow help us understand these effects by highlighting the consequences of violence for neighborhood identity, for the structure and strength of peer networks, for socialization of adolescent boys, for the calibration of expectations, and for trust in our society's basic institutions. While social scientists frequently study the causes of violence in poor neighborhoods, the social and cultural *consequences* of violence have received little attention. These social and cultural consequences cause "the drama" to have spillover effects in other domains.

Here "drama" also has a second meaning, as it evokes my arguments about neighborhood cultural context. As explained above, this work is not built upon Wilson's social isolation theory, which emphasizes the mainstream isolation and negative normative values of poor neighborhoods. Rather, it proposes an alternative framework for understanding the cultural context of poor neighborhoods: cultural heterogeneity. I posit that competing and conflicting cultural models—some that are mainstream or middle-class, and others that are locally developed alternatives—characterize the social life of poor neighborhoods. In the chapters that follow, I document some of the dimensions along which poor neighborhoods are culturally heterogeneous. I look especially at the conflict and contestation that surround sexual behavior, romantic relationships, work, and schooling. Adolescents growing up in poor neighborhoods must contend with a cultural environment in which there is an abundance of drama.

In making these arguments I rely heavily on illustrations from the experiences and perspectives of the adolescent boys who so generously participated in this study. In presenting this material in book form for public consumption, I have endeavored to portray my subjects neither as heroes who summon strength in the face of unbelievable adversity nor as victims of structural forces beyond their control, though at times they are both. In the pages that follow, the reader will encounter examples of behavior both deplorable and commendable, of decisions both foolish and wise beyond the teenage years, and of observations both juvenile and remarkably acute. These include sexist comments, violent behavior, emotionally abusive relationships, and greed, but also valiant attempts at responsible fatherhood, incredible turnarounds, generosity, and bravery. Too often, social scientists portray young men from disadvantaged backgrounds as feathers blowing in the strong winds created by social forces far beyond their control—racism, poverty, violence—and too often popular media portray them as violent predators damaged beyond repair. Such accounts, either oversocialized or overindividualized, do little to help us understand the decisions that lead them to success or failure. I approached the writing of this book believing that, to learn from their participation in this study, we must take them seriously as individuals with human agency, but at the same time we must endeavor to understand the social, economic, and cultural constraints that limit that agency. To whitewash or sanitize their experiences out of fear of stigmatization will merely blind us to the realities that they face. These are the realities that we as responsible adults need to know about and address if we want to support and protect our most vulnerable young people. I ask the reader to keep in mind that no matter what they say or do, these boys are essentially children, and as might any individuals confronted by horrible circumstances, they sometimes do horrible things—and other times are astounding in their poise and bravery.

There are those who would say that a well-educated white male from a middle-class background cannot hope to understand, much less convey, the experiences and perspectives of African American and Latino boys growing up the inner city. I am sensitive to such issues of social distance and include in the appendix a discussion of them as they relate to the collection of data in in-depth interviews. And I recognize that in some sense no person can fully understand and convey the experiences of another. However, I reject the notion that racial and class identities are inherently impenetrable barriers to honest and insightful communication and true human connection. I also reject the corollary of such an argument that qualitative research on poverty, race, and inequality must be left to only certain social scientists. Indeed, if we are ever to move toward solutions to these problems, we must all be willing to engage with them. In the end, readers must judge for themselves whether the arguments and accounts in the pages that follow ring true and are compelling. I ask only that judgment be reserved until the data and arguments are presented.

Fieldwork Neighborhoods

Roxbury Crossing

"Roxbury Crossing" is a high-poverty area located on the border of the gentrifying South End and the traditionally black district of Roxbury.[23] It is a study in contrasts and transitions. Along Washington Street, gleaming bus shelters with digital kiosks for the new Silver Line bus rapid transit system reside in the shadows of deteriorating buildings with shabby and barren-looking storefronts. Yet Roxbury Crossing is only blocks from renovated South End brownstones and some of the city's most chic restaurants. Newly renovated Northeastern University buildings are visible from "the bricks," the local public housing developments that have seen only minor updates since their construction in the 1940s and early 1950s. Camfield Estates, a recently rebuilt affordable housing complex of townhouse-style units with neatly manicured lawns, sits across the street from the Lenox/Camden public housing development, a cluster of 376 three-story walk-ups built in 1939 and 1949 and surrounded by glass-strewn parking lots, cracked sidewalks, and bare dirt. When I was conducting my interviews, the grounds at Lenox/Camden were undergoing a much-needed renovation, and a few enterprising residents tended a community garden that produced flowers and vegetables.

Roxbury Crossing is home to a unique blend of public, private, and cooperative housing.[24] The Whittier Street public housing development, constructed in 1953, is a cluster of medium-rise brick buildings set in a no-man's land between a busy four-lane thoroughfare and the grounds of two public high schools. After especially heavy rains a putrid marsh appears around the development's cheery blue and gold Boston Housing Authority sign. The area in the center of the buildings, once a playground, is now a patch of dirt and concrete, all that remains of a renovation stopped midstream when funds dried up. Inside are overheated apartments with cinder-block walls and noisy, smelly stairwells. Roxbury Crossing is very unusual in its high concentration of tenant-run cooperative affordable housing. During the 1990s, with backing from the U.S. Department of Housing and Urban Development (HUD) and state and city housing agencies, tenant groups won control of the large private housing developments in the area, renovated them, and now manage them as affordable housing under tenant management and ownership.[25]

Roxbury Crossing is relatively well-served institutionally in comparison to Franklin, the other high-poverty area I studied. Public transportation is available at three Orange Line subway stops and at the Dudley Square bus terminal for MBTA (Massachusetts Bay Transportation Authority) buses. Nearby are several important city and state institutions, including the Boston Police Headquarters, Northeastern University, the Boston University Medical Center Hospitals, the Reggie Lewis Track and Field Center, and Roxbury Community College. Two public high schools (Madison Park Technical Vocational High School and O'Bryant High School of Mathematics and Science, an "exam" or magnet school) sit on a common campus on the south side of the area. Jim Rice Field and portions of Southwest Corridor Park provide green space for the community. Neighborhood health services include the Whittier Street Health Center as well as nearby hospitals, some of which are among the finest in the nation. Finally, the Dudley Square commercial district is an important center for black commerce in Boston. Still blighted by a few vacant buildings and boarded-up storefronts, it is nevertheless undergoing revitalization and is home to important social services such as the Roxbury Boys and Girls Club and Youth Opportunity Boston, a city-run agency that primarily serves youth involved in the criminal justice system. The Roxbury YMCA is also nearby.

Like the rest of Boston, Roxbury Crossing has undergone considerable demographic change in the last decade. The once overwhelmingly black neighborhood now has a large population of Latinos, particularly in the two public housing developments where, between 1993 and 2003, the resident composition shifted from majority black to majority Latino.[26] These rapid changes, coupled with language barriers, have resulted in racial

tensions among residents that have dampened involvement in tenant organizing and community activities. Community activists see their neighborhoods as jeopardized both from gentrification, which threatens to dis-
place residents from what is now highly valuable land near the center of a
growing city, and from the violence and drugs that threaten to reverse the
recent revitalization efforts.

Lower Mills

The "Lower Mills" area of Dorchester is just north of the Boston border
with Milton, a mostly white working- and middle-class suburb.[27] Homes
in Lower Mills tend to be small single-family and two-family dwellings,
with comparatively few of the more traditional Boston triple-deckers.
The streets are wider and yards larger than in much of Dorchester. To the
north of Lower Mills is Ashmont Hill, a mixed-race middle-class neighborhood known for its concentration of gay residents and its majestically re-
stored Victorian houses. Dorchester High School and the Dorchester YMCA
are also located just to the north. Were it not for the vintage of some of
the housing, one might easily mistake Lower Mills for any lower-middle-
class American suburb, with leafy, quiet streets and well-tended lawns.
Yet one does not have to go far before the landscape changes drastically.
Much poorer sections of Dorchester are to the north and in Mattapan to
the west.

The Ashmont MBTA subway stop on the Red Line serves the Lower Mills
area, as do a series of trolley stops on the line that runs between Ashmont
and Mattapan Square. Carney Hospital is located here, and Dorchester Avenue ("Dot Ave" in the local parlance) and Washington Street are the main
commercial streets. There are only a few churches in Lower Mills, the most
prominent of which is St. Gregory's, a Catholic church that supports a K–8
school. Lower Mills is also home to much open and green space, including
Dorchester Park and Walsh Park. Today, the area of Lower Mills to the west
of Dorchester Avenue is majority black, and middle-class African Americans and West Indians have begun to move east across Dorchester Avenue.[28] Though today it is considered a racially integrated neighborhood,
Lower Mills is largely split into two parts, the black Lower Mills to the west
of Dorchester Avenue and the mostly white Lower Mills to the east.

Demographic changes created strains on St. Gregory's parish, a long-
standing institutional hub of Lower Mills, and led to a weakening of the
community's institutions. As the white Catholic population was gradually replaced by non-Catholics, participation in church activities declined.

St. Gregory's was forced to close its all-girls high school and to reduce its programs and services, once central to the community, when the new mostly non-Catholic residents did not step in to run them. Current residents, who decry the lack of community institutions and youth programs, often rely on social support organizations in other parts of the city.

Despite these changes in Lower Mills, the community's vitality has been maintained through the economic and cultural resources of its large working- and middle-class population. A civic association was active until recently, and a business group seems to be gaining momentum. The former Baker Chocolate Factory, located in the southernmost corner and near the banks of the Neponset River, is being renovated into condominiums and artist lofts. A new supermarket has opened within the last year, and the commercial strips along Washington Street and Dorchester Avenue remain lively and well-kept, populated by bank branches and a mix of chain restaurants and local shops selling ice-cream, hardware, and reasonably priced haircuts.

Franklin

The high-poverty "Franklin" area is in the southwest corner of Dorchester on the Mattapan border. The geographic center of this area is the large open space that includes Franklin Field and Harambee Park. To the west is Franklin Park, home of the much-maligned Franklin Park Zoo and a buffer between Dorchester and the white parts of Jamaica Plain. Unlike Roxbury Crossing, Franklin is surrounded by other disadvantaged neighborhoods. Poor areas in Dorchester are to the east and in Roxbury to the north. Mattapan is to the south, where poverty rates are somewhat lower at 15–25 percent. Franklin has many signs of disorder and blight: trash-filled lots, boarded-up houses, abandoned cars, and dirty streets. Cars are double- and triple-parked along the main commercial street, Blue Hill Avenue; young men loiter outside the local pizza joint and small grocery store at the corner of Blue Hill and Talbot Avenue. Many small businesses line Blue Hill Avenue, and the residential areas are also dotted with small car repair and auto body shops, take-outs, and bodegas.

Construction on what would eventually become the Franklin Field housing development began in the late 1940s in the form of temporary housing for veterans, and was completed in 1954.[29] Today the Franklin Field housing development is a wide swath of low-rise brick buildings connected by winding streets and pedestrian pathways. The Franklin Hill housing development, located on the other side of Blue Hill Avenue and adjacent to Frederick Olmsted's Franklin Park, was completed in 1951 (Vale 2002; Gamm 1999). Franklin Hill's age is abundantly clear from the rusting clothesline poles, relics of a previous era, that still occupy some parts of its main courtyard. Additional public housing for the elderly was constructed in Franklin Field in 1962 and 1964, but the Franklin Hill housing development has never had a major renovation. The Boston Housing Authority, which attempted to secure funding for redevelopment from HUD under the HOPE VI program in 2004, was unsuccessful in its bid.[30]

Between 1969 and 1971, the residential composition of Franklin Field changed rapidly from about 65 percent white to 90 percent black. New tenant families were more likely to be headed by a single parent and more likely to rely on welfare. It was also at this point that the commercial district along this portion of Blue Hill Avenue began to deteriorate, and many empty storefronts remain to this day. During the 1970s, neighborhood decline continued, and the two public housing developments became increasingly isolated from their neighbors. Conflicts between youths from the two developments were first reported in the late 1970s. The community was hit hard during the late 1980s and 1990s by violence spurred by the crack cocaine epidemic. The Franklin area, particularly its two public housing developments, became synonymous in the public mind with drug dealing and deadly violence (Vale 2002). A lengthy and contentious renovation of Franklin Field, completed in 1987, failed to significantly improve the lives of its residents (Vale 2002). And though a combined police and community effort reduced youth violence considerably during the 1990s, the area remains on the Boston police list of the city's worst "hot spots" for violence. Residents complain that they still cannot convince fearful relatives from outside the neighborhood to visit them at their homes.

Today, Franklin is an area on the margins and in transition. Since the late 1960s, when the population began to shift from predominantly white to predominantly black, community cohesiveness and identity has declined. Emblematically, this area lacks even a neighborhood name—the term "Franklin" is my own. Unlike most other parts of the city, Franklin does not have a strong community development corporation (CDC) to advocate on its behalf, though the Lena Park CDC is now reemerging after a long decline. The area also lacks large churches with an institutional history in the area. In the last few years, the Greater Love Tabernacle Church of God in Christ and the Faith Pentecostal Church moved to the area, but, like most large Boston churches, these churches draw their membership from all over the city. The larger African American churches are mostly to the south in Mattapan or to the north in Roxbury. The Franklin area is also somewhat geographically isolated. The old streetcar line that once ran down Blue Hill Avenue is long gone, and now the only public transportation is the bus, by which it is at least a twenty-minute ride to any subway station. Franklin's dynamic state is evident in the demographic changes that are occurring, driven by larger changes throughout the city of Boston, particularly increases in immigrant populations. Haitians and West Indians are moving to the area from Mattapan, and Latinos are moving in from other parts of Dorchester and Roxbury.[31]

Despite its problems, the Franklin area is not devoid of local institutions and services. Just to the south is the Mattapan-Dorchester District B3 police station, constructed within the last ten years. Health services are available at the Harvard Street Neighborhood Health Center or nearby Codman Square Neighborhood Health Center. The area is also home to the Perkins Community Center at the Lee School and the Blue Hill Avenue Clubhouse of the Boys and Girls Clubs of Boston (located on Talbot Avenue near Blue Hill Avenue), both of which have a number of recreational, educational, and cultural programs for adults and children. In addition, the area has smaller programs targeting youth, such as the Urban Dreams program that runs summer and after-school activities for youth and job readiness and GED programs for older youth and adults, and Project FREE (Franklin Residents Efforts for Equality), a collaboration between Franklin Hill and Franklin Field residents run in cooperation with the Committee for Boston Public Housing. Unfortunately, the youth centers supported by each housing development were closed after the Boston Housing Authority cut funding for teen centers across the city in 2002. (Through Herculean efforts by a small handful of neighborhood volunteers, the Franklin Hill center managed to stay open for a few more years.)

Outline of the Book

Chapters 2 through 4 focus on the social organization of violence in Boston neighborhoods and the consequences of neighborhood violence and crime for adolescents. In chapter 2 I describe the social organization of violence in Boston's poor communities, especially the role of cross-neighborhood rivalries, the ways in which neighborhood is a form of social identity, and the ways violence structures adolescent boys' safety and their use of space in the city. I argue that neighborhood violence serves to level expectations among both youth and parents and focuses attention on safety at the expense of other concerns.

Chapter 3 explores the consequences of violence for boys' peer networks. The strategies that boys use to provide some measure of safety for themselves in violent neighborhoods, coupled with the ways in which violence alters local adolescent status hierarchies, leads to greater cross-age interactions in poor neighborhoods and strong bonds based on mutual protection. Adolescent boys in these neighborhoods are often socialized by older peers on the street—cross-cohort socialization—and tend to develop strong loyalties to neighborhood friends. They are also exposed to cultural models from which their more age-segregated peers in safer neighborhoods remain relatively insulated.

Chapter 4 widens the lens to assess other aspects of the social world of adolescent boys, particularly those that relate to social ties to others in the neighborhood. Virtually all investigations of neighborhood effects assume that place of residence is a significant determinant of the development of social networks, but this assumption has never been examined empirically among adolescents. This chapter examines boys' conceptions of neighborhood boundaries and the role of neighborhoods, neighborhood violence, and parenting practices in structuring connections to same-sex friends, girlfriends and other sexual partners, nonfamily adults, and organizations and institutions. Understanding the relationship between neighborhoods and social networks is critical to understanding which adolescents are likely to be affected by their neighborhoods and which are not.

Chapters 5 through 7 focus on the cultural context of disadvantaged neighborhoods. Chapter 5 provides a primarily theoretical discussion of past scholarship on culture, poverty, and neighborhoods and introduces cultural heterogeneity and its consequences. Chapters 6 and 7 use cultural heterogeneity as a lens to understand decision making and behavior in two domains: romantic and sexual behavior (chapter 6) and schooling (chapter 7). These chapters describe some of the ways in which poor neighborhoods are culturally heterogeneous and connect this heterogeneity to the boys' behavior and decision making.

Chapter 8 concludes by tying together the arguments in this volume and proposing a model of neighborhood effects on adolescents that includes both structural and cultural elements, as well as a role for individual agency. It also discusses the policy implications of my findings.

CHAPTER TWO THE SOCIAL ORGANIZATION OF VIOLENCE IN POOR NEIGHBORHOODS

Around 9:30 p.m. on June 18, 2003, eighteen-year-old Mikeal Harris was shot in the back of the head three times from close range. Police found his body the next morning in the third-floor hallway of one of the low-rise apartment buildings of the Franklin Hill housing development in Dorchester. Mikeal had lived with his mother and brothers in Franklin Hill until the age of ten, and lived on nearby Talbot Avenue at the time of his murder. He was known to visit friends frequently in the public housing development.[1] Two years later, his murder remains unsolved, apparently lost in a torrent of shootings, stabbings, and fistfights that plagued Boston's poor neighborhoods that summer. Elsewhere such a horrible event would be the focus of community and law enforcement attention for some time, but in a neighborhood in which there were at least four other shootings within a few weeks of Mikeal's death, his shooting was remarkable only for its relative brutality.

Murders like Mikeal's don't happen everywhere. Violence of this kind is one of the most spatially patterned social phenomena, concentrated in the nation's poorest neighborhoods. In Boston, two of eleven police districts accounted for half of all homicides, 40 percent of all nonfatal shootings, and 40 percent of all firearm seizures during a fourteen-month period in 2003 and 2004.[2] It should come as no surprise that these two districts, C11 (covering part of Dorchester) and B3 (covering Mattapan and part of Dorchester), encompass some of the city's poorest neighborhoods (including Franklin), but they also contain upper-middle-class enclaves and working-class sections of the city (including Lower Mills). Within these districts, however, violence is concentrated in what police call "hot spots."

TABLE 2.1. Violent crime counts and rates per 1,000 residents by study area and for City of Boston as a whole

	Franklin		Roxbury Crossing		Lower Mills		City of Boston	
	2003	2004	2003	2004	2003	2004	2003	2004
Homicide	4	8	1	0	0	3	39	61
	0.34	0.67	0.16			0.31	0.07	0.10
Robbery	76	68	48	46	26	23	2759	2433
	6.39	5.71	7.78	7.46	2.72	2.40	4.68	4.13
Aggravated	171	157	83	90	58	44	4113	4151
assault	14.37	13.19	13.46	14.60	6.06	4.60	6.98	7.05

SOURCE: Author's calculations from incident data provided by Boston Police Department.
NOTE: Denominator for rates is 2000 census total population.

In a city the size of Boston, even over a distance as small as a few blocks, the character of a neighborhood can change drastically.

The most striking difference between the two poor areas in which I conducted fieldwork, Roxbury Crossing and Franklin, and the relatively advantaged area of Lower Mills is the sheer frequency of violence.[3] Table 2.1 shows violent crime rates and counts for the three study areas and for Boston as a whole for the two years in which I conducted fieldwork. Because they are rare events, homicides provide indications of only the most severe violence. By this measure, Franklin is the most violent of the three study areas. Though it contains only 2 percent of the city's population, Franklin accounts for over 10 percent of the city's homicides in both years.[4] Rates of robbery and aggravated assault, much more frequent events, illustrate the distinction between Roxbury Crossing and Franklin, the two high-poverty areas, and Lower Mills, the low-poverty area. By both measures, Roxbury Crossing and Franklin have much higher rates of violence than Lower Mills or the city as a whole.

For the boys living in Roxbury Crossing and Franklin, violence is an almost constant presence, and the threat of victimization or physical confrontation casts a permanent shadow. Shots echo frequently, though mostly at night; confrontations are common, and the ability to fight is a valuable skill (see also Anderson 1999). On a regular basis a young person, usually a male, is shot. In contrast, for the boys of Lower Mills, violence and fighting occur, but they are not a regular fixture of neighborhood life and rarely rise to the level of murder.

Neighborhood differences in fear of victimization and violence are also evident in nationally representative data. Add Health (Harris et al. 2003)

asked adolescents age twelve to eighteen during the 1994–95 school year whether they agree with the statement "I feel safe in my neighborhood." Ninety-three percent of boys and 91 percent of girls in low-poverty urban neighborhoods (those that are 0 to 10 percent poor) said they felt safe in their neighborhood, but as the neighborhood poverty rate increases, fewer and fewer adolescents say they feel safe. In the most disadvantaged neighborhoods (those that are over 40 percent poor), only about two-thirds of boys and slightly less than two-thirds of girls feel safe. These differences are even more remarkable when we consider that adolescents in dangerous environments, especially males, may be hesitant to admit fear or weakness. Suburban neighborhoods show a similar relationship between neighborhood poverty and feelings of safety, though the gradient is smaller. There appears to be no such relationship in rural areas.[5]

To an outsider watching the evening news or reading the local section of the newspaper, the kind of violence that claimed Mikeal's life seems random and chaotic, a symptom of a "Wild West" atmosphere in which bullets are flying in all directions and predators roam the streets. Most of the time, though, violence in poor urban neighborhoods is socially patterned, not random. These patterns, well understood by the young people involved, are not always apparent to even long-time neighborhood residents. At a small community meeting on a muggy August evening, tenant leaders met with youth from a Boston antiviolence group in the basement meeting room of a low-rise pubic housing development in Franklin. During the day, the room serves as an informal day-care and after-school center. The children's drawings that covered the walls contrasted sharply with the evening's topic, the summer's shootings in and around the neighborhood, an annual spate of violence of which Mikeal Harris was only the most brutal example. One elderly tenant leader, clearly exasperated, lamented that the kids today will beat each other up for a baseball hat or pair of sneakers. Their parents aren't raising them to have any respect for others, she explained as she shook her head. Unable to contain herself, a young teenage girl from the antiviolence group chimed in, "It *ain't* about the hat . . . but it *is* about respect."

She proceeded to describe to her elders what Elijah Anderson (1999) calls "the code of the street," a set of informal rules for public behavior in poor, violent neighborhoods. Though Anderson's account of the code of the street comes from years of ethnography in a poor Philadelphia neighborhood, it would be instantly recognizable to adolescents and young adults in Franklin, Roxbury Crossing, and many other urban neighborhoods across the country. Poor youth, particularly males, are angry about their deprivation and have few ways to express and validate their self-worth other than through "campaigning for respect" on the street—asserting their masculinity, confidence, and social status through posturing and fighting. A reputation for toughness must be honed through public displays of ferocity and ability that only fighting or intimidation of others can provide. To be the loser of a public confrontation means a loss of respect and status in a world where other forms of status are hard to come by. Far worse is to be "punked"—as Boston youth call it—backing down from a fight, no matter how long the odds. Being punked signifies weakness, someone who will not stand up for himself or his friends, and invites future attacks, robberies, and harassment. There is little confidence in the willingness or capacity of police to control violent behavior in the community, so one must be prepared to defend oneself. Taking someone's baseball hat is not at all about the monetary value of the hat, but about the respect that comes from taking the hat from another by force or intimidation. Ongoing conflicts are set in motion when the losing party attempts to regain status with revenge. When these conflicts escalate, friends and relatives are enlisted, and someone can indeed be murdered over what seems—at first glance—like a conflict over a hat.

But these interpersonal dynamics are not the only important way in which violence is socially organized. Conflicts and confrontations are based on ordered social relationships and social identities, relationships and identities that—at least in Boston—are closely connected to neighborhoods. I focus on the role of neighborhoods in organizing violence and on differences between poor and nonpoor neighborhoods in how the boys experience and relate to violence and fear of victimization. The neighborhood-based social organization of violence is important because it structures many aspects of the social lives and the geographic mobility of adolescent boys in poor neighborhoods. Thus this chapter also sets the stage for later chapters that delve more deeply into the effects of such violence.

"The Drama": The Social Organization of Violence in Boston Neighborhoods

Chris sits on the steel railing outside his Franklin Hill apartment, only a few hundred yards from where Mikeal Harris was killed three months earlier. An acquaintance of Mikeal, Chris, like many of his neighbors, attended Mikeal's funeral. When teens from a nearby street started "talking trash" about Mikeal and about Franklin Hill outside the funeral home,

Chris and his friends got into a fight, and another one of his friends suffered a superficial knife wound. Violence ebbs and flows in poor neighborhoods in Boston as young men "rep" (represent) their neighborhoods, defending their reputations and exacting retribution for previous losses and signs of disrespect. Chris feels a strong loyalty to his neighborhood and its territory, so much so, he explained to me, that he is considering skipping a family trip to live down South for the summer with relatives, lest he is needed in the neighborhood during the long, hot Boston summer, when neighborhood conflicts flare up:

> CHRIS: I can't go out there. I can't leave the projects. [There's] too much stuff happening . . . If I leave and if something happens, I've got to come right back.
> INTERVIEWER: What kind of stuff might happen?
> CHRIS: Somebody might get killed, get hurt; I've got to come back.

Chris's experiences offer a window into the "the drama," the system of ongoing neighborhood-based rivalries and conflicts that structures central aspects of youth violence in Boston. Baggy jeans and a long white T-shirt hang off Chris's tall, lanky frame. It is a warm fall day after a cold snap, and an oversized winter coat dangles across his neck. Late-model sedans and SUVs line the street alongside clunkers and "hoopdees." A burned out mid-1980s GMC minivan sits incongruously across the street from a gleaming Lexus sedan. Soda bottles and discarded candy wrappers clog the gutters, and a few blades of grass struggle to grow in the trampled earth between the apartment building and the sidewalk. Chris is surrounded by three friends who eye me warily as I greet him for our second interview. Barely fourteen, Chris's height and cold "street" stare make him look seventeen or eighteen. With more of a grunt than a greeting, he motions slightly toward his apartment building, a red-brick three-story structure that spans almost an entire block. We climb up a dimly lit stairway with a cracked linoleum floor and past a newly installed set of mailboxes. Once inside the small, dark, smoky apartment he shares with his mother, Chris's demeanor changes.

Now he smiles and talks in an animated fashion, describing an incident that occurred over the weekend at Chez Vous, a roller rink and teen dance club about a mile or two down Blue Hill Avenue. Chris and his friends go there frequently on the weekends to dance and "bag" girls, to get their phone numbers. "The Vous," as Chris calls it, is a weekend gathering place for teenagers from Dorchester, Roxbury, Mattapan, and other sections of Boston, so there is always potential for neighborhood rivalries to erupt.

Soon after Chris and "his boys" arrived, they had an encounter with a group of young men from a nearby street who insulted a girl from Franklin Hill.

> CHRIS: We almost got into a fight. Some Lucerne kids was there . . . They were just making mad noise. 'Cause in the Vous they're like, "Lucerne, Lucerne." I know the name is Lucerne. I don't know where it's at though. There was all kinds of kids there though. The Point was there and the Head was there. D Block was there. They had a dance contest and the girl that was from [our neighborhood], she was dancing. And they was talking mad trash [about her] so we almost got in a fight with them. They was scared. They left . . . We was there like twenty deep.
> INT: If those guys had stayed, would you guys have fought them?
> CHRIS: Probably. But they were scared, they left. They want to collaborate with us, but they punks so we won't collaborate with them.
> INT: Why do you say they're punks?
> CHRIS: 'Cause they scared. They be scared every time something happen.

Standing and fighting when challenged is the essence of manly behavior in Chris's circle. Displaying very openly one's reputation for toughness is a critical part of the street repertoire (Anderson 1999), and it is expected behavior from "his boys." Chris looks down upon the boys from Lucerne Street for leaving rather than fighting, even though they were hopelessly outnumbered. They are "punks," people who will not defend themselves or their neighborhood.

As this account illustrates, neighborhood is a central organizing category in Chris's life. "The Point," "the Head," and "D Block" are terms he uses to describe other boys, using local slang for the neighborhoods where they live. Chris and the twenty other adolescents from his neighborhood are not being chivalrous in defending "their" girl. Rather, they are defending their own neighborhood from insult by outsiders. The youth from Lucerne Street announce their presence by chanting the name of their street. Then one of them challenges Chris's neighborhood by insulting the girl.

There is nothing particularly inevitable or "natural" about the centrality of neighborhood in this conflict. An outside observer might have expected an older brother, cousin, or boyfriend to challenge the individual who insulted the girl, but the conflict quickly became a conflict between neighborhoods rather than individuals. Chris mentions that Lucerne Street youth would like to "collaborate" with the youth from his neighborhood, meaning that they would like to form an alliance of mutual support and protection. "D Block" is one such alliance between two housing developments in another part of the city.

"Beefs" between neighborhoods, ongoing disputes with escalating confrontations, have many characteristics similar to the beefs between individuals described in the literature (e.g., Anderson 1999; Dance 2002). Beefs between neighborhoods are to some extent about a neighborhood's reputation and the relative safety that comes from being known as a rough neighborhood (Anderson 1999). A youth who lives in a neighborhood that does not have a reputation for being tough and for standing up for itself is at greater risk of victimization when he ventures beyond its borders. When young men know that neighborhood-based retribution will be forthcoming if they attack or rob an individual, they are likely to leave him alone. On the other hand, zones that are not well defended are understood to be targets for street crime. Young men in Franklin and Roxbury Crossing frequently assured me that failing to stand up for their neighborhoods and to control who could enter them or the activities within them would lead to criminal activity in the neighborhood such as drug dealing, car theft, and vandalism. This in turn would attract undue law enforcement attention.

Beefs between neighborhoods are also about status. Young men in high-poverty neighborhoods know that American culture measures status according to residential location, and that their neighborhoods, with dirty, unsafe streets and high poverty rates, are at the bottom. Yet among themselves, an even more fine-grained status system has emerged. Neighborhoods filled with "punks," unwilling or unable to mount a defense, lose face. Defending one's turf is an important end of its own, and not usually for the reasons typically assumed, such as the need to defend particular drug markets (though in a few situations that is the case, as I will describe below). Neighborhood rivalries are the basis for much of the more serious violence that occurs in Boston. Beefs between neighborhoods often go back years, before today's teens were even born, and their exact origins are almost always unknown by the current participants. In Roxbury Crossing, for example, youth from the Lenox/Camden public housing development often have beef with those from Ruggles Street, those from the Mandela Homes apartment complex, or those from the apartment complex at "1850" (Washington Street), also known as Grant Manor.

In Franklin an ongoing feud simmers below the surface between the Franklin Hill and Franklin Field public housing developments, located within sight of one another on opposite sides of Blue Hill Avenue. In the early 1990s this conflict peaked with a rash of drive-by shootings, knife fights, shoot-outs, and murders. Efforts by community activists and police, in cooperation with the young men involved, managed to end the conflict. When I spoke with Chris in the fall of 2003, calm prevailed, but when I revisited him in the spring of 2004, "the drama" was ready to explode again. As Chris remembers it, it was at a party in February 2004 that the conflict surfaced again:

> It was over some girls at this party. Me and my boys bagged these Franklin Field girls, and the guys from Franklin Field got mad. So they brought [the fight] to us. We beat them up a little bit. Then the older mens came, then we got our older mens, so that it looked like a go. But then the girls called us like, "We don't want drama." So I was like, "All right, forget it."

As Chris made his way home from the party, he was jumped by young men from Franklin Field riding in a car driven by one of the "older mens." They were looking to settle the score and win back some pride for their neighborhood. As Chris tells it, he took a number of punches but never fell down and even managed to get in a few good blows himself before escaping. As his mother confirmed, Chris was beaten fairly badly but suffered no serious injuries. At this point, there was considerable potential for the conflict to escalate into serious violence, as Chris would be expected to rally his boys from Franklin Hill and attempt to exact retribution. As it turned out, though, the cooler heads among the "older mens" prevailed, and the beef was "squashed," at least for the time being:

> Then [the young men from Franklin Field] started riding through here [Franklin Hill]. So me and my little niggas told our older niggas, and then they got involved. Once they got involved, [Franklin Field] didn't want it. Our OGs, they didn't even get involved. There was just me and the older niggas. It was just a couple of niggas from [Franklin Hill], and [Franklin Field] couldn't handle it. They said they didn't want it no more. Because if the whole [Franklin Hill] team came together, it would have been a problem. And they only had half their team fightin'.

The young men from Franklin Field made a strategic decision: they brought the conflict to a halt, fearing that if it escalated, the Franklin Hill youth would call in more support from the older men in their neighborhood and easily gain the upper hand in any fight. Franklin Field youth would undoubtedly give a different version of this conflict, but Chris's account illustrates another aspect of the social organization of neighborhood conflicts. Age-segmented groups have merged for the purposes of a cross-neighborhood conflict.[6]

Three sets of neighborhood actors who differ in age and experience are involved in this story. "Little mens" (or "little niggas") are teenagers growing up in the neighborhood. "Older mens" are in their late teens or twenties and, as veterans of previous "beefs," have honed their reputations based on past deeds. They may be hustling or dealing drugs, or they may be working legitimate jobs these days, but they are a continuous presence on the streets. "OGs," or "original gangsters," are in their thirties and forties, survivors of the worst days of violence in Boston. Many have known the inside of prison walls. OGs grew up in the neighborhood and were leaders in their day. Their place at the top of the social hierarchy is cemented by their legendary reputations, but their daily connections to the neighborhood are often less strong now, as many have moved away from the street life. Still, they are reliable in times of trouble. As we will see in the next chapter, the "older mens," and to some extent the OGs, play an important role in socializing adolescents in poor neighborhoods.

Public street life unfolds differently in Lower Mills, a low-poverty neighborhood less than a mile away from Chris's Franklin neighborhood. Darnell is Chris's thirteen-year-old half brother. Neither Darnell nor Chris knew of one another's existence until a week before I first interviewed Darnell, when a chance meeting of long-lost relatives brought the two together. Their mothers both dated their father during high school. Darnell lived in a suburban town before moving back into Boston, though he continues to attend school in the suburbs. Their father plays little role in either young man's life, and their mothers both finished high school, did some postsecondary schooling, and worked until recently.

Like most of the other adolescents whom I interviewed in Lower Mills, Darnell is familiar with the system of neighborhood rivalries. He recounts how youth from certain neighborhoods have beef with other neighborhoods and how those entering the wrong neighborhood risk a confrontation. Like other adolescents from Lower Mills, Darnell is subject to the "code of the streets" (Anderson 1999) when he ventures out of his own neighborhood, either into poorer neighborhoods or into neutral territories. However, the similarities end there. While Chris has to contend with a nearly constant threat of violence, Darnell could recall only one fight in the three years he had lived in Lower Mills. Darnell and his friends see no need to defend their neighborhood from outsiders, mainly because Lower Mills stands outside the system of neighborhood rivalries. Youth from elsewhere do not recognize Lower Mills as a potential rival or as an area with a reputation and little reason to visit or pass through. Indeed, a street worker I met at the beginning of my fieldwork who works with adolescent males involved in violence told me there were no youth in Lower Mills. While the density of young people is indeed lower there, what he meant was that he never had occasion to come into contact with the young men from that part of the city. They did not "have beef" with any of the youth he deals with in the city's poorest neighborhoods.

One can measure the distance between Darnell and his half brother Chris where violence is concerned by contrasting their responses to my questions about what a "thug" is.[7] In keeping with the definition that adolescents from the two poor neighborhoods gave me, Chris described a "thug" as someone who engages in violent or risky behavior without considering the consequences and often without provocation. Clothing and mannerisms are secondary markers of a thug, but not defining characteristics. When I asked Darnell this question, he gave a different response, one that was typical of boys from Lower Mills. To him, being a thug is primarily a way of presenting oneself to others, rather than a description of one's actions. Dress, style, and fashion are key.

> INT: What about when somebody calls somebody a thug?
> DARNELL: That's like when people say "gangsta." The way you spell it is s−t−a. It's kind of like, what you do, and like stuff you wear. It's not being in a group. It's just like . . .
> INT: It's more of like a fashion sense?
> DARNELL: Yes. Like a white tee. Some Air Force Ones [a type of sneaker], pants and a hat. You're like, oh yeah, he's gangsta. It's just the way he look. Somebody say you're a thug. It's the same thing, your fashion sense, and all that. It's how cool they are.

The meanings that boys attach to terms such as "thug" and "punk" provide a subtle window into their thinking about violence by revealing the social categories that are salient in their minds. Recall Chris's explanation of a punk, someone who shies away from a fight and is easily taken advantage of or does not stand up for himself or his neighborhood. Cyril, a sixteen-year-old resident of Lower Mills, had a very different and vague definition of the term, suggesting that the street violence typical of areas like Franklin and Roxbury Crossing is far less relevant to Cyril's daily life. Even though he attends a Boston public high school with many fellow students from poorer neighborhoods, Cyril described a punk as "like a person who likes to use weapons, punch somebody in the face when they're not expecting it."

Similarly, when I asked Jason, an eighteen-year-old resident of Lower Mills, about gangs, he dismissed the notion as if it were a passing phase that younger adolescents engage in, not a real neighborhood problem:

I don't know if it's just me, but gangs are kind of like eighth grade. Nobody is in a gang any more . . . Don't see them wearing their bandannas any more.

I mean there are gangs but it's not that serious any more. Like you won't hear anyone like, "Oh yeah, a whole bunch of Crips jumped some old lady" or something. It'll be just a couple kids. It's not really a gang any more 'cause when it comes down to it, people are mostly for theirself. And it's kind of hard to find somebody that's gonna be there like that. Where if you had problems with somebody, they're gonna step up and make your problem theirs and stuff.

Violence does not touch Darnell, Cyril, and Jason very often. When it does occur, it is both less serious and more likely to be based upon interpersonal disputes rather than ongoing neighborhood conflicts. If a young person from Lower Mills ventures outside his neighborhood, he must avoid encroaching on others' turf, but he need not fear encountering someone with whom his neighborhood has beef. Lower Mills is outside the system of neighborhood beefs.

Neighborhood as Social Identity

A direct consequence of the neighborhood-based system of violence is that neighborhood is a powerful form of identity for many of Boston's adolescent boys, a dividing line between insiders and outsiders. When one's friends and enemies are determined by neighborhood residence, neighborhood becomes a potent social marker. As Chris's account above illustrates, neighborhood rivalries are intergenerational, passed from cohort to cohort on the streets.[8] The power of neighborhood distinctions is illustrated by Marcus, a sixteen-year-old African American who lives in a public housing development in Roxbury Crossing. Another kid from Marcus's development owed him a small amount of money. Marcus wanted to get it back, but did not want to fight this neighbor for the money. Instead, he told his debtor that if he did not give Marcus the money, Marcus would rob his friend from another neighborhood:

A kid owed me four dollars. He lives in this development, so I didn't want to do nothing to him, because I knew it would cause problems. And I said, "I see you coming around here with a kid that you hang out with on a daily basis, and I really don't care for the kid, 'cause the kid's not from around here. So," I said, "It's either I get my money, or we're going to have problems." I told him, "I'll rob your friend the next time I see him around here." So, I had my four dollars in my hand the next day . . . We just shook hands, and we left it at that. I seen him today, and we said, "What's up?"

Conflicts between neighborhood insiders are often different from those that divide youth from different neighborhoods. Conflicts among neighbors are resolved quickly, though often with a physical fight. Third parties from the neighborhood take on a mediating role, attempting to resolve the dispute before it escalates into an ongoing beef. There is often intense social pressure to resolve the dispute, shake hands, and "leave it at that." When conflicts between youth from different neighborhoods emerge, however, much more is at stake. Each boy becomes a representative of his home space; the neighborhood's reputation is at stake. Others may become involved, either to seek retribution and redemption for the neighborhood or to protect its reputation.

The salience of place-based identity is so great that lying about one's provenance is a known ploy for avoiding a fight with a kid from a rival neighborhood. This strategy often elicits scorn from others, for it goes against the notion that neighborhood is an unshakable social category. It is similar to pretending to be of a different race or ethnicity, simultaneously suggesting shame or abandonment of one's own and disrespect for the other. Daniel, a seventeen-year-old African American from Roxbury Crossing, referred derisively to this practice as "hood hopping":

Dudes might be hood hopping. "Oh I'm from Mission." But then five minutes later you ask the same dude that question, "Look, where you from?" "I'm from Brunswick." And you're like, "How are you from Brunswick? You just said you're from Mission." That's how this dude was in my school. I'm like, "How you from Brunswick, then you said you're from Mission. Then you said you're from Lenox." I'm like, "So how do you do that?" He's like, "Oh, no, it's not even like that." I'm like, "You're hood hopping."

In Roxbury Crossing and Franklin, violence, neighborhood identity, and community membership are closely linked. Violence generates mutual obligations, as Tyree, a seventeen-year-old African American youth from Roxbury Crossing, explains:

If you're not willing to help in the neighborhood, when someone is in need then you really can't be here. We had a circle of people. If you wasn't in that circle, you was outside that circle, that's where you had to be . . . There's people in the neighborhood that live on the same street and could see you getting jumped that wouldn't care. They put it as, "Oh it's not my problem." But if you was really tight, grew up together, been through ups and downs, know family members, then there's always a chance of help. But I put it as, "I always got to help the people in my neighborhood because you never know when it's going to come back to you." I could be outside the neighborhood getting ready to get jumped, and he could walk by and [help me].

Those who do not help their friends in physical confrontations or defend the neighborhood cannot rely on others for other forms of assistance. Though not all boys see things this way, for adolescents like Tyree, participating in this system of obligations defines membership in the community, including access to such benefits as mutual protection.

In contrast, the adolescents of Lower Mills, the more advantaged area, do not link identity and community membership to mutual obligations of protection. Lower Mills teens tend to look to sources of membership other than the neighborhood for identity. Small friendship groups, interests such as particular sports or music styles, and involvements in religion or ethnicity-based groups are more important. For example, Isaac is thirteen and lives in Lower Mills. An avid athlete, Isaac is the quarterback of the Pop Warner football team. He can also frequently be found playing football either at the park near his house or at the after-school program he attends. He has one or two friends from the neighborhood, but most of his friends are from his football team or his after-school program. He describes himself as someone who "doesn't have any enemies," by which he means that unlike some of the other kids who attend his public middle school, neither he nor his neighborhood have beef with anyone.

The importance of neighborhood as a form of identity in Roxbury Crossing and Franklin means that adolescents in these neighborhoods come to see their neighborhoods as "defended communities" (Suttles 1972). These notions of territory are also passed down from previous cohorts of young people and reinforced by the experiences of daily life in the neighborhood. Youth from Roxbury Crossing and Franklin often understand geographic space in terms of a territory frame, in which the city is divided into small areas that are controlled by certain groups of youth. These territories affect their conceptions of their neighborhoods.[9]

It should come as no surprise that Chris defines the boundaries of his neighborhood according to the territory that is controlled by young men from Franklin Hill. This includes the development itself, the commercial strip along Blue Hill Avenue just up from Talbot Avenue, and the mostly residential area a little way down Harvard Street. (Maps are available in the appendix.) It also includes the Lena Park Community Center on American Legion Highway, but does not include the Boys and Girls Club on the corner of Talbot and Blue Hill. Chris does not venture into the club, even though it has superior facilities, because it is considered the territory of the young men from the rival housing development, Franklin Field. Again, the comparison between Chris and his half brother Darnell from Lower Mills is instructive. Chris talks proudly about "reppin' the Hill," his Franklin public housing development, but when I asked Darnell how he describes his neighborhood to others, he just says "the Pan," short for Mattapan. Mattapan is a whole section of the city, not a specific neighborhood, apartment complex, or street. A strong sense of neighborhood social identity is largely absent among Lower Mills youth like Darnell.

Jerome, thirteen, and his fourteen-year-old cousin Jamar, who live in Roxbury Crossing, also understand their neighborhoods in terms of territory. Neighborhood boundaries are governed by notions of territoriality and enforced with violence:

> You can't go on that side of the street. We can't go on a certain side of a street or you can't go out across that street. Can't do nothing about it. For example, "This is my territory, and if you step over my territory, I have the right to beat you up." That's what they [are] trying to say.

Similarly, Jamar explained that there are nearby places that he cannot go without being jumped and that people from his neighborhood prevent outsiders from entering their territory:

> INT: What are places that are near here where you wouldn't go?
> JAMAR: 1850 or Ruggles.
> INT: Why wouldn't you go over there?
> JAMAR: 'Cause they'd probably try to jump me.
> INT: If they didn't know you?
> JAMAR: Yeah.
> INT: Does the same thing happen around here? Like if somebody from down there came up here would they get jumped?
> JAMAR: Yeah.
> INT: What about gangs and stuff like that? Is that the issue?
> JAMAR: Nah, it's just territory.

Neither Jerome nor Jamar has thought very much about why territory is so important. It just is what it is, "can't do nothing about it," as Jerome says. Territories and their boundaries existed long before they moved to the neighborhood and, in their minds, are a permanent and taken-for-granted part of neighborhood life.

Tavon is eighteen and currently living in Lower Mills. He recently moved there with his mother and sister but spent most of his childhood and adolescence in another neighborhood in Dorchester, one known for violence. He prefers Lower Mills, describing it as peaceful and quiet, a place where people do not know him and will not try to "start trouble" with him. He explained the importance he and his friends once attached to keeping others out of his old neighborhood, lest they bring "drama":

> TAVON: It wasn't quiet, but we made sure everything was cool around there and we made it quiet. It was good, but I like over here better, because too many people knew me over there . . . We made it quiet because a lot of people come hanging around, and they don't even live around there and hanging around making drama. We let them know that we stay here, I mean, this is our property, and so we quieted it down . . . People like to go other places and make trouble that they won't do in front of their own spot.
> INT: What kind of trouble were people making?
> TAVON: You get a group of people in front of one house and just chillin', I mean, there's going to be noise . . . Cops are going look at it like they sitting over there doing something, like they are a gang or something. We had to stop all that because we want a quiet street. We have a lot of little kids that used to live around there, so I mean, everybody is doing everything in front of them and we don't like that.

These neighborhood rivalries and conflicts are not just in the minds of adolescents. Physical safety is involved, and parents take rivalries seriously as well. For instance, two parents cited neighborhood rivalries as affecting decisions about which public high schools to request for their sons. When Terrell, now sixteen and living in a Franklin housing development, and his mother were deciding on which schools he preferred, she insisted that he not include either English High School or Madison Park High School on his list of preferences because she thought many youth from a rival housing development attended them, and he would be at risk of getting attacked at school. When Manuel, now fourteen, and his mother were making the same decision, she put a particular high school on the top of his preference list because she knew many other youth from their Franklin housing development attended that school. He would have friends from the neighborhood to help keep him safe at school and while traveling there and back.

In contrast, when Charles, a fifteen-year-old from Lower Mills, and his mother were making his high school choices, they focused on the academic programs at the various schools. Charles was struggling in middle school with behavior problems. He seemed uninterested in doing his schoolwork and was acting out in resistance to teacher demands and in response to his poor grades. He just did not want to be there. However, Charles has a strong interest in working with animals when he grows up and is thinking about becoming a veterinarian, so his mother decided his first choice should be a school that offers a marine biology program in the hopes of increasing his interest in school.

Instead of worrying about violence, victimization, and involvement in crime, Lower Mills parents have the time and energy to worry about the other challenges that most adolescent boys will undoubtedly face, like staying focused on school, avoiding fatherhood at a young age, and avoiding sexually transmitted infections. Darnell's mother dismissed violence as a worry of hers, instead focusing on her fear that her thirteen-year-old son will get "sidetracked" from school by girls:

> Violence? This neighborhood, not too much. Most of the kids, they basically play at the park and my son is not the fighting type. He is real quiet, he is real friendly. That is not one of my concerns, just because of his personality and the way he is . . .
>
> I don't want him to get sidetracked. Girls, no. Girls and falling into the wrong crowd. Not that I think he's a follower, but I just think if he sees people doing things that they think is fun but is stupid, that he might want to try it too, just 'cause everybody else is having fun, so I just don't want him to just fall into that trap of getting caught in everybody else's whirlwind.
>
> He spends a lot of time by himself just by choice. Like sometimes I have to tell him, go outside and play, but he is in his room writing and reading . . . So sometimes I have to kick him out the door, like to get some sun.
>
> I think he's getting into girls. He is looking at the girls a little bit more now too, just by the way he talks. So he's turning into a little man there. I just think that is the only thing that will change him. Once he really gets into girls and things like that, I try and steer him away from that, sex and getting girls pregnant, diseases and just all the little things that can go on between teenagers. Girls getting into trouble with other guys because they have a boyfriend already.

While Franklin and Roxbury Crossing parents worry constantly about their sons becoming enveloped in the neighborhood's dangers, Darnell's mother makes it a point to encourage him to go outside and interact with his neighborhood friends. She can focus her parenting energy on other issues: education, romantic relationships, and risky sexual behavior.

The strength of neighborhood identities and the desire to defend neighborhood territories from outsiders is not unique to the adolescents and young men in Boston's poor neighborhoods. Americans have long viewed neighborhoods as sacred ground, measures of a person's status, and boundaries to be enforced. For example, Sugrue (1996) documents the efforts of white Detroit home owners to resist the integration of their neighborhoods by newly upwardly mobile blacks during the 1950s and 1960s. White Detroiters resorted to legal, political, and violent means in attempts to keep out those they viewed as threatening their property values and their moral order. The young men discussed here are not, of course, defending property values and do not have access to legal or political means of protecting their neighborhoods, but they do see themselves as keeping order and defending identities based on categories of moral worth.

Safe and Unsafe Spaces within Neighborhoods

Though territories are enforced and defended by violence and threats of violence, safety plays another role in how adolescents think about neighborhoods and the use of space. Even within one's territory, spaces come to be known as safe or unsafe, not because of conflicts with outsiders but because of how the space is used by insiders. In particular, certain areas become known as unsafe because older men hang out there on the street or because a space is controlled by drug dealers. Within a neighborhood, individuals self-segregate according to their activities, and groups tend to use different spaces for different purposes. Youth who regularly engage in illegal activities—or socialize with those who do—spend time in the parts of the neighborhood associated with those activities, while youth who do not want to engage in such activities exclude the "unsafe" areas from their regular routines.

In Roxbury Crossing, the block on Shawmut Avenue between Lenox Street and Kendall Street contains a social club where the members' activities often spill out onto the street and into a neighboring pizza joint. At all times of day and night, cars are double-parked, and older men can be found socializing on the benches at the playground in Jim Rice Field, sometimes intoxicated. For Malcolm, a thirteen-year-old who lives nearby, this place is the most dangerous part of his neighborhood, especially after dark. Cheap pizza and a park with a playground would otherwise make this space attractive to him, but its use by the older men rules that out: "At night, it always happens and stuff. And my grandfather is always telling me if I go outside, don't come on that side or nothing down there. So I stay over here a lot."

Most neighborhoods have such danger zones. In Franklin Hill the drug dealers congregate by the entryway of a particular building. Near Whittier Street in Roxbury Crossing, older men congregate behind the development along Cabot Street, working on cars, playing cards, smoking, and drinking. In Franklin Field the area near the entrance of the development on Blue Hill Avenue has become known as the place where the "gangstas" and drug dealers hang out. Reed, fifteen, walks past this area almost every day to pick up his younger brother after his brother is dropped off by the day-care van. He hates going anywhere near there:

> It's just like when you're up there people, they're not from where I live, they come down like, "You've got drugs. Can I buy some?" And I'm like, "I'm not even a drug dealer, nothing like that." I don't like it, because I'm not a drug dealer, and I don't want nobody thinking I'm a drug dealer. There's nice people around here, but when they see somebody asking you [for drugs], they don't want you to be around their kids. My friend's mom once heard a guy saying that to me, and then she didn't want me hanging around with him. But then I told her the truth, that I didn't do it.

For Reed, the unsafe space and its inhabitants provide a foil. The drug dealers who occupy a certain space are negative role models for him. He defines himself in contrast to them. Staying away from this space or clearly defining his purpose for being there (picking up his little brother from the bus) provides him a way to enact his identity as someone who is one of the "nice people," someone who is "not a drug dealer."

Even relatively advantaged Lower Mills has spaces deemed unsafe, though they tend to be just outside the area. Marshall, seventeen, describes an area near the Gallivan Housing Development that he considers unsafe:

> I feel pretty safe around here. The further you go down Morton Street, the less safe you'll probably feel because the badder stuff happens over there . . . But nothing really happens over here . . . Plus, there's the projects right there. Stuff happens sometimes over there, but it never really leaks out over here.

Marshall's father described how his son came to the conclusion himself that this was not a good place to hang out:

He would venture into the Gallivan apartments [a public housing project] and play basketball, but there was too much inappropriate activity going on in there, and he made his own choice not to hang in that area. And further down Morton, there are a lot of businesses that create a lot of traffic, and there's a hustle, bustle about that area that doesn't appeal to [his mother and me] and doesn't appeal to Marshall either.

Because such unsafe spaces are fewer and farther between in Lower Mills, Marshall can choose to avoid them. There's another basketball court in a public park without the "inappropriate activities" that Marshall's father wants him to avoid. For Reed, in contrast, there is no way to steer clear of the drug dealers and gangstas in his Franklin development. They control certain sections of public space through which he must pass.

Consequences of Beef between Neighborhoods

Only a small proportion of youth actively police neighborhood boundaries, defend territory from intrusion by others, confront youth from other neighborhoods in neutral territories, and carry out the retribution and revenge that keep beefs going. Indeed, the community and policing strategies that were at the core of the "Boston Miracle," the amazing decline in youth violence and youth homicide in the 1990s, succeeded because of the relatively small number of central actors in the conflicts. By targeting "impact players" with both social services and law enforcement sanctions, police, community leaders, and religious leaders stemmed the tide of violence by "squashing" the beefs (see Berrien and Winship 2002; Braga and Kennedy 2002).

Nonetheless, beefs affect all the young people in afflicted neighborhoods. Venturing outside one's own neighborhood to go to school, to the store, or downtown to see a movie means risking confrontation with youth from other neighborhoods just by passing rival enclaves or neutral territories. Neutral spaces such as schools, public transportation, and downtown or commercial areas become sites of contestation and conflict. Confrontation between youth from different neighborhoods is always a possibility, and often youth will ask each other where they are from as a challenge or physical threat. Most young men prefer to travel in a group to avoid being jumped or harassed when going outside their immediate neighborhood. Even those who never start fights with youth from other neighborhoods are enveloped in the system of place-based antagonisms.

Manuel, a Latino Franklin resident, is fourteen years old. He talks tough, but his short height and slim frame make him look at least two years younger. Manuel has gotten into only one fight in his life, with another boy from the neighborhood (over a conflict that started in school when the other boy became jealous of the attention Manuel was getting from a girl). He describes himself as "not a troublemaker," not someone who starts fights or "talks trash" to seem tough. However, Manuel is well aware of the conflicts between his development and Franklin Hill. A friend of his was beaten up by youth from "the Hill" in a nearby park.

> MANUEL: We still have problems with Franklin Hill because they started a lot of stuff. Like one day they jumped one of my friends. They were talking trash, and this time my friend said something back to them, and they beat him up. He was walking home like late at night, and he was crossing [the park]. And they used to like just like come down here [to our development] and just talk trash, and just like leave. Because [my friends and I] really don't try to like start trouble . . . The things I do to try to avoid it is like I'll just like ignore them, or like don't answer their questions. And I will just like walk away. Like just be the better man, and just like leave it be.
>
> INT: And what happens when you do something like that?
>
> MANUEL: They'd just probably like talk trash, saying that I'm a wimp, or that I'm a little girl or something, which I really don't care what they say, because they're not hurting me and stuff. I just get mad, and hold in all my anger. And I just leave, walk away.
>
> INT: So some people would say if someone kind of challenges you like that, and you walk away, then you're going to get a reputation as someone who's scared.
>
> MANUEL: Yeah, they do say that, but I really don't care, because to me, I'll fight a kid if I was really, really mad. But if I wasn't like really that mad, I would just like leave it be. They could think whatever about me, but I know my real personality.

By refusing to fight, Manuel is risking his reputation. It is a risk he is willing to take, but the need to make such a calculation is further evidence of what is at stake. Manuel avoids going near Franklin Hill, at least when he is not with an adult. He explained what would happen to him if he went there:

> Say if I was in front of Franklin Hill, they'd be like, "You know where you're at?" And I'd be like, "Yeah, I'm in front of Franklin Hill." He'd be like, "Where you live?" I'd be like, "I live in Franklin Field." He's like,

"You know this is my neighborhood?" I'll be like, "And it's not really your neighborhood because you don't own it." And they'd be like, "What? You gettin' smart?" And they would just like talk more trash.

These confrontations, however, can quickly become more than just trash talking. The talk itself is often a prelude to physical altercations or at least is often designed to provoke one. Terrell, a sixteen-year-old African American from Franklin, described an incident that occurred when he went to visit a friend who lived near the Bromley Heath public housing development in Jamaica Plain. His development and Bromley Heath had beef at the time, but Terrell was never involved in any of the fights or other confrontations. He is unusual in that he tries to avoid socializing with youth from his development. This does not, however, provide him with much insulation from the conflict:

Just from us living around here, sometimes it's a safety issue, because, we gotta watch our backs. [People from our development] step on a lot of people's toes, and get a lot of people riled up against them. So they want revenge in any way. And they don't care if you hang with them or you don't hang with them, as long as you live around here, you're a target to certain people.

I was actually with one of my friends, that doesn't live around here, and we were going to [a grocery store] in Jamaica Plain. And some people asked me where I was from, so I told them. And then they pulled out a handgun on us. They was just trying to seem tough, so I didn't like panic and overreact. I just walked away from it. It was broad daylight too.

And it's more than just trying to ignore it, you gotta watch your back too. You can't just say, "Well yeah, I'm from around here, but I don't mess with those guys [who are involved in neighborhood beefs]." [The kids from other neighborhoods], they're gonna say, "So what!"

Contrast Terrell's experience outside the narrow confines of his neighborhood with that of Delbert, fourteen and from Lower Mills. Like his counterparts in Franklin and Roxbury Crossing, Delbert always tries to travel with a group of friends when he leaves the neighborhood, even to take the train to go downtown to go shopping or to the movies, but because his Lower Mills neighborhood is outside the system of neighborhood beefs, his chances of victimization are far lower than Terrell's.

DELBERT: I remember I was on the T [the Boston subway] one day and I was with somebody. I was coming from downtown, the movies . . . And I was sitting there and these three kids who were like seventeen came

over to me and was like, "Where are you going, where are you from, do
you know the big gangs that are around there," and questions like that
and I answered no to all of them.

INT: And then they left you alone?

DELBERT: Yeah, 'cause I said no.

As Delbert's story suggests, the youth who confronted him were looking for people from certain neighborhoods, and approached him because
they suspected he was from one of these areas. As a resident of Lower Mills,
he has no connection to the neighborhood conflicts that the youth on the
train are trying to draw out, and so he was left alone. Neighborhood identity does not structure Delbert's safety as it does for Terrell.

The consequences of neighborhood beefs can also persist over time,
limiting where in the city a young man can go and still be safe. Eduardo,
age seventeen and Latino, grew up in a public housing development in
Roxbury Crossing and "ran the streets" in his early teenage years, stealing
cars, carrying a handgun, and selling drugs. He was eventually arrested
and incarcerated at the Division of Youth Services (DYS), Massachusetts's
juvenile jail. He has since moved to a calmer neighborhood, earned his
GED, and plans to apply to college. During the time when he ran the
streets, his development had beef with two housing developments located
in the nearby South End. Though it is now years later, he must still be
careful where he goes.

EDUARDO: Can't go to the South End to this day. I can go around Back Bay.
I can go around Newbury Street, but I can't go towards the Villa Victoria
[housing development], around that area. Also more towards Cathedral
[housing development], I can't go around there. If I were to go around the
South End, near Cathedral, something would happen to me regardless
whether I'm living that type of lifestyle or not.

INT: What would happen if you went to, say, near the Villa?

EDUARDO: [That beef], it was over something serious. It's not over a female. It's over murder. I had nothing to do with that . . . If you're from
that area, you can have nothing to do with it, and you still have problems
if you go around that area.

INT: I also could imagine you dress like that [in slacks and a tie] and say
walk down Tremont Street, how would anybody even know that you
weren't on your way to the Prudential Center or working in an office?
How would they know where you were from?

EDUARDO: A lot of them recognize me. There's a couple that actually have
recognized me, have stared me down like they're about to do something,

but haven't 'cause they see I'm not living that type of lifestyle. I want nothing to do with you or [my old development] . . . I just want to live my life in peace.

The consequences of neighborhood beefs and defended territory for a young man's freedom of movement are amplified by the relatively small size of the neighborhoods involved. Boston's official city neighborhoods, such as Dorchester, Roxbury, South End, East Boston, South Boston, Charlestown, Back Bay, Fenway, Hyde Park, West Roxbury, Roslindale, Jamaica Plain, Beacon Hill, Allston, and Brighton, are really sections of the city rather than functioning neighborhoods. (Dorchester, in which Franklin and Lower Mills are located, contains nearly one-quarter of the city's population.) The geographic areas in which the above described dynamics play out are quite limited. Boston's relatively small public housing developments, usually not more than several hundred families and covering only a few blocks, are natural organizing units. Many of the most well-known and dangerous neighborhoods are housing developments, such as Orchard Park, Warren Gardens, Mission Hill, Franklin Field, Franklin Hill, Lenox/Camden, Whittier Street, and Bromley Heath. Other natural geographic areas are large private or co-op housing developments, such as Grant Manor or Mandela Homes in Roxbury Crossing near the South End. However, many of the geographic areas are single streets only one to three blocks long. Examples include Castlegate Road, Intervale Street, Brunswick Street, Ruggles Street, and Copeland Street. Intervale Street and Brunswick Street, located in the Grove Hall section of Dorchester, run parallel to one another and have had beef for years.

Residential neighborhoods are not the only context in which neighborhood beefs can flare into open conflict. Boston is a small city with a very good public transportation system, making it relatively easy to get around. Riding public transportation can also be dangerous for youth, however. Boston's public high schools are all "citywide" schools, meaning their attendance areas cover the entire city. Thousands of students ride the buses, trains, and trolleys of the MBTA (the T) to and from school every day. Between 6 and 7 a.m. and 1:30 and 3 p.m., major subway stations and bus lines near the schools and the city's poor and minority neighborhoods are teeming with high school students, pressed against each other in train cars and buses as they travel to their distant schools. In an environment in which holding a glance too long, stepping on someone's toes, or brushing up against a shoulder can be interpreted as a sign of disrespect, these tight quarters can be the spark that ignites the flame.[10]

Almost all high school students and many middle school students learn to ride public transportation while traveling to and from school, thus opening up greater opportunities for geographic mobility. The downtown and Fenway movie theaters are recreation spots for city teens. They also frequent the Cambridgeside Galleria Mall, Downtown Crossing, and the Copley Mall to go window shopping; travel throughout the city to visit family members living in other neighborhoods; roller skate and dance at Chez Vous, a roller rink in Dorchester; and visit the Good Times Emporium, a giant amusement center featuring video games, carnival games, pool, laser tag, and go-carts located in a strip mall near the Sullivan Square subway stop on the border between Somerville and Boston's Charlestown neighborhood.

Miguel, sixteen, is particularly mobile. He moved to Roxbury Crossing as a preteen, and initially most of his friends were from his neighborhood. After a summer job gave him a little more spending money, he began going to Good Times on a regular basis to play video games and now visits several times a week because it is only a short subway ride from his family's apartment near the Orange Line. His friendship group slowly shifted from neighborhood friends to the people he met at Good Times, particularly as he became quite good at a video game, "Dance Dance Revolution." One of these friendships led him to a weekend job selling newspapers in another subway station, where he developed a work history that eventually allowed him to get a regular after-school job working as a courier downtown. Now, with the heavy demands of both school and work, he spends almost no time hanging around his neighborhood.

However, the free range that Miguel enjoys is relatively rare. Except for school, most teens venture out of their neighborhoods only a few times a month, in part because they cannot afford it. Without a little spending money, trips to Good Times, the mall, or the movies are not really an option. However, the most common reason was a concern about safety beyond the neighborhood boundaries. Even if one's destination is not a defended neighborhood, there is always the risk of confrontation over a dirty look, a perceived insult, or neighborhood conflict.

Because their neighborhood is not a part of the system of neighborhood rivalries, Lower Mills youth can enjoy a broader range of movement if they so choose. While sixteen of twenty Franklin boys and nineteen of twenty Roxbury Crossing boys discussed the role of potential conflicts with other youth in determining where they went and with whom, only four of twenty Lower Mills boys considered these risks, and those who did so either lived on the edges of Lower Mills close to poorer neighborhoods or had lived in a more violent neighborhood in the past. In comparison to many of his counterparts from Roxbury Crossing and Franklin, Charles does not usually come back to his home neighborhood immediately after school. Instead, he goes to visit friends in a nearby Dorchester neighborhood where he lived when he was in elementary school, or he goes to see other friends he knows from a summer program he attended at a university in another section of the city. He and his friends like to "meet up" and hang out at pizza shops in various parts of the city for an hour or two when they get out of school, after which he heads home. Though he has seen fights in other neighborhoods, he is not worried he will get sucked into these conflicts. My questions about where he feels comfortable going and where he does not—which usually sparked extended conversations among the Roxbury Crossing and Franklin boys—seem odd to him. "I usually go everywhere," he shrugs.

In contrast, Terrell's experience illustrates how simply being associated with a particular neighborhood known for violence and enmeshed in ongoing neighborhood beefs can limit one's freedom of movement. Many adolescents in Franklin and Roxbury Crossing adopt a survival strategy of remaining in their home neighborhood as much as possible, geographically constricted as it may be, and avoiding interaction with males from other neighborhoods.[11] Simon, a sixteen-year-old Franklin resident who has experienced many altercations arising from such situations, now rarely leaves what he perceives to be the safe confines of his own neighborhood. He explains how leaving his neighborhood can easily lead to a violent confrontation if he is not with a group of friends for protection.

INT: So how safe do you feel on the streets in the neighborhood?

SIMON: I don't feel safe at all. Well, probably a little bit, like in my neighborhood, it's all right. But other places? Noooo, I don't really go out of my area that much . . . People, just from looks, get murdered . . . Because you're like an alien, you're not known over there. So the first thing you do when you walk through there, all eyes is on you. And it's not friendly, like a "Mr. Rogers neighborhood." It's not like that [laughs]. So it's like, "Where you from?" and if you say the wrong area . . . If they got problems with that area . . . They just set it off with you right there . . . That's happened to me a lot of times.

INT: So what's your strategy for staying out of trouble?

SIMON: Basically, there's not even a strategy. You just have to watch the streets, you have to duck. The best thing to do, if you're not with people

you know, you have to be at the [local community center], because that's
the most safest thing. That's about it if you're not with a lump sum [large
group] of people.

Even riding public transportation poses a risk for Simon, and it is most
dangerous when traveling to and from school:

That's crazy, taking the [public] transportation. The buses be packed in the
morning. There's a lot of kids going to school and you step on somebody's
sneaker, they ready to kill you, there's a fight breaking out there. In that
train station, there always be fights. You have a lot of schools, and all
these kids be meeting up at Ruggles, Jackson Square, Forest Hills [subway
stations], and that's how stuff be happening. I take the bus [to school]
right now. That's the main reason why I don't like taking the bus because
it's always a problem. That's why I like to drive to school. I feel much safer.
I told my mother. When I first went to [my high school], I didn't feel safe
there. I had to fight my way to get respect. So now I've got the respect, it's
still little problems, but not that much.

After Simon got in a few fights at school, he developed a reputation as a
tough fighter, and other students began to leave him alone.

Public transportation is one venue that even Lower Mills youth have to
watch out for, however. Seth, a fourteen-year-old African American from
Lower Mills, also tries to avoid public transportation, particularly during
the peak time after school. He takes the trolley and the train to his middle
school in another part of Dorchester in the morning, but prefers to take
the school bus home in the afternoon with the younger kids to avoid problems with fellow students his own age.

SETH: I take the train in the morning. I have a school bus but I don't want
to catch it. So I'll take the train in the morning and my school bus in the
afternoon. So many people from my school be on the train [in the after-
noon]. So I get on my school bus. They fool around too much on the train.
They push each other. They stand by like the little yellow line [on the edge
of the platform] and they push each other. Somebody could fall.
INT: And are there people getting in fights and stuff on the T also? Is that
an issue?
SETH: Almost, but it didn't happen. Police break it up. There's like one
[officer] on each [platform].

Several months after my interview with Seth, a student at his school was
stabbed in the stomach outside the train station after school.

A Note about Gangs

The purpose of this chapter is not to describe gangs in Boston (and indeed whether we characterize the social organization of violence described here as gang violence is irrelevant to my larger argument). However, it is useful for those familiar with research on gangs to draw some parallels where possible.[12] It should be clear from the above discussion that the dynamics of group violence in Boston bear considerably more similarity to "classic" street-corner gangs (loosely knit groups of young people who frequently fight with other groups and sometimes engage in crime) than to the "corporate" gangs found in some larger cities. Such corporate gangs are characterized by clear boundaries between members and nonmembers, formal leadership hierarchies and roles, and organized involvement in crimes such as drug dealing.[13]

However, there are also elements of neighborhood beefs common to both classic street-corner groups and corporate gangs, including territory defended by violence and the use of symbols or colors to advertise membership, in this case neighborhood of residence. In Boston, young men wear the athletic jerseys or hats of different college and professional sports teams to signify that one is "reppin'," or "representing," a particular neighborhood: Mission Hill wears Minnesota Twins, Orchard Park wears Portland Trailblazers, Ruggles Street wears North Carolina Tar Heels, and Franklin Hill wears San Francisco Giants. (Local teams such as the Boston Celtics or New England Patriots are not claimed by any particular neighborhood and are therefore safe.) They also engage in tagging and graffiti. Finally, like members of corporate gangs in larger cities, the young men who actively participate in neighborhood beefs and in defending their neighborhood are often referred to as gangsters or gangbangers by residents, police, and the young people themselves. Nevertheless, the term "gangster" (or "gangsta") has largely come to take on a different meaning among Boston youth from neighborhoods like Roxbury Crossing and Franklin. Rather than denoting someone who is in a gang, it denotes a certain attitude and "hardness," a willingness to use violence and a lack of fear or conscience (see also Dance 2002).

Yet in other ways groups in Boston are quite different from gangs in larger cities such as Los Angeles and Chicago. Young men from some Boston neighborhoods are associated with national or international gang organizations such as the Latin Kings, the Crips, the Bloods, and the Salvadoran gang MS13, but most geographic areas have no such tie, and young people who are associated with such groups are only loosely affiliated. None of the youth I interviewed knew of anyone from their neighborhood claiming membership in these so-called corporate or named gangs. The young men described here who are defenders of their neighborhoods and engage in conflicts with others do not fit this model of a gang. There are no initiation rituals or stark distinctions between members and nonmembers, and these groups have little or no formal organization. Most of the groups are not actively engaging in criminal activities such as "corporate" drug dealing for collective economic benefit, though certainly some young men do so as individuals. The result is that defending one's territory is almost never about defending economically valuable turf.[14]

There are exceptions, of course. Tyree, a seventeen-year-old from Roxbury Crossing, relates the story of a beef reignited by conflict over drug-dealing turf. When he was fourteen and selling drugs, young men from his neighborhood and those from a nearby housing project had beef when they started encroaching on each other's corners:

> Even though it was right across the street, [the project] and [my] street really didn't get along. 'Cause I would say, everybody in that neighborhood was selling the same thing and it was either I'm taking your money or you're taking my money. There's not enough money out here for all of us to eat. I mean it was like, there was like two sides of the street, you stay on your side, we'll stay on our side . . . It was real crazy but you had to defend your neighborhood and you had to defend yourself most of all because if they see that you're scared, it makes them feel like a bigger person. "I can intimidate him from school all the way home." If you didn't defend yourself it was just gonna get worser and worser and worser.
>
> We took our chances. We went over there and they came over here but as long as they didn't say nothing to us and we didn't say nothing to them there was never really a problem. But until they started coming on our side trying to make money and then we started going on their side trying to make money, that's when the controversy really started.

This description does not rise to the level of organization of a corporate gang, however. While Tyree and his friends were involved in drug dealing and defending drug turf, their dealing was for personal rather than group benefit.[15]

Violence, Negative Role Models, and the Leveling of Expectations

What are the consequences of neighborhood violence and its social organization for the boys who live in the neighborhoods of Franklin and

Roxbury Crossing? Often answers to seemingly simple questions such as "What is the most important decision you have made in your life so far?" can be extraordinarily revealing about boys' expectations and evaluations. Fifteen-year-old Dalton is a slender, soft-spoken boy whose braids, plain white oversized T-shirt, and baggy jeans drape his body. A long-time resident of his Franklin public housing development, Dalton spends almost every day after school hanging out in and around the development. The basketball court is a favorite locale. When we talked the summer before he was to start high school, he explained that "staying out of trouble. Staying off the streets," was the most important life decision he had made so far.

> Like I'd be out on the corner, and there'd be a lot of people doing one thing, and some people doing another thing, and like I don't know which one to pick. Should I stay with this group or this group? . . . They'd be smoking and stuff. They'd be doing all types of things. Because I seen some of them—they be having a lot of money so, I just was like I could make money working. So, instead of trying to get in trouble trying to do drugs and stuff, I do the right thing instead of the bad . . . So, I decided to stay playing basketball and get off the streets and all that other stuff.

"The streets" serve as an important reference point for the boys of Franklin and Roxbury Crossing as they struggle to understand their actions and identities. Violence, drugs, and crime characterize "the streets," and the individuals that Dalton associates with "the streets" are salient on his block. Dalton compares himself to "bad kids," those involved in violence and other criminal behavior who are a fixture of public life in Franklin and Roxbury Crossing. Their presence in his immediate surroundings has the potential to affect him through their role in framing his own decision making and behavior.

Growing up in Franklin and Roxbury Crossing, a boy observes—and often interacts with—gangbangers and dope slingers on a regular basis, even if he is not involved with either. The salience of these figures is magnified by their public presence, the way they call forth police attention, and the danger that they attract, not to mention the dope fiends and crackheads who seek them out. Some residents tend to withhold judgment of these young men—often only adolescents themselves—because they are "doing what they have to do" to survive, but they are crystal clear about the negative example that they set for younger boys. Gangstas and dealers can seem glamorous and exciting; at the same time the urban poor know all too well that these lifestyles are failures in mainstream culture. Violence and drug dealing are not consistent with the educational and family aspirations of most boys in the neighborhood. As such, deviant figures serve as a foil for ordinary boys growing up in the neighborhood, a low standard by which to measure one's own successes and failures.

The young men who populate the streets stand as stark reminders of the potential pitfalls that boys in the neighborhood face, and of how easy it is to fall off track. The dangers of engaging in "street" behavior—incarceration, injury, or even death—are given concrete meaning by example. They are, in this sense, a source of motivation, a daily reminder of the costs of failure. Paul, fourteen and from Franklin, described how he compares himself to the high school dropouts hanging out on the corner all day:

> I know I'm gonna finish [high school]. I don't want to drop out of school. I don't want to grow up to be no dummy . . . We seen some kids in our class that dropped out of school already, last year . . . They just never came back to school . . . Now when we see them, they just be sitting on the corners and stuff, getting harassed by the police . . . I don't want to be on the corner.

Gangbangers and drug dealers serve as *negative role models,* examples of what not to do with one's life.[16] While the concept of role model is traditionally used to denote those who set positive examples for children to aspire to, poor neighborhoods contain plenty of negative examples. These negative role models have particular salience because of their public visibility. Tyree, seventeen and from Roxbury Crossing, is a former drug dealer himself. He learned some serious lessons from the local dealers. The near death and permanent injury of a family member was a rude shock and powerful motivator:

> If I put myself in that situation, I could be dead or in jail, and I don't want to be dead or in jail ten years from now. I want to be in school, something positive, so I just really use it as a motivational tool, as I really have to do something better than what they're doing . . .
>
> What really got me was my uncle. He got shot up by some people over some drugs. He's still in a wheelchair now, and he still wants to be outside in the street with all his friends and running the streets, selling drugs and being the top guy. And I tell him like, "See what doin' all that got you? It got you in a wheelchair. I mean, I'm not saying you was a bad person, I'm not saying you was a good person; I mean, you did what you had to do and now look where it got you?" When I first heard that he got shot, I was only like eleven, and it really hurt me, because where he got shot at was outside of a school, there was kids and after-school programs . . . It really hurt me because I really didn't want to see him laid up in the hospital. He was in a coma for about three months.

Negative role models do more than make the costs of failure clear. They also redefine what success and failure mean. When one's neighborhood peers are frequently involved in violence and crime, when they suffer the consequences, including arrest, incarceration, injury, and death, merely avoiding those activities and consequences becomes an achievement. A new calibration emerges based on neighborhood standards, *leveling expectations* to the local comparison group and thereby heavily influencing the frames that boys use to understand and evaluate their own actions. In Roxbury Crossing and Franklin, success is partly—though by no means only—avoiding the troubles of the street. Like Dalton, thirteen-year-old Elijah from Roxbury Crossing thinks success means "staying out of trouble."

> INT: So if you were to meet somebody on the street, how would you tell if that person is successful or not?
>
> ELIJAH: If he's nice and treats people right and if he's not always outside playing a lot, or outside with his older friends and all that, or he's always doing something, always being in good places, doing something, then I'd know he's a good person, a successful person.
>
> INT: Would you look at how much money he made or what type of job he had?
>
> ELIJAH: Not really. Just the way he is, his personality. Because if you're doing what you're doing, staying out of trouble, then you're successful to me.
>
> INT: So do you know anyone who you would say is successful in this way?
>
> ELIJAH: Me! 'Cause I'm getting things done. Staying out of trouble. I choose basketball as my number one goal. I stay out of trouble. I use that as a goal to stay out of trouble.

Notably absent from Elijah's idea of success is going to college. Avoiding the corner is also a benchmark of achievement for Fernando, fifteen, from Franklin.

> INT: If you see a grown man walking along the street, how do you tell if he's successful or not?
>
> FERNANDO: If he's not on the street on a corner, I guess he was successful . . . How he dresses. An unsuccessful dude would dress all bummy and stuff. A successful person would dress like perfect; they'd not dress bummy at all . . . You finished college; you've got a job. You work for your own stuff. You don't depend on nobody.
>
> INT: Who do you know who's successful in that way?
>
> FERNANDO: Who do I know? Nobody.

While they punctuate the dangers of failure, negative role models do little to illuminate paths to success. Observing peers engaging in violent or other criminal behavior tells a boy nothing about how to go about doing something else that he views as more positive. Like Fernando, boys in Franklin and Roxbury Crossing often knew of no one they would consider emblems of achievement in terms of relationships or schooling.

Negative role models shift the frames that boys use to interpret their behavior and that of others. When boys are faced with negative exemplars, they focus on avoiding their mistakes rather than doing what is necessary to achieve more exalted goals, such as going to college. Energy and attention are diverted to staying out of trouble. Zach is fourteen and from Roxbury Crossing. He talked about how important it was to him to go to college, but when we discussed the challenges that he would have to overcome to attend college, rather than keeping his grades up or taking standardized tests, he focused on staying away from neighborhood violence, the temptations of which he experienced firsthand.

> INT: What are the challenges you might face in the next few years along the way to achieving those things?
> ZACH: People who distract me, and gangsters I guess. They might try to like get peer pressure to join in the gang or something and then I might get shot.
> INT: And so have you ever been approached by anybody and asked to join a gang?
> ZACH: Yeah. My friend. When I was in sixth grade. We was really, really cool and stuff. Started hanging with each other and backed him up in fights. And then he joined this gang like a few months after. Then like two weeks after, I went with him somewhere and then he introduced me to his friends that was in the gang and he wanted me to join with them . . . Like it'll be really fun and stuff. We'll go out to bad places and we won't have to fight just us two, it will be a whole group. I was about to join because me and him were really, really tight. And so I spoke with another one of my friends. He was like, "Don't do it. Don't do it. That could mess up your life right there." Like a gangster dies like half of his life that's normal than someone that's not in the gang.

The low estimation of violent characters predisposes other boys to think of themselves in a positive light just for staying clear of the worst. This is the process by which negative role models level expectations. Boys' descriptions of college admissions requirements are a case in point. Boys from all three neighborhoods talked about grades, but the boys from Roxbury Crossing and Franklin also focused on good behavior as a key criterion for college admissions. By staying out of trouble, they could set themselves apart from their neighborhood peers. College applications do indeed contain questions about suspensions or expulsions from school and about criminal records, but that is not what the boys from the two poor areas have in mind. They are focused heavily on behavior and conduct issues. Take, for example, Jamar, age fourteen and living in Roxbury Crossing, who aspires to attend a local university like Northeastern or UMass-Boston. When asked what he thought colleges like these would look at to decide who they wanted to admit, he focused on test scores and good behavior: "Who follows rules, directions, high test scores, um like listening abilities, following directions." (Jamar's reference to test scores here is to the Massachusetts Comprehensive Assessment System (MCAS), the state's standardized test for high school graduation.)

Contrast Jamar's emphasis on good behavior with that of the boys from Lower Mills. Sixteen-year-old Cyril from Lower Mills wants to be a computer engineer or graphic designer. When asked what might stand in his way of going to college, notably absent is any worry about drugs, violence, or behavior: "Work, money, school, family . . . Like something might happen and I'd have to come out of school and, then, go back into school, and it would be harder to get back into school." Cyril is worried about becoming a father too early and how that could interrupt his education. When asked about what colleges look for in applicants, he gives the answers we might expect to hear from middle-class adolescents: "Grades. And what school you came from. That's it." Similarly, thirteen-year-old Reynard explains that "grades and athletics" are important for going to college, and that "goofing off" in school might prevent him from getting a good job later in life. Finally, fourteen-year-old Delbert, from a different section of Lower Mills, explains what might prevent him from achieving his goal of having his own auto repair shop: "Taking drugs, smoking, getting bad grades in school, and getting arrested." Yet when I ask him why he is worried about getting arrested, he explains that he has a friend who smokes, and they could both get arrested if his friend is caught by police smoking underage: "If I hang out with one of my friends, like Dave, sometimes I'm worried about getting arrested 'cause he's underage smoking." For the boys of Lower Mills, the reference point for "bad behavior" is far different than that for the boys of poor neighborhoods. Among the twenty Lower Mills boys, only five expressed any concern about neighborhood violence, crime, or drugs as a challenge in their lives. In contrast, twelve of twenty boys in Franklin and sixteen of twenty boys in Roxbury Crossing talked about these potential problems as realistic threats to their educational and career goals.

Because of their salience in the neighborhoods of Roxbury Crossing and Franklin, the potential consequences of violence and drug dealing are starkly felt, and the perceived chances of involvement are magnified. Ramon, a seventeen-year-old from Roxbury Crossing, dropped out of high school because he could not handle both attending school and working his minimum-wage job at a grocery store. Ramon aspires to attend college and knows he will need to graduate from high school to do so, yet he chose to prioritize his job over school. Why? Having spending money from a legitimate job insulates him from the temptation to turn to the streets to make money. Drug dealing would be easy, as crackheads and fiends already approach him looking for drugs. Yet becoming a drug dealer would mean he would be a disappointment to his family and would risk being incarcerated, with all of its long-term consequences. He knows that life is not for him:

> Last year, there were a lot of kids out here, like thirteen years old, selling weed and selling crack, making mad money. They was making way more money than I would make at [the grocery store]. Getting paid minimum wage, I would make at most $150, and they would have $300, $400, just all off of like selling weed and crack. So I decided to keep the job because I kept telling myself, if I leave this job I'm gonna end up getting eaten up by the streets. I wouldn't want to put myself in that predicament where it's just getting arrested for selling drugs. Spend time in jail, and then have my little cousins ask, you know, where's Ramon? Jail's not a good place to be at. Even though I should have left [work] for school, after school there's always a place I got to go, and it's called home. Or on weekends I'm always gonna have to see the face of the streets, see these fiends, crackheads. Come up to me, "Yo, you got some stuff?"
>
> Dealing is way easier than working. I feel even though working's harder, it's much more worth it, 'cause of the future, when I want to move on. I got this big-time dream, it's just I want to become a detective. I want to be a cop. I have a resume to take along with me. I'm not gonna be in [the grocery store] forever. I want to be the kid that everybody knows did good . . . My family has always looked at me as the good one, as the one that didn't go bad, as the one that actually has a future ahead of him, and can actually do things.

Ramon's comments also reveal why the drug dealer is a negative role model while the drug addict is not. The income provided by drug dealing allows a young man to be independent, to not have to rely on others for support. (This type of independence was also cited by other boys as part of being successful, e.g., Fernando above.)

It's all about money. Nowadays, without a dollar in your pocket, you ain't going nowhere. Without this job, I would be broke, living off child support. I hate having to depend on somebody. Waiting for my father to send his check every week to get my money. I want to be my own man. I want to buy my own things. I don't want to have to wait, save up, and then buy it. I don't have to go out there and ask my mother to buy it for me.

For Ramon, the negative role model presented by the drug dealer is the wrong way to go about achieving the right goal, financial security and independence. (Correspondingly, violence may be viewed as the wrong way to go about gaining respect and identity.) Drug addicts, on the other hand, are simply crazy or sick—"fiends" and "crackheads." Ramon and the other boys do not worry about becoming fiends or crackheads in the way they worry about getting caught up in neighborhood rivalries or in drug dealing, and thus becoming a drug addict is not a legitimate negative role model. To be viewed as a negative role model, the potential comparison's lifestyle and decisions must be seen as realistic alternatives.

Keeping Sons Safe and Out of Trouble

For parents too, neighborhood violence and crime are salient features of neighborhood life and represent the strongest threats to the well-being and future prospects of sons. The streets of Franklin and Roxbury Crossing, populated by drug dealers and gangbangers, level the expectations parents hold as well. They calibrate their success as parents by their ability to keep their sons safe and out of trouble in an environment in which many adolescent males end up dead or behind bars. One Franklin mother of three grown men explained why she considered herself a successful parent, even though two of the three fathered children as teenagers and none has been to college: "None of my boys got killed, hurt anyone, or ended up in jail."

It is no easy task to raise adolescent boys in a violent neighborhood. Safety and supervision absorb tremendous energy when violence and crime are ubiquitous. Less energy and attention remain to manage other challenges, such as education or sexual relationships. Duante is seventeen and living in Roxbury Crossing. His mother described her worries about Duante and his thirteen-year-old brother:

The violence that occurs every now and then, it's really bad . . . They just start shooting and don't care. And all the kids are right there. That's the one thing that I would change, the violence that they bring in here. A lot of trouble that goes on in here is started from people who don't even live here . . . It just makes the neighborhood bad. You know the kids can't go out there and play in fear there might be bullets being shot. Or somebody might jump out and just start beating up on somebody. I mean, that has happened.

Duante's mother is keenly aware of the organization of violence in Boston's poor neighborhoods (described above), the parameters of which her son must navigate on a daily basis. He is at risk for injury not just from his own confrontations, but those of his friends and neighbors:

People who don't live in the neighborhood cause problems. I guess those people say, "This person's hanging around here. So why don't we just go over there to where they're at." They come over here, cause problems; and then that individual leaves, but those people are still coming back here because they're like, "This is where I've seen him at. So we'll just keep coming around here until we run into him again." Or you know maybe they'll see somebody that he's hanging with and they'll just take it out on them. You know, make the feud bigger.

Duante's mother tries to keep her son away from these dangers and temptations, but adolescent boys crave independence and adventure, so maintaining control and supervision is hard. At some point, a parent must "send them out there into the world and just hope for the best":

It's a mess. And I tell Duante, "You don't need to be out here." Duante's a good boy, but all boys get into trouble. I mean he's hardheaded at times, because he thinks because he's taller than me I won't kick his ass. You know he gets into trouble every now and then. But I tell him, "Be a leader, not a follower. Just because they're getting away with it doesn't necessarily mean that you'll get away with it. It'll just be your luck that you'll be the one ending up getting caught . . . "

Everyone's biggest fear is they don't want to lose their child, especially at a young age. And with everything going on out here anything can happen . . . But you got to let them go, send them out there into the world and just hope for the best. That's all I can do for them.

Duante's mother assuages her worries by reminding herself that Duante is "not a violent person," someone who does not exhibit much aggression and stays close to home, preferring to spend time on video games, on reading, and with his girlfriend than out in the streets. Spending a lot of time on video games or in private with a girlfriend become positive when the alternatives involve life-threatening danger or getting into trouble with police:

Duante is not a violent person. He's a clown, a really silly person. He likes playing his video games; he's into, you know, rapping. He likes the music. He likes reading too. I notice that a lot, that he likes reading lately. That's really cool. And his grades in school have improved. But other than that, no, he's not a violent person. He has a girlfriend who comes over, visits him. Other than that, he doesn't go anywhere.

Even more than school dropout and teenage pregnancy, parents are keenly aware of the threat that incarceration places on their sons' economic future. Prison time reduces employment and wages, as parents of Franklin and Roxbury Crossing know all too well.[17] Marcus's grandmother, his primary caretaker, worries that her sixteen-year-old grandson will be caught up in the drama and end up in prison:

> I know of one person that has a son, and he grew up all wrong. The parents don't pay attention to him. I guess she's alcoholic, and then the child get hooked on the drug wars and say, "OK, my mom don't buy me new sneakers." And he got big drug boys or whatever you call them. They go and say, "I'll buy you a pair of sneakers." The child got hooked up with them, you know, this child going the wrong way . . . Now this child is in prison. And that's where a lot of these kids are. That's why I be yelling at Marcus. "Watch what you do 'cause sometime you could be with the wrong people at the wrong time and you are . . . "
>
> You don't mean to be nagging at them, but you nag because you see what happened to kids in the 70s and 80s . . . The kids of the 90s, oh they're looking at fast money, nice cars, fancy clothes and they don't give a doggone how they get it. And you are the parent, you work. Your kids is falling by the wayside. Your child is history. So I made sure I yelled at my kids. I made sure they got a high school diploma and I made sure they was OK. I tell the kids, "Look. It's easy to get into trouble and like hell to get out of it. Once you get in it, you can't get out 'cause people won't let you get out. They'll see you in the big house." If you got a record, you ain't gonna get nothing. And you can't get an apartment, you can't get nothing.[18]

Neighborhood violence and crime also frame how parents evaluate their sons' friends and peers. Parents judge their sons' friends according to their involvement in "trouble." Even parents who were confident that their sons were of good personal character and judgment worried that peers could easily draw them into trouble. It is often difficult for parents to tell whether a new friend is going to be a negative influence, as teenagers are mature enough to know how to present themselves one way to parents and in another way on the street. Emilio's mother finds it hard to judge which of his Roxbury Crossing peers will be good for her thirteen-year-old son and who might drag him into drugs or violence:

> There's a lot of young teenagers that be selling drugs, and if you are within the crowd, they'll say, "Well, you want to do this?" And you'll make fast money. With drugs you make fast money than a job . . . They just say, "Oh yeah, if I sell drugs, I could have $200 a day." But that's not even right because if you want to really do good yourself, you try to get a job. I mean you work hard. Your money is clean . . . You either get caught by the cops or you get shot. But some of that depends who you hang out, and who are your friends. You gotta pick your friends. I mean there's good friends and bad friends . . . They could be good kids in front, but then in the back, they turn around and they be doing the wrong thing. So it's kinda hard because teenagers, they can't really tell. It's not easy. It's tough for teenagers growing up in the projects.

Mothers from Franklin and Roxbury Crossing prepare their sons for the decisions they will inevitably encounter when faced with problematic peers who threaten to get them into trouble. Paul's mother explained how she prepared her fourteen-year-old son for the decisions he would face in their Franklin neighborhood:

> I can let him know that "listen, make sure when you choose, that this person is not having you do anything negative or get yourself in trouble." You can never come up to me and say, "Well this person got me in trouble." No. You allowed them to get you in trouble. You get yourself into trouble. So I always tell him, "Sit and think about something. Is it gonna cause you to go to jail? Is it gonna cause you to get in trouble with me? Think about it before you do it."

In a violent environment, confrontations occur with great frequency. Often they cannot be avoided, as walking away means risking losing status and thus placing oneself at greater risk for future victimization. Since adolescent males often carry knives (and occasionally guns), the potential consequences of these confrontations can escalate into serious injury or death for the loser—and prison for the winner. Marcus's grandmother explains her attempts to guide Marcus in how to deal with these circumstances before they happen:

> My call is defend yourself, but like not with no knives or guns or anything, because you fight your way out with your fingers. These days kids want knives. Marcus has a knife. I tell him, "Don't go out with no knife. If

they hit you, you fight with your hands. No weapons." Fight on the dirt on the ground. But these kids, "Oh, I want him gone. Go get my gun." He was talking the same way. I said, "Look, we're not having it. We're not talking no guns. We're not gonna have knives" . . . They say you're a punk, you're a punk. At least you not worrying about killing somebody. You serve in jail and then you really gonna be a punk human being. Messed up. Or in jail where you don't know who is gonna try to hurt you.

The parents of Lower Mills provide a stark contrast to those of Franklin and Roxbury Crossing. Instead of worrying about violence, victimization, and involvement in crime, Lower Mills parents have the time and energy to worry about the other challenges that most adolescent boys will undoubtedly face, like staying focused on school, avoiding becoming a father at a young age, and avoiding sexually transmitted infections. Recall from above how Darnell's mother, herself a mother for the first time in her teens, was worried about teenage pregnancy, and encouraged her son to go outside to get some exercise and play with neighborhood friends. Similarly, when asked about the major challenges facing young men these days, Cyril's father, a Lower Mills resident, focuses not on violence or crime but on what he calls "fashion," and the short-sighted viewpoint that boys like his sixteen-year-old son have when it comes to spending money.

> INT: What do you see as the major challenges facing young men these days?
> CYRIL'S FATHER: Peer pressure. They're more materialistic. They want to look fancy now, but looking fancy, getting dressed up and looking all sharp now, is just a short-time thing. They don't look at the future as they should. They would spend a whole lot of money just to buy sneakers, and within two days that same sneakers they paid $100 for is in the closet piled up with junk on it. They should focus on things that's going to benefit them long term, although it might not be as fancy they want it. But in the long run, their stuff is going to be more fancier than their friends.

Cyril's father does worry about violence, but only when Cyril spends time at his mother's house in a poor neighborhood in a nearby inner-ring suburban city, where drug dealing and violence are more common than in Cyril's paternal home in Lower Mills. Cyril is ill-equipped to deal with the "aggressive people" in his mother's neighborhood, his father says, because Lower Mills is a more "calm and peaceful atmosphere," where confrontation and drug dealing are not part of public life.

> INT: Every parent worries about their son sometimes. When you worry about Cyril, what kind of things do you worry about?

CYRIL'S FATHER: The area where [his mother] is at is not the greatest. They're selling drugs on the street, so it's kind of hard for you go to one area they're not dealing with drugs and then you're got to jump back into another area, so you have two lifestyles. One, you have to try to fit into a calm and peaceful atmosphere and at the same time when you go to this other area, then you got to flick a switch on and you gotta be more aggressive to the people that's there, and I worry will he switch over at times ... There was one time when I heard that somebody was bothering his sister so they went over there, and they was going to beat the guy up with a bat. So I think that kind of made him, by me talking with them, realize that might not be the best thing.

Without the dangers of the streets to contend with, parents in Lower Mills have much less to worry about than their counterparts in Roxbury Crossing and Franklin, and can focus their parenting energies on the schooling and early childbearing outcomes that will structure their sons' lives for years to come.

Conclusion

This chapter has explored the social organization of violence in Boston's poor neighborhoods. It has long been recognized that rates of violence and victimization are higher in more disadvantaged neighborhoods.[19] But less well understood is the way that this violence is socially patterned according to neighborhood identities. I have built upon the work of previous researchers who have developed concepts such as status contestation (Anderson 1999; Dance 2002), age segmentation (Suttles 1968; Horowitz 1983), defended territory (Suttles 1972), and respect, reputation, and honor through violence (Anderson 1999; Horowitz 1983).[20] However, unlike previous research that describes the interpersonal dynamics of violent conflict, I focus on the role of neighborhood identities in structuring youth violence. Cross-neighborhood rivalries take on different forms and call for different responses than interpersonal conflicts and conflicts between corporate gangs.

For the young men of Boston's inner-city neighborhoods, neighborhood serves as an important form of social identity, one that defines insiders and outsiders, friends and enemies. This analysis highlights the symbolic importance of neighborhoods among youth in disadvantaged neighborhoods. For most youth in poor communities, the neighborhood is more than just a place to rest one's head at night. Closely coupled to these identities is a system of place-based antagonisms that have been passed down from previous cohorts, neighborhood rivalries that wax and wane in their intensity and violence, created and maintained by acts of revenge and retribution. Young men act to defend the territorial integrity and the social status of their neighborhoods. These neighborhood beefs are at the heart of much serious violence involving Boston youth.[21]

It is important to emphasize that only a small minority of youth create and maintain neighborhood conflicts, acting to defend their neighborhoods or to exact retribution on rivals. Adolescents like Chris and his friends are the exception rather than the rule. Yet ongoing neighborhood conflicts affect all youth in communities like Franklin and Roxbury Crossing. Youth from rival neighborhoods do not distinguish between participants and nonparticipants in selecting their targets or policing the boundaries of their neighborhoods. Venturing outside one's own neighborhood, even to neutral territories like shopping centers, public transportation, and school, means risking a confrontation. In response, many young men, especially those from the poorest neighborhoods, limit where they go and prefer to go out in groups.

Another consequence of both high rates of violence and victimization and a strong focus on home neighborhoods in Franklin and Roxbury Crossing is the leveling of expectations. Boys in poor neighborhoods are presented with many negative role models who starkly illustrate the risks of involvement in drug dealing and violence, but they are presented with few options of how else to achieve their goals. As a result, both parents and boys calibrate their success by comparing themselves to their neighbors, particularly those few whose involvement in the streets puts them in public view. With these individuals as foils, simply surviving to adulthood unharmed and staying away from crime, violence, and prison comes to be viewed as success, irrespective of early childbearing or school dropout. With violence an ever-present threat, parental attention focuses on keeping sons safe. The next chapter delves further into the effects of neighborhood violence, turning to the consequences of neighborhood rivalries for the social lives of adolescents. By structuring social identities, use of space, and peer groups, neighborhood-based violence affects not just those directly involved in the conflict but all youth in the neighborhood.

In the early evening of Valentine's Day 2004, fifteen-year-old Shawn Adams was stabbed at the bus station in Roxbury's Dudley Square during a fight between two groups of teens. Shawn and eight other boys ranging in age from ten to seventeen, residents of the nearby Orchard Park housing development, were waiting for the Silver Line bus to go downtown to see a movie when they were approached by six youth ages sixteen to nineteen from the Ruggles Street area. The Ruggles group noticed that one of Shawn's companions was wearing a Portland Trailblazers jacket, a symbol of association with Orchard Park since the days in the 1990s when the Orchard Park Trailblazers were a feared gang. On that night, the long-standing beef between Orchard Park and Ruggles Street claimed another young life, as Shawn, slowest to flee, was grabbed from behind and stabbed in the heart. He stumbled two blocks and collapsed. Transit police, usually present at the station, had been called away to respond to a stabbing at another station.[1]

By all accounts, Shawn was "a good kid from a good family," not someone who was involved in violence or "gangbanging." His only fault was hanging out with a friend with the wrong type of jacket. Though this is the usual refrain anytime a young man falls victim to Boston's neighborhood violence, in this case it was likely true. As one of Shawn's cousins told the *Boston Globe,* "These were little kids that were scared. If they were really gang-bangers, they would have stayed there" and fought. Shawn's assailant, an eighteen-year-old who had been released from a juvenile correctional facility only two months earlier, was arrested nine days after the murder. A twenty-one-year-old accomplice, who helped his friend dispose of distinctive clothing, was also arrested.[2]

Nevertheless, for the adolescents of the neighborhoods involved, the arrests did not mean the end of the drama. James is fourteen and lives in Roxbury Crossing, only a few blocks from Dudley Square and in the territory considered part of the Ruggles Street area. He attends a charter school and spends most of his free time playing basketball, either at school, in special basketball programs, or in the park near his house. After Shawn's murder, James worried that youth from Orchard Park would come to his neighborhood to exact revenge:

> The stupid stuff that other people do makes other people from different neighborhoods come to our neighborhood. That's what makes the neighborhood bad . . . Like the boy who recently just got killed in Dudley [was killed] by another kid who lived down the street [from me] . . . We got people from over there coming over here, sit on the steps, on the basketball court at night and waiting for people to come by, like older kids, like into their midteens. Probably some are my age but looks older. They try to mess with people or shoot. They're from probably Orchard Park . . . But people always want revenge on other people in our neighborhood.

A friend of James's escaped attack by running to James's house.

> **JAMES:** A boy I know, older boy about sixteen, seventeen, came to my house and had to wait in my house for a good hour for the people to [leave]. Because we went outside, and they was like a cage. [After a while,] he was like, "All right. They're gone. They ain't there no more." And we look at the gate at the end of the street near the court, and they're right at the corner, and they turned and look. And he just turned around and started running back in the house. So we just had to drive him home.
> **INT:** What kind of things can you do to avoid getting in that kind of situation?
> **JAMES:** I have no idea. 'Cause most of the time they're everywhere. I feel safe mostly, but I stay in the house. I go outside to play basketball in the day. When it gets dark, I come in the house.

Even daylight does not always offer protection, however. James described another incident in which there was a shooting near the basketball court:

> Recently I was at the basketball court playing, and some kids at the end of the street were down there. Some guy was in his car talking to his girlfriend while his kid was playing basketball. And he started screaming to his kid, telling him to get in the car. And then he goes, "Somebody is shooting at the end of the corner." So everybody drops the ball and just starts running . . . I ran straight home.

After the security service of his private development stepped up their pa-
trols, James began to feel safer, but this was not the first time he was exposed to danger because of neighborhood-based conflicts in which he was
not directly involved. Four years earlier, when youth from Ruggles Street
had beef with the nearby Lenox/Camden public housing development,
he witnessed a drive-by shooting: "I was walking up the street with my
babysitter, and some guy got shot right in front of me on a drive-by. Right
across the street, and died. It sounded like firecrackers to me. And [the car]
just drove off."

While James talks as if the violence does not bother him when matter-
of-factly describing his experiences, his mother explained his fears,
and hers:

> Right now I think he's scared, and I'm scared. Because recently there's
> been like several shootings. I think there has been about seven or eight
> kids his age that have died or got injured. And I'm scared to send him
> to the basketball court. If you got a police report of all the killings that
> happened, there's probably several out of this area around this basketball
> court. And that's really scary to me . . . And he's pretty scared he can't go
> to Ruggles [train] Station. You know, like I used to be able to get on a train
> and go downtown and not worry about some of my peers beating me up
> or giving me dead stares—that's what they do nowadays. You can't really
> look at nobody.

What is striking about James's experiences is not his description of any
one incident, but the sheer number of them, especially given his limited
interactions with others in his neighborhood and his lack of direct involvement in neighborhood beefs. In the previous chapter I discussed the
social organization of violence. This chapter delves more deeply into the
effects of neighborhood violence on the teenage boys like James who live
in the poor neighborhoods of Franklin and Roxbury Crossing. Previous
research has documented the biological and social-psychological consequences of living in the chaotic and stressful environment that violence
creates, but here I focus on the effect of violence on the social lives of
adolescents. Young men find ways to create some measure of protection
for themselves; these strategies are adaptations to their violent environments. These strategies involve seeking protection through relationships
and interactions with peers.

Peers have long been thought to influence adolescent decision making
and behavior. As young people mature into adolescence, the focus of their
social world generally shifts from family to peers, and recent research

has found strong associations between peers' characteristics, attitudes, or behavior and a wide range of outcomes ranging from crime and delinquency to sexual behavior to school performance and drug and alcohol use (e.g., Matsueda and Anderson 1998; Bearman and Bruckner 1999; Haynie 2001; Maxwell 2002; Haynie and Osgood 2005; Gaviria and Raphael 2001; Hanushek et al. 2003). Although the idea of peer effects is intuitive to researchers, teachers, parents, and youth themselves, statistical associations between peers are not definitive proof that peers actually affect an adolescent's behavior. If teenagers choose their peers based on common interests, priorities, preferences, or activities, then these "selection" processes could, in theory, account for observed associations between an adolescent's outcomes and the peers with whom he associates.

These methodological issues, which are similar to the selection problems in neighborhood effects research discussed in chapter 1, mean we should be cautious about inferring that peer associations indicate causal peer effects. One way to be more confident that peers truly have causal effects is to study individuals in situations in which they cannot choose their peers, thus eliminating the possibility that selection problems are biasing results. Economists have discovered several such situations, and their research suggests that peer effects are real. One such situation is assignment of first-year college students to dorms and rooms within dorms, which is often done at random. Zimmerman (2003), Sacerdote (2001), and Carrell, Fullerton, and West (2008) have used such research designs at three different colleges and found that the characteristics of randomly assigned roommates and dorm-mates affect an individual's college grades. Another such situation is the assignment of juvenile offenders to correctional facilities. Bayer, Hjalmarsson, and Pozen (2007) studied juvenile offenders in Florida who are randomly assigned to juvenile correctional facilities and found that the characteristics of fellow inmates predicted whether an offender committed a crime again in the future. While these studies focus on somewhat narrow sets of young people, they suggest that peer effects are indeed real, at least in certain circumstances.

Despite the importance attributed to peers in research on delinquency, education, and drug abuse, peers and peer cultures have only rarely been invoked to understand neighborhood effects (exceptions include Anderson 1991, 1999; South and Baumer 2000). Moreover, the importance of the social processes governing the selection of peers suggests that we also need to better understand how neighborhoods affect the types of peers with whom different adolescents interact. In other words, for peers to play a role in neighborhood effects, we need to understand how neighborhood environments structure peer networks. Yet little previous research has investigated the role of neighborhoods in the formation and character of peer networks.[3] In this chapter, I link the level and pattern of violence in disadvantaged neighborhoods to both the intensity of friendships between boys from the same neighborhood and to the age structure of peer networks.

Building on the description of neighborhood violence in the previous chapter, I argue that boys in more violent neighborhoods form intense friendships and interact more frequently with older peers because of both the need for protection and the role of violence in limiting social contact with others outside the neighborhood. Young men are forced to adapt to violent conditions and to protect themselves from victimization. Peer groups serve as an important form of protection, and shared experiences with violence and the need for high levels of trust intensifies ties to peers. Moreover, the social organization of violence leads to peer networks in poor neighborhoods with far more cross-age interaction and to far more friendships and acquaintances with older youth than we find among youth in more affluent areas. These dynamics elucidate one mechanism through which disadvantaged, violent neighborhoods shape the choices that adolescents make in seemingly unrelated domains such as romantic relationships and education, a mechanism I term *cross-cohort socialization*. Violence is one of the key characteristics of poor neighborhoods when it comes to adolescent outcomes, as it structures the peers with whom they interact on a regular basis.[4]

Neighborhood Violence and Bonds of Mutual Protection

For youth in Franklin and Roxbury Crossing, the neighborhood is a much more important context for the development of friendships than for youth in Lower Mills. This difference is linked to the neighborhood violence that youth in poor neighborhoods disproportionately face. While violence can lead to the breakdown of social networks among adults, as individuals retreat into their homes to avoid victimization, for adolescents the opposite often occurs. Neighborhood violence reinforces strong loyalties among neighborhood-based friendship groups.[5] As discussed in chapter 2, the social organization of violence magnifies the salience of neighborhood identities. In addition, trust can come not just from repeated and ongoing interactions but from shared experiences. As I discuss in chapter 4, though adolescents spend long periods of time at school with classmates, their bonds with them are considerably less strong, and at times nonexistent.

Particularly in poor neighborhoods, adolescents perceive their neighborhood peers to have a common set of shared experiences and to face the same daily challenges. These shared experiences and daily challenges often have to do with navigating the perils of street violence. A desire for safety and protection is often cited as the reason boys join gangs, but a formal gang is not the only way to seek protection through association.

Many adolescents rely on neighborhood friends and associates to help them defend themselves and to feel safe. Recall Simon from Franklin, who in chapter 2 explained that he does not like to leave his neighborhood without a "lump sum of people." David, seventeen and from Franklin, described how fights can break out between groups of adolescents at school:

> There's always somebody who think they ain't gonna like you. So, it would start off like, they'd be in a group; we'd be in a group. One of them don't like one of our friends, so we end up fighting. Then another one try to get big [act tough], and try to bring on something, [and it] just turns into a brawl. Then, we end up not liking them. Then, they finally hang out with some new people. They don't like them. That turns into more fights and more fights. That's basically how fights start. People that's walking the hallway like, "I don't like him 'cause he always looking at me."

Wherever a fight breaks out, David can expect his neighborhood friends to help him, and he knows his friends expect the same from him. One cannot abandon one's friends in a confrontation, even if it means risking injury. Friendships dictate that everyone must take the same beating, if it comes to that:

> When I got into a fight at the park, but my friends just jumped in. We all claim each other as cousins and all just tight friends. We just feel like, that's my friend. I can't see him getting beat up . . . We just all stick together. If there's a group bigger than us, we'll take an ass whipping. It doesn't matter as long as you just don't think you're gonna hit one of us, and we gonna [do nothing]. We gonna hit right back . . . Sometimes we go home bruised up.

Further evidence of the importance that adolescents in poor neighborhoods attach to mutual protection comes from a vignette about school effort that I discussed with many of the interview subjects. In this story, a boy has a very important test in school the next day, a test he must pass in order to be promoted to the next grade. The object of the discussion is to determine the situations under which the adolescent would choose to do something else rather than study for the test and thus to gauge how adolescents prioritize school effort when faced with potentially competing demands. Of course, putting school first is clearly the normative response, and so we may question whether an interview subject would really follow through as he claims he would. Yet precisely because studying is the strongly normative choice, any scenario under which the boys say they would choose not to study indicates that they attach strong importance to the competing demand. Other than a family medical emergency, the only scenario in which subjects consistently said they would skip studying (or take a break from studying) was when a friend came to their home and asked them to walk with him to the store because he was worried about getting jumped. These reactions to the vignette reveal the importance that adolescents attach to obligations of mutual protection that come with friendship.

Obligations of protection among neighborhood friends and peers can trump other considerations, such as interpersonal conflicts. Chris, who described in the previous chapter his experiences with neighborhood-based conflicts between Franklin Hill and Franklin Field, also noted that other boys from his neighborhood with whom he did not get along personally would still "have his back" in any conflict with neighborhood outsiders. Chris says they often talk negatively about him to others and try to "hit on" the girls Chris and his friends were seeing. However, when Chris got into an argument with a young man outside the local pizza joint, these young men stepped up to show their support for Chris in case the argument escalated into a physical fight: "They have our back, but they talk behind our back too. That's why I hesitated because it's like three or four people that will talk behind your back and try to take your girls. They just hate on you. But they have your back because they know you'll have their back."

When youth from the same neighborhood are called upon to defend one another and to defend the neighborhood, bonds form quickly. Trust in friends is essential if you must rely on them for your physical safety. Loyalty is not merely prized, it is a prerequisite for membership in peer groups. In extreme cases, commitment to neighborhood friends is akin to the closeness of soldiers who face combat together. As one mother put it, when describing her son's group of friends, "These kids, it's like they were in Vietnam. And nobody understands that. These kids are not bad kids, none of them. They are scared."

The notion that one's friends should "have your back" was common to boys in Lower Mills as well, but there these obligations were largely unnecessary, and such professed loyalties went largely unproven. In another vignette, one's friend is approached on the street by another boy itching for a fight. The aggressor's friends are there to back him up, and the subjects were asked what to do if they were in a situation in which their friend was challenged in such a way. In all three neighborhoods, most boys explained the importance of trying to avert a physical confrontation by talking through the conflict, but also said they would jump into the fight if either (1) their friend was being beat up badly or (2) the other boys' friends entered the fight. More telling, however, was what the boys thought of the vignette itself. All the boys in Roxbury Crossing and Franklin thought the story was realistic, something that had either happened to them, had happened to a friend, or might happen to them at any point. In contrast, the story sounded totally implausible to half of the Lower Mills boys. Delbert, fourteen, was one of those Lower Mills boys for whom the vignette seemed unrealistic. "It sounds like something more that would happen in a movie or a TV show, but I've never seen something like that happen in real life," he explained. When I asked how people in his neighborhood "look out for one another," he cited an example where a friend got hit by a car while riding his bicycle, and neighbors came out to help him and called both an ambulance and the police. For Delbert, looking out for one another is not about obligations of mutual protection, and he does not understand his friendships in that way.

Cyril, sixteen and from Lower Mills, also expressed support for the abstract notion that one should help one's friends in a fight. But when pushed on how such a scenario would really unfold, he insisted that one should just walk away or break up the fight, and that there would be no negative consequences to doing so.

INT: You said earlier that there aren't really very many fights around here, but how important is it to help out friends in a fight?
CYRIL: You just try to break it up because you want people to become friends again. You don't want to have them enemies.
INT: Are there situations where you would feel like you had an obligation to get involved in a fight?
CYRIL: Yeah. If there were like two on one. I'll help the person or try to break it up.
INT: And what do you think your friends would expect of you if they were in a fight?
CYRIL: They would expect me to help them or break it up.
INT: And what sort of things do people do around here to avoid getting into fights in the first place?
CYRIL: Walk away.

INT: Are there consequences to just walking away? I mean, is that usually going to solve the problem?

CYRIL: Yeah. That will usually solve the problem.

INT: Do people around here ever try to represent the neighborhood or defend the neighborhood from people if they talk trash about it or stuff like that?

CYRIL: No. Because this is just people you'll be around—play basketball with them.

INT: I see. So, stuff like that doesn't really happen?

CYRIL: No.

Contrast Cyril's perspective with that of David above. To Cyril, a fight is a onetime event with no potential for igniting a cycle of revenge and retribution, and it is unrelated to neighborhood or other group loyalties. Cyril seems unworried about someone being "punked" because he walked away from the fight. For David, walking away from a fight is not an option. One should get beat up along with one's friends rather than be punked.

Shared experiences with violence lead many Roxbury Crossing and Franklin boys to think of the neighborhood as more than just a collection of homes, but rather as a community or a family. Marcus, a sixteen-year-old resident of Roxbury Crossing, described his neighborhood as a "family," even though his neighborhood is a public housing development with high resident turnover and considerable ethnic diversity:

> Every neighborhood has its drug dealers, gangbangers, and it has its kids that go to school and do their normal thing. I done involved myself with a little bit of everybody, so I pretty much have a feel for how everybody has done lived in this neighborhood, and pretty much it's peaceful around here . . . because everybody knows everybody in this neighborhood. Everybody is pretty much family, so I've got to think this is one of the good neighborhoods actually to be in, because it's pretty much all family members.

This notion of neighborhood as family also generates pressures to go along with the family and support others, even if that is not in one's best interest. We met Tyree, seventeen, in the previous chapter when he explained the obligations he felt to his neighborhood peers in Roxbury Crossing and how these obligations were connected to neighborhood violence. Tyree is now living in a calmer neighborhood in Boston, but he grew up in Roxbury Crossing and felt strong connections to his friends in the neighborhood from an early age, even though he now realizes he did not know some of them very well. Their close connections evolved out of shared experiences and the mutual protection that developed through their common adventures and encounters on the streets. Tyree was a fairly good student in elementary school, but as he matured into an adolescent, he became more involved with his friends on the streets. In what his mother described as a particularly shameful incident for Tyree, his bike was stolen by a neighborhood youth, and his mother had to get it back for him. This incident was one of many that taught Tyree what Anderson (1999) calls the "code of the streets":

> If I walked away from a fight today, and I came back the next day on the block, people would really talk trash about, "You is a punk, you didn't want to fight." Until you fight that person, your reputation would go down. I'm not saying you have to live for a reputation, but sometimes you really have to defend yourself because if you didn't fight, you was gonna end up fighting anyway. Even your friends would talk about you if you didn't fight. So it's either you're fightin' your friends or you fightin' your enemy . . .
>
> If you're considered a punk in the neighborhood, everybody would pick on you, you know what I mean? You'd get jumped because you're a punk. Like if you walk down the street and you didn't fight Joey from up the street three days ago, they're going to mess with you. "I can take his money; I can take his shoes."

Tyree began to struggle in school when he stopped doing his homework so he could spend more time in the neighborhood. Through older adolescents and young men in the neighborhood, he became involved at age eleven or twelve in drug dealing, drinking alcohol, and smoking marijuana, "running with the in-crowd," as he described it. As he explained in chapter 2, he felt pressure to stay out on the streets with his friends, lest he lose the protection that the in-crowd provided. Tyree's connections to his neighborhood friends were about more than camaraderie or hanging out or playing basketball. They provided mutual protection, others who would "have your back" in a fight or confrontation, as long as you demonstrated that you had their back as well. Failure to participate in this system would result not just in loneliness or isolation but would mean a loss of respect on the street and a greater risk to Tyree's safety:

> I was out there running with the in-crowd, just to stay alive. When I really think back about it, it really is just silly to me, but that's just the way it was. That was the neighborhood I was living. I had to make sure I fit in with everybody else, [otherwise, I'd get] no respect. I'm not saying that respect from people you barely even know counts, but sometimes it

helps you. Like not having no respect from the people around the neighborhood, you really couldn't come outside, because you would get made
fun of, get picked on. So it was basically like, if you wasn't with everybody
else, you wasn't with nobody . . .

Under the system of mutual protection, commitment to the group and
willingness to put others' needs before one's own are constantly tested.
Those who fail these tests in more mundane matters cannot be relied
upon when loyalty really counts. Tyree continues:

> Say if I needed $30, no matter what I needed it for, if I asked you for $30
> and you had it on you and you didn't help, the people would really put it
> as, "Oh, you're really worthless. Why should we let you make money out
> here on this corner if you can't help me when I'm in a time of need?" We
> basically put that as a number one rule: always give on to the others.

These intense relationships were based on mutual protection, and once he
was no longer participating in that system, he was cast aside. It was not
until his family moved away that he realized the nature of his friendships
in Roxbury Crossing:

> I would say when I moved out of the neighborhood, I realized that they
> wasn't really my friends. You don't know who is your friend until they
> come and really care about you and ask about how you are doing after
> the matter. Because once I moved out the neighborhood, nobody called
> me. I told them, "I don't want to just stay out here late [until] twelve, one
> o'clock. I go in at ten o'clock." People are, "Oh, you are a punk. You go in
> early, da-da-da." So I realized, are these my real friends? Your real friends
> don't down you for the good things you do. They help you succeed with
> the good things you do . . . Basically nobody really cared about me no
> more because I wasn't in the neighborhood. So it made me realize that
> nobody cared from the beginning.

Once Tyree indicated his disinterest in participating in these mutual obligations (by failing to accompany friends in a dangerous neighborhood at
night), he was no longer in the "in-crowd."

Because loyalty among friends is highly prized and because friendship
groups provide protection as well as camaraderie, demonstrating loyalty
trumps other interests when they clash. Spending time on educational activities can come at the expense of maintaining these strong friendships.
Adolescents from poor neighborhoods like Franklin and Roxbury Crossing
take risks with schooling to protect friends and preserve ties.

Terrell, age sixteen and from Franklin, was in the tenth grade at a Boston public high school when an incident occurred that now threatens to derail his educational career. Terrell and his friend Shawn were entering school one day in April when Shawn was stopped by two school police officers. Shawn was ushered into a small conference room and asked to empty his pockets:

> I didn't know he had a knife. But he was going into his pocket. They said, "Empty out your pockets." And so, he emptied them out, and when he went to his pocket, bam! Got hit, before he even had a chance to do anything. The cop just didn't like him. When my friend went into his pocket, and the cops started hittin' him, I went into the room . . . I really didn't think anything would happen to me because I didn't do nothing to nobody. I went in the [conference] room, and I put my hands up, and they still arrested me . . .
>
> I wasn't really trying to interrupt nothing. I just wanted [my friend to be able to say,] "You know, there's somebody besides the two officers and the principal that seen what happened." I was pretty sure my friend was going to get arrested because he was fighting with the cop. But I didn't think anything would happen to me, I backed up against the wall. They said I hit the two officers, when I didn't hit anybody. I'm not saying I did, but I might have, very, very, very small chance of when I put my hand up, I hit the guy.

Terrell was arrested and taken to the police station where he spent the day and night in jail. The next day he was released to his mother because he had never been in trouble before. It took weeks for the court to hear his case, but in the end his offense was forgiven, provided he did not get into any further trouble for eighteen months. In the meantime, however, he was expelled from school. Assigned for two weeks to an alternative school for violent youth, Terrell did not receive a new placement until the end of the school year. Unable to attend school, he automatically failed all his classes and was forced to repeat the tenth grade. Terrell's split-second decision to try to protect his friend put him a year behind in school and greatly increased the risk he will join the ranks of Boston's high school dropouts. Terrell had been on the edge of failure that year, but he was on track to make a recovery. This incident pushed him over the edge:

> I was just on the verge of pulling myself together in school. I had kind of messed up the first marking term; I was like Ds. I started staying after school to do the homework, so I'd just do it right after school, and get it out the way. If I stayed after school there was no way I could get it wrong, because the teacher was always there to help. I got extra-credit work, and

the day it happened, I had an essay in my book that I was passing in for extra credit. It was gonna give me the points that I needed to pull my grades above a C. Then, this happened, and I didn't get to pass it in . . . If I'd just kept myself out of that room, I'd have passed, I would still be at [that school], I'd be playing football. But as it is right now, I don't know if I'm eligible yet.

Terrell's mother is worried that this incident will put him off track from going to college, though she is thankful he will not end up with a criminal record:

I was very surprised when the police called me. I couldn't believe they were talking about my son. Because as big as Terrell is, he has never been aggressive . . . So when they told me that Terrell went in there swinging at them, I didn't believe that.

You know how people say there are three versions—their version, their version, and the truth? I don't know if I fully believe Terrell's version of it either. I think that when Terrell came into the room—you see the size of Terrell—and the adrenalin was pumping and everything, I think that the officers might have been a little bit intimidated.

Could have been worse. He could have been charged with assault. It's nice he wants to help, but you have to think about yourself . . . We talked about this when I talked about him repeating the tenth grade. I said, "Terrell, you say you want to go to college," and I told him, "You know what? You're going to have to get there on your academics, because I don't have any money." I told him that this was like a second chance for him. So he's going to do the best he can—well, better than what he did before. So we'll see.

Contrast Terrell's experience of friendship loyalty with that of fifteen-year-old Charles from Lower Mills. Charles calls the boys whom he hangs out with in his neighborhood "associates" rather than "friends." They are available in the neighborhood, so they play basketball together sometimes after school. His real friends, he explained, live in other neighborhoods and are boys he has known for a long time from after-school programs and from another neighborhood where he lived when he was in middle school. But even these closer friends would not warrant a significant sacrifice of the type that Terrell made to help his friend or that David described above, regarding fighting for a friend. Charles does not anticipate doing such things out of friendship loyalty:

If you know it's real dangerous, and you think yourself is gonna get hurt, obviously, look out for yourself before you look out for other people. But if you don't think it's that dangerous, and you could do something to stop something . . . Like let's say you see someone on the street about to get shot, and you could tell them to put their head down so the bullet would miss them, you would tell them that. So, it's just like helping someone out so that you'd know that you did something to help it instead of just sitting there and just watching it all happen.

For Charles and many of his neighbors in Lower Mills, friendship carries fewer obligations.

Neighborhood Violence and the Age Structure of Peer Groups

The social organization of violence in poor neighborhoods also affects the age composition of the peer networks of the young men of Franklin and Roxbury Crossing. Compared to their counterparts in Lower Mills, the youth in these two neighborhoods interact more often with both older adolescents and young adults from their own neighborhoods. Recall, for example, that when Shawn Adams was stabbed, he was with a group of youth ages ten to seventeen, all from his public housing development. The peer networks of Roxbury Crossing and Franklin boys include individuals considerably older than them, sometimes as close friends but more often as acquaintances. Seventy-five percent of boys interviewed in Franklin and Roxbury Crossing reported older males from outside their families as part of their peer networks. These older males were typically at least two years older and sometimes as old as their midtwenties.

In contrast, the youth in Lower Mills were much less likely to interact with older adolescents and young adults outside their families; only 15 percent reporting doing so. Besides family members or friends of family members, they usually could not even name older adolescents or young adults, let alone describe meaningful interactions with them. When they could, these interactions often did not occur within their own neighborhoods. For example, thirteen-year-old Reynard, who had been living in his Lower Mills neighborhood for a few years, described his local peer network as all boys who are his own age. When asked about older boys, however, he described the older boys who live near his cousin, whom he visits once or twice a week. His cousin lives in a Franklin public housing development. Similar patterns are evident in nationally representative data. In an analysis of data from the National Educational Longitudinal Study of 1988, I found that tenth graders in disadvantaged neighborhoods are more likely to report interacting regularly with older individuals than their counterparts in more advantaged neighborhoods, controlling for individual and school characteristics (Harding 2009c).

Because their neighborhoods are part of a larger system of place-based violence, the boys in poor neighborhoods face real constraints in choosing friends. Though a small minority are more mobile, most tend to stay inside their own neighborhoods to avoid confrontation or victimization. Youth outside the neighborhood are more often potential enemies than potential friends.[6] This leaves as potential friends only those who live in the same neighborhood. Since the social space in question is quite small, same-age peers are not always in abundance, and older peers often fill the gap. Marcus, a sixteen-year-old from Roxbury Crossing, described how the lack of same-age peers in his housing development led him to socialize with the "older guys" who are a fixture of the sidewalks and streets. These older guys dispense advice to Marcus and his friends and try to keep them out of trouble with the police or with youth from other neighborhoods:

> [My two friends and I are] the three younger individuals that live around here, so we're forced to be around nothing but older guys . . . We're put around older guys that done been through it, that tell you—that tell you what to do, and what not to do, and when it's appropriate to confront somebody, or that you've got a problem with, and stuff like that . . .
>
> All the older guys around here, they said don't stand in one place for too long, because that's how you end up getting harassed [by the police], so I don't stand in too many places for too long.
>
> We just hang out, talk about the past, things that done happened— laugh, joke with each other. One person might be fixing on their car; one person might be fixing on their bike, listening to music, and we all just go gather around there, and just talk.

For Marcus, a dearth of same-age peers in his housing development leads him to a hang out with older males in the public spaces of the neighborhood. The scene he describes is frequently visible to any observer who spends much time in the neighborhoods of Franklin and Roxbury Crossing. Hanging out in a mixed-age group (with older individuals at the center and younger at the periphery), usually on the basketball court, a stoop, or the corner, older adolescents and young adults recount their experiences and dispense general advice.

Previous ethnographic work has described the extensive use of public space in poor neighborhoods, owing to overcrowded apartments and lack of air conditioning in the summer and leading to "street interaction and informal meetings" (Horowitz 1983, 39). The neighborhoods of Franklin and Roxbury Crossing are no different. For adolescent males, basketball courts, parks, and corners are a venue for cross-age interaction. Limited from venturing outside their local area by violence, they come into frequent contact with older males in these settings, and these males become part of their social networks, not necessarily as friends but as acquaintances. Joseph, age fifteen and from Franklin, frequents the basketball court and nearby athletic fields to play ball and to hang out, where he encounters individuals of every age, some older and some younger: "I know little kids and older, like adults, like in their twenties or so. Teenagers my age. I know most everyone on that court. And we made our own field a long time ago. They made it, the older people, and we all just play with them. And now we play with our own age and stuff like that. So it carries on through the ages, like a legacy." For Joseph, the neighborhood "legacy" is passed down to him from the older cohorts, and he will pass it on to the younger boys he encounters as well.

The interaction patterns and peer networks of similar youth in Lower Mills are quite different. Lower Mills youth tend to have age-homogeneous friendship groups. Their peer networks are more similar to those of middle-class children in the bureaucratized and age-graded social settings described by Lareau (2003). As a consequence, the streets and parks of the neighborhoods in Lower Mills present a stark contrast. Compared to Franklin and Roxbury Crossing, the regular observer of Lower Mills will witness far less activity in the neighborhood's public spaces. Boys are often willing to venture farther to seek out same-age peers, and they associate much less with older adolescents in the neighborhood. In addition, greater family economic resources mean that more youth participate in formal programs after school and on the weekends, or have the pocket money to venture outside the neighborhood to the movies or the arcade. This affects even those without such resources, as there are simply fewer others of any age hanging around the neighborhood with whom to interact. For example, when I asked fourteen-year-old Seth about the older guys in the neighborhood, he explained that he did not really know them. When pressed as to whether he had any interactions with them, he complained that they push the younger kids off the basketball court when the school gym is open on Friday nights: "They be trying to take over the court. They play full so everybody else don't get to play, we just sit there and watch."

When the youth of Lower Mills do associate with older peers, their interactions are more often family-based and take on a qualitatively different character. When age-inappropriate discussions or activities arise—for example, those about romantic relationships, sex, and drug or alcohol use—younger adolescents are pushed away. Delbert explains his experiences with older neighborhood peers.

> INT: So are there any older youths in the neighborhood, people that are a little older than you? You said the older youths would be your brother and his friends?
> DELBERT: Yeah. His friends about like a range of seventeen, eighteen, and nineteen. Some of them are twenty . . . They don't let us hang out with them. And then if we try hangin' out with them, they'll say, "Get out of here."
> INT: Why?
> DELBERT: Because they don't want us to do bad things. They want us to live our own lives and not copy what they do and to be ourselves.
> INT: What kind of bad things might you be doing if you were hanging out with them?
> DELBERT: Smoking [marijuana] probably.
> INT: And why would you guys want to hang out with them? It seems like you guys have tried and they said no.
> DELBERT: 'Cause they're older and they're more experienced and some of them . . . [pause], but most of them look like they're going in the right direction.

Older peers are also valuable for the protection they provide. We have already seen, in Chris's account of the conflict between Franklin Hill and Franklin Field in chapter 2, how the "little mens" called upon the "big mens" when the conflict became heated. Older youth or young adults can be protectors or intervene in conflicts before they become fights. James, who above described the violent incidents he witnessed near his home in Roxbury Crossing due to neighborhood beefs, explained how the older neighborhood youth he knows might be able to protect him:

> I know mostly everyone 'cause I've grown up with everyone. So kids who are eleven and I was seven and eight, I was probably outside playing basketball with. So now they're probably about sixteen, seventeen . . . The kids who you think was doing bad things, I know most of them. So I wouldn't feel bad walking down the street . . .
>
> I know most of them with a good relationship; I could talk to them and hold a conversation, but that's about it . . . I'm littler than most people. If somebody was like trying to jump me or do something stupid, [or] if somebody older was trying to jump me, they'd probably come in and stop it.

Association with older friends can also provide status and respect. This, of course, is an end in itself, but the respect that older friends provide translates into a measure of protection. Miguel, a sixteen-year-old Latino who grew up in a housing development in Roxbury Crossing, describes his relationships with older youth, which started when he moved to the development at age thirteen:

> MIGUEL: Most of my friends are a lot older than me. Probably like, maybe twenty [years old].
> INT: The ones from around the neighborhood, how did you get to know them?
> MIGUEL: Hanging out, like in the summer time we go out you know, we just sit down on the steps and chill, we talk and stuff like that. People playing baseball. They just tend to come over and they start playing, and you get to know them.
> INT: So why would someone who's younger want to be friends with people who are older?
> MIGUEL: Well probably a lot more people will respect the younger person. They wouldn't mess with him because he has a lot of older friends.

Younger adolescents' need for protection does not explain why older youth and young adults would befriend younger teens. In *All Our Kin* (1970), Carol Stack describes the cooperative survival strategies of the poor, African American residents of a ghetto neighborhood in a midwestern city. The strategies include swapping services such as child care as well as the development of "fictive kin" in which nonkin take on kinlike relationships. A similar dynamic is occurring in Franklin and Roxbury Crossing. The older adolescents and young adults see it as their duty to look out for the younger adolescents and children in the neighborhood. They have learned this behavior from adults and from those youth who have come before them. They also see this guardian and friendship behavior as a way to keep the neighborhood safe, to keep the peace and prevent the "drama" that conflicts can create.

David, a seventeen-year-old from the Franklin neighborhood, describes how he watches over younger adolescents as part of his role as a member of the community. Others who came before protected him, and the youth he looks out for will grow up to do the same.

> If I look after somebody, then they can probably grow up and look after somebody else—*that's basically what makes it a community*—everybody looking after somebody. So, if something happens in your neighborhood, you can like stop it before it gets worser. Like somebody coming in here, selling drugs, shooting, he know before those folks moved in, there was none

of that stuff going down. Like none of that stuff came to our neighborhood. And, basically, just watch out for your kids.

These caring behaviors are learned early. Younger adolescents take the
example that is set for them by older adolescents and practice it with the
children of the neighborhood. Jerome, a thirteen-year-old from Roxbury
Crossing, describes how he cares for the children in his neighborhood.

> JEROME: If the boys and the girls [are] fighting, you got to separate them,
> you got to go bring the boy to his mother and the girl to her mother.
> INT: When did something like that happen?
> JEROME: Four weeks ago. 'Cuz, the boy hit her too hard with the ball and
> she smacked him. And then he punched her and he didn't want to let her
> go. I had to separate them and bring them home.

Caring for younger children and adolescents extends beyond simply
keeping the peace. Older adolescents recount with pride how they help
the younger ones by giving them a dollar or two when the ice cream truck
comes around or when they want a bag of chips from the corner store. As
Stack (1974) has described, those who have money or other resources are
obliged to share it with others in the neighborhood. This set of norms extends to adolescents as well. For Marcus, who learned from his elders the
importance of not standing in one place for too long, relationships with
younger adolescents are about creating a family. Marcus correctly observes
that only a minority of the youth in disadvantaged neighborhoods have
fathers who play a regular role in their lives.

> MARCUS: Some kids don't know who their father is. With me, I know who
> my father is, but . . . ever since I was little, me and him never was able
> to get along with each other. I never had a big brother, so I never had an
> older person to look up to, to throw a football around with . . . So, when
> a younger guy comes and asks me he want to run and play ball, I'll be
> happy to play basketball with him; because I want him to feel like he
> has an older person to hang out with. If he doesn't have a father, or older
> brother, he knows that he can come outside and there's a guy outside that
> would like to play ball with him.
> INT: So what are some of the things that you try to impart on the younger
> kids?
> MARCUS: Just like the older guys tell me: Don't hang out in a place for too
> long. So, I tell the little dudes that are maybe like thirteen, twelve, don't
> hang out in one spot for too long, because that's going to make it look bad
> on you, and then now it's going to make it look bad on us, because now
> they think that we have you all out here doin' stuff.

The relationships and interactions that older boys have with younger adolescents are about more than altruism. By taking responsibility for their juniors, Marcus and David are also gaining the higher status that comes with adult roles. Whether it is breaking up a fight, providing a dollar for the ice cream truck, offering instruction on how to shoot a basketball, giving a lesson on avoiding police harassment, or, as we will see below, sharing knowledge about handling romantic relationships, Marcus and David gain a positive reputation among younger kids in the neighborhood as well as the respect of others who play the same role. In an environment in which mainstream sources of status and respect—work, education, and money—are in short supply, this status is meaningful.

Alternative Explanations?

This analysis has emphasized the importance of neighborhood violence in understanding the composition of friendship groups that link young adolescents to young adults in disadvantaged communities. Yet there could be alternative explanations for greater interaction with older peers in more disadvantaged neighborhoods.

One such explanation is the role of older family members in connecting younger adolescents with older peers in the neighborhood. In addition to older siblings, Lareau (2003) has argued that among working-class or lower-class families there is a great deal of interaction with extended family members such as cousins or uncles. Yet when my subjects described their interactions with older peers, these relationships were not typically family-based, nor was there a difference between adolescents with large extended families in their neighborhood and those without such families.

Another alternative explanation might be age mixing in schools. Given the large numbers of students from disadvantaged communities who are held back in school, sometimes multiple times, classrooms rather than neighborhoods might provide the context in which such cross-age relationships are formed. However, as chapter 4 will discuss in more detail, adolescent males from Boston's poor neighborhoods rarely form close relationships with classmates or interact with them outside of school unless they also live in the same neighborhood. Furthermore, when adolescents described older friends or acquaintances, these older youth or young adults were never former schoolmates.

A third alternative explanation is that relationships that formed prior to adolescence carry through to later years. In disadvantaged neighborhoods where many young children play together outside, cross-age relationships may be formed between ten-year-olds and seven-year-olds in the course of pickup games of football, basketball, and capture the flag. However, when discussing older friends and acquaintances, only one of the adolescents interviewed met them prior to adolescence (James, discussed above).

Older Peers and Cross-Cohort Socialization

The consequences of relationships with older peers depend on who these older peers are. Higher than average rates of male joblessness mean that the older youth and young adults who are both available and visible in high-poverty, high-violence neighborhoods are not always the most positive influences, though not for lack of good intentions.[7] For example, Marcus, who tries to be an older-brother figure to the boys in his neighborhood, is an occasional drug dealer, and at sixteen already has two young women claiming they are pregnant by him. He says he tries to hide these activities from younger boys, but it is hard to see how that is really possible. While previous research has noted the role of older adolescents and young adults in teaching younger boys how to commit crime and in bringing them into criminal apprenticeships (e.g., Thrasher 1927; Cloward and Ohlin 1960), my focus here is on the influence of older peers on how adolescents make decisions about other matters, particularly school and sexual relationships.

Not every older adolescent and every young adult male in the neighborhood deals drugs, impregnates multiple partners, or has dropped out of high school and stands on the corner. Indeed, the majority do not. Even in neighborhoods with high male joblessness rates, many males are not jobless (Newman 1999). In Franklin and Roxbury Crossing, the male joblessness rates in the 2000 census were 45 percent and 51 percent, respectively. The working- and lower-middle-class neighborhoods of Lower Mills have fewer idle young men and older adolescents of working age with whom younger adolescents might pass the time. (The male joblessness rate in Lower Mills was only 35 percent, very similar to the citywide rate of 31 percent.)[8] However, those who might serve as more positive role models are often not available to youth because they are working or in school.

Tyree, now age seventeen, described the characteristics and behaviors of the older peers in the Roxbury Crossing neighborhood where he grew up:

I'd say they were extended from like sixteen to like twenty-two. They was basically not going to school, selling drugs, shooting guns, and really basically doing all the negatives opposed to the positives. Like they would rather sell drugs than go job hunting. They would rather buy a gun than buy their mother some shoes or something, you know what I mean?

It seems like the older you get the worser it gets. Like if you're living in the neighborhood, if you started off young, the older you get, the harder it is to leave the neighborhood because you feel that's where you're from and you got to hold the neighborhood down. I would say it gets harder as you get older.

As a younger teen, Tyree did not see those older peers who were working or in school, as they were not hanging around the neighborhood. As a result, the older males who were actually present seemed more and more disadvantaged as they got older. He began to see himself becoming more like them as he hung around them and was involved in neighborhood rivalries, what he calls "holding down" the neighborhood. Tyree's experiences are consistent with research from nationally representative data. Drawing on survey data from Add Health, I find that adolescent boys in more violent neighborhoods are more likely to be friends with individuals who do not attend school (Harding 2008).

Older peers who might provide protection or status are likely to be those who are present on the streets on a regular basis, and not those in school or working. Miguel, now sixteen, described how he became friends with older teenagers when he first moved to his Roxbury Crossing housing development at the age of thirteen. These older friends spent a lot of time hanging out in the development, occasionally smoking marijuana. Miguel described how they almost led him to begin smoking as well.

MIGUEL: When I was younger and stupid, I used to be with them [older boys], while they were [smoking marijuana]. I never did it myself, I just used to be on the side.

INT: What age were you?

MIGUEL: Like maybe thirteen or fourteen. When I probably first moved around here. You know they were my friends and stuff, so if they wanted me to go with them somewhere, I would. I wasn't just going to let them go by themselves. I wasn't really into [smoking marijuana] but . . . I was like, I wonder how it works, and stuff like that. 'Cuz I've always been around it but never actually experienced it myself.

INT: And how old were these guys?

MIGUEL: About four or five years older.

INT: And how did you become friends with them?

MIGUEL: From hanging around the development.

Before Miguel got involved in drug use himself, one of these friends was arrested for selling marijuana to an undercover police officer, and Miguel decided to stay away from this group. While Miguel of course had some choice as to who he would associate with, as he explained above these older boys were the peers who were available locally and hanging around in front of the entrance to his building. He got to know them in particular because both he and they spent most of their time hanging out in the development.

Eduardo, now seventeen, recalled how, at age twelve, older friends in the neighborhood introduced him to drinking, smoking marijuana, and stealing cars. At about the same time, he became considerably less interested in education and stopped going to school for a time in the eighth grade.

> EDUARDO: I turned thirteen in fall of '99. That summer of 2000—that's when everything went downhill. By the time eighth grade came around, I went to school for maybe about a week.
> INT: If you could think back to that time, when you first started to lose interest in school, why do you think you weren't interested?
> EDUARDO: The peers around me. [We were] smoking [marijuana], drinking. We were always around girls. Those type of things. Stealing cars. Selling car parts.
> INT: How did you get into doing those kind of things?
> EDUARDO: The so-called friends around me, they knew how to steal cars. I just got into it. At first, I just started breaking car windows 'cause I didn't know how to steal a car; then, slowly, I learned.
> INT: Were they your age or were they older?
> EDUARDO: Maybe a little older, but I considered them my age. Now that I look back at it, though, they weren't my age, but when I thought about it [at the time], they were my age. It's confusing.
> INT: You thought of them as, kind of, being in the same spot as you?
> EDUARDO: Same age. Exactly. The other guys that were fourteen or fifteen were still acting younger. At twelve, I was into girls. I was into going out, partying, taking a girl out to a restaurant. I grew up too fast because I was around older people, older guys, my whole life . . . I just ended up acting mature. The other twelve-year-olds, they were thinking about, Mommy, buy me some sneakers. At twelve years old, I was thinking [about] how to get 'em myself.

Miguel and Eduardo were actually imitating the behavior of older friends with whom they were hanging out. Older friends and acquaintances can also have more subtle influences because of their cultural power to frame or contextualize daily life, a process I call cross-cohort socialization. Through both their words and their deeds, they expose younger adolescents to cultural models that often differ from those privileged in mainstream or middle-class culture. The older adolescents and young adults who are respected in the neighborhood because of their mastery of the streets regularly dispense advice about girls, school, and staying out of trouble. Often this advice is in keeping with mainstream cultural models, but at times it is not.

Younger boys talk about getting advice from these older friends, and older boys reveal the advice they got when younger, but none of this chatter is very specific. Young teens do not go to older ones with specific problems on which they would like guidance. Nor do they typically have one-on-one discussions about a particular problem with which the younger adolescent is grappling. Rather, the guidance comes in the form of general statements that can be interpreted and applied to future situations. As Marcus described above, hanging out in a mixed-age group (with older individuals at the center and younger at the periphery), older peers recount their experiences and dispense general advice, such as the wisdom of not standing in one place for too long lest the police think you are a drug dealer, and the need to watch out for girls who are simply after money and gifts rather than a relationship.

General admonitions have little traction when they come from teachers or parents. But older males, especially those with status that has been earned on the streets, command attention because they are seen as role models who have "been through" experiences similar to those their younger counterparts will soon face. By virtue of their reputations for toughness, their exploits in previous conflicts, and often their resources from dealings in the underground economy, these young adults sit atop a "street" status system that confers upon them cultural power, particularly in the eyes of adolescent boys (see also Anderson 1999).

Through these discussions with older peers, younger adolescents are exposed to ways of thinking about problems, solutions, and decisions that are sometimes at odds with mainstream or middle-class convention. Fernando, fifteen and a resident of a public housing development in Franklin, became friends with his seventeen-year-old neighbor, Ben, who lives across the hall. Fernando sees Ben as someone who will have his back if there is a conflict. Ben then introduced Fernando to his group of friends, who are mostly twenty-one and twenty-two years old, and Fernando began hanging out with this group on a regular basis. The most frequent topic of conversation, according to Fernando, is girls. Fernando moves back and forth between staying with his mother or his father and stepmother, which produces an often difficult home life. The result is that Ben and his group of older friends are a frequent source of information and advice about romantic and sexual relationships for Fernando.

Daniel, a seventeen-year-old from Roxbury Crossing, described how he was first approached by Reggie, an older male from the block. Reggie is well respected in the neighborhood, and Daniel gained the respect of other men Reggie's age by his association with Reggie. Reggie in turn gains status among his peers by developing a following among the boys Daniel's age. Daniel's and Reggie's discussions include romantic relationships and the history of the neighborhood.

> DANIEL: My man [Reggie] is pretty cool. And he's an old guy with a lot of wisdom. [Reggie] is like twenty something. He be like, "Stay out of trouble. Don't go do things like that." Like don't go start any problems with anybody. "Follow your dreams and be true" and stuff.
> INT: And how did you get to know him?
> DANIEL: Just chillin' outside one day and he came over and, "What up you all?" We're like, "What up [Reggie]?" We knew his name and everything 'cause people used to talk about him.
> INT: And are there advantages to being friends with some older people like his age?
> DANIEL: Yeah. You get like a little bit of clout 'cause you know someone a lot older than you. And like most people really respect that, like, "Oh he knows what's his name. He's cool." Like some older dude you might not know, but he know. Be like, "This is my little mans right here." And you be like, "Whaddup" and stuff and they start talking to you. So it's pretty cool.
> INT: So what are the kind of things you talk about with him?
> DANIEL: How life is; girls and cars and everything and how the block is. He's like, "If your woman starts yelling at you for nonsense, don't get mad about it." Like stuff that you need to know when you get older . . . [Also,] don't mess with a girl that has kids. 'Cause she might have you try to pay child support or just have you be attached and the kids like you, then up and leave one day . . . Like don't try to be a father figure to a kid that you know is not yours, he's like, "Don't get too attached or nothing" . . . He used to tell us a lot of things about our block, how it used to be very known in history and stuff. How [a local store] stayed open during the riots. It's like history class outside of school.

Chapter 6 addresses in greater detail the role of money and material resources in romantic relationships among youth in different types of neighborhoods, but we begin to see here how ideas about women using relationships with men for economic gain are passed from older to younger males in the neighborhood. While Daniel's own experiences certainly inform his attitudes, when I spoke with Daniel two weeks later about romantic relationships, some of the same ideas populated his current thinking. He described how fully half of the young women he might meet are "gold diggers," just out to get a man's money, making it difficult to have a real relationship.

> INT: So how do you tell whether a girl is going to be a gold digger?
> DANIEL: When girls ask you for money all the time, like, "Can I have $5?" Like they ask for $5 and you have like $100 in your pocket, and you be like, "Here's $5, what's $5? I have $100, that's nothing." Or they always want something, like, "You gonna buy me this?" It's like, "I'm not a ATM card, nor a bank." It's like, "You have a job. Go pay for your own stuff."

By contrast, boys from Lower Mills offer more conventional views of the challenges of girlfriends and relationships. They are less worried about girls who are just interested in sex or money and more worried about making an emotional connection. Darnell, thirteen and from Lower Mills, explains how he thinks about the traits girls are looking for in a boyfriend, and bases it on what he looks for himself in a girlfriend. He explicitly rejects the idea that most girls are interested in a man's money.

> INT: What do you think girls your age are looking for in terms of a boyfriend?
> DARNELL: Just somebody they could feel comfortable with, that's what I would want. Somebody that's just cool, that's not talking a lot. They just want somebody to listen to them, talk back to them. Somebody you're gonna have a good time with, that you can respect.
> INT: Some people say that girls are more after looks or a guy who's got money or stuff like that?
> DARNELL: No. I don't think it's the case. I don't have any of those problems . . . On TV, they always say the bad girls always get the good guys. I figure myself that's what I try and be. One of those good guys. That's why I try to stay away from the bad girls.
> INT: So what's someone who is a bad girl and what are they like?
> DARNELL: Just somebody that disgusts you. They just do like rude things all the time. I was with one girl that did that, so it didn't work . . . It's like basically the main thing was every time I talked to her, she would kind of like push me away. It's like she wouldn't try to leave. It's just she always talked about something different and I didn't like that . . . Like her and me and stuff, but she'd always change the subject to something else . . . It was nothing like personal.

Darnell's concerns about relationships have more to do with the inter-personal connection he might establish with a girlfriend than with the trust issues surrounding money and sex that figure so prominently among the boys from Franklin and Roxbury Crossing. For the boys of Lower Mills, the "gold-digger" category that Daniel described carries very little salience because it is not constantly reinforced by the tales of older peers.

Another example of the role of older youth in framing romantic and sexual relationships comes from Chris, the fourteen-year-old Franklin resident who described the conflicts between Franklin Hill and Franklin Field housing developments in chapter 2. Older adolescents and young adults play a major role in those conflicts. Chris turns to them for information about sex as well.

> CHRIS: I've had sex without a condom twice. Twice when I was younger, because I didn't know how to do it when I was young . . . Then the condom broke once on me, but I was young! So, I'm just like, "All right, now I've got to get my head straight."
> INT: How did you get your head straight?
> CHRIS: Started talkin' to people. Now I'm like, "What? Oh, it's chlamydia. How can you get it?" "How do you get AIDS?" "Blood to blood transmission . . . Fingering chicks with an open cut is not good." I'm like, "Oh yeah? I didn't know that." Just started listening. If you start listenin' to people, they'll open your eyes.
> INT: So who did you learn this from? You learned a lot of this from your father?
> CHRIS: No. A couple from my mom, my uncle, my older niggas out here [in the neighborhood]. I asked them too like, "Yo, you ever been burnt [had a sexually transmitted infection] before?" Like, "What's chlamydia?" They'll tell me like it just burn a lot, because it happened to them. Like, "Don't go raw [have sex without a condom], it's not good." I'll never go raw again, I'll tell you that much.

Chris's account illustrates the complexity of the messages that adolescents receive from their older peers. On the one hand, he gets good advice about avoiding sexually transmitted infections and using condoms. Yet he is also being told that if one takes the proper precautions, it is appropriate and even desirable for boys his age (recently turned fourteen) to have sex, even with someone he does not know very well.

Chris's mother encouraged him to refrain from sex until he is older, but he is getting the opposite message from his "older niggas" on the street. Peers who present one's children with competing messages are a common lament among parents, rich and poor alike, but when those competing messages are coming from older peers with considerable status on the streets, parents are at a significant disadvantage. Chris's mother, who tried in vain to get him to wait until he was a little bit older, gave up and changed her focus when he told her at age thirteen that he had sex. When we spoke a few months later, Chris's mother described her new perspective: "At one point I [disapproved of him having sex], but now I'm at the aspect that I [don't], because we talk about it. He hasn't had sex since that one time. I think he found out he wasn't ready." She then focused on making sure he used a condom if he had sex again, a viewpoint that Chris interprets as approval, though his mother thinks of it as being realistic.

Interactions with young adults also influence the frames that adolescents bring to their school experiences. Though these educational frames will be discussed in detail in chapter 7, one such frame that adolescent boys from Franklin and Roxbury Crossing hear a lot about is that it is the rare teacher who actually cares about students. The vast majority of teachers are merely there for the money—to "collect that check"—or because of the pleasure they get from the power and authority that they wield in the classroom.

Simon, growing up in Franklin, was sixteen and about to start his sophomore year at a public high school when we discussed his experiences during the previous academic year, his first at the school (he would later drop out of high school). Simon had struggled in middle school, and he and his mother had hoped that high school would mean a new beginning. Simon explained his view of the typical teacher in his high school:

> You can tell they are just there for the check. They are like, "I don't give a hell, I got my high school diploma." That's all they care about. They're getting their check at the end of the day, they got their high school diploma already. But these kids don't. When they get sent home, that's a day less of education they just lost right there. I know that's what the teachers think like.

When Simon observed students being suspended from school, and when he himself was suspended for fighting and missed several days of school, this frame informed his interpretation of these events. From this perspective, teachers and staff do not care enough to create a school environment in which students feel safe, so fights break out as students jockey for status. Teachers are eager to remove students from the school because that makes their jobs easier; they have one less student to deal with. Notably absent here is the alternative notion, held by most teachers, administrators, and many parents, that students who use violence in

school are a threat to other students and disrupt the learning environment for others.

Simon's frame does not come from his mother, who expressed considerable satisfaction with the school and its staff, nor does it derive from
the church-run summer programs and community center in which Simon
occasionally participates. When not at school or the church programs, Simon spends most of his time in the local neighborhood park, where boys
his age play basketball, where the neighborhood's unemployed young
adults hang out to pass the time, and where, according to both Simon and
his mother, some sell and use drugs. While Simon's own experiences have
certainly informed and reinforced the frame though which he views his
teachers, the amount of time that Simon spends in the park with these
young adults, most of whom themselves dropped out of high school, suggests their views and experiences in the Boston public schools are playing
an important role as well. Simon himself implicitly recognizes the influence of older peers: "There's generations at that park. I can't help that I'm
in it, but I'm also trying to go above it."

Father Absence and the Influence of Older Peers

Adolescent boys who do not have regular contact with their fathers are
especially susceptible to the influences of cross-cohort socialization. For
them, older adolescents and young adult males in the neighborhood can
play an important social and emotional role because "your mother cannot teach you to be a man." In addition to role modeling, attention from
older males also provides an emotional affirmation. Father absence was a
particularly painful part of the lives of the boys whose fathers were dead,
incarcerated, or simply not around, having moved away from Boston or
started a new family with a new partner. Boys who talked freely about violent behavior, drug use, sexual behavior, and school failure often found it
too uncomfortable and distressing to discuss their limited or nonexistent
relationships with their fathers.

Boys without fathers in their lives frequently gravitate toward potential male role models, both for the information and advice they can provide and the attention that affirms their value as someone worth caring
for. Hence Marcus described how his own poor relationship with his father
motivated him to play a father or big-brother role with younger kids in the
neighborhood. His assessment of the frequency of father absence among
children in poor neighborhoods is correct. According to the 2000 census
(summary file 3, table P16), about two-thirds of children under age eigh-

teen in both Franklin and Roxbury Crossing live in a household without an adult male. The comparable figure for Lower Mills is 41 percent.

Jared of Franklin is now eighteen, and looking back on his experiences growing up without his incarcerated father and as the oldest of four children, he explained the appeal of the older guys who his mother tried desperately to shield him from. These days he has a relationship with a mentor from his church, but before that he craved attention from male role models. Like Marcus, he also now finds himself playing the big-brother role to younger kids, though Jared is likely a better role model than Marcus, having graduated from high school, taken college prep courses, landed a job, and been accepted at a local community college:

> I know for myself one reason why I always talked to guys who were older than me, was because I wanted a father figure or a big brother . . . And I have friends who are younger than me, or they consider themselves my friends . . . They were like people who I taught, spoke to, and people who I learned stuff from as well because they would explain something to me and I would listen . . . If you have someone who's older than you, you have someone who's going to be able to back you up, especially if they're a good friend of yours, rather than someone who's younger. They're older than you so they're protecting you. You have some friends who are younger than you and you're protecting them. So it's like trying to gain people's back. [As] if you were to try and develop a family in a manner that will not be disrupted.

Montel is fifteen and lives in Franklin. He described his relationship with an older friend, Jay, who is eighteen and just finished high school. Jay always pays for things for Montel and his twin brother when they go out, and Jay looks out for them like an older brother or a father would.

> MONTEL: Me and my brother and Jay go to places. And since he got a job and everything, he'll pay most of the stuff. He always looks out for us, like a big brother. Like he worked at McDonald's so he used to help us out all the time when we'd go up there.
>
> INT: Has he ever protected you or anything like that?
>
> MONTEL: Yeah. He does it all the time. I can't remember any fights or anything like that, but he's always helping me out. I remember one time we was on the roof. And I hate heights. It didn't look that high when we were on the ground, but when we got up there, I wasn't getting down from there. So he came up there and he helped me get down. So he helped me out a lot of times.
>
> INT: Do you think it's different being friends with Jay than with [a friend your own age]?

MONTEL: Maybe it's a little different because Jay is older, so he's always looking out for us more.

Montel in turn helps out the younger boys in the neighborhood, engaging in father or big brother-like behavior with them, such as fixing bikes and playing ball: "The kid downstairs [age eight], he asks me to fix his bike. I help him fix his bike, I put some air in his tires. And my cousin, he's younger than me, I help him out. We always play together. Oh, and sometimes when me and my friends we go and play football in the park behind the school. There are some little kids we play with."

Jay is an example of an older neighborhood peer who provides a more conventional influence than Daniel's friend Reggie, Chris's "older niggas," or Simon's "generations" at the local park. With a high school diploma and a job, even one in the low-wage service sector, Jay comes closer to modeling decisions and behaviors consistent with mainstream views about the importance of education and work. Together, these heterogeneous older peers expose boys in poor neighborhoods to conflicting cultural models, which is discussed in chapters 5 through 7. Chapters 6 and 7 also provide additional examples of socialization by older peers.

Neighborhood Violence, Institutional Distrust, and Cultural Resonance

The cultural power of the older males who display mastery of the street life is not the only reason that younger boys take their cultural messages seriously. Another reason is that these messages often resonate with the daily experiences of boys from Roxbury Crossing and Franklin. Michael Schudson (1989) defines "resonance" as the extent to which a script or frame is compatible with others already in play.[9] Because older boys can help younger boys make sense of their own daily experiences in the neighborhood, their messages carry greater weight. As residents of violent neighborhoods, one particularly salient neighborhood experience for boys in Roxbury Crossing and Franklin is dealing with the police.

Boys from Roxbury Crossing and Franklin see the police in their neighborhoods on a daily basis. The media and popular culture portray the African American community as antagonistic toward law enforcement. However, opinions of the police are actually more varied and nuanced, at least in Boston. Indeed, the boys in Franklin and Roxbury Crossing are often frustrated that the police, with their considerable power, do not do more to keep their streets safe and their neighborhoods free of drug dealers and drug addicts. For many, the police are too scarce. Yet there is also anger over harsh police tactics and lack of respect from some officers. Police too often abuse their powers. A kid who has escaped mistreatment or disrespect knows many others who have seen the rogue side of the law. Experiences with police and advice on how to deal them are frequent topics of conversation. Recall for example, Marcus's description above of the lessons he got from older peers on the street about avoiding police harassment, and how he in turn passed that advice on to younger adolescents.

When Manuel, age fourteen, talked about the police in his Franklin neighborhood, he made it clear that police were slow to respond to trouble and not around enough to prevent it. But he also described how police mistreated him.

> MANUEL: Police don't come around here often. They just come here like every other day, and patrol it, and come back. Like every bad thing that might happen with the shootings, the next day the police would just drive by, get very suspicious about people . . . They should just like really drive by in the police cars so we know that they're around . . .
>
> People get more nervous when the police are around. So the police would get more suspicious about them. I think they should like just like come here like just drive by, like once or twice around here every day, because like people like, "Where are the police at?" Especially when something bad happens, the police take like five hours just to get down here. As if they're not in a rush to help . . .
>
> I think some [people] are police officers because they like to help other people. But some police officers are real mean. They'll like ask you personal questions, and they'll make you answer it, [even] if you don't want to.
> INT: Have there been situations that have happened to you or to your friends where the police were mean?
> MANUEL: No. Because we basically like, if there's a police patrolling by, we'd basically like try to ignore the police, instead of like just waiting until they drive by . . . They really sometimes get on people's nerves, because they would ask you the same question every other day. They do kind of get annoying because they'll stop in your way, and just look at you like for five minutes, and then leave.

Officers stop youth on the street and "profile" them by asking a series of questions about where they live and what they are doing. If they suspect that the boys might be carrying weapons, drugs, or other contraband, the officers will also search them. Being searched is a particularly humiliating and frightening experience, especially for the younger boys. Because most youth crime and violence takes place in groups, small crowds of young minority males hanging out on the street are a frequent target for police observation, questioning, and searching. Manuel and his friends try to ignore the police as they circle the neighborhood, but they feel watched.

The police are "just doing their job," boys would explain, but this did not diminish the anger that they felt over police treatment. To be questioned or searched is to be accused of criminal activity or other wrongdoing. It is doubly unsettling to be disrespected in the process. Police officers insult them, detain them, and manhandle them without consequence. Their size, experience with violence, weapons, and power to arrest means that cops seem to be in total control of the situation. The boys, on the other hand, are made to feel powerless, demeaned, and embarrassed. Neighbors, friends, and enemies witness the humiliation. In a social environment in which status and respect are highly prized, public episodes of powerlessness—even at the hands of the police—are particularly distressing, as one of Ramon's (seventeen and from Roxbury Crossing) experiences suggests:

> It was embarrassing. It was me [and four friends]. And we just coming out the store. We obviously looked like a large group. Everybody has something to eat in their hand. We sitting there and we're just trying to have a good time, and they gonna stop us for no reason. And the thing that makes it embarrassing is that everybody was out there. Before we had went to the store there was these girls that we just started to talk to, and they was out there too, and we're sitting there getting our pockets searched and checked, and they sitting there laughing at us. Out here in the projects, when people see the police, everybody's gonna come out there. We was like the center of attention. They just had to do it for a show. They probably checked us 'cause we was running in a crew. So they surrounded us. It's a big crew, a whole bunch of black kids out there just chilling. I felt like my pants had fallen down, and everybody was laughing.

In contrast, Lower Mills youth had much less to say about the cops. For them, police presence was adequate given the rarity of public violence and crime, and their interactions with police officers were minimal. A typical account was provided by thirteen-year-old Kevin, who had been living in Lower Mills for almost a year. Kevin had nothing negative to say about the police in his neighborhood, and even recounted a story in which a police officer mediated a dispute between two of his friends.

INT: How are the police around here?
KEVIN: Good, 'cause at night they have like the cops just looking and every time you look at the corner, you see another cop there . . . My friend, he was getting into a fight and then the cops came and stopped it. And he told

him to shake hands and that was cool . . . Snowball fight. He beat this kid around his face, and then my friend got mad and hit him. And the cops stopped and said, "Hey, hey, no fighting." And he came and talked to them and said, "What's the matter?" And then I didn't hear what he was saying 'cause he told them over there. Then all I saw was them shaking hands.

INT: Do you think the neighborhood is better off when there's more police around, or worse off when there's more police around?

KEVIN: Better off with cops here.

In Franklin and Roxbury Crossing, police come to symbolize the dual failure of institutions in mainstream society. They fail to protect young people from violence and crime, and compound the problem by failing to treat neighborhood residents, particularly young minority males, with dignity. The natural conclusion for the boys of Roxbury Crossing and Franklin is that an important subset of police officers do not actually care about their safety or general well-being and abuse their power rather than use it to advance the public good. A cynicism about motives grows: Police officers take their jobs only for the salary or for the power that they wield. The rest of law enforcement and other government officials allow this to happen and are therefore implicated as well.

That these experiences—often the first the boys have with the institutional mainstream outside of school—are overwhelmingly negative serves to reinforce the notion that the larger society does not care about them; it does not take their interests into account and does not care what happens to them. The result is a frame of *institutional distrust,* a lens that negatively colors future interactions with not just the police but also other important social institutions and actors, like a veil of suspicion and doubt. I specifically avoid using the term "oppositional" here because I do not wish to suggest that experiences with the police lead boys to reject mainstream values such as the importance of education, hard work, and marriage. Rather, the institutional distrust frame refers to a lack of confidence in the capacity of mainstream institutions and the individuals who run them to aid boys from places like Roxbury Crossing and Franklin to realize mainstream values. Boys with this frame are then much more willing to listen to the words of older peers on the street who "tell it like it really is" and "done been through it" and who offer other unconventional or alternative cultural frames and scripts.

The institutional distrust frame influences boys' interpretations of their experiences in other contexts, such as school. The idea that teachers and other school staff are not interested in the well-being of their students but rather in getting paid and in wielding power—described above by Simon—colored their interpretations of school experiences. Junior, age fifteen and from Franklin, made the link between teachers and police officers explicit as he described an incident in school in which he felt disrespected by the authorities:

> Teachers, they're just like cops, the way they talk to you. They talk to me like I'm a nobody. Like I was in class talking to my friend. I started laughing. My teacher doesn't like it when I smile. So she sends me out of class, goes to [the administrator] and he's like, "You have to go home." While I'm walking out and he's still talking, he's like, "Oh, you think you're a tough guy? You think you're a tough guy?" I just felt like punching and hitting.

Based on his experiences, Daniel also sees the parallels between teachers and cops. Both are capricious power mongers who do not care about young men like him:

> The detecs [detectives] usually come out their cars and start frisking people or start asking the harder questions like, "Do you know what time it is?" When you can see all of them got watches. Or they'll stop you for no reason. Hop out and like, "Oh, you're violating parole." But I never been to jail. Or they try to run your name in the computer and they don't come up with nothing, they get mad about that. And it's like they really don't have no respect for anybody 'cause they think they're the police and they're above the law. But you guys are supposed to enforce the law, but yet you all are breaking it.
>
> They would see a group of us sitting on the stoop. As soon as they see us, they'd be real slow. You can tell they looking. They looking like you about to go run or something when they come back around. They come back around like six times.
>
> It's like most police sure do their job, but other police it's like, "Oh, I don't care about this job. I don't care about the kids on the streets. If they go to jail, that's more money for us." And if someone gets shot in the neighborhood, they're like, "We don't care." It's like, "Oh, that's less people we have to worry about."

For Daniel, high school teachers are cut from the same cloth. They are disrespectful and abuse the power they have over young people for their own ends:

> Some of the teachers really didn't care about their students. They'll tell you straight up, "If you don't pass this class, you're gonna be a burger

flipper." You're supposed to give us encouragement, enthusiasm. But they don't do that. They just, "You're gonna be a low life. You're gonna be someone's garbage picker." They just push you like that.

Tenth grade, it was all right. I got to know the school better, people got to know me better. But it was the same problem, teachers not devoted to their work . . . It was like 70/30. It was like more teachers really didn't care what the students did . . . Teachers play favorites. If they don't like you, you probably not gonna make it that far in that school 'cause they're gonna set up things to bring you down. But if they do like you, they're gonna have everything in their power to do for you to succeed and everything.

If a teacher doesn't like you but you're able to do good work, they're not gonna accept it. Cause I remember I had a teacher that told me in eleventh grade if I don't do this one project she's gonna fail me for the rest of the term. And the other three terms following them. And I'm like, "You can't do that 'cause I don't do one project." I said, "My grade right now is a B, so one project is not gonna bring me down to an F." She said, "Oh yes it is. If I say it is, it is." I'm like, "So you're gonna jeopardize my schooling so I can do better in different grades and stuff, so I can go to college or something just 'cause you don't like me."

Boys' frequent and negative interactions with police, a result of living in poor neighborhoods where crime and violence rates are high, reinforce distrust of social institutions. This frame is then available for interpreting their experiences in other domains including schooling, coloring their perceptions of the behavior and motivations of other actors such as teachers and administrators. It also magnifies the salience of cross-cohort socialization, as the messages of older street peers resonate with the institutional distrust frame, particularly those messages that conflict with mainstream messages, whether they be about violence or about other domains such as school.

Conclusion

This chapter has presented two ways in which the level and social organization of violence in Boston's poor neighborhoods affect the same-sex peer relationships of adolescent boys. Because adolescents must rely on peer groups for protection and safety, adolescents in poor neighborhoods form particularly close bonds with male friends. Group membership is important because without it an individual is more susceptible to victimization. Through shared experiences with violence and strong needs for loyalty in the face of confrontations with other youth, trust is developed among groups of neighborhood friends, much in the same way that close bonds form among soldiers in combat. These close bonds of mutual protection have the potential to amplify peer effects among youth in poor neighborhoods. One must go along with the crowd to ensure one's safety. Youth in more advantaged neighborhoods face fewer risks of victimization and tend to have more same-age friendships based on interests and more school ties than place-based ties.

Because of cross-neighborhood conflicts, the neighborhood becomes one of the only geographic spaces where a young man is safe from challenge or victimization at the hands of youth from rival neighborhoods, regardless of whether one is actively involved in neighborhood beefs. The result is a restricted set of peers who are candidates for friendship. With fewer options one's own age, older peers become a more attractive choice. Older friends also become a source of protection, both indirectly through the reputational advantage that comes with having older friends and directly through their capacity to intervene in disputes. Notions of community based on the cooperative survival strategies employed among adults and the status benefits of caring for others provide the framework through which older adolescents understand their associations with younger youth.

These interactions between older and younger youth expose younger adolescents to local frameworks and understandings regarding not only crime and deviance but also school, work, and romantic and sexual relationships. Because those older youth and young adults who are visible and available in disadvantaged neighborhoods often present models at odds with those of mainstream society, these relationships have the potential to adversely affect younger adolescents' later decision making around education, sex, and romantic relationships. Adolescent boys who have little or no relationship with their fathers, the norm in poor neighborhoods, are particularly susceptible to the influences of older peers. In addition, the position of these older peers atop the street hierarchy gives them cultural power to frame and contextualize life in the neighborhood and beyond for younger adolescents. Moreover, their messages resonate with the daily experiences and frames of institutional distrust of the younger boys in the neighborhood. This cross-cohort socialization constitutes one mechanism by which growing up in a poor neighborhood affects adolescent decision making and behavior.

Despite my emphasis here on the cultural power of older adolescents and young adults on the streets, I do not wish to argue that adolescents in disadvantaged communities are *only* exposed to the cultural models presented by older friends and acquaintances or that the models that older adolescents provide are always deviant. They are, perhaps, more likely to be so because there is a degree of "reflection onto the street." The working men or college students are less available to play this role. Instead, the social processes I have described here explain how adolescents encounter—and why they take seriously—local cultural models that can be at odds with more mainstream models held by others in their communities and elsewhere. As chapters 5 through 7 argue, adolescents in such neighborhoods must contend with an environment with a wide range of cultural models. Cross-cohort socialization is an important source of such models, but it is not the only one.

Violence in disadvantaged neighborhoods often pulls adults apart, making them afraid to venture out or make connections with others, for fear of becoming entangled in conflicts or of being victimized. Ironically, violence can serve to unite adolescents in the same neighborhood, as they come together against outsiders and as they find their own geographic and social space constricted. Anderson (1999) has written that adults often do not understand the code of the street and so have trouble helping or relating to the young people who must deal with it on a daily basis. A similar dynamic is at work here. Adults, especially those of the grandparent generation, have trouble understanding the neighborhood-based organization of the violence with which their sons and grandsons must contend.

Previous work on the social organization of inner-city neighborhoods has highlighted the age segmentation of street-corner groups (Suttles 1968; Horowitz 1983). While Suttles and Horowitz disagree on the sources of age segmentation, they both argue that it is an important element of social life in these environments. Young people are described as associating primarily with others their own age, though occasionally combining across age groups when conflict with other territories demands it. In contrast, the account I have given here, while recognizing that some degree of age segmentation does occur, emphasizes that disadvantaged neighborhoods, *in comparison to their more advantaged counterparts,* have a relatively high rate of cross-age social interaction, and that this interaction has important consequences for the young people of the neighborhood.[10]

Anderson (1990) writes about the decline of the cultural authority of the "old head," older men who work hard and attempt to socialize younger men and adolescents to norms and values around work, responsibility, and respectability, and about the rise of the "new" old heads, largely drug dealers whose flashy material success appeals to their younger neighbors

and sends the message that work does not pay and that taking responsibility for one's children is unnecessary. My account is similar to Anderson's in that both highlight the importance of adult men in socializing
adolescents in poor communities. However, there are important differences. First, Anderson locates the source of a drug dealer's cultural power
in the decline of the labor market for low-skill men and the lure of the
quick money of the drug trade, while I locate older peers' cultural power
in the social organization of violence in poor neighborhoods, in their role
in navigating the dangers of street violence and protecting younger boys,
and in the salience of neighborhood as a form of identity for adolescents
in poor neighborhoods. As I argued in chapter 2, most boys in Franklin
and Roxbury Crossing understand drug dealers and gangbangers to be
negative role models whose actions and biographies are to be avoided if
possible. The older peers who are the sources of cross-cohort socialization
in Franklin and Roxbury Crossing need not drive new cars (or any cars at
all) and flash gold jewelry; they merely need to be present in the neighborhood on a regular basis and available for protection and mentoring in the
ways of the street. It is not clear that Anderson and I are talking about the
same actors when it comes to cross-cohort socialization.

Second, Anderson's analysis has drug dealers acting as role models
from afar and primarily influencing younger peers through their modeling of success from participation in the underground economy rather
than legitimate work. He employs a norms-and-values view of culture in
which the drug dealer's success undermines mainstream values regarding work and responsibility, drawing boys into a deviant subculture that
valorizes fast money and early fatherhood and rejects schooling and work
in the formal labor market. In contrast, my account of the role of older
peers in neighborhood socialization suggests a greater level of interaction,
in which advice and experiences are passed from older to younger cohorts
through direct, repeated contact. Rather than instilling oppositional values, older peers provide their younger counterparts with ways of thinking
about the world, lenses through which they understand their own options
and decisions. Indeed, a close reading of the examples above suggests that
the messages boys get from their older peers are frequently consistent in
important ways with those from teachers and parents, particularly when
it comes to schooling, work, and contraception. As I discuss in chapter 5,
I rely on a more cognitive theory of culture (see DiMaggio 1997) that leaves
greater room for individual agency, in which older peers provide cultural
frames through which younger adolescents interpret and understand
their experiences and observations in the neighborhood and in outside

social institutions such as schools. (The content of such frames and scripts is explored in more detail in chapters 6 and 7.)

This chapter has focused on same-sex peer relationships among adolescent boys, with a particular emphasis on the role of violence in structuring these relationships. The next chapter widens the lens to consider other aspects of boys' social lives, such as girlfriends, organizational participation, and nonfamily adults as well as the roles that violence, parental control, and other social forces play in structuring their social relationships.

Joseph is fifteen years old and has lived in Franklin his entire life. His social life revolves around his immediate neighborhood, the two or three square blocks that make up his public housing development. Every day after school, he heads outside in search of his friends, who can usually be found on the basketball court playing ball or hanging out in the development's interior courtyard. Joseph has known these four or five boys almost his entire life, since they grew up in the same development. Unable to find a summer job, his entire summer is also spent hanging out and playing basketball with his neighborhood friends. Joseph rarely leaves the neighborhood, except for school and the occasional trip to visit a relative. When asked whether he has any close friends from school, Joseph mentions only one. His school peers are mostly acquaintances rather than close friends. Other than the one, he never spends time with them outside of school.

Tamarr, fourteen, lives on the other side of the housing development, only a few hundred yards from Joseph. Tamarr avoids socializing with most of his peers from the neighborhood, afraid of "getting into trouble" or becoming caught up in conflicts and violence. He spends a lot of time indoors with his many brothers and sisters, playing video games and watching television and movies. Tamarr has only a few close friends, and some of these he met in school. He recently began spending more time outdoors when one of his friends from school moved into the neighborhood, though they tend to stick together and avoid others. Tamarr spends his summers at a camp in New Hampshire. Though Tamarr has lived in the development since he was four years old, his social world is radically different from Joseph's.

The comparison between Joseph and Tamarr has important implications for the study of neighborhood effects. Underlying almost all theories of the effect of neighborhood context on individuals is a set of strong assumptions about the correspondence between residence and social life, particularly institutional and organizational involvement and the composition of social networks.[1] The dominant theories of neighborhood effects—social isolation and social organization—rest on the idea that where one lives determines whom one interacts with on a regular basis and therefore also profoundly influences the cultural environment one experiences. This link is most obvious for social isolation theory, which holds that adolescents growing up in disadvantaged neighborhoods have considerably less contact with middle-class or mainstream individuals and institutions than their counterparts in more advantaged neighborhoods. It is this lack of interaction that is thought to lead to localized or "ghetto-specific" cultures that have important consequences for future well-being and life chances (Wilson 1987; Massey and Denton 1993). Social isolation, conceived of more generally, may also refer to the social separation of neighborhood residents from people in other neighborhoods.

Social organization theory argues that disadvantaged neighborhoods are poorly organized to regulate the behavior of young people, but it also rests on the assumption that the neighborhood has a meaningful influence on whom a young person interacts with on a regular basis. If adolescents were interacting primarily with people outside their neighborhoods, then it is difficult to see how the capacity of their own neighbors to regulate behavior occurring within their own neighborhood would be of any consequence.

In short, theories of neighborhood effects require social interaction with neighborhood peers and adults or exposure to neighborhood-specific cultural environments.[2] Yet we know very little about the relationship between an adolescent's geographic neighborhood and his social life. There have been almost no systematic attempts to understand the degree to which adolescents' friendship networks are limited by their neighborhood of residence, how geographic location is related to the organizations or institutions with which an adolescent has contact, or whether adolescents in different neighborhoods have contact with different adults outside their families.[3] On the one hand, we might expect neighborhoods to become more important during adolescence when social lives become unglued from nuclear families. On the other hand, it is just as plausible that neighborhoods become less important during adolescence, as the overlap between school attendance areas and neighborhoods weakens, as young people become more involved with other institutions or contexts (such as schools and workplaces), and as adolescents become more mobile.[4]

Previous research points to the importance of neighborhood-based social interaction for adolescents. For example, Turley (2003) finds that neighborhood effects on test scores, self-esteem, and behavior problems are larger for children who say they know more peers in their neighborhood and for children who have been living in the neighborhood longer. In a housing mobility study in Yonkers, New York, Briggs (1997) finds that social attachments to home neighborhoods are strong, even after moving to a new neighborhood. Finally, the classic urban literature emphasizes the importance in poor communities of local same-sex peer groups, which form the primary basis for socializing among adolescents and many adults (e.g., Gans 1962; Whyte 1943; Suttles 1968).

Yet these studies are merely suggestive, and most prior research on neighborhoods and networks focuses entirely on adults, so many questions still remain about the social networks and institutional attachments of adolescents in poor neighborhoods.[5] This chapter investigates the relationship between geographic neighborhoods and "social neighborhoods" among the boys of Franklin, Roxbury Crossing, and Lower Mills—in other words, the degree to which they are socially attached to their geographic neighborhoods. It examines the friendship and dating networks of adolescents, their involvement with institutions and organizations, and their contact with nonfamily adults to assess their social isolation. It attempts to answer the following questions: How are adolescents' neighborhood boundaries socially constructed? What is the relationship between neighborhood and peer networks, organizations, and nonfamily adults? What social processes produce these relationships? For whom is neighborhood an important determinant of social connections and participation, and for whom is it not?[6] Differences within neighborhoods in the degree to which adolescent boys are socially attached to the neighborhood can contribute to our understanding of which adolescents are likely to be affected by their neighborhoods and of within-neighborhood variation in outcomes. This analysis focuses less on comparisons across the study areas than the other chapters in this book, instead emphasizing patterns that are common across all three and noting key differences where they occur.

The Social Construction of Neighborhood Boundaries

Any attempt to understand the relationship between geographic neighborhood and social life must first grapple with the definitions of the neighborhoods themselves. When young people and their parents talk about their neighborhood, what do they mean? What spaces and places do they consider to be inside and outside their neighborhood? Previous scholars have noted that residents' conceptions of neighborhood boundaries vary considerably and rarely correspond to official census or other administrative definitions of neighborhoods (Hunter 1974; Coulton et al. 2001; Furstenberg 1993; Furstenberg and Hughes 1997; Tienda 1991), but there have been few attempts to understand the sources of individuals' conceptions of neighborhood boundaries, particularly among adolescents.[7] Among adults, the geographic size of perceived neighborhoods is thought to vary by age, income, involvement in local community life, and the characteristics of the community (Hunter 1974), but the perceptions of youth remain unexplored.[8] As we will see, neighborhood definitions are largely socially constructed, often through the same processes that determine the role of neighborhoods in adolescents' social lives. Neighborhood boundaries and social networks are, for many, mutually reinforcing.

Neighborhood boundaries are constructed from building blocks that are part physical and part social.[9] As Lynch (1960) argues, the construction of one's mental "image of the city" is a two-way process based on both physical features and the meanings that individuals attach to them. Geographic features of the city provide "natural" candidates for boundaries, but individuals decide which ones will serve as boundaries based on salient social categories (Keller 1968). In some cases, such as public housing developments (examples of what Suttles [1972] calls "contrived communities"), borders create stark social distinctions of membership and nonmembership. Residents of public housing are often stigmatized as lazy, poor, and dirty, even by their neighbors across the street. In Boston, public housing developments are often referred to as "the bricks" for the brick facades of the apartment buildings, and their residents are sometimes derisively known as "brick people." Housing developments, especially those built prior to the 1970s in Boston, are set apart from surrounding residential housing by their appearance—unadorned low-rise brick apartment buildings. In other cases, physical features such as major thoroughfares, highways, and railroad tracks create restrictions to movement that provide the basis for neighborhood boundaries, carving out what Grannis (1998) calls "tertiary street communities."[10] Finally, parks and other open spaces can be boundaries because they are unpopulated on a regular basis. At the same time, however, smaller parks can be thought of as being part of the "territory" of a particular neighborhood. As Keller (1968) notes, socially determined "functional distance" (such as the ways an intermediary space can be used) is more important than physical distance.

In Roxbury Crossing, the railroad tracks on the west side of the neighborhood (which carry the MBTA's Orange Line and commuter rail as well as Amtrak trains) provide a boundary, though some adolescents regularly crossed over these tracks at Ruggles station to visit the fast-food restaurants and video-game arcades around Northeastern University. (Neighborhood maps are in the appendix.) In Lower Mills, Gallivan Boulevard, which runs approximately east-west through the area and carries heavy traffic in four lanes, creates a boundary. In Franklin, Blue Hill Avenue, which runs north-south, plays a similar role.

Most residents of public housing developments consider the borders of the development to bound their neighborhood as well, though this is not universal. In some cases, a young man limits his neighborhood to a particular section of a development or includes neighboring streets outside the development. For example, Manuel, fourteen, considers his neighborhood to be the part of Franklin Field that is farthest from Blue Hill Avenue. Chris, fourteen, considers his neighborhood to be all of the Franklin Hill housing development plus a few surrounding streets, primarily the commercial area along Blue Hill Avenue near the intersection with Talbot Avenue.

Landscape features matter as well. In developments that are cut off from other residential areas by open space or main thoroughfares, the young people are much more likely to simply name the development itself as their neighborhood. Both the Franklin Hill and Franklin Field developments are largely cut off from other housing. Franklin Hill is bordered on one side by a steep slope down to Blue Hill Avenue and on the other by Franklin Park and American Legion Highway, a busy four-lane thoroughfare. The streets that access Franklin Hill only serve the development itself and a small set of privately run subsidized apartment buildings along Franklin Hill Avenue (which are considered to be part of the development by residents even though they are separately managed and owned). Franklin Field is bordered by Harambee Park, St. Mary's Cemetery, and Blue Hill Avenue on three sides. In Roxbury Crossing, the Whittier Street development is bordered by Tremont Street, two large churches, and the high school ball fields, which almost completely separate it from other residential areas. In contrast, the Lenox/Camden development in Roxbury Crossing is nestled within other private housing. Young people living there are much more likely than their counterparts in the three other developments to include streets and areas outside their developments as part of their neighborhoods.

Despite the importance of physical features, both natural and artificial, neighborhood boundaries are also socially constructed (what Hunter [1974] calls "symbolic communities"), the product of ongoing social interactions involving both groups and individuals. Next-door neighbors have very different understandings of the geographic areas that comprise their neighborhood, as do parents and children within the same household.[11] Even when public housing developments such as Franklin Field seem to provide clear boundaries for neighborhoods, there is variation.

The City of Boston's official neighborhood designations produce little consensus on neighborhood boundaries, mostly because they are too large to represent real neighborhoods. East Boston, South Boston, Dorchester, Roxbury, Roslindale, Hyde Park, West Roxbury, Jamaica Plain, the South End/Back Bay, Charlestown, Allston, and Brighton more closely resemble sections of the city than neighborhoods.[12] Names for subsections of the city have emerged over time. Residents think of their neighborhoods as Lower Mills, Ashmont, Codman Square, Fields Corner, Ashmont Hill, Uphams Corner, Four Corners, Grove Hall, or Neponset, before they imagine Dorchester as a neighborhood. However, these enclaves carry no official status, and there is little agreement among residents on their boundaries.

Adolescents think of their neighborhoods in very small terms, areas of no more than a few square blocks, sometimes even less. Older adolescents who have access to automobiles or are no longer attending school and working think in broader terms, which is consistent with a classic finding that those who are more mobile perceive their neighborhoods to be larger (Hunter 1974).[13] Since high schools are citywide, and each elementary and middle school attendance zone currently draws from one-third of the city, one might expect that the large school attendance areas in Boston might broaden young people's conception of neighborhood. Yet young people's travels to and from school or school-based social interactions do not seem to influence their conceptions of their neighborhoods. Figure 4.1 shows the Franklin area map with outlines of the neighborhoods of five adolescents as they described them (two are centered on Franklin Field, two on Franklin Hill, and one in the private housing in the upper right section of the map).[14]

One factor that influences how adolescents see their neighborhoods is the notion of territory and its connection to neighborhood violence. As I have already suggested, some adolescent boys in poor neighborhoods view their neighborhoods as territories to be defended from outsiders. The boundaries of these territories match closely the neighborhood defi-

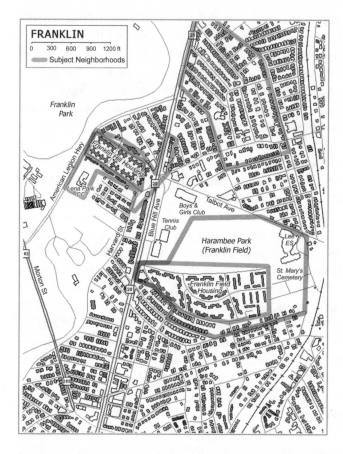

Figure 4.1.
Five adolescents' conceptions of neighborhood in Franklin

nitions that they employ. Certain parts of a neighborhood can become associated with the activities and people regularly found there, whether they are winos drinking in a park or drug dealers conducting business on a corner or out of a house. Areas deemed unsafe were often excluded from adolescents' definitions of their neighborhoods and avoided unless absolutely necessary.

Finally, daily activities matter as well (see also Keller 1968). When he spends time in a location on a regular basis, a boy develops a comfort level as he sees the same people repeatedly and as neighborhood features become more familiar. For example, Isaac, thirteen, lives in Lower Mills and spends a great deal of time at a local community center. When asked to describe his neighborhood, he included his own street, a few neighboring streets, and the main street he walks down to get to the community center, but only as far as the community center itself.

Neighborhoods, Networks, Organizations, and Adults: Using Daily Activities to Understand the Social Worlds of Adolescents

Almost every young man in this study participated in some sort of after-school or summer program, if not currently, then in the past. Even in disadvantaged neighborhoods, city-run and nonprofit community centers offering athletics, homework help, and computer rooms are available, sometimes at little or no cost.[15] Almost without exception, boys in all three areas stay away from community programs or formal organizations other than schools that are not located in (or just outside) their own neighborhoods. They avoid teen programs and community centers (such as the Boys and Girls Club, YMCA, and city-run centers based in schools) that are located in a particular building or other physical space and are not in their own neighborhood. Only one boy, a thirteen-year-old from Lower Mills, participates in a teen program outside his neighborhood, and it is conveniently located across the street from his middle school. When neighborhoods are narrowly conceived and great importance is attached to membership, opportunities outside one's home turf are considered off limits. Even though the Boys and Girls Club on Blue Hill Avenue is about equidistant from the Franklin Hill and Franklin Field housing developments, adolescents from Franklin Hill do not consider it part of their neighborhood. Franklin Hill boys use the Lena Park Community Center on American Legion Highway instead. Community centers, after-school programs, and even basketball courts and playing fields beyond a short walk are also generally ignored. The boys often did not know about these activities even though they take place only a short distance away.

There were four exceptions to this general rule. First, parents sometimes took the initiative to find programs for their sons that fill a specific need or remove the young man from the neighborhood because of concerns about negative peer effects. For example, one mother registered her son for an anger-management therapy group in another part of the city, and another enrolled her son in after-school and summer basketball programs in the suburbs because she was worried about his safety on the local basketball court. Fifteen of the sixty boys participated in such after-school or summer programs outside their neighborhoods at the time of the interview or within the last year (five in Franklin, five in Roxbury Crossing, and five in Lower Mills). Churches are a second exception, as they are generally not neighborhood-based (see McRoberts 2003), and hence involve interaction with people from other parts of the city. Only five boys were heavily involved in church activities and programs (two in Franklin, two in Roxbury Crossing, and one in Lower Mills). A third exception is educational programs. Four boys age seventeen or eighteen who had dropped out of high school attended GED or job-training classes in other parts of the city, but they thought of these programs as a replacement for school, which they were used to traveling long distances to attend. The fourth exception is citywide athletic leagues, though these often have neighborhood or organization-based teams. Six boys participated in these basketball or football teams (one in Franklin, two in Roxbury Crossing, and three in Lower Mills). In addition, nine boys participated in school-based athletics such as the football, basketball, and track teams or in school-based extracurricular activities such as ROTC and student government (two in Franklin, three in Roxbury Crossing, and four in Lower Mills).

Insiders and Outsiders

Jordan, thirteen, and Esteban, seventeen, both live in Lower Mills and come from families in which the adults have low levels of education. Jordan attends a public middle school in another section of Dorchester and gets home from school every day around two o'clock in the afternoon, sometimes does his homework, and goes to find his friends in the local park. There he and his friends play basketball and football and ride their bikes. Occasionally they go to the library a few blocks away to use the computers or to get help on a school assignment. Jordan comes home around eight in the evening for dinner, a shower, perhaps some homework or television, and bed. On the weekends, he also plays with his friends, and they sometimes go to Chez Vous roller rink (outside Jordan's neighborhood) if they can get a ride from a parent. Jordan considers his closest friends to be two brothers who live next door and attend the same school as he does, as well as four other young men who live on two nearby streets and who go to school in other parts of the city.

Esteban attends a Christian school in the suburbs, where he plays on the school's basketball team and leads devotions in the morning a few days a week. Most days, he returns home from school in the evening after basketball practice, eats dinner, and does his homework. Esteban is also very active in his church, located outside the neighborhood, as a peer leader, youth minister, and member of the step dance team. He spends most of his weekend either at basketball games, step team practice, or church, and Wednesday evenings are also spent at church. During the past summer, Esteban went on a mission trip with his church's youth group. The only local institution he is involved with is a community center, where he once worked as a summer counselor and where he goes to work out in the fitness room from time to time. Esteban's closest friends include another student from his school who also plays on the basketball team and lives in another section of Dorchester, near Roxbury, as well as the members of his step team. Esteban is also close to some of the youth ministers and peer leaders at his church. I asked Esteban why he does not seem to be very involved in things going on in the neighborhood:

> Because I occupy my time with productive, positive stuff, I guess. I go to the [community center] down the street. I don't know if that's being involved in the neighborhood a lot, but . . . I don't go to school with any of the kids around here. I go to church. That's where I spend a lot of my time. So it's like I'm not really here much. People just see my face, and they just know that I live here.

Esteban's situation is anomalous. Most young men have friends in their neighborhood, and unless they spend almost no time nearby, their closest friends usually live nearby. This was particularly true of the adolescents in the two disadvantaged neighborhoods. In Franklin and Roxbury Crossing, thirty-two of forty boys (80 percent) reported that more than half of their friends lived in their neighborhoods, and twenty-two of the boys (55 percent) in these areas had no friends from outside their neighborhoods. Only three of forty boys reported no neighborhood friends. In Lower Mills, thirteen of twenty boys (65 percent) reported that more than half of their friends lived in their neighborhoods, and seven of the boys (35 percent) had no friends outside the neighborhood. Four of twenty Lower Mills boys reported no neighborhood friends.[16]

When a young man's friends live very close by, and most people spend their time hanging out in the neighborhood, it can be difficult to end a friendship. A boy sees his former friend frequently, and both are embedded in the neighborhood's social network, with mutual friends and acquaintances. Fernando is a fifteen-year-old Franklin resident. When he decided that he should not be hanging around a particular friend anymore because he was drawing Fernando into a lot of conflicts, he tried to distance himself. This proved impossible. The friend was always around and always with Fernando's other neighborhood friends.

Activities and friendships are mutually reinforcing. The context where time is spent affects who becomes friends, and the composition of a friendship group affects where (and how) one spends time. As discussed in the previous chapter, the desire to remain close to neighborhood friends meant that Tyree was spending more time out in the street with them.

So too with Seth, fourteen. Seth's family is planning to move from their Lower Mills apartment to another part of Dorchester, in the neighborhood where his grandmother lives, because they need a larger apartment. He is worried about being an outsider in the new neighborhood. He explained that after he moves he will not have any friends in the neighborhood, so he will spend most of his time indoors:

> The neighborhood we're moving to is loud. Like there's a lot of fights over there. Last time I been over there, there was fights. But when I be over there, I be at my grandmother's. I just be watching from off her porch. I won't go outside to play . . . I'll probably end up playing ball less. I play more over here, but when I move to that neighborhood, I'm not just gonna jump out and go play 'cause I don't know nobody like that around there.

Young men steeped in the neighborhood do sometimes have friends from elsewhere. These exceptions come about in two ways. Sometimes family members who live in other neighborhoods open up opportunities for friendships with kids from that neighborhood as well. A boy is not viewed as an outsider if he has a cousin or uncle in the neighborhood who can vouch for him and bring him into the local social group. Joseph, a fifteen-year-old who has lived in the same area of Franklin his entire life, is an example. Almost all of Joseph's friends live in his neighborhood, but his best friend is actually a cousin who lives in another part of Dorchester. Joseph has integrated his cousin into his own friendship group in his Franklin neighborhood, and his cousin is a regular fixture in the neighborhood. Family ties can trump neighborhood boundaries. Nine of the forty boys living in either Roxbury Crossing or Lower Mills had friends from outside their own neighborhoods that they had initially met through family members. This was also the case for three of the twenty boys in Lower Mills.

A second exception comes from teens who move from one neighborhood to another one nearby, especially in late adolescence. Strong friendships have already been created with peers from the former neighborhood, and friendship groups in the new neighborhood are well established by late adolescence. As Briggs (1997) noted in a study of adolescents whose families participated in a housing mobility program, often a neighborhood newcomer will retain his attachment to the old neighborhood and hang out there most of the time (especially if it is close by), returning to his new community at night only to sleep or spend time with family. Duante, seventeen, now lives with his mother and younger brother in Roxbury Crossing, but spent most of his childhood and adolescence living with his grandmother in a housing development in another part of Roxbury before his mother was able to care for him. His closest buddies live in his grandmother's housing development, which is a fifteen-minute walk from his current home. The only friend he has in his new space also used to live near Duante when they were younger. He does not socialize with young men from his current neighborhood.

Finally, there are school friends. Boys spend more time in school than anywhere else. Why then does school not figure more in the development of friendships? The boys typically do have one or two friends they met sometime during their school careers (but who do not live in the same neighborhood), but school friends were far less common than neighborhood friends, particularly in the high-poverty areas. While only one-quarter of boys in Franklin and Roxbury Crossing reported having *any* friends from school who did not also live in the neighborhood, 55 percent of boys in Lower Mills had made friends in school with boys from other neighborhoods. Similar patterns are evident in nationally representative data. Adolescent boys in more violent neighborhoods report fewer friends who attend the same school as they do (Harding 2008).

Peers from school are typically not "real" friends in the eyes of the Franklin and Roxbury Crossing boys, and they rarely spend time together outside the school context. Why? The way time is structured in schools, particularly middle and high school, is partly responsible. Instruction takes up most of the day, and since the composition of classes changes each period and class schedules change each semester, there is only a short window for making new friends. School assignment also likely plays a role. In Boston, students do not move from school to school together as in some systems in which elementary schools feed into middle schools that feed into high schools. Students are assigned to schools individually (based on parents' ranked preferences), so they end up with a mostly new group of classmates at each school level. In addition, many students change schools multiple times during their school careers. Of the sixty boys in this study, at least fifteen attended more than one elementary school and at least nine attended more than one middle school. Of the thirty-six who had reached high school (many of whom were only in ninth or tenth grade), at least eleven had attended more than one high school.

The safety climate of Boston's middle and high schools impedes school-based friendships. Like the malls, buses, trains, parks, and movie theaters, Boston schools are a context in which strangers from different neighborhoods meet and interact. The same potential for confrontation makes it difficult to make friends (of course in cities with neighborhood-based schools, this is likely to be less of a problem). When a new Boston public middle school was to open in the 2003–4 school year in the Grove Hall section of the city (on the border between Dorchester and Roxbury), there was great concern that the new school would bring together youth from rival neighborhoods, and security was tightened. It was even difficult to name the school, eventually temporarily named the New Boston Pilot Middle School, because many of the suggested names were associated with particular streets or neighborhoods from which rival groups hail.

Simon, the sixteen-year-old Franklin resident who described the dangers of public transportation in chapter 2, got into a number of conflicts with other students when he started his freshman year of high school. Without other people from his own neighborhood at school, there was no one there to "have his back." Simon quickly adopted a strategy of minimal interaction with his classmates, talking to almost no one unless spoken to and avoiding places where others congregated. Simon's reaction to this climate is extreme but, nevertheless, revealing. He explained to me what he does at lunch when others are socializing:

> I don't hang out with nobody. At lunch, I only eat. I did it for one whole year straight. I could do it again. I just stand up near the table. I had one friend who went to middle school with me, and that's just one. Me and him, we talk, but we both stand up every day. Because there's so much stuff going on in the cafeteria. You could be walking by somebody, and they could stab you.

Girls and Girlfriends

Other than same-sex friends, perhaps the second most important part of a young man's social life (at least in his eyes) is his relations with girls and girlfriends. Relationships with members of the opposite sex were less dependent on neighborhoods. Boys in all three neighborhoods were more likely to meet romantic or sexual partners outside the neighborhood than they were to make friends with males outside the neighborhood. (Indeed, for some young men a primary motivation for leaving the neighborhood was to meet girls.) The young men I interviewed met girls in any location where they spent a considerable amount of time, including their own neighborhood, family members' neighborhoods, school, after-school activities, shopping districts, and even using telephone or Internet chat lines.

Why? Girls inside the neighborhood are less available. If one thinks of one's neighborhood as a family, then some of the potential romantic or sexual partners in the neighborhood are thought of as "sisters" or "cousins." Chris is close friends with a girl his own age who lives a block away and whom he calls his "sister." The two are almost inseparable at times, though they are not romantically or sexually involved. Given the close ties between neighborhood friends and the small size of neighborhoods, conflicts over girls and girlfriends have the potential to strain male friendships. One way to minimize this potential problem is to pursue girls outside the neighborhood, where there is less chance that neighborhood friends will be interested in the same girls.

Romantic or sexual relationships in which both partners are members of the same local networks face considerably more social regulation and control than relationships that are free of these encumbrances.[17] When partners have overlapping social ties, those connections can be called upon to influence a partner's behavior. It is also more likely that information about one's prior or ongoing romantic and sexual activities will be spread around. For example, Marshall, seventeen and from Lower Mills, described a relationship he had with a young woman from his school: "In-school relationships are wack because everybody knows about it and then like most of the time the girl doesn't want to go on with things because, 'Oh what are my friends gonna think?'"

A fair number of young men (though by no means a majority) make it clear that long-term monogamous romantic relationships are not for them. One-time sexual encounters, simultaneous relationships with multiple girlfriends, or long-term purely sexual relationships appeal more. Carrying on with partners who are from the same social context is risking one's reputation or ties to others. News travels fast, and potential partners in the neighborhood quickly learn of a young man's multiple or short-lived relationships. Elton, seventeen and from Lower Mills, described having two girlfriends at the same time when he was attending a summer camp when he was fourteen:

> I was slick, and they were both from the same group, too. I was real slick. Maybe they knew, and they didn't care. There really wasn't even any problems. I think the one girl was scared of the other girl so she didn't even want to tell her so it basically worked better for me . . . I did it for just that week 'cause I was never going to see them again.

Finally, cross-neighborhood rivalries are gender-specific and much more frequent among males than females, so even though young men are very rarely friends with males from rival neighborhoods, young women from rival neighborhoods are potential romantic or sexual partners. When approaching a young woman he does not know, a young man is not risking a physical confrontation (at least not with her), as he would be by talking to an unknown male. If that male is from the wrong neighborhood or interprets the interaction as a threat, a fight will likely ensue. Though a young man takes a risk by visiting a girl in another neighborhood, meetings can be arranged in somewhat safer neutral locations. Nevertheless, even though adolescent boys are pursuing girls from outside their neighborhoods, these girls often live in structurally similar neighborhoods because those neighborhoods are typically nearby.

Adults outside the Family

Close relationships with adults outside the family are fairly rare for boys in all three neighborhoods.[18] Only eight of the sixty boys reported sustained relationships with nonfamily adults whom they regularly spent time with and could talk to about problems or advice (four in Franklin, three in Roxbury Crossing, and one in Lower Mills). Even those who see unrelated adults in after-school programs, school, or church tend not to think of them as people with whom they can discuss important things. Interactions of this kind occur in group settings where forming personal ties is hard, or the relationships did not last long enough for the adolescents to see them as close. Boys distrust the motives of individuals who are being paid for their work with youth, believing that they do not really care but just need a job. High staff turnover at many local youth agencies reinforces these views. When a local youth worker had to move out of state because his wife found a new job, Reed, fifteen, interpreted this as a sign that the worker was indifferent to the kids in Franklin. "He was working at the teen center," Reed recalled, "and then he left, then they shut it down. And I knew he was going to do the same thing [with the new program] . . . You can't trust everybody. He said he was going to be there for like a of couple years. It wasn't even a year, and he left."

Kids do occasionally come to know and trust adults outside their families. Esteban, who spends almost no time in the neighborhood, was close to ministers at his church because he spent many hours there each week and considered their motives as church leaders to be beyond question. James, a fourteen-year-old resident of Roxbury Crossing, developed a close relationship with a teacher from his school who was also a volunteer basketball coach. They saw each other all the time on the court, and interaction in multiple contexts provides the opportunity for closer bonds, so-called multistranded ties (Keller 1968). Finally, the parents of friends or long-term girlfriends can also become part of a boy's social network. Fernando, fifteen and from Franklin, spends a considerable amount of time at his girlfriend's house with her family, and sees her mother as an adult he can talk to about his problems. He says he would go to her with a problem before going to his own mother or father. Yet these bonds were relatively infrequent, and most boys could name few—if any—unrelated adults who mattered in their lives. Even when the definition was broadened to include any nonfamily adult they could seek advice from, only one-third of boys were able to name a single adult over age twenty-five. The lesson is that socialization by nonfamily adults from the neighborhood is not a likely source of neighborhood effects.

The Role of Parents and Parenting Strategies

Some parents control their sons' time use and daily activities, and hence condition the role that neighborhood plays in their children's social lives.[19] In turn, neighborhood contexts affect parenting strategies. In socially organized environments, parents trust other adults in the neighborhood to monitor their children. In resource-rich environments, formal institutions will promote achievement and positive developmental outcomes. But in resource-poor environments, parents are forced to go it alone (Furstenberg et al. 1999; see also Furstenberg 1993).[20]

Many parents in Roxbury Crossing and Franklin did indeed act to limit the effects of neighborhood peers and adults in their sons' lives. However, social organization is in the eye of the beholder. Some parents see their neighborhoods as fine places to live and raise a child, rather than as risks to be managed. They take advantage of local resources and dwell on the need to manage the safety issues and risks created by *outsiders,* such as rival youth or the police. Recall Simon, the sixteen-year-old Franklin resident who discussed the dangers of leaving his neighborhood by himself. Simon's mother thinks of their neighborhood as a family. Community members care for one another and for each other's children. She is the self-described neighborhood aunt:

> If I could have my choice, I would still live here, because I know what everybody is about . . . Everybody here is family. You know how there is people in your family you just don't like but you have to deal with? That's just how this neighborhood is, because the majority of us have been living here our whole lives. Our kids are friends, basically family.
>
> Like, on a school night, I could wake up and I have three kids in my

house on a school night. They all go to three different schools, but they will all get up and go to school. If you [visit] over there, you stay the night. If you go over there, you eat over there. It's just a big family . . .

You got some assholes, but that's everywhere . . . It's just like a big distant family. Everybody gets into arguments, and quarrels, but it's not to where you have to fight like you would fight with somebody from Mattapan or Mission Hill. It's just different . . . It's like an argument—might be a little squabble, but then it's nothing. It would be altogether different because you don't know them and you have no love for them. It's just like the Wild Kingdom. You know how you protect your grounds? That's just it.

Simon's mother trusts the residents she knows—including the winos in the park and drug dealers on the corner—to watch out for her son, just as she watches out for her neighbors' children. In fact, moving would lead to more danger, not less, because Simon would be an unknown in a new place: "I wouldn't feel safe for my son because it would be a testing period, just like mating season with the animals. They have to see who the big male is, and he would have to go through that again. Whereas, where he's at right now, he doesn't have to go through that because he already has a spot." Neighbors can be another set of eyes and ears for monitoring a boy's behavior. Information about his actions is expected to come in from neighbors who know the family. Simon's mother believes her neighbors will tell her if they see Simon in trouble and depends on them to intervene on Simon's behalf.

"Street smarts" are critical if black and Latino men are to prosper in a hostile world, according to parents. Holding one's own in a fight, reading a situation to predict when violence will occur, and developing the capacity to sense another person's intentions are survival skills. "When you live in urban America," a middle-class father from Lower Mills explains, "you [hear] people saying so-and-so is street smart, or so-and-so is not street smart."

Little things, for example, going on public transportation, [my son] needs to get. There is no book. You just experience and you learn.

I used to take [my sons] to the park and watch them interact with other kids from afar . . . I would watch [my older son] get into a little tussle with some of the girls on the playground when he was smaller, and I would not intervene. That's a life experience. He has got to learn how to deal with the situation.

In suburbia, you may have a parent, they may be livid when they see something like that, pushing and tussling. They want to run in instantly and break it up. But when you live in urban America, there is so much of it. You are not always going to be there, and they have to know how to handle themselves.

A parent can provide guidance and reflection, but street smarts must be learned through experience. A key lesson is the importance of standing up for oneself; failure to do so means others will take advantage of you, not just in the moment, but afterward as well. Backing down quickly translates into a reputation for weakness, as this father explains:

> My youngest boy, he has gotten into a number of situations at school; kids picking on him on the bus, and little things like that, and, we drill into him, tell somebody. It continues. Tell him to stop. Just let them know you are not happy with it. Tell somebody again. After that, that's twice. So it is noted that you have told this person, who is overlooking everybody, maybe a bus monitor.
>
> At that point, you are not going to be bullied by anybody. You have to stand up for yourself because, if you don't, [they] will ride you the entire school year. Kids are cruel . . . You have to establish yourself, and you have to let them know that. Because if you hit me, I am going to hit you back. So, stop. You might beat me up, but know what? I am still going to hit you back. That's what you almost have to say.
>
> And some people may be mortified. It's like, "Oh my God, why is he teaching his kid this?" My kid has to survive where he lives. And I am not saying life and death, but what I am saying is, what are you going to do, living where you live and getting pushed around and bullied?
>
> One thing he doesn't do is start trouble. There's a difference. I am telling him, defend yourself.

This father lives in Lower Mills, but Franklin and Roxbury Crossing parents have even more to worry about. Parents worry about fights, stray bullets, friends who are involved in crime or drug dealing, and drug use. How do they deal with these threats? One strategy is total separation from those who live in the neighborhood. Jared, now eighteen, grew up in Franklin, and his mother rarely let him leave the apartment except for school and church. He played indoors with his older and younger siblings. In his teen years, Jared got involved in a peer leadership program at a nearby health center. He did not have a single friend on the block, though he occasionally got into fights with neighborhood kids on the way to and from the school bus stop.

Parents with more resources often use after-school and summer programs to occupy their sons' time and thereby limit free time to simply hang around the neighborhood. When Tyree was twelve, his mother noticed that he had new sneakers and new clothes that she had not purchased for him. She suspected that he and his friends had joined the older boys on the corner in selling drugs in Roxbury Crossing. She knew that simply forbidding him to hang out on the corner would not solve the problem, so she enrolled Tyree in after-school programs at the local Boys and Girls Club and signed him up for karate classes at the YMCA. The following summer, she sent him to live with his aunt and cousins in a small town on the North Shore, far from Boston, where he worked as a busboy in a seafood restaurant.

This strategy is harder to implement as boys age. At fourteen, they "age out" of many after-school and summer programs. Only a few can be kept on as staff members or summer counselors, and most private-sector employers in Boston are not willing to hire anyone who is under sixteen (the one exception seems to be grocery stores, which will hire children as young as fourteen to bag groceries). Every year there are far fewer jobs in the city's summer jobs program than there are applicants. The result, as parents and youth workers know all too well, is that during an age when teenagers exercise the worst judgment and are most vulnerable to peer influences (fourteen to sixteen), they have the least structure in their lives.

Sometimes parents happen upon the organized-activities strategy by chance in the process of trying to find better schools for their sons. For those with few resources, the only real alternatives to a traditional Boston public school are charter schools, of which there are now many in the Boston area, or the Metco program, which buses minority Boston students to suburban schools throughout the region. Boston public middle and high schools end the school day between 1:30 and 2:00 p.m. and offer few extracurricular activities other than selective athletic teams. Boys who attend these schools are home and hanging out in their neighborhood by 2 p.m. In contrast, charter schools usually start and finish the school day later, often around 3 p.m., and have longer academic years. Many require after-school tutoring for students with low grades, and they are sometimes far from students' homes, lengthening their travel times. Metco students tend to return home much later in the day because they spend one to one and a half hours on the bus coming home. The result is that most charter and Metco students are not home until 4 p.m., and sometimes much later.

Edwin's mother removed her five sons, of which Edwin, fifteen, is the oldest, from the Boston public schools after elementary school. Hence when we first met, Edwin attended a charter school in another section of the city, about an hour's ride on public transportation from his Roxbury Crossing home. He was required to attend the after-school program because he had a below-C grade in one of his classes, which kept him in the building until 5 p.m. It was often 6:30 p.m. and time for dinner when he got home. As a result, Edwin had little time to make friends with the other teenagers in his neighborhood, and all of his close friends were schoolmates. A few months after we first met, Edwin was expelled from his charter school for bringing a knife to school, which he said was for protection on the subway. He began carrying the knife after someone threatened him on the subway with a knife while on a school field trip. Banned from his charter school, Edwin began attending a Boston public high school, and his schedule changed dramatically. He now returns home from school by 2:00 p.m. He also has no more contact with his former school friends, who live all over the city. With four or five more free hours each day, Edwin now spends his afternoons at the local basketball court, and he has started to become friends with the other neighborhood teenagers. Edwin's mother worries about whether these new friends will draw him into dangerous activities, but, with five mouths to feed, there is little she can do to provide Edwin with an alternative and little time to keep a close eye on his behavior.

Some parents choose instead to provide a competing set of influences, an alternative framework for thinking about daily life that will keep their sons out of trouble and help them see the wisdom of avoiding friends that may draw them toward violent behavior or drug use. Religious or church-based programs are good examples. Junior is fifteen and a Franklin resident. With a father who is incarcerated and a mother who is a recovering addict and a former victim of domestic violence, Junior has a difficult home life, and he has had behavior problems at least since middle school. He has trouble managing his anger, acts out in school, skips class, and gets involved in fights and crime in the neighborhood. His mother has tried an alternative school and therapists, and even got him put on probation, but nothing seems to work, so she enrolled Junior in a church-based program for troubled teens, which he attends a few days a week. It looked promising for a while:

> He's very angry and he's been into the [alternative school]. I had a probation officer for him. Finally, I found a good program . . . He's real happy about it, and I'm real happy about it, too. It's a church atmosphere . . . It's young men, no girls. Just guys and they talk about issues. I just want him to do well, but he's kind of like a follower, whatever the guys are doing, he wants to be a part of it. If there's any negativity to it, I think he

thinks that that's the group to be with . . . In the beginning [the program was helping him] but then, in the end, he started getting [punished] for different things. I figure the new kids coming in were doing little sneaky things and he became involved with that crowd, too . . . I think he's really confused.

Letting boys spend time in the neighborhood under close watch is another way parents try to manage their sons' lives. They set firm rules about curfews, friends, girls, and where in the neighborhood a son is not allowed to go, keeping close tabs on him through cell phones and preestablished "check-in" times. This is an exhausting regimen, especially for working parents. It is also hard to enforce in the face of adolescents who want more and more independence. Manuel is fourteen and lives in Franklin. His mother has strict rules for him: in the house by 9:00 p.m., no going to the pizza shop, no leaving the neighborhood without permission. Only friends whose parents she knows are allowed in her apartment, and Manuel is only allowed to go into the homes of friends familiar to his mother. Manuel must also call her every day at work when he comes home from school. As Manuel has gotten older, he has begun resisting these rules. "I think parents should have all the control," his mother notes:

> But sometimes you don't have that control. Like, I tell my son, "I don't want you hanging over there." He's gonna go hang over there. Like I said, "I'm not telling you for my own good. I'm [safe at] home. I'm telling you for your own good." But sometimes they want to learn their way; they don't listen. So when things happen, I say, "Hello! I told you so!"

Setting these sorts of rules can be especially difficult when other parents do not follow suit. Elton is seventeen and lives at the edge of Lower Mills, where it borders a more disadvantaged neighborhood. Many of his neighborhood friends are from the more disadvantaged area. Elton's mother tries to set and enforce rules, just like Manuel's mother, but runs into problems:

> It's hard to find groups of kids that are making good choices . . . They are around, but because they're making good choices they're not just like hanging out on the street, it's hard to find them . . .
>   The curfew, that's just such a foreign thing. Elton challenges me and says, "They don't have any curfew. Nobody tells them to come into the house." So well, I'm going to call one of your friends' mothers and see. She expressed that her son should be in the house at X time, but he just doesn't

listen. And then I went and asked the kid and said, "When are you supposed to be home?" "Oh, my mother never tells me any time to be home." There's so many kids where even the parents tell them but don't expect them to actually do it. Or they don't tell them anything. It's just such an influence. So that makes it hard in this neighborhood right now. 'Cause you try to find kindred spirits with parents, but the folks that your kids are hanging around with, their parents don't seem to have those kind of expectations.

Conclusion

This chapter has addressed the relationship between geographic neighborhoods and social neighborhoods among adolescents. As classic accounts of urban neighborhoods (e.g., Hunter 1974; Keller 1968; Lynch 1960) would lead us to expect, neighborhood definitions are partly constructed from building blocks based on physical features, but they are largely socially constructed. Consistent with these classic accounts, time use, mobility, and routine activities structure neighborhood attachment, for example when more time in school limits exposure to the neighborhood or when parents work to keep sons in programs or in the house rather than in the street. Also important in classic accounts are individual characteristics such as age, as most adolescents in urban communities see their neighborhoods as small (compared to what we would expect of adults), and family characteristics such as income, which affects the resources available for programs and for travel outside the neighborhood.

What is unique for adolescent boys, particularly in Roxbury Crossing and Franklin, is the importance of violence in structuring their use of space and their relationships with same-sex peers inside and outside the neighborhood. Cultural notions of territory passed down from previous cohorts and policed by threats of violence, daily routines and activities, and safe and unsafe spaces all affect the boundaries that adolescents construct for their neighborhoods and where they spend their time. Boys in disadvantaged neighborhoods spend most of their nonschool time within the neighborhood.

How attached are they to this space? It depends on how such attachment is measured. Few young men are involved with local organizations outside of their immediate neighborhoods other than schools. Bonds with same-sex friends from the neighborhood are strong; connections to boys they meet in school are weak. This is in part due to the amount of time they spend in the neighborhood, but also to the importance attached to shared experiences and to the bonds created through commitments to mutual protection discussed in chapter 3. Yet boys search for romantic and sexual partners outside the neighborhood. Cross-neighborhood violence restricts same-sex friendships but does not hinder opposite-sex relationships to the same degree, and romantic or sexual relationships with partners outside the neighborhood are not subject to the same social control, surveillance, and reputational concerns. Few of the young men have much contact with older nonfamily adults, so this is not a source of neighborhood attachment or much help in understanding neighborhood effects.

Nonetheless, attachment to neighborhoods is quite variable. The social lives of most adolescents are closely intertwined with others in the area, but for some the neighborhood is considerably less important and other social contexts, such as school, church, or family, matter more. Sources of this variation include the parenting strategies used to manage adolescents' exposure to others in the neighborhood and the way in which school schedules structure adolescents' free time. Neighborhood means very little for a subset of boys. We would expect neighborhoods to have less effect on them, so variation in neighborhood social attachment is a potentially important explanation for within-neighborhood variation in neighborhood effects on longer-term outcomes.[21]

Most theories of neighborhood effects assume that residential areas are the primary sites of social interaction. This appears to be largely correct for boys' friendships with same-sex peers, particularly for those in disadvantaged neighborhoods. However, this seems to be less true for romantic and sexual relationships. Adolescents are much more willing to choose romantic and sexual partners from outside. Not that neighborhoods are unimportant in shaping these relationships, however. Partners from outside the neighborhood were often from structurally similar communities, and local culture can still influence relationships whether or not one's partner is from the neighborhood.

These findings also suggest that neighborhood-specific opportunities are important. Adolescents rarely used local resources available in other parts of the city, despite the availability of public transportation. Even when adolescents' social worlds are not limited to their neighborhoods, they may lack access to mainstream individuals and organizations. Social isolation and geographic isolation do not necessarily go hand in hand. Small (2004) concurs: residents of a South End housing development surrounded by wealthy whites had little social interaction with them, as racial, class, and spatial barriers trumped geographic proximity.

Social relationships and interactions are important, but alone they are not sufficient to explain young men's decision making and behavior. We need to understand the *content* of the ideas that are conveyed through these social connections and to figure out how the messages sent are interpreted. The next chapter shifts the focus from the organization of boys' social lives to the cultural context of their neighborhoods.

CHAPTER FIVE THE CULTURAL CONTEXT OF DISADVANTAGED NEIGHBORHOODS

Sitting across the kitchen table from me in his mother's apartment in a Franklin housing development, fifteen-year-old Reed, a freshman at a Boston public high school, describes his goals for the future. The Formica tabletop is well-worn, and deferred maintenance by the housing authority has left a few holes in the walls and some missing tiles on the kitchen floor. Still the apartment is well-kept and orderly. Our conversation transports us away from "the projects" to Reed's vision for himself:

> I want to go through high school, and I want to get my bachelor's degree in college. I want to have a good job, a good-paying job, minimum $100,000 [a year] ... Designing stuff. Designing artwork, designing a new sport, designing new kind of clothes, designing cars ... If you don't finish high school, you only get a certain amount of money. Go through college, the whole thing of college, you get a lot more money than you would like a dropout. My father gets $400 a week. Someone with a high school diploma, probably $900. Someone with a doctorate would get like $4,000 a week.

For Reed, a college education is the way to ensure his economic future, to guarantee a middle-class salary and a job with status, one that will allow him to exercise his artistic creativity.

For the vast majority of boys and parents I interviewed, in both the poor neighborhoods (Franklin and Roxbury Crossing) and the lower-middle-class neighborhood (Lower Mills), college was an important goal. Even the youngest boys, age thirteen and still in middle school, understood the economic benefits of higher education and the economic costs of failing to graduate from high school. At the request of a social worker at a community center, I conducted several interactive workshops on the monetary value of education, asking teams of youth to guess the average yearly earnings of a high school dropout, a high school graduate, a graduate of a two-year college, and a graduate of a four-year college. In various types of neighborhoods throughout the city, young people tended to *under*estimate the wages of high school dropouts and *over*estimate the wages of college graduates. There was no question that they appreciated the value of education and aspired to college.

"Conventional" or "mainstream" ideals such as the importance of education dominate the thinking of boys and parents in all three neighborhoods. When asked what it would take to have a successful life, hard work was the most common response. Skin color, luck, connections, and coming from the right family were never raised as determinants of future success in the labor market.[1] The dominance of conventional ideals extends from education and work to other domains such as romantic relationships, childbearing, marriage, and family life. Tamarr is fourteen and lives with his father, two siblings, and two half siblings in a Franklin housing development. His father started having children as a teenager and has had children with three different women. He does not work, so that he can be home for his children, and the family relies on welfare, food stamps, and public housing. Tamarr explained that having a child at a young age would make it impossible for him to go to college and have a career, and so he wants to wait until he is finished with college to become a father. He worries about having to drop out of school to support a child. He also pointed out that having a kid at a young age would be harmful to the baby as well: "If the child's dad was sixteen, the child might end up growing up wrong because the father won't be able to spend a lot of time and teach the child things 'cause he have to worry about school, getting a job and all those things, a career. But if the child's dad was twenty-six, they could probably just focus on the child."

Frames such as these, which define the consequences of early childbearing as negative, are commonplace, even among boys in the poorest neighborhoods, where early childbearing is all too common. Boys in poor neighborhoods hold very conventional views on issues like marriage, the importance of father involvement in children's lives, condom use, and trust in relationships.[2] They aspire to marry, but hold a very high standard for financial and emotional preparedness for marriage. Condoms are viewed as essential, both because they offer greater protection against sexually transmitted infections, especially HIV, and because they prevent pregnancy. Fatherhood is a serious responsibility, since one must reorient one's life around providing for children, spending time with them, and "being there."

These cultural frames, scripts, and goals drawn from poor communities would be instantly recognizable to middle-class adolescents. They stand in stark contradiction to the prevailing view in the literature on poor neighborhoods and on neighborhood effects. When culture is invoked to understand the consequences of growing up in disadvantaged communities, the emphasis is often placed on the isolation of ghetto residents from mainstream social networks and mainstream culture. Wilson (1987, 1996) argues that the out-migration of the black middle class and the decline of manufacturing produced neighborhoods in which life is no longer organized around work. Social interaction in isolated neighborhoods leads to the development of cultural repertoires that are "oppositional" or "ghetto specific," adaptations to blocked opportunities in the labor market and society generally. For example, Anderson (1990, 1991, 1999) invokes an alternative status system among adolescents from underclass neighborhoods to understand high rates of teenage pregnancy and single parenthood. Massey and Denton (1993) argue that racial segregation and the concentration of poverty lead to an "oppositional culture" in inner cities in which conventional norms and values are upended as a response to blocked opportunities. "As intense racial isolation and acutely concentrated poverty have continued, ghetto values, attitudes, and ideals have become progressively less connected to those prevailing elsewhere in the United States. More and more, the culture of the ghetto has become an entity unto itself, remote from the rest of American society and its institutions, and drifting ever further afield" (Massey and Denton 1993, 172).

A new way of thinking about disadvantaged neighborhoods is required in order to understand the role that culture plays in the lives of adolescent boys such as Tamarr and Reed. In this chapter and the two that follow, I attempt to reorient the study of culture in poor neighborhoods and to shift our understanding of the relationship between cultural context and adolescent decision making. I reintroduce an idea that was once a staple of theorizing about poor neighborhoods—they are characterized by a wide array of competing and conflicting cultural models (Shaw and McKay 1969; see also Kornhauser 1978), or what I term *cultural heterogeneity*.[3] Instead of emphasizing the separation or isolation of residents of poor neighborhoods from mainstream or middle-class culture, the concept draws attention to the multiple cultural models that are present in poor neighborhoods (see Newman 1999, chap. 7). Some of these models are conventional, and some are "deviant" alternatives developed locally (though these locally developed models often have their roots in mainstream ideas as well).[4] Understanding the contribution of the cultural heterogeneity perspective on the cultural environment of poor neighborhoods first requires placing it in the context of prior explanations for neighborhood effects.

Explaining Neighborhood Effects

Much of the early literature on neighborhood effects was fairly atheoretical, emphasizing categories of influences on adolescents—peers, institutions, or neighborhood adults—rather than the social processes by which these influences have their effects (see Jencks and Mayer 1990b for a review). However, recent scholarship is beginning to coalesce around two separate but linked theoretical models: social isolation theory and social organization theory. Both these theories identify key social and/or cultural characteristics of poor neighborhoods and posit how these characteristics affect individuals, though one could argue that the latter contribution is less developed than the former in both theories.

Social isolation theory argues that residents of concentrated poverty neighborhoods live in isolation from middle-class or mainstream social groups, organizations, and institutions (Wilson 1987). The joblessness endemic to high-poverty areas means many residents are not connected to the mainstream labor market, an important link to the culture of middle-class life (Wilson 1996). A general lack of resources also means that sustaining neighborhood institutions is more difficult, further isolating neighborhood residents from mainstream institutions and lessening the contexts available for creating strong social networks within the community. In neighborhoods with high rates of joblessness, many children do not experience life organized around work, and reliance on illegitimate sources of income reduces attachment to the labor market. In short, social interaction in isolated neighborhoods leads to the development of cultural repertoires that differ from the mainstream. In its most extreme form, this theory posits that ghetto neighborhoods have developed alternative and "oppositional" subcultures (see Massey and Denton 1993). These cultural repertoires are thought to significantly affect adolescent outcomes, presumably through their influences on decision making.

At the heart of social isolation theory is a conceptual distinction between what is usually termed "mainstream," "middle-class," or "conventional" American culture and "alternative," "ghetto-specific" (Wilson 1996), or "oppositional" culture (Fordham and Ogbu 1986; Massey and Denton 1993). This distinction is usually made in reference to domains such as work, education, sexual behavior, family life, alcohol and drug use, and crime. "Culture" is defined broadly to include "common modes of behavior and outlook" (Wilson 1996, 66). One challenge for social isolation theorists is to specify what elements of culture are important and to identify how "mainstream" and "alternative" culture differ from one another. We also must be careful not to valorize mainstream culture when using it as a foil to understand the cultural life of poor neighborhoods (Valentine 1968; Young 2004).

The assumptions of the social isolation model have not gone unchallenged. As Newman (1999) illustrates, even in neighborhoods with high rates of joblessness, the majority of people are still in the labor force or going to school and experience daily life structured around these institutions. Therefore it may be more profitable to ascertain which residents of disadvantaged neighborhoods suffer negative outcomes from social isolation, rather than to assume it is a universal liability. Cultural isolation, the development of alternative or "ghetto-specific" cultural models that differ from the mainstream of American culture, is assumed to accompany social isolation. Yet, as will be discussed below, the available empirical evidence indicates that poor urban neighborhoods are not as culturally isolated as this theory suggests.[5]

The notion that poor urban neighborhoods lack organizational and institutional resources has also come under scrutiny. For instance, Small and Stark's study of child-care centers in New York (2005) finds that in poor neighborhoods where the market fails to provide institutions, the nonprofit sector fills the gap. Also, Small and McDermott (2006) show that, while racially segregated neighborhoods that have experienced depopulation suffer from lower levels of organizational resources (retail stores, banks, child-care facilities, and restaurants), neighborhoods that are merely high in poverty do not. Swaroop and Morenoff (2006) find that social organization in poor neighborhoods depends on a number of other community characteristics, including stability, disorder, and the nature of surrounding neighborhoods. Sánchez-Jankowski (2008) documents the continuity and change among five types of institutions in five poor neighborhoods over ten years, and shows how institutions provide order and consistency in such neighborhoods.

While social isolation theory emphasizes social and cultural disconnections between neighborhood residents and the outside world, social organization theory focuses primarily on internal neighborhood processes. Disadvantage is said to lead to difficulties establishing and maintaining order. Lack of resources, ethnic heterogeneity, and population turnover lead to fewer social ties and therefore diminished social control—the capacity of a community to regulate the behavior of its members (Park and Burgess 1925; Shaw 1929; Shaw and McKay 1969). Communities with denser social networks are better able to articulate and enforce common norms and values. While the original work within the social organization framework focused on crime and juvenile delinquency, the approach might also be used to explain variation in other adolescent outcomes, such as sexual behavior or education. Neighborhoods with low levels of social organization may have difficulty regulating adolescent behavior other than crime and delinquency.[6]

Bursik and Grasmick (1993) add an institutional component to this classic model. They suggest that local formal institutions, such as neighborhood organizations, and informal institutions, such as community conventions regarding public behavior, affect the ability of neighbors to maintain social control by influencing norms and expectations and providing contexts within which social ties are developed. External institutions, such as police, city government, and markets, affect the resources that are available for both formal and informal methods of social control. From the time of Whyte's work on street-corner groups (1943), the notion of community disorganization has been criticized for failing to distinguish between different forms of social organization. Poor neighborhoods may simply have different ways of organizing themselves and maintaining cohesion (see also Sánchez-Jankowski 2008).

Sampson's research on neighborhood collective efficacy follows from the Chicago school tradition of social organization theory. Collective efficacy, defined as "social cohesion among neighbors combined with their willingness to intervene on behalf of the common good," is thought to mediate the relationship between concentrated structural disadvantages (residential instability, ethnic or racial heterogeneity, and poverty) and crime rates (Sampson, Raudenbush, and Earls 1997). The concept of collective efficacy more clearly specifies what elements of social organization matter, and takes into account both internal and external resources. Thus far, however, this kind of theory has largely been used to account for neighborhood differences in crime, violence, and delinquency.[7] The underlying theoretical premise of social organization models is that without some form of social control, individuals will readily engage in behavior that the wider society views as deviant or destructive. But we lack a full account of individual behavior, especially in domains for which deviance and conformity are less clearly defined and less public than violence and crime, such as schooling and sexual behavior.

Neighborhoods, Culture, and Individual Behavior

How can culture in general and cultural heterogeneity in particular help us understand neighborhood effects? Cultural concepts have already been incorporated into social isolation theory and social organization theory to different degrees.[8] Though social organization models are not usually thought of as cultural models, they do incorporate cultural elements. In the classic formulation, social organization matters because socially organized neighborhoods are better able to enforce common values. Collective efficacy can be thought of as a cultural concept, insofar as it captures residents' commonly held expectations or beliefs about how others around them will behave when faced with nonnormative behavior. Small (2002, 2004) shows how cultural frames regarding the neighborhood and its origins can influence residents' willingness to engage in the common activity and institution building that lead to collective efficacy and social organization.

While social organization theory focuses primarily on processes internal to the neighborhood, social isolation theory emphasizes social and cultural disconnections between neighborhood residents and the outside world. As discussed above, youth are thought to be socialized into a "ghetto-specific" or "oppositional" cultural environment that promotes behaviors, such as teenage pregnancy and dropping out of high school, that are viewed as detrimental in the outside world. Most research on social isolation theory investigates the social connections of neighborhood residents by examining whether neighborhood poverty is related to organizational participation or to network ties to employed or college-educated individuals, after controlling for individual characteristics. This research tends to find that neighborhood poverty does predict such social ties among adults, at least to some degree.

Meanwhile, the cultural predictions of social isolation theory have been left largely uninvestigated.[9] Social isolation theorists have relied heavily on the notion of "oppositional culture" from ethnographic research on racial differences in educational performance by Fordham and Ogbu (1986), extending the concept to apply in domains other than education (e.g., Massey and Denton 1993).[10] Fordham and Ogbu (see also Ogbu 2004) argue that poor black students develop an oppositional culture in which behaviors that promote academic achievement, such as speaking standard English, doing homework, and engaging in class discussion, become defined as "acting white" in response to inferior schools, discrimination, and blocked opportunities.[11]

However, survey research has rejected the claim that blacks devalue education compared to whites or are sanctioned by their peers for academic effort (Cook and Ludwig 1998; Ainsworth-Darnell and Downey 1998). These findings are reinforced in qualitative interviews and survey research by Carter (2005), who shows that behaviors unconnected to school achievement are at the heart of notions of "acting white" among poor black and Latino youth (see also Jackson 2001). Newman (1999) cautions that even in the face of structural disadvantage, mainstream notions of work, family, and respectability may win out because there are multiple contexts in inner-city neighborhoods (the streets, the workplace, the home). Moreover, the cultural isolation and development of a "ghetto-specific" or "oppositional culture" in poor neighborhoods is further challenged by both survey-based and ethnographic research on attitudes among the poor that finds very strong support for conventional views about education, work, welfare, and marriage (Young 2004; Newman 1999; Edin and Kefalas 2005; Solorzano 1992; Goldenberg et al. 2001; Dohan 2003; Hayes 2003; Carter 2005; Waller 2002; Duneier 1992). In short, there is little evidence that cultural isolation is an accurate description of the cultural context of poor neighborhoods.

Yet analyses of the role of culture in explaining behavior in poor neighborhoods still largely rest on subcultural models. They tend to identify subcultures that promote or justify particular behaviors, and membership or adherence to the subculture is offered as an explanation for those behaviors. Group memberships, whether they be peer groups or residential neighborhoods, are assumed to map onto coherent and distinct subcultures with particular cultural values or orientations. In other words, as in Fischer's subcultural theory of urbanism (1975, 1995), there is an assumption that patterns of social interaction and cultural logics are tightly coupled.[12] Membership in a particular group—which when applied to neighborhood effects translates to residence in a particular neighborhood—leads to adoption of a particular subculture, which then structures decision making and behavior through its effects on values and orientations. When applied to neighborhoods in social isolation theories, this is often accompanied by an assumption that an oppositional cultural logic dominates the subcultures of poor neighborhoods. For example, Anderson (1990, 1991, 1999) explains adolescent sexuality, gender relations, and teenage pregnancy in disadvantaged neighborhoods with the development of a subculture in which early sexual activity and early parenthood are normative. For young men, "sexual conquests" without being tied to any particular partner bring status within the peer group. For young women, a baby signifies adult status and brings adoration and attention from peers and older women.

In sum, subculture-based theories of neighborhood effects fail on two fronts. First, as a simple matter of empirical accuracy, they fail to recognize the diversity of cultural models and ideas in poor neighborhoods. Most prior research—both qualitative and quantitative—as well as the data presented in this book, is not consistent with the idea that poor neighborhoods are dominated by oppositional subcultures that value nonmarital early childbearing, denigrate education, or are tolerant of crime and violence. As I will argue below, adolescents growing up in poor neighborhoods are exposed to these ideas, but not exclusively so. Mainstream or conventional ideas also hold considerable sway. Second, subculture-based theories rely on an overly deterministic model of the effect of culture on behavior. In this model individuals are assumed to belong to a single subculture (defined in terms of group membership with a common and coherent set of cultural values) that defines which behaviors are normative and which are nonnormative. Instead, I hope to illustrate in this chapter and the next two how adolescent boys in poor neighborhoods do not just follow the normative prescriptions and proscriptions of their immediate peer group but rather actively navigate and manipulate multiple sources of cultural messages about how to understand their world, what to do, and how to go about doing it as they make important decisions about schooling, romance, and sex.

Yet perhaps because poverty researchers have few other conceptual tools in their theoretical tool kits, the "dominant deviant subculture" theory persists, and as a result, the literature contains two incompatible theoretical models. In one model, poor neighborhoods are described as containing a mix of nondiscrete cultural groups. Individuals are not just members of one group or another; they draw cultural content from multiple groups. The second model relies on cultural subgroup explanations of behavior in which individuals behave according to the norms of their subgroup, downplaying or ignoring the norms and values of other groups.[13] The confluence of these two theoretical models creates an analytical conundrum: If individuals draw from multiple cultural lifestyle models, how can subcultures hold such sway over behavior, action, or decision making? I propose that cultural heterogeneity provides a better understanding of the relationship between culture and behavior among adolescents in disadvantaged neighborhoods. It does so by breaking the assumed link between social groupings and coherent cultural logics and by challenging the capacity of subcultures to narrowly structure behavior.

The development of the cultural heterogeneity concept draws on ideas developed in cultural sociology over the last two decades.

Bringing Cultural Sociology Back In

For many years, culture was the "third rail" of scholarship on urban poverty. To invoke culture to understand the intergenerational transmission of poverty was to blame the poor themselves for their predicament because cultural explanations suggested that a defective value system—one that did not value (for example) education, hard work, and marriage—was the root of the problem. This type of explanation is most associated with the work of Oscar Lewis and his "culture of poverty" concept (Lewis 1966, 1969). Most social scientists preferred more "structural" explanations, those that emphasized blocked opportunities, low levels of resources, and discrimination. Gradually, however, cultural arguments have crept back in, particularly as Wilson (1987, 1996) emphasized the role of culture as a product of structural circumstances and blocked opportunities, and therefore as a mechanism through which structural circumstances affect behavior.[14]

In the last two decades cultural sociology has moved away from a view of culture as an internally coherent set of values and toward a view of culture as fragmented and composed of "disparate bits of information and . . . schematic structures that organize that information" (DiMaggio 1997, 263). This view posits that in any social context, individuals may choose from a variety of available cultural models. These models may be overlapping or contradictory, and reflect ideas about how the world works, what appropriate goals are, and how to go about accomplishing things.[15] The "cognitive" theoretical perspective implies a loose coupling between interaction patterns and cultural logics. As we try to understand what is and is not unique about the cultural context of poor neighborhoods, a key distinction between the "cognitive view" of culture and the "values view" of culture is how cultural variation is understood. Under the values conception, culture is viewed as internally coherent, and cultural differences imply distinct subcultures with their own systems of values. In contrast, the cognitive view of culture allows for cultural variation, since any social context offers the individual multiple contradictory or overlapping cultural models from which to choose (Swidler 1986; Quinn and Holland 1987; Holloway et al. 1997; Fuller et al. 1996).[16]

In the remainder of this book, this cognitive view of culture takes center stage in unraveling the pathways by which structural disadvantage

turns into behavioral choices—choices that determine life chances in powerful ways. I rely on three conceptualizations, culture as repertoire or tool
kit (Hannerz 1969; Swidler 1986, 2001), culture as frame (Goffman 1974;
Benford and Snow 2000; Small 2002, 2004), and culture as script (DiMaggio 1997).

Swidler (1986, 2001) draws upon the idea of cultural repertoire to develop a general conception of culture that recognizes its causal role in
influencing action.[17] Swidler sees culture as a "tool kit" of symbols, stories,
and worldviews that people use to solve different problems. It is a cache of
ideas from which to draw rather than a unified system of values or norms.
In her view, culture provides the components used to construct "strategies
of action," defined as "persistent ways of ordering action through time."
The elements that make up one's tool kit come not just from direct experience or social interaction, but also from the wider milieu through institutions such as the media, schooling, and religion. Variation in repertoires
across groups or across individuals will lead to divergent behaviors, and it
is in this way that culture plays a causal role in influencing action.[18]

The cultural analyses in this volume are largely based on two types of
cultural objects that may be present in an individual's or group's cultural
repertoire: frames and scripts. Frames are ways of understanding "how the
world works" (Young 2004). They encode expectations about consequences
of behavior and the relationships among various parts of the social world.
A frame structures how we interpret events and therefore how we react
to them. Benford and Snow (2000), writing from a social movements perspective, emphasize that frames are collectively constructed. They identify
problems and assign blame, suggest solutions or strategies, and provide a
rationale for engaging in action. Like repertoires, frames allow for cultural
heterogeneity. Individuals can have multiple contradictory or competing
frames that they deploy in different situations. Small (2002, 2004) shows
that individuals in the same neighborhood can employ different frames.
He also develops what he calls "neighborhood frames" to explain the decline across cohorts in participation in community activities in a Puerto
Rican housing project in Boston. Such frames are the product of historical conditions experienced by different cohorts. Small shows that frames
are not fixed, demonstrating that young people's neighborhood frames
change through interaction with the neighborhood activists of earlier
generations.

Scripts are conceived as cultural templates for the sequencing of behaviors or actions over time. They are akin to Swidler's "strategies of action"
in that they prescribe how to solve problems or achieve goals. Because

individuals or groups may adopt multiple scripts and frames that are inconsistent or even contradictory, frames and scripts are not necessarily hierarchically nested or systematically coherent. In this view, people of a common culture share not a coherent monolithic culture, but available frames and scripts, objective structural conditions, and knowledge of what others do and think. Sewell (1999) characterizes this level of consistency as "thin coherence."

This more cognitive (as opposed to values-based) view of culture has some advantages for understanding the role of context in the form of neighborhood effects. First, it broadens the scope of potential avenues for neighborhood socialization. Rather than just observing and mimicking other local individuals, following particular behavioral edicts, or striving toward the goals defined by particular values, individuals are socialized via a broader set of influences. Frames and scripts conceptualize more general and contingent ways that individuals understand their behavior and that of others, perceive their options and the consequences of their actions, and process information. Second, because the cultural environment is viewed as a determinant of one's repertoire rather than one's actions, it permits more room for individual agency, allowing for variation in behavior among those who experience the same contextual environment. It helps us understand why, even in a neighborhood with high rates of teen pregnancy, most teens do not get pregnant.

Conceptualizing Cultural Heterogeneity

I define cultural heterogeneity as the presence of a diverse array of competing and conflicting cultural models. It is a characteristic of a neighborhood (or perhaps some other social context, such as a school or firm) rather than an individual, though it has consequences for the individuals embedded in that setting. By the "presence" of a cultural model, I mean that there is *social support* for that model among at least a significant number of the individuals who make up the neighborhood. However, one need not be enveloped in a cohesive subculture for cultural frames or scripts to be socially supported. Individuals publicly exhibit behavior motivated or explained by that model; people profess allegiance to it, either in their words or in their deeds. Social support may also come from larger social institutions that transmit messages, such as the media, religious institutions, and educational institutions. The simple knowledge that some people somewhere sometimes employ a particular cultural model is not enough to grant it social support. Particularly for unconventional cultural models that do not enjoy broad support in the wider society, social support must be in some way locally reinforced, for example by members of a neighborhood-based social network. However, social support does not require universal acceptance or approval, only enough to sustain the viability of the cultural model in question.

Cultural heterogeneity may be measured on a continuous scale but is itself the mix of multiple discrete cultural models. The tipping point at which increasing cultural heterogeneity produces more problems than benefits is an empirical question. Heterogeneity is not necessarily synonymous with a mix of discrete groups, such as those with Anderson's "street" versus "decent" orientations (1999) or Hannerz's lifestyle groups (1969). Under a cultural heterogeneity framework, individual members of such groups need not be completely enveloped within them. Individuals can draw from the various cultural models that are available to them. It is the mix of various available orientations or lifestyles that creates a culturally heterogeneous neighborhood environment.

High cultural heterogeneity can be thought of as the neighborhood-level (or more generally, group- or organization-level) counterpart to a diverse cultural repertoire or cultural tool kit. Like the repertoire or tool kit, cultural heterogeneity as a concept is possible only under a theoretical framework that conceives of culture as fragmented and conflicting rather than internally coherent, a perspective compatible with the cognitive view of culture. There is no assumption that in a particular neighborhood context the available cultural models will be compatible with one another or form a coherent whole. As discussed above, under a values view of culture, contradiction is handled by the splitting off of subcultures. Cultural heterogeneity can be thought of as a concept that plays an analogous theoretical role in a more cognitive view of culture.

Thinking about culture in terms of frames, scripts, and goals (rather than values) allows for cultural heterogeneity. Individuals can have multiple contradictory or competing frames that they deploy in different situations, and frames may have various levels of specificity. Similarly, there can be various scripts to accomplish the same goals, and goals may conflict across domains. Maintaining a romantic relationship can interfere with schooling, for example. In addition, there need not be consistency, as individuals are often able to live with many contradictions and inconsistencies. Therefore, one should not think of cultural models such as frames, scripts, and goals as hierarchically nested (though they can be), and individuals or groups may possess or employ multiple contradictory cultural models.

This way of thinking about variation can be contrasted with the more traditional view of culture in the urban sociology literature that accounts for variation via subcultures. Early work on urban neighborhoods rested largely on a view of neighborhoods as culturally homogeneous. For example, Park and Burgess (1925) viewed urban neighborhoods as immigrant receiving areas. Between-neighborhood differences were the consequences of cultural differences between immigrants' home countries, and the culture that immigrant groups brought with them was thought to be the basis of local neighborhood cultures (for a more class-based argument, see Gans 1962). Park and Burgess viewed behavior as determined by "custom and code," much of which is passed on through the family from generation to generation. Within this culture, subcultures are organized sets of responses to opportunities and deprivations, informed by parental or other childhood influences.[19]

Yet the notion that culture is a unified system works poorly to understand variation within societies or within neighborhoods. As discussed above, this type of theory explains action by identifying the different norms and values that motivate it, and membership in different subcultures is the basis for differences in behaviors. If everyone in a neighborhood is exposed to the same set of norms, and if norms determine behavior, then there should be little variation in behavior. When there is behavior that varies from local norms, it is understood as deviance—behavior that would not be considered acceptable by most of the community and would likely result in sanction or punishment. Sociological notions of culture that are based on norms and values allow for cultural differences, but only through the concept of subculture. But are there profound cultural differences between the poor and the middle class? Do the poor have a distinct subculture? "Culture of poverty" models (Lewis 1966) fell out of favor when critics (e.g., Valentine 1968) argued that the poor are no less likely to value education or hard work than their more advantaged counterparts, and that structural constraints limit their access to resources and opportunities. When culture is viewed as heterogeneous, variation in behavior can occur when different individuals interpret and deploy different cultural models, since individuals are active and selective consumers and manipulators of cultural frames and scripts.

Even when the subculture concept is used by poverty researchers or when analysts argue that there are indeed some elements of culture among the poor that are unique to those experiencing poverty, they do not find that the poor have a completely different value system from the rest of society. Sánchez-Jankowski (2008) describes what he terms the unique "value-orientations" of the poor in five poor neighborhoods in two cities, New York and Los Angeles, that develop as individuals "make a life for themselves" under conditions of constant material scarcity. Those who maximize excitement prioritize pleasure in personal life because it is so hard to come by when one is poor. Those who maximize security adopt a frugal lifestyle intended to minimize the risks and consequences of poverty. While Sánchez-Jankowski argues that these orientations are "built without reference or deference to the dominant moral position outside poverty" (22), he notes that both are based on deep-seated moral beliefs about responsibility that are "not specific to class" (244).[20]

Cultural heterogeneity provides an alternative way of thinking about variation that is more consistent with the reality of life in poor neighborhoods, particularly as experienced by young men trying to make their way toward adulthood. For adolescent boys, cultural heterogeneity can lead to cultural repertoires that contain competing and conflicting cultural models. These cultural models can come from a variety of social sources. Direct social interaction with others is one. This includes family members, friends, and nonfamily adults such as teachers, youth workers, and neighbors. These sources of influence may be—but are not necessarily— neighborhood-based. As discussed in chapter 4, some adolescents are heavily involved in their neighborhoods while others are not. Moreover, even adolescents who are equally involved in the neighborhood may, based on prior experiences and viewpoints, take more or less seriously various frames and scripts available in the neighborhood.

A second source of cultural models is observation, especially direct observation of others in the neighborhood or in school. However, cultural models do not just come from immediate ecological factors or interpersonal interactions. Institutions that are decoupled from everyday interactions, such as the media, religion, and politics, also contribute to cultural repertoires. They are particularly rich sources of ideas and ideals drawn from mainstream or middle-class culture. For example, youth draw role models from television and radio (Carter 2005, chap. 5). The American dream provides a cultural template for many of the poor (Hochschild 1995). Feminism shapes how young mothers think about economic independence and marriage (Edin and Kefalas 2005). And religion provides a repertoire for constructing strategies of action in black communities (Patillo-McCoy 1998).

Adolescents do not passively embrace a cultural repertoire that simply reflects the social and cultural world around them. They evaluate this world, selectively drawing upon or rejecting cultural models. How do they choose between competing possibilities when it comes to making decisions? "Resonance" matters: the extent to which a script or frame is compatible with others already in play (Schudson 1989), particularly those within the same domain, such as education or romantic relationships. A cultural model that fits with an adolescent's preexisting ideas is more likely to be adopted or employed than one that challenges them. Resonance can help us explain individual variation within neighborhoods, as different adolescents bring different preexisting ideas and experiences to their neighborhood interactions and observations, and can help us explain cross-neighborhood variation. For example, as discussed in chapter 3, the frame that identifies teachers and other school personnel with power and money rather than the welfare of their students will have greater resonance to an adolescent in a poor, violent neighborhood in which he and his peers view other authority figures, such as police, as guided by similar motives. As discussed above, Tamarr rejected teenage fatherhood because it contradicted both his frame about the requirements for effective parenting and his script for educational attainment. However, whether an adolescent sees a contradiction depends on the information he has available. We will see in chapters 6 and 7 how adolescents in poor neighborhoods often hold simultaneously (and even combine) multiple cultural models that others might see as contradictory and incompatible.

Social support for a cultural model is important as well. The extent to which others adopt and employ the model in their words and actions helps adolescent boys evaluate their choices. When others worthy of respect adopt a cultural model, an adolescent evaluating his options will be more likely to follow suit. For example, in chapter 3 we saw how Daniel adopted Reggie's frame to understand women's behavior in romantic relationships as often motivated by material gain. Reggie's reputation, gained by navigating the violence of the streets, made him an authority. However, social support can operate negatively as well. The negative role models discussed in chapter 2 do not find a receptive audience among kids who have rejected their example. Drug dealers often serve as an available foil for adolescents in poor neighborhoods, and their emphasis on short-term economic gain and flashy displays of materialism can actually motivate some youth to reject frames that emphasize short-term over long-term material well-being.

The material conditions of daily life, the opportunities that a young man has at his disposal, and the barriers he perceives all affect the practical feasibility of enacting a particular cultural model and lead to the rejection of scripts or goals that are out of reach.[21] Edin and Kefalas (2005) show how poor mothers reject a family formation script that puts marriage before childbearing because they see the material requirements for marriage as unattainable given their economic circumstances. Even so, they embrace the legitimacy of the "marriage before childbearing" script for others with the required resources. However, the calibration process is itself a cultural product. For example, the perceived availability of athletic scholarships for college makes a script that involves a more middle-class path to college appear attainable to those with limited means.

Underlying this conceptualization of cultural heterogeneity and individual cultural repertoires is a theoretical model that views adolescents as individual actors who are purposeful but not necessarily rational. In other words, they are not rational calculators who carefully consider the costs and benefits of various actions before acting. Nor are they focused exclusively on economic considerations in evaluating the costs and benefits of various potential actions. (Indeed, anyone who has spent much time with teenage boys can attest to their lack of rationality, particularly in domains such as sexual and romantic relationships.) Yet they are purposeful. They act to achieve their own aims, not simply to mirror the prescriptions and proscriptions of social norms. Adolescents also have many competing needs, including material, emotional, sexual, and status-based needs. Balancing these often conflicting needs can be particularly difficult. Adolescents lack full information for making accurate predictions about the costs and benefits of their actions (predictions that are themselves based on interpretation of cultural models).

In sum, while the subculture model (1) rests on a values view of culture and assumes (2) the dominance of "oppositional" culture in disadvantaged neighborhoods and (3) strong links between peer groups, coherent cultural logics, and decision making, the cultural heterogeneity model (1) rests on a cognitive view of culture and assumes (2) the presence of both "mainstream" and "oppositional" cultures in disadvantaged neighborhoods and (3) the fluidity of cultural logics across groups as individuals draw from multiple cultural models in their repertoires or tool kits.

Poor Neighborhoods and Cultural Heterogeneity

Why are adolescents in poor neighborhoods presented with a more heterogeneous array of cultural models from which to fashion their beliefs and actions than their counterparts in more advantaged neighborhoods? They are exposed to a greater diversity of lifestyles or cultural orientations among their neighbors. Even in the poorest neighborhoods, 20 to 50 percent of the families are poor, not 100 percent. Though many of the non-poor in poor neighborhoods have family incomes barely above the poverty line, most high-poverty neighborhoods still have a sizable working-class or lower-middle-class population.[22] In other words, among disadvantaged neighborhoods, all but the most extremely poor neighborhoods have a mix of people who are working and people on public assistance or involved in crime, people who are high school dropouts and people who have attended college, and people who have middle-class incomes and people who are struggling below the poverty line. As Patillo-McCoy (1999) notes, though many middle-class blacks left inner-city neighborhoods in the 1970s, many also remained there. Institutions such as the media, schools, and churches reinforce mainstream cultural messages. This diversity means that adolescents in poor neighborhoods will come into contact with adults who endorse or practice a wide array of cultural models.[23]

Recent research has demonstrated that within disadvantaged neighborhoods, multiple cultural models are available.[24] For example, Newman (1999) shows that even in neighborhoods with high levels of joblessness, most people are pursuing activities consistent with mainstream ideologies, such as working or going to school. Anderson (1990, 1999) documents the presence of both "street" and "decent" orientations among those living in disadvantaged neighborhoods. Though they are in the numerical minority, those with a "street" orientation dominate public space and public life in inner-city neighborhoods. With the decline of low-skill jobs that command reasonable pay and the rise of the drug economy, the "old heads," older working men who uphold "decent" values such as the work ethic, have lost the cultural high ground to drug dealers who have access to the material signs of status that entice young people used to growing up without material comforts. MacLeod (1995) documents the contrasting educational aspirations of two groups of adolescent boys, the "Hallway Hangers" and the "Brothers," in a single public housing project. Sánchez-Jankowski (2008) describes the two "value orientations" in his ten-year ethnographic study of five poor neighborhoods in two cities, "maximizing security" and "maximizing excitement," both of which are present-oriented but represent different ways of responding to the material scarcity of poverty.

Hannerz (1969) also provides evidence for cultural heterogeneity, not just across groups residing in a single neighborhood but also in the use of culture by individuals. For Hannerz, there are multiple forms of culture—norms and values, meanings, and modes of action—and each individual has a repertoire of these. Local subcultures can add to or substitute for items in the mainstream cultural repertoire and thereby provide adaptations and reactions to a given set of opportunities. Like Liebow (1967) and Anderson (1978), Hannerz sees local culture as helping individuals come to terms with contradictions between the wider society's culture and the individual's position in the social structure. Yet Hannerz makes clear that "ghetto culture" is not a monolithic entity but rather a heterogeneous mix of fluid ideal-type lifestyle groups (which he calls "mainstreamers," "swingers," "street families," and "street corner men"). In ghetto neighborhoods, members of these groups live in close physical proximity, which often leads them to construct exaggerated social hierarchies and distinctions (see also Newman 1992). However, family ties and spatial proximity pull individuals with divergent lifestyles into regular contact and confrontation, diminishing the divisive moral judgments between lifestyle groups.

A culturally heterogeneous neighborhood is one in which both mainstream and alternative cultural models are socially supported, so it is necessary to account for the presence of both types of models. A long line of previous social science research has illustrated how poverty and blocked opportunity result in the development of alternative cultural models, as individuals adapt to their circumstances by developing new status systems, new interpretations of their circumstances, and new ways to "get by." In other words, urban ethnography has complicated the stark divisions of "ghetto culture" and "mainstream culture" implicit in social isolation theory, tending to see culture in disadvantaged neighborhoods as derived from mainstream culture but modified or reinterpreted to serve local needs and in response to blocked opportunities. For the men in Liebow's *Tally's Corner* (1967), Anderson's *A Place on the Corner* (1978), and Duneier's *Slim's Table* (1992), failure to live up to values of the larger society (e.g., masculinity, marriage, economic self-sufficiency) because of blocked opportunities leads to the creation of a local status system that interprets the ideals of the larger society in light of those constructed locally. The local culture is less a new set of values than a set of alternative ways for locals to realize them.[25]

Social organization theory also provides a clue as to why poor neighborhoods are culturally heterogeneous. The social-control capacity of those who endorse mainstream or conventional cultural models is often too low in poor enclaves to keep alternative or unconventional cultural models underground and out of public view. A lack of such strong social ties in poor neighborhoods means social control of alternative behaviors is diminished; local institutions are weak and collective behavior is more difficult (Shaw and McKay 1969).[26] Sampson, Raudenbush, and Earls

(1997), for example, show that low collective efficacy in poor neighborhoods accounts for much of the increased violence that these neighborhoods experience. Residents of poor neighborhoods lack confidence that their neighbors will intervene to stop public disorder and hesitate to do so themselves. Such breakdowns of public order can be self-perpetuating, as residents lose touch with neighbors and retreat from the streets, further weakening neighborhood social ties (Venkatesh 2000). Similarly, Wilson (1996) argues that the lack of social organization in these neighborhoods makes "ghetto-related" behaviors more acceptable while the lack of opportunities makes them necessary for survival. As the number of individuals pursuing "ghetto-related" behaviors such as early parenthood, reliance on public assistance, and street hustling increases, the stigma attached to these behaviors declines.

Of course the mere presence of alternative lifestyles in disadvantaged communities does not necessarily mean that adolescents will interact with individuals who engage in them. Deviant behavioral patterns may have more salience than sheer numbers would lead us to expect. As discussed in chapter 3, in contrast to young adults with more mainstream lifestyles who leave the neighborhood for work or school, those with "street orientations" have a daily presence in poor neighborhoods. The level and organization of violence in poor neighborhoods leads to greater cross-age interaction, as younger adolescents seek out older adolescents and young adults for protection and revere them for their status atop the street hierarchy. Because of their cultural power, these older peers provide social support for alternative or unconventional cultural models in other domains such as education and romantic relationships. Strong peer attachments, also a product of the level and organization of violence in poor neighborhoods, serve to diffuse the messages of the older peers to an even wider range of adolescents.[27]

Cultural Heterogeneity in Franklin and Roxbury Crossing: A Brief Illustration

Compared to their counterparts in Lower Mills, the young men of Franklin and Roxbury Crossing are exposed to and employ a wider array of frames, scripts, and goals. Teenage pregnancy is a case in point. Multiple frames inform adolescents about the consequences of becoming a father or mother at a young age. Tamarr recognizes that early parenthood is a hindrance to schooling and future success. The responsibilities of providing for and caring for a child may make it impossible to continue high school and will certainly preclude attending college. In a post–welfare reform world, these boys never saw reliance on public assistance as a viable alternative to their own responsibilities toward a potential child, both because of the failure that such assistance represented and because of the difficulty of obtaining public assistance.

Tamarr also thinks that having a child at a young age will be bad for the child because a young parent is unable to be a good parent. Yet an opposing frame was often invoked by boys in Franklin and Roxbury Crossing. In a male version of the "weathering hypothesis" (Geronimus 1996), some of the boys felt that a parent who is too old will have trouble relating to his child and understanding the child's experiences. A man who fathers a child at age thirty will be forty by the time the child is ten years old, they explained. A parent that age will not have the physical energy to play with the child, particularly in sports such as basketball and football that are popular among these boys. Opportunities to bond over shared activities will be lost, and the parent-child relationship will not be as close, reducing the parent's influence over the child. In addition, an older parent will not be able to understand and relate to the experiences of the child. The greater the age gap between the parent and child, the more different the social worlds of the parent and child. This also means that the parent will be less able to help the child through the trials of childhood and adolescence.

Another frame highlights the status that comes from fatherhood. A child has the power to boost a young man's masculinity and to instantly grant adult status to a new parent. A father has new, adult responsibilities to care for and protect another human being. It means that it is time to "get serious" and "stop playing around." The responsibilities that come with fatherhood are perhaps the only legitimate excuse to abandon one's close-knit peer group and stop "running the streets." A young man who fathers a child and fails at his responsibilities—both providing materially for the child or "being there" for the child—is looked down upon. However, the young man who succeeds in fulfilling his responsibilities, even if only partly, is held up as an example. In other words, having a child at a young age is only a failure if you make it so by not fulfilling your fatherly responsibilities. By contrast, those who achieve success are owed considerable respect. These examples are only meant to illustrate how heterogeneity of cultural models related to romantic and sexual relationships is manifested in the interview data. These models and the consequences of heterogeneity for behavior will be explored further in chapter 6.

There is also considerable cultural heterogeneity in the education scripts that boys of Franklin and Roxbury Crossing were exposed to and used to understand their own educational trajectories. Most boys knew of individuals who had achieved economic success through a variety of means. Even the conventional path to success, attending a four-year college, has multiple variants. One can study hard in school and receive a scholarship or financial aid. One can be a star basketball or football player and be recruited to play for the college team. One can take remedial courses at a community college, earn an associate's degree, and then decide whether to go on for a bachelor's degree at a four-year college or university. Alternative educational models are also available, however. If one is frustrated or bored by high school, one can drop out, get a GED, and attend community college. Advertisements for technical trade schools in computer repair, automobile technology, medical record keeping, and heating and cooling systems maintenance are ubiquitous on public transportation and in the media, and they include promises of financial aid. There is Job Corps, a residential education program that emphasizes GED prep, literacy, and learning a trade or craft. Finally, though none of the boys planned to "turn to the streets," there is always the possibility of dealing drugs (an opportunity that is often only yards from one's home), at least temporarily until some other opportunity comes along. Street-level "entrepreneurs" can enter the game temporarily to make some money to pay for college or training or to start a legitimate business. From a distance this may seem like fanciful thinking, but for many boys such scripts seem like real options. These examples illustrate the heterogeneity of cultural models relating to education in Roxbury Crossing and Franklin. These models and the consequences of heterogeneity for educational decision making and behavior are discussed further in chapter 7.

Unconventional or alternative pregnancy frames and educational scripts are rooted in mainstream or middle-class cultural ideas and values. The notion that younger fathers can make better fathers is at its core based on the importance of fatherly responsibilities and the expansion of the father's role from merely providing material support for his family to being a nurturer. Similarly, an emphasis on masculinity (and fulfilling parental responsibilities as evidence of masculinity) is rooted in very conventional ideas of manhood that involve supporting and running a family. The value of learning a trade or a skilled craft, becoming an entrepreneur, or pulling oneself up by one's bootstraps by any means necessary are all based on widely available rhetoric in American culture. Though these mainstream ideas and values are not usually prioritized when considering decisions about early fatherhood or educational trajectories, they make it easier to understand alternative frames and scripts as connected to—and in accordance with—mainstream American life.

Another way to illustrate neighborhood cultural heterogeneity is to measure adolescents' allegiance to different cultural frames, scripts, and goals and then examine differences across neighborhood types in the diversity of responses in these measures. Though survey data are not equipped to examine diversity of cultural models within individuals, we can test one prediction of the cultural heterogeneity model: If more disadvantaged neighborhoods have greater cultural heterogeneity, then we would expect to see greater variation or diversity in cultural models across adolescents in more disadvantaged neighborhoods. Data from Add Health allow us to examine such diversity for cultural models relating to college goals, teenage pregnancy frames, and romantic relationship scripts.[28] Add Health is a nationally representative survey of adolescents in grades 7 through 12 during the 1994–95 school year (Harris et al. 2003). As part of the Add Health in-home survey, respondents were asked about their views on college goals, frames regarding the consequences of teenage pregnancy, and their ideal romantic relationship scripts. A simple descriptive examination of differences across neighborhoods reveals that adolescents in more disadvantaged neighborhoods exhibit greater heterogeneity in college goals, teenage pregnancy frames, and relationship scripts than those in more advantaged neighborhoods (defined by poverty, unemployment, and other sociodemographic neighborhood characteristics from the census). While there are differences between the typical adolescent's frames, scripts, and goals across neighborhoods, there are also sizable differences within neighborhoods as well. Across all three measures, poorer neighborhoods tend to have greater cultural heterogeneity than wealthier neighborhoods (Harding 2007, 2009b).

There are at least two potential criticisms of this type of analysis. First, one might reasonably ask whether there are other characteristics of poor neighborhoods that are really producing cultural heterogeneity. For example, poor neighborhoods may be more racially and ethnically diverse than more advantaged neighborhoods, and poor neighborhoods tend to have higher rates of residential turnover. They may also have a greater mix of immigrants, who bring different cultural backgrounds from their home countries. A second criticism is that combining neighborhoods with similar levels of disadvantage may mask differences across neighborhoods that fall into the same category of a neighborhood-disadvantage scale. For example, if all neighborhoods in the top quintile of neighborhood disadvantage were internally culturally homogeneous, but there was great variation across these neighborhoods in cultural frames, scripts, or goals, the same patterns in the data would be produced. To eliminate these possibilities, I calculated neighborhood cultural heterogeneity measures for each of the cultural measures for individual neighborhoods and examined the relationship between neighborhood cultural heterogeneity and neighborhood disadvantage, controlling for other sources of diversity. These regression models confirm that in a nationally representative sample, adolescents in poor neighborhoods exhibit greater cultural heterogeneity (see Harding 2007, 2009b for further details).

Finally, it should be noted that cultural heterogeneity is an analytical concept generated by a social science researcher to develop stronger theoretical models of neighborhood effects, not a "folk understanding" articulated by the research subjects. While its utility rests on whether it accurately describes the cultural context of poor neighborhoods (or at least some poor neighborhoods), it does not necessarily accord with how the boys or their parents would describe their neighborhoods. It need not, in order to be theoretically relevant. (Indeed, sociologists would not expect research subjects to articulate a theory of symbolic boundaries [Lamont 1992], for example, even though such a theory is based on an empirical analysis of those subjects' views and experiences. Developing theoretical concepts and relationships is the analyst's task.) For instance, in chapter 4 we saw how parents act to keep their sons away from the negative peer effects of "the street." They are implicitly developing their own categories of safe and unsafe places and positive and negative influences that help them organize their social worlds. These categories are important sources of *data* for the social scientist, but subject's categories should not be unreflectively adopted as the social scientist's *analytical categories* in generating and evaluating theories.[29] Thus the reader should not expect to see subjects articulating a lay version of the concept of cultural heterogeneity in the chapters that follow.

The Consequences of Cultural Heterogeneity for Adolescent Boys

What are the consequences for adolescents who face a wider array of cultural models in their social environment? If an individual's cultural repertoire is constructed from what he observes among the people with whom he interacts and from the broader cultural ideas to which he is exposed through media and institutions, then the average adolescent in a disadvantaged neighborhood will have a wider repertoire of possibilities. Even more critical, the social environment contains less information about choosing between these cultural models. When it comes to choosing a course of action from among available scripts, to prioritizing various goals, or to considering the various frames that define the pros and cons of particular life events, adolescents in disadvantaged neighborhoods have much more to grapple with than those in more affluent areas.[30] This can have consequences not just for how they talk about their plans and options but also for their decision making and behavior.

Model Shifting, Dilution, and Simultaneity

It is hard to process multiple competing and conflicting cultural models, particularly for adolescents, who struggle to find their own identities. In the presence of cultural heterogeneity, the advantages and disadvantages of various options are more poorly defined than in a more homogeneous cultural environment. The social environment provides a weaker signal about what option is best, because there is social support for many different options. Since there is less consensus or agreement where there is greater heterogeneity, it will be harder for the adolescent to choose between competing options. The result may be weaker commitment to the chosen option and a lower likelihood of follow-through. With a weaker commitment, it is easier to change one's mind when a particular option does not seem to be working out. Another option is available—with local approval. There are always others one can look to who appear to be surviving (or even thriving) while engaging in behavior consistent with various competing cultural models. Furthermore, those individuals will tend to defend the decisions they have made. In a culturally heterogeneous environment where there is considerably less than unanimous social and cultural support for particular frames and scripts, individuals will also face frequent challenges to their chosen cultural models.[31] Obstacles or setbacks may be more likely to push the adolescent off track. In other words, cultural heterogeneity can result in a lack of anchoring to a particular frame, script, or goal. I use the term *model shifting* to refer to problems of weak commitment to cultural models due to cultural heterogeneity. In contrast, in more culturally homogeneous neighborhoods, a narrower range of alternatives will be seen as viable and acceptable, leaving adolescents with few options besides persevering according to conventional cultural models.

In the short term, model shifting can facilitate necessary adaptations to difficult circumstances, but it can have negative long-term consequences. For example, when a romantic partner is not serious about contraception, one can downplay the "pregnancy as roadblock" frame and adopt the "parenthood as status" frame to understand one's options and behavior. Similarly, when high school becomes unpleasant, the GED route to college is also available. In chapter 7 we will see that when some boys in Roxbury Crossing and Franklin begin to struggle in high school, they quickly abandon that route to college and attempt to gain access by earning a GED and then attending a community college. For example, Daniel, seventeen and from Roxbury Crossing, began to fall behind in his classes during his junior year of high school when he frequently skipped school to hang out with his friends downtown. Often he would go to school for one or two periods, but get tired of being there and leave. Faced with the prospect of being held back if he did not quickly make up the work he had missed, Daniel took another available option. He dropped out and enrolled in a free GED class with plans to attend college after getting his GED. He might even be a year ahead of his former classmates who still had to finish their senior year in high school. Yet this route can easily backfire if the GED exam is too challenging or the adolescent fails to enroll in community college and is left with only a second-rate educational credential.[32] Though adolescents in more culturally homogeneous neighborhoods like Lower Mills may also know in the abstract that a GED plus community college is an option, such a path would be a major deviation from what is conventional among their peers, making it seem less viable in practice.

A second type of information problem is that, for any particular cultural model, there will be on average less information about how to carry it through. In a social environment in which many options are present and visible, there will be fewer who have taken a particular path. Because fewer individuals have followed a particular script, there will be fewer examples of how to do so. In other words, the details of the available scripts will be less clearly defined or developed, which will make it more difficult to successfully carry out the script. For example, college enrollment requirements and admission and financial-aid procedures will be more difficult to figure out when fewer neighbors have previously successfully completed the process. Those who want to follow a script for college attendance and know the broad contours of that script will be less likely to know in detail the actions required to successfully realize the script. I use the term *dilution* for problems relating to knowledge of cultural models when there are many heterogeneous models. In contrast, more culturally homogeneous neighborhood environments present adolescents with far fewer socially supported pathways and therefore more examples of how to successfully follow any particular path.

Another example of dilution is the power of multiple competing frames for romantic relationships to dilute boys' understandings of committed long-term relationships. As discussed in chapter 6, boys in Roxbury Crossing and Franklin categorize girls and relationships in multiple ways, and some of the most salient categories are those in which girls will try to take advantage of a boy either sexually or financially. The prominence of this distrust dilutes the definition of a strong, committed relationship. Relationships that last and are characterized by some degree of trust look strong in comparison to the alternatives boys see around them, resulting in thin conceptions of committed relationships. David, seventeen and from Franklin, expects the girls he meets to be after sex or money, rather than a "real relationship," so when this did not prove to be the case with his current girlfriend of eighteen months, he decided he trusted her enough to be less careful about using condoms. She is not going to give him a sexually transmitted infection, and if she gets pregnant, he believes the two of them have a strong enough relationship that they can raise the child together. Cultural heterogeneity in relationship frames has influenced his evaluation of his own relationship.

In the next two chapters I present examples of adolescents who seem to be concurrently employing multiple scripts, multiple frames, or multiple goals. In some cases they are unaware of the contradictions and are combining different aspects of incompatible cultural models. The result is that none is enacted successfully. In other cases they are fully aware of the contradictions but are unable to resolve them. They sometimes operate in accordance with one model and at other times in accordance with another, often based on the immediate situation or context. In addition, these contradictions can be paralyzing and confusing when it comes to taking action or making decisions, resulting in delay of action or decision making, which appears to outsiders to be a lack of initiative or "drive." I use the term *simultaneity* to refer to problems caused by holding multiple cultural models at the same time. Too much information can be overwhelming and confusing for adolescents, especially when they do not have adults who can help them navigate it and separate the useful from the distractions. In contrast, with a narrower range of choices and more clearly defined options, adolescents in culturally homogeneous neighborhoods are less likely to be trapped in the vagaries and contradictions of multiple options.

An example of the simultaneity problem comes from Reed, fifteen and from Franklin. As discussed in chapter 7, boys like Reed in Roxbury Crossing and Franklin are exposed to a wide array of competing and conflicting scripts for educational attainment. As Reed begins high school and is thinking about his educational future, he mixes elements from various scripts. He believes that his participation in football will give him the "points" he needs to graduate from high school even if he does poorly in his classes and on standardized tests. Unbeknownst to him, he is mixing a script for admission to elite colleges and universities, for which extracurricular activities can improve one's application, with the graduation requirements of his public high school, where only passing grades in required courses and the state's "high stakes" proficiency tests in math and English determine whether he actually gets a high school diploma.

One implication of the problems associated with model shifting, dilution, and simultaneity is that young men will be less likely to behave in accordance with the cultural models that they articulate than otherwise similar adolescents in more culturally homogeneous environments. They will be less likely to achieve their goals, less likely to act in accordance with their frames, and less likely to follow their scripts. Using the Add Health data described above, I investigated this hypothesis with regard to college goals, pregnancy frames, and romantic relationship scripts and found this prediction to be correct. Among those adolescents living in neighborhoods with greater heterogeneity of college goals, there is a much weaker relationship between one's own college goals and whether one actually enrolls in college, even holding constant one's own family resources and the characteristics of one's school. Among adolescents in neighborhoods with greater heterogeneity of frames regarding teenage pregnancy, there is a much weaker relationship between what one says about the consequences of teenage pregnancy and whether one has premarital sex. Finally, among adolescents in neighborhoods with greater heterogeneity of romantic relationship scripts, one's ideal romantic relationship script differs more from one's actual relationships (Harding 2007, 2009b).[33]

When Does Cultural Heterogeneity Matter?

Not all cultural heterogeneity matters, and poor neighborhoods are not necessarily more culturally heterogeneous than wealthy ones in all (or even the majority of) domains. Middle-class neighborhoods may exhibit greater diversity of religions, fashions, musical tastes, and political views, for example. Such diversity is probably beneficial for most people, allowing them to connect with others who share cultural interests or worldviews or to access a wide variety of experiences. However, my argument is about cultural heterogeneity in domains with direct bearing on life chances and well-being, particularly schooling and early childbearing. It is not just the sheer number of cultural models available to an adolescent that matters, but the content of those models.

Cultural heterogeneity matters when three conditions are met. First, when cultural models are truly contradictory, not just diverse. One can enjoy multiple styles of music, for example, but one cannot both drop out of high school and join Job Corps, and complete high school and go to community college. Second, as discussed above, cultural heterogeneity matters when various competing models receive social support. It is not enough to know that some students drop out of school and get a GED. Examples must be locally available within one's social world. Third, cultural heterogeneity matters when different models actually lead to different pathways. Middle-class neighborhoods of course have multiple family forms, particularly in urban settings: traditional breadwinner and homemaker, dual-earner couples, homosexual couples with children, and divorced single parents. Yet all these forms involve long-term committed relationships and fatherhood in later life stages. Even divorced single parents at least tried marriage, and likely had their children after they married, and rarely as teenagers. Thus they are not heterogeneous in a way that provides adolescent boys with mixed messages about the timing of fatherhood.

Adolescents like the boys of Franklin and Roxbury Crossing may be especially susceptible to the effects of cultural heterogeneity. Because of their developmental stage, adolescents from all class backgrounds are different types of decision makers than mature adults. Without reference to adult forms of status such as occupational or educational prestige, they are particularly concerned with their social identity and social place in the world of their peers. Seeking to establish themselves as adults independent of parents and other family members, alternative cultural ideals may seem especially attractive, at least to consider. They are also often impulsive, focus on the short term, and have difficulty prioritizing. Most important, they are experimental, seeking out new experiences for their own sake. Adolescents are willing to "try on" various available cultural models and may be more open to alternative frames and scripts. These characteristics of adolescents make them particularly susceptible to problems associated with cultural heterogeneity.[34]

Conclusion

This chapter has developed the concept of cultural heterogeneity from a theoretical perspective and reviewed some initial evidence from both previous ethnographic work and nationally representative survey data that shows that poor neighborhoods are characterized by greater cultural heterogeneity. Conceiving of poor neighborhoods as culturally heterogeneous rather than culturally isolated from the rest of society represents a significant break from how recent social science has understood the cultural context of such neighborhoods. It also provides a new mechanism to explain the effects of poor neighborhoods on adolescents. By exposing adolescents to a wide array of competing and conflicting socially supported cultural models, neighborhood cultural heterogeneity affects their decision making and behavior through processes of model shifting, dilution, and simultaneity. Yet the findings I have reviewed have only scratched the surface of the implications of cultural heterogeneity for adolescent decision making and behavior. The next two chapters draw on the fieldwork in Franklin, Roxbury Crossing, and Lower Mills to more fully explore the contours of neighborhood cultural heterogeneity and how it affects the lives of adolescent boys.

CHAPTER SIX CULTURAL HETEROGENEITY, ROMANTIC RELATIONSHIPS, AND SEXUAL BEHAVIOR

Elijah, thirteen, has been living in his Roxbury Crossing neighborhood his entire life. His interest in girls has been growing, though his parents do not want him to begin dating until he is much older. One of his cultural frames is quite traditional, emphasizing the importance of abstinence until marriage. Here the imprint of both his parents and sex education in school is clear: sex before marriage is dangerous because of the potential failure of contraception. When a baby is born to young unmarried parents, the father is likely to leave the mother and baby behind, resulting in a difficult childhood for the baby. Sexually transmitted infections (STIs) are also a possible consequence of sex before marriage:

> I think you should only have sex when you are like married . . . It's when you have a commitment and you have a baby and you and the wife can take care of the baby. 'Cause mostly other chicks have babies and the father runs away. And the baby is stuck with the mother only and the grandmother or grandfather . . . No one-night stands. 'Cause condoms are not good protection . . . 'Cause people can have a baby when they do have a condom on. They can have a disease when they are having a condom on.

Yet this is not the only frame that informs Elijah's understanding of girls and romantic relationships. His "tool kit" simultaneously contains another competing model derived from his dealings with peers: sex can be freely arranged outside of a long-term relationship and without commitment as long as contraception (a condom) is used. The way to meet potential sexual partners is to talk to them on the street, at school, or anywhere else, and to get their phone number. The beginnings of this script are visible to anyone who spends time in Roxbury Crossing or Franklin,

as young men practice "hollering at girls" or "spitting their game" in full
public view and as girls compete for the public attention of boys.

> If I see a cute girl walking down the sidewalk, then I'm gonna holler at
> her [laughs]. "Come here." And then if she turns her head, and then I just
> walk over there and like, "What's your name?" She tells me her name and
> I'm like, "Where do you live?" She be like, "I live so and so." I tell her my
> name, and it's like, "What school you go to?" If she's older than me, I tell
> her a fake school, fake age. And I just keep talking about other things.
> Hoping that she gives me her number at the end. You always say, "Can I
> get your number?"

The next stage is more private, but at age thirteen Elijah already knows
what is involved. Boys talk to girls on the phone over a period of days
or weeks to establish some level of familiarity, and then they meet to
have sex. (While this particular script does not seem to be so far from the
middle-class script for the "one-night stand," we must remember that Elijah is only thirteen.) "Boys will do anything to have sex; older boys," Elijah
says. A boy will often tell the girl that he loves her in order to move the
relationship along, even if he does not. On his own, Elijah mixes the behavioral implications of these two frames. Like all thirteen-year-old boys, he
is very curious about sex and has begun "hollering" at girls, having done
so five times so far by his own count. He has succeeded in getting a phone
number twice, both times from thirteen-year-old girls in his neighborhood
whom he met on the street. After talking to one girl a few times, the girl
brought him to her friend's house while the parents were away at work.
Elijah was prepared with a condom, but according to his own account he
insisted on stopping short of having sex. He left when things got to that
point. Shortly afterward, the girl's family moved away from the neighborhood, and he never saw her again. He has now been talking to the second
girl for about two weeks.

Elijah is experiencing the simultaneity problem firsthand, and these
multiple scripts are evident in his behavior. He simultaneously employs
two conflicting frames, struggling to remain true to both at once but
acting in accordance with neither on a consistent basis. The abstinence
frame suggests that condoms are not foolproof and therefore sex should
be avoided outside of marriage, but Elijah arranges encounters with girls
and brings condoms with him as if he plans to have sex, which the "hollering" script calls for. He follows the "hollering" script, but he does so only
partially, stopping short of having sex, at least so far. His compromise is to
not tell the girl he loves her, lest that lead to sex:

I never said I love you to a girl because you never know if you really love her. You just like her. If you say, "I love you," then they're really gonna take off their clothes. Once you say that, they think you're gonna stay with them until you get married, and you don't want that. 'Cause you want to just go out with her for a couple of months.

When asked about the contradiction, Elijah admits that his curiosity about girls and sex can get the better of him: "'Cause it's boring when you're just seeing the girl. Kiss them and, 'Bye.' Can't do that. When you feel horny, that's when it happens."

Elijah is not alone in confronting a cultural world in which an array of competing cultural models regarding romantic relationships and sexual behavior is available. Compared to their counterparts in Lower Mills, the boys of Franklin and Roxbury Crossing live in a sea of cultural heterogeneity when it comes to girls and sex. This chapter attempts to understand the worlds of romantic relationships and sexual behavior in Roxbury Crossing, Franklin, and Lower Mills from the perspectives of these adolescent boys. The boys' views often involve at best unflattering appraisals of many of the adolescent girls they interact with. Even when we object to the attitudes and understandings of these boys, it is important to understand their perspectives and where they come from, for these perspectives play an important role in driving their decision making and behavior.

Stunts, Gold Diggers, and Good Girls: Framing Girls and Relationships

Eduardo, a seventeen-year-old who grew up in a large Roxbury Crossing public housing development, classifies potential romantic or sexual partners in a mix of attractive and unflattering ways: "stunts," "gold diggers," and "good girls" populate his intimate world. While boys sometimes use different terms for these categories or have less or more fine-grained distinctions, Eduardo's categories are in use among his peers.

A "stunt" is a girl who is primarily interested in sex rather than a relationship. Boys think of these girls as the ones who enjoy sex for its own sake and do not connect sexual behavior with emotional intimacy. Nor is a stunt after money or the status that comes from associating with particularly popular or high-status boys. Since she is mostly interested in sex, a stunt is easy to get into bed, and accordingly she is most likely to respond to the guy who is "hollering" at her in the way Elijah describes. She is also extremely likely to cheat on a boyfriend or husband because relationships are not a priority for her. Eduardo explains:

Stunts, they are easy to do anything with. They look like good girls. Any female could be a stunt. It has nothing to do with age. It has nothing to do with you. You can have a female that's working who has a kid, pays all her bills, amazing credit. It has nothing to do with money. Example: I was working with this lady at [my job]. One of [my coworkers], she's maybe twenty-nine or thirty. She's a stunt. She's married and has a kid, but was still trying to feel on me. Well, a horny female. That's what you would call a stunt.

Traditional gender roles inflect the way that young men think about stunts. Boys are revered for being "players," reveling in sexual relationships with multiple girls without the entanglements of emotional commitment. Stunts, the female equivalents, are stigmatized. They are "hos" (whores). A girl who is (or once was) a stunt is not a good candidate for a romantic relationship, and boys who get too involved with stunts are made fun of:

I was looking for a lot of stunts just for pleasure. But if I ever got into a relationship, I would always look for a good girl . . . Jay, he had a kid with a stunt. Everybody's laughing at him. How you gonna have a kid with the girl who's been around everywhere . . . What are you doing? What is wrong with you? I don't understand why would anybody look for a relationship with a stunt.

"Gold diggers" are girls who are, according to the boys, interested in a man's money or other resources. She looks for a man with a car and a job (legitimate or not) and seeks to extract gifts, rides, and money from him, using the relationship with him to that end. She wants a boyfriend who will take her shopping, out to eat, and to the movies. She will have sex with a young man in order to create and preserve a relationship, but unlike a stunt, a gold digger is not interested in sex for its own sake. Rather, she uses it to extract resources from her boyfriend and to control him. Since the gold digger is interested only in a man's resources, she is very likely to cheat on her boyfriend with another boy who has a thicker wallet. She will also end a relationship when a partner loses his job or runs out of cash, or when another partner comes along with a nicer car or more expensive gifts. As discussed in chapter 3, it is the gold digger who seeks to trap men into a relationship as a way to support herself or her children. However, not every girl who is swayed by a boyfriend's material displays of affection falls into this category. To be a gold digger she must consider material resources a primary factor in the relationship. Other girls may simply view a boyfriend's gifts as a sign of affection or find themselves enjoying spending time with a boyfriend because he can provide a pleasant lifestyle. It is a fine line, as Eduardo explained: "Gold diggers are a little different from when the female thinks she loves that person, but she loves him because she's getting treated with all this."

The gold-digger frame resonates with the poverty of the families living in Roxbury Crossing and Franklin.[1] Boys witness on a daily basis how their own families and others around them struggle to scrape together the material resources for survival. The notion that someone might use a romantic or sexual relationship as part of this struggle for material survival fits with these observations and experiences.

Finally, Eduardo explains, there is the "good girl," who is focused on her future, not on boyfriends or parties. She goes to school regularly, studies, and has plans to go to college or at least some sort of job training after high school. She probably has a job of her own, so she does not need a man's money. The good girl is watched over by her family, close to her mother or father, attends church regularly, and is usually uninterested in a boyfriend. She does not have time for a boyfriend, at least not until she graduates from high school. This makes the good girl inexperienced, as she usually has never had a boyfriend and has at most one prior sexual partner. There is no chance the good girl is going to let herself get pregnant. She is the one a boy could bring home to meet his mother. She will be a positive influence because she has her own priorities "straight." The good girl is the type of girl you could have a long-term relationship with:

> What I mean by a good girl is a home girl. That's one big difference. You can tell if she's after your money or not. You can tell if she wants to get pregnant or not . . . She does what she has to do—school, job . . . Half of them don't want to get into a relationship. Half of them are scared. They've never been in a relationship. They say they're too busy.

Just as Eduardo and his peers hold various frames describing types of girls, there are also different cultural models for romantic relationships. Tavon, eighteen, moved to Lower Mills with his mother, older sister, and one-year-old niece only a few months before our interview. He had spent most of the rest of his life growing up in a poor neighborhood adjacent to Franklin. Tavon's relational landscape is populated by "wifeys" and "shorties." The wifey is the primary girlfriend. She takes priority over others, the shorties. Tavon spends the most time with the wifey, and she is the girlfriend with whom he is having a long-term relationship, based on emotional as well as sexual intimacy. She is a protowife, the girlfriend he might someday have children with and someday marry, and, as the name suggests, this is the type of relationship that comes closest to an idealized "middle-class" romantic relationship. A young man also devotes more of his financial resources to the relationship with the wifey. The shorty relationship is casual, intermittent, and nonexclusive, but it is not a "one-night" stand and it is not only a sexual relationship. A young man can have multiple shorties, girls he "talks to" (spends time with) and has sex with from time to time, without the level of commitment or the long-term orientation of a wifey. Tavon helps out a shorty with a ride or a gift when he can, but never at the expense of his relationship with his wifey:

> Wifey's home now, I mean your wifey, you do without it for your wife. She asks you, that's to only show you she can get whatever she wants. You gotta spoil a wifey. She asks you to come pick up, you do it. "I gotta go pick my girl up" . . . Shorty's just some chick. "That's my shorty."

If the wifey begins to suspect that Tavon has a relationship with a shorty, he breaks off the shorty relationship and denies that the relationship ever happened.

> INT: So what do you think about having different girls at the same time?
> TAVON: As long as you don't fuck up home. They can find out about each other. As long as they're home. Wifey, you don't fuck up there . . . Keep the happy home . . .
> INT: What about if one of these girls you have on the side finds out, then she might tell the one at home?
> TAVON: Oh, you can always deny that shit. "Who is she? I haven't been fucking with her. She asked for my number every damn day. I told her I've got a girlfriend at home."

Though older adolescents like Eduardo and Tavon are best able to articulate the distinctions between the various frames for girls and for relationships, much younger adolescents talk the same language. Even those with virtually no experience employ the diverse frames underlying stunts, gold diggers, and good girls to understand their social worlds. The frames exist outside their own individual experience and have been transmitted to them by older boys who really have "been there and done that." Deon, age thirteen and from Roxbury Crossing, has never had what he would describe as a real relationship with a girl, though he began talking to a girl a few weeks before his first interview. Yet Deon is well aware of the categories Eduardo and Tavon employ, and uses them to evaluate girls. Deon described what a stunt is and why he would avoid one, and in explaining how a "booty call" works, he reveals his knowledge of the shorty type of relationship.

DEON: I wouldn't have a girl for just a night. If you're a slut I'm not gonna go out with you.

INT: What is a slut?

DEON: A stunt. I don't go out with girls that had sex before. I'm not gonna have no sex with no stunt girl. Anytime I have sex is when I feel like it at the right time . . . 'Cause I'm not gonna rush into it . . .

INT: What about having a sexual relationship with someone you are not really interested in having a girlfriend/boyfriend relationship with?

DEON: No, 'cause it's actually a booty call. Calling a girl, "What you doing?" She says, "Nothing." "I'm coming over right now."

Though the boys in Franklin and Roxbury Crossing take these frames very seriously, it is important to keep in mind that they are cultural interpretations and perceptions and do not necessarily accurately describe the attitudes or behavior of the girls who are their potential romantic and sexual partners. First, different boys categorize the same girls in different ways based on their own perceptions. A girl who is a "stunt" to one boy may be a "gold digger" to another. Second, and more important, the notion that girls can be neatly categorized according to these frames and that any particular girl or any particular relationship objectively fits into only one frame is clearly incorrect. To see this, we need only imagine what would happen if we were to turn the categories around and use them to categorize the boys based on their behavior (setting aside the question of how the girls in Franklin and Roxbury Crossing would categorize the boys they interact with). Tavon, for example, acts like the male equivalent of the stunt and sometimes the gold digger in his shorty-type relationships, while he also plays the male counterpart of the good girl in the context of his wifey-type relationship. In short, it is important not to reify these categories and to keep in mind that these are the categories of the boys themselves, not analytical categories.[2]

How do Lower Mills youth differ from their counterparts in Roxbury Crossing and Franklin? What matters is not the content of the categories but their relative salience. Like their counterparts in Franklin and Roxbury Crossing, the boys of Lower Mills understand that some girls may be only after sex, that other girls may be only after money, and that still other girls want a long-term, emotionally intimate romantic relationship. Yet these first two frames carry very little salience because the boys of Lower Mills tend to believe that the vast majority of girls are looking for love. In other words, the boys of Lower Mills saw most girls as "good girls." They rarely talked about girls being "stunts," and they were much less worried about girls using a relationship to extract resources from them.

When I asked the boys in Lower Mills what proportion of the girls they meet are interested in money rather than a "real relationship," the typical answer in Lower Mills was that 10 percent to 30 percent of girls are interested in money. Consider Timothy, who is fourteen years old and has lived in Lower Mills his entire life. Timothy's mother gave birth to him when she was nineteen, and she and Timothy's father run a child-care business out of their home, which they inherited from Timothy's grandmother. When asked what girls his age were looking for in a boyfriend, Timothy explains that they consider 50 percent looks, 20 percent personality, and 30 percent money. He thinks that only about 30 percent of girls would cheat on their boyfriends. He gave an example of the type of girl who might cheat:

> Let's say I buy her a sweater. There's three scenarios. One would be like she says, "Oh, it's OK. You don't have to buy it for me." That's like modest. The other is, "Thank you," and accept it. So it's like in between. And the other is, "Where's my matching pants?" So that's the one you better watch out for.

When asked about his ideal romantic relationship, Timothy described a fairly conventional one, involving going out on dates alone and with friends, kissing, exchanging presents, telling other people about the relationship, meeting each other's parents, having sex, getting married, and having a baby. Timothy did not think it would be very hard to find someone to have this type of relationship with.

Franklin and Roxbury Crossing boys see the world differently. Fifty percent to 70 percent or sometimes up to 90 percent of girls are primarily interested in a man's money, according to these boys. For them, gold diggers and stunts are just as salient, if not more so, than good girls worthy of a wifey-type relationship. Boys in poor neighborhoods are much more concerned about girls being faithful to their boyfriends. This is connected to the idea that girls are interested in money and will quickly abandon a boyfriend for another boy with more money or a nice car. Franklin and Roxbury Crossing boys hold the same ideals for romantic relationships that Timothy outlined, but they were almost universally pessimistic about the prospects of finding someone to have that relationship with. In their view, finding the good girl is a huge challenge, and something they may never be able to do. Though they hold mainstream values regarding long-term relationships, they are very pessimistic about their prospects for realizing those goals.

Elijah, thirteen, of Roxbury Crossing, whom we met above, explains his worries when it comes to romantic relationships:

INT: What do you think girls your age look for when they are looking for a boyfriend?

ELIJAH: Really they just look for a macho man . . . They're really looking for sex.

INT: And why do you think they're looking for sex?

ELIJAH: Because that's all they know. They see it on TV. Mostly they see people kissing and stuff. So they figure, "I want a boyfriend to see how it is." Once they see how it is, "Oh, I don't want that boyfriend no more."

INT: So do you think they care about how much money someone has or how someone looks or their personality?

ELIJAH: Money.

INT: Do you think they care about personality?

ELIJAH: Some do. Those with a good personality are nice girls.

INT: And why do you think girls care about money?

ELIJAH: 'Cause that's what they want, they want boys to buy them stuff.

INT: And how many girls your age do you think would be faithful to their boyfriends?

ELIJAH: Like 45 percent. Not all girls are really . . . how can you say, really trustful. They can say they like you and then go to a different boy and say "I like you" to that boy.

INT: So how do you think you can tell when a girl is going to be someone you can trust?

ELIJAH: She has to show it. She has to be caring. She don't have to be asking for money all the time . . . She can be calm and say, "Let's go to a movie." She doesn't have to be the type of girl that says, "Oh, buy me this and buy me that."

INT: So what type of things do you look for when you're looking for a relationship?

ELIJAH: I'm looking for a girl who really cares about me.

Elijah's account reveals the multiple frames that he draws upon to understand the behavior he observes in girls. He identifies two types of girls to stay away from, those interested in sex and those interested in money. In his view, the majority of girls cannot be trusted to be faithful, and the sign that a girl will not be faithful is whether she asks a boy to buy her things. Note that his view that many girls are just interested in sex is not what we would think of as the conventional view of gender and sexuality. In mainstream culture it is girls who are warned to watch out for boys who are just after sex and will say anything to get it. Elijah is looking for a girlfriend who "cares about [him]," but girls motivated by sex and money are what he expects to encounter most often.[3]

The role of the local environment in shaping the frames that boys bring to romantic and sexual relationships becomes clearer when we look at boys who have moved between neighborhoods. Eduardo grew up mostly in a Roxbury Crossing public housing development, but his family recently moved to a more working-class section of Boston. It was only after spending time in his new neighborhood that he developed a new perspective on what to expect of girls and of relationships:

> That time maybe three or four years ago, I always used to think that 90 percent of the females are stunts. Now, I think, maybe, 30 percent of the females are stunts. Why? Because I'm around different people. I just have a different point of view now. I'm not just in that circle where all the hustlers are, [Roxbury Crossing]. I see things in a wider [way]. My vision at that time was [local]. Now, I can actually see the world.

When Eduardo moved out of his Roxbury Crossing housing development, his view changed from expecting girls to be gold diggers or stunts to expecting the typical girl to be a good girl. Boys from Lower Mills offered such conventional views of girlfriends and relationships, even at a young age. They were less worried about girls who are just interested in sex or money. Darnell, age thirteen, explains how he thinks about what girls are interested in from a relationship, and bases it on what he looks for himself.

> INT: What do you think girls your age are looking for in terms of a boyfriend?
> DARNELL: Just somebody they could feel comfortable [with], that's what I would want. Somebody that's just cool, that's not talking a lot. I figure the way I think about girls is they just want somebody to listen to them, talk back to them. Somebody you're gonna have a good time with, that you can respect.
> INT: Some people say that girls are more after looks or a guy who's got money or stuff like that?
> DARNELL: No. I don't think it's the case. I don't have any of those problems . . . I'm probably what they would call on TV, they always say the bad girls always get the good guys. I figure myself that's what I try and be. One of those good guys. That's why I try to stay away from the bad girls.
> INT: So what's someone who is a bad girl and what are they like?
> DARNELL: Just somebody that just like disgusts you. They just do like rude things all the time. I was with one girl that did that, so it didn't work.
> INT: What kind of things was she doing specifically that you didn't like?
> DARNELL: The main thing was every time I talked to her, she would kind of like push me away. It's just she always talked about something different, and I didn't like that.

INT: What were some of the things you wanted to talk about that she didn't want to talk about?

DARNELL: Her and me, but she'd always change the subject to something else. Or about an object or something that was coming up. It was nothing personal.

Darnell's concerns about relationships have more to do with the interpersonal connection he might establish with a girlfriend, fairly typical teenage relationship concerns, than with the issues surrounding money and sex that figure so prominently among the boys from Franklin and Roxbury Crossing. While his counterparts in Franklin and Roxbury Crossing bring multiple salient girlfriend and relationship frames to any encounter, Darnell approaches possible partners expecting a good girl.

Similarly, Jason, eighteen and from Lower Mills, does not approach relationships with the suspicion that is characteristic of the boys from Roxbury Crossing and Franklin, who must juggle multiple frames. Jason explained that cheating sometimes happens in relationships, because all relationships have their problems: "There's no way you can go through a relationship without an argument, like a serious issue or something. I mean there's always an obstacle in there." But he does not approach all relationships expecting that the girl could be a stunt or gold digger who will cheat or otherwise take advantage of him.

JASON: I don't go in there expecting it to happen, but I won't say, "Oh this person will never do that." You can't put anything past anybody because everybody's capable of doing something wrong. You just hope it doesn't happen.

INT: How forgiving would you be if someone had cheated?

JASON: It depends on the situation, how it happened, who she was with.

Frame Heterogeneity, Relationship Trust, and Contraceptive Use

Heterogeneity of frames leads to low levels of trust and can have consequences for contraceptive use and therefore for understanding teenage pregnancy. The presence of competing and conflicting models contributes to an almost poisonous atmosphere for adolescent romantic relationships.[4] Compared to their counterparts in Lower Mills, the boys of Roxbury Crossing and Franklin approach romantic and sexual relationships with a great deal of distrust, which derives both from the content of the frames—gold diggers and stunts—and from cultural heterogeneity itself. When there are competing and conflicting frames rather than one dominant model, the chances that a potential romantic partner will approach a relationship with the same frame declines dramatically to the point that one must assume, until proven otherwise, that one's partner is looking for something different in the relationship. Even if boys expected all girls to be stunts or all girls to be gold diggers, their romantic lives would be much simpler, since they would know how to approach the relationship and could trust their understandings of the girl's intentions, even if those intentions were to take advantage. Instead, they approach relationships with a great deal of distrust and suspicion of the potential partner's motives. The result of this distrust is that the boys in the high-poverty neighborhoods expect such a mismatch when they approach a new romantic or sexual relationship.

Franklin and Roxbury Crossing boys worry out loud and in private that girls will trap a man into a relationship—or at least into paying child support—by tricking him into fathering her child. One way that a gold digger might trick a man into a pregnancy is by claiming that she is taking birth control pills when she is really not. She will tell him it is okay not to use a condom because she is on the pill. Another warning sign that the boys watch out for is a girl who wants to put on the condom herself or to use a condom that she has provided, lest she has tampered with it to make it ineffective. We first met Chris, age fourteen and from Franklin, in chapter 2 when he described the conflicts between the Franklin Hill and Franklin Field housing developments. He is particularly worried about girls and condoms:

> When like they'll actually put on a condom, and they'll just poke a hole at the top, so the semen can go up. That's why I don't let girls do nothin' for me. I'll put on *my* condom. "I'll do it." If she say that, I'm like, "Never mind, I'm not havin' sex with you. Get out. You were just tryin' to set me up."
>
> I know, because I learned it from my older niggas. They told me like, "Don't ever let a girl do that. I got a kid from that right now." My mother even told me that's how I was made[5] . . . People are really doin' that . . . Max, he's fifteen. He's got a kid too. Let a girl put on a condom, and that was it . . . Some girls just want to know how it is to have a baby. Some girls want to keep that man. Some girls, it just happens by accident . . .
>
> [The father has] got to pay child support no matter what. They've got to see their kid, so she sees him once in a while. Some niggas just say forget it, and leave. They call that "deadbeat dad." Ain't no deadbeat dad. That's a dad that didn't want a kid so early. And you had it, so you take care of it on your own.

Almost every boy in Franklin and Roxbury Crossing expressed this set of fears about girls who trick a man into fathering a child, but only

Chris and one other boy actually knew someone who had this experience. Yet even boys with zero personal knowledge believed it was a common problem and something they needed to be suspicious of girls about. Being tricked into fatherhood is a sort of urban legend that takes on importance because it is widely perceived to be true, even if it is rare. It is believable in part because it resonates with boys' frames about girls. In Lower Mills, however, boys rarely voiced this concern. While they were familiar with the idea that a girl might trick a boy into fatherhood, they did not see it as something that girls would actually do because it did not fit with the dominant frame regarding girls. One boy explained that this sort of thing would happen with "like 1 in 800" girls, and did not know anyone who had been tricked into fatherhood. For Lower Mills boys, being tricked into fatherhood is something that happens on television on *The Jerry Springer Show*, as one boy put it, not in real life.

For example, Charles, fifteen, has lived in Lower Mills for three years. He had certainly heard of the idea that a girl would try to trap a man into a relationship by getting pregnant with his child, but he did not know anyone who had such an experience. Charles explained that a condom was the way to have safe sex, to prevent pregnancy. When I asked him what he would do if a girl said that she was on the pill and that he did not need to use a condom, Charles explained that he would still use a condom, but not because she might be lying or might have an STI.

> INT: If a girl told you, it's okay, you don't have to use a condom because I'm on the pill, what would you think about that?
> CHARLES: I wouldn't care that she's on the pill. Because she might forget to take it.

Charles is worried, perhaps correctly, that a girl his age might not be responsible enough to use the pill correctly. His prediction that he would still use a condom is not based on suspicion of girls' intentions, even after our extensive conversation about such problems. When I asked whether these issues affected which girls he might want to go out with, he said no, "'Cause everybody's not like that."

Of course boys often behave in ways that make them unworthy of a partner's trust as well. As Anderson (1999) notes, boys will often tell girls they love them, promising a long-term relationship, in order to have sex with them. Dustin, age fifteen and from Roxbury Crossing, explained how he and other boys try to do this in order to get a girl into bed without having a relationship with her. But Dustin only does this if he is not interested in a relationship with a particular girl.

DUSTIN: Some dudes might just say "I love you" so they can have sex and all that. So, the girl can feel like you really do, and it makes her feel special, and they'll probably end up having sex with you.

INT: So, does that kind of thing happen a lot, would you say?

DUSTIN: Yes.

INT: How many guys out of ten would you say would use that tactic?

DUSTIN: Eight!

INT: How about you? Would you do that?

DUSTIN: Yeah, I would in certain cases. Like probably where I don't want to go out with her, but she want to go out with me, and she looking right.

INT: Is there a situation in which you wouldn't do it?

DUSTIN: If I really liked the girl.

Franklin and Roxbury Crossing boys also worry that girls who are stunts will have sex even if they have an STI. Since a stunt is interested in sex and does not care about her partner, she is willing to risk his health to satisfy her desires. Stunts who have sex frequently and with multiple partners are likely to have STIs and not even know it. (The sexual education curriculum of Boston schools and public health campaigns ensure that most boys are aware of STIs. Lessons from these programs stuck in the boys' heads.)

Though he is only fourteen, Chris has developed both from experience and from talking to friends and older peers a list of warning signs when it comes to girls and sex:

I wouldn't [have sex without a condom], period. I [would] tell her, "If you're not willing to have a condom, you've got to get off. I'm not having sex with you if you're not having sex with a condom. Because if you did it with another nigga, anything could happen . . . "

If a girl do something sneaky to me, I'm not having sex with her, because either she's got somethin' or she want to have a kid, and I don't want to have [a kid] that way. I don't want to be burned [get a disease] . . .

I don't ask for sex. I test it. Like if a girl actually wants to have sex, I'm not having sex with her, because she's a stunt. But if it's been like six months, and she ain't said nothin' about sex, I could go there [have sex with her] . . .

No girl begs for sex. Like, "Come on, let's go in the room, let's go in the room! Why don't we do it?" I had one of those girls . . . They're stunts, a skeezer, a ho. And they're doin' it to somebody else too. That's how you know girls are cheatin'. If for like a week, and all of the sudden it just stop, they ain't askin' for nothin', like why they stop so quick? They're gettin' it from somewhere. That's why.

This is not just idle talk. Boys take additional precautions to avoid getting STIs from girls they do not trust completely. Local neighborhood health clinics offer free tests for STIs, and boys avail themselves of this service sometimes, insisting that their sexual partners do the same.[6]

Lower Mills boys are less worried about getting an STI because they expect to encounter "good girls" and trust girls to tell them if they are infected. When Seth, age fourteen, explained how he imagined his next romantic relationship progressing, he did not include talking to his partner about STIs. When I asked why he left that out, he said it was not necessary for him to bring it up: "Because if they have a disease, maybe they would tell you before they would want to get a relationship started." Seth's expectation is that the girl is interested in a real romantic relationship and cares about a partner enough to protect him from an STI.

Greater gender distrust among boys in Franklin and Roxbury Crossing is a product not only of the content of the frames that they bring to romantic relationships but also of their heterogeneity. While they are looking for the good girl to have the wifey relationship with, in their minds the girls they meet will rarely be good girls, and they will often be stunts or gold diggers. When they are looking for the stunt for a casual, primarily sexual relationship, the girls they meet may be gold diggers instead. The high likelihood of a mismatch between what a boy is looking for in a relationship and what he perceives the typical girl is looking for means that in most nascent relationships the partners' goals will appear to be different. In this situation, distrust follows directly from the assumption that the partner will try to take advantage of the relationship. Boys use that expectation to justify their own attempts to take advantage of the relationship for personal ends, material or sexual.

Having multiple models of girls and girlfriends caused trust problems in the boys' relationships, another example of the model shifting engendered by cultural heterogeneity. Even when a boy believes he has found a girl of a certain type, when other frames are also available, events or observations can trigger these alternative frames. Eduardo described how he was dating a girl he thought of as a "good girl" when he was fourteen and fifteen, but he had trouble treating her in a way that was consistent with that frame because the stunt and gold-digger possibilities were also on his mind. His inability to reconcile the relationship with these two competing frames led to the end of the relationship. He accused her of cheating on him, even though in retrospect he now says that did not make sense. Most of the girls he was around in the neighborhood were—in his view—stunts. His accusations lead to the end of their relationship, though now, over two years later, he still regrets breaking up with her, the only true good girl he has ever dated. In retrospect, Eduardo describes her as trustworthy and a good girl who would not cheat on him, but at the time, he was very confused:

> She was a home type of girl. She had a lot of friends. She had a lot of guy friends, but if she ever did hang out with one of the guy friends, I would be with her. She'd call them to hang out with us together . . .
>
> I thought she was cheating on me. She wasn't. I thought it was with someone from church. I found out she really wasn't. They proved it to me that she wasn't. After we broke up, she wanted to get back with me. I kept saying no. It wasn't going to work out. But I really wanted to say yes, but I was saying no . . . I was so upset about it. I wanted to say yes because she didn't do anything wrong. But I don't know . . . I thought she was. That's where the trust issue comes in.
>
> She ended up leaving church. But she's still the same person. She doesn't do anything wrong. She doesn't smoke. She doesn't drink. She has a job. My mother sees her. I don't know how they see each other so much. Why can't I run into her?

Another example of the role that multiple models of girls and girl-friends play in romantic relationships—the simultaneity problem—comes from Rico, age sixteen and from Franklin. Rico's girlfriend of five months did not seem to fit into any one particular model. At times, Rico saw her behavior as consistent with the good-girl frame. She told Rico that she loved him, was very cautious about sex because she did not want to get pregnant, and even got along well with Rico's mother because she was a friend of the family before they started dating. However, the girlfriend's past behavior also seemed to indicate that she had a habit of "talking to" (dating) multiple boys at the same time. When Rico heard a rumor that she was cheating on him, he remembered "what type of girl" she was, and he broke up with her, though now he is not so sure the rumor was true.

> RICO: My mom, she was really liking her. They was always together . . . 'Cause we knew her for a long time. [My mom] was asking me, why did I break up with her? She wasn't faithful. I haven't seen it, but there have been rumors . . . She broke up with her ex, that's always been the talking, and her ex go to the same school. So I was hearing that they was still mess-ing around. So I didn't like that and as soon as I heard that I thought it can't be no more . . . She still want to be my girlfriend. I always tell her, no.

INT: So how confident are you that she was actually cheating on you?
RICO: Sort of in between. 'Cause I know what type of girl she was, too. But she said she would never want to do it while she was with me.
INT: What do you mean by, what type of girl was she?
RICO: Like if she had a problem with her boyfriend while still going out with him, she'll talk to another [guy].

In contrast, the boys of Lower Mills primarily bring a single frame to potential relationships, and their expectations are that a potential partner is not going to take advantage of the relationship for her own purposes. As discussed above, the boys from Roxbury Crossing and Franklin, faced with multiple scripts and frames for relationships and girls, were pessimistic about their prospects for finding a girl whose goals and motivations for a romantic relationship matched their own and for finding a girl to have a long-term relationship with who could potentially become a wife or permanent partner. The boys of Lower Mills are much more optimistic about their chances of finding such a girl because their primary and dominant frame is that of the good girl.

These differences in expectations are reinforced by the observations that boys make of their immediate environments. The boys of Lower Mills were more likely to know people, either in their extended families or in the neighborhood, who had successful long-term relationships. Though single-parent families are common in Lower Mills, single mothers often had long-term romantic partners, or at least did not have a string of short-lived relationships. In contrast, the boys in Roxbury Crossing and Franklin frequently saw failed relationships all around them. As they attempt to understand their own interactions and relationships, an environment in which successful long-term relationships are rare reinforces alternative cultural models such as the stunt, gold digger, and shorty, providing a weighty counterpoint to conventional ideals.

Consequences of Gender Distrust for Contraceptive Use

Such a cultural environment, filled with gender distrust and expectations of relationship failure, has consequences for contraceptive use that are at times counterintuitive. To understand these dynamics, it is necessary to step back and examine the circumstances in which the boys were responsible for teenage pregnancies. These circumstances generally fall into two situations of failure to use contraceptives (or to use them effectively). In the first type, failure to use contraceptives effectively occurs very early in a romantic relationship or in a short-term, purely sexual relationship. Sometimes partners who have little sexual experience either do not use a condom or fail to use it correctly. (Condoms are the only forms of contraception being used by the boys.) This was more common among the younger boys. Other times, a lack of trust or understanding between partners, combined with strong biological urges, make negotiating effective contraception difficult in the heat of the moment. In the second type, a couple in a long-term relationship gradually becomes complacent about using condoms consistently. This was more common among the older boys, who were more likely to have longer relationships. Both can be understood as consequences of a culturally heterogeneous environment in which there is considerable gender distrust.

In the first case, in which the partners are either new to a relationship or involved in a casual or one-time sexual encounter, the existence of multiple cultural frames around romantic and sexual relationships makes it more difficult for sexual partners to negotiate effective contraceptive use, particularly for inexperienced sexual partners. When a boy and girl barely know one another, the sexual encounter itself is the stage in which the scope and nature of the relationship are worked out. Add to this situation—challenging for anyone, but particularly so for adolescents—an element of gender distrust. When one suspects one's partner of ulterior motives or intentions for the relationship that are different from one's own, contraceptive behaviors become meaningful not just for the instrumental purposes of preventing pregnancy or transmission of an STI, but also for the nature of the relationship itself. In the context of the encounter, multiple frames become salient, and boys look for indicators of the "type of girl" they are with. As Sobo (1995) finds in a study of condom use among black women in Cleveland, condom use can indicate lack of trust in the faithfulness of one's partner and is sometimes inconsistent with monogamous romance narratives.

In an environment in which gender distrust is common, not using a condom with a partner can serve as an indication of love and trust. Because of the risks involved in not using a condom, risks of both STIs and pregnancy, not using one is an indication that one trusts one's partner to be both disease-free and to be responsible and committed to the relationship should a pregnancy occur. Chris described the meaning of not using a condom as part of our conversation about STIs. He gave an example of a friend who betrayed a girl who loved him so much that she was willing to have sex with him without a condom. Chris suspects his friend gave her chlamydia and gonorrhea.

I be tellin' all these little niggas out here [in the neighborhood] and in my school, "Don't have sex with everybody, because girls be burnin'." They could be carryin' anything: gonorrhea, chlamydia. I know a girl right now in my school, she has chlamydia. And I know for a fact she had sex with my man [my friend], and my man [gave her] gonorrhea and chlamydia. And they did it raw [without a condom]. So she has it, and she don't know though. And she's talkin' to this other nigga, and I keep tellin' him like, "Yo, don't have sex."

Three weeks ago she was up here having sex with my man. When he came out of the room like, "I did it raw." I'm like, "Why would you do that? You just gave a girl a disease. You're burnin'!"

That's why we got into a fight. I was like, "You just burnt an innocent girl. Because she loves you, she had sex with you. You couldn't wait. You can get rid of chlamydia and gonorrhea." Like, all right, you got burnt. It happens sometimes to people. But you didn't get nothin' you can't get rid of. Be happy you didn't get herpes or somethin'. You've got gonorrhea, chlamydia. He went and had sex while he got it. That girl find out, her life's going to be crushed, because that was her first time ever goin' raw, because she loved him. And he was like, "I don't like the way condoms feel." She said, "All right, I love you. We can do that."

Of course, one could say that if the partners cannot negotiate the effective use of contraception, they should not have sex, but as we will see below, this is easier said than done, especially when adolescent emotions and biological urges are involved. An example of this type of pregnancy comes from Marcus, sixteen years old and a resident of Roxbury Crossing. Marcus recounts how he met a girl for a casual sexual encounter that led to a pregnancy when they had sex without a condom:

I guess she was a freak. I got a phone call from her saying that she was in the area and she wanted to hang out with me. She came through and we started messing around. She said she was allergic to latex condoms, and I knew there was condoms out there that weren't latex, but I didn't have that at the time. And I told her, "I don't have that type of condoms," she was like, "OK then . . ." She said something smart, "Well that's bad for you then." So I was like, "All right." So then I turned to watch a music video [on television], and I'm laying on the bed. She gets on me and unbuckles my pants and starts feeling around, and she takes off her clothes. So then to my mind I just lose it, and just one thing led to another.

So I ended up sleeping with her without a condom on. I didn't figure that I had got her pregnant because when I was finished I pulled out and I went to the bathroom. So I really didn't think that I had ejaculated inside of her. I was like, "Damn, I done screwed up. Now I'm kind of scared. I might get that phone call."

A few weeks passed and I got a phone call. And it was her sister on the phone. So I guess her sister pretended to be her and called me up and told me that she was pregnant. I thought, "OK. I have to accept my responsibilities now." I said, "Well, are you going to keep it?" And the sister said, "Yeah, I'm gonna keep it," pretending to be her. So I was like, "Well if you're thinking about not keeping it, me and my family will go half on an abortion." She said she didn't believe in that, so I understood that.

Marcus's account reveals a number of important details about how he is thinking about this encounter. When he describes the girl as a "freak," he is using a synonym for "stunt," a girl who likes to have sex. He views this as a casual sexual encounter rather than the beginning of a relationship, and, as will be further revealed below, one that he did not expect to repeat. Marcus also did not intend to get the girl pregnant, since he initially refused to have sex with her without a condom and tried to use the withdrawal method. He had no intention of fathering a child, as his offer to help pay for an abortion suggests, but the urges of a sixteen-year-old took over in the heat of the moment. There is also evidence of conflict in the encounter, illustrated by Marcus's initial refusal to have sex resulting in a "smart" comment. The rest of Marcus's account reveals how differently Marcus and the girl were thinking about the sexual encounter and about their relationship. A few weeks later, Marcus received another phone call:

She was like, "Well, that's kind of messed up that I had asked you to come and chill with me Wednesday now that I'm pregnant and you told me you had something else better to do." And I said, "Well, we wasn't planning on talking after this [seeing each other again] anyway were we?" She said, "No." So I said, "OK. If it doesn't involve the kid or anything, I have nothing much to say to you." She was like, "Well that's fucked up. How you gonna get me pregnant and now not be able to have a conversation with me?" I said, "Well, from the get-go, we just made that clear that we was never gonna talk to each other again after that, regardless if you was pregnant or not. So what were we gonna have to say to each other when I came down there Wednesday?" So she couldn't answer me that question.

The conversation continues, and Marcus becomes even more frustrated with what he sees as her unreasonable interpretation of their encounter. He decides to make his own understanding perfectly clear:

So I told her, "All I wanted was sex from you." And I guess that made her cry and stuff. Somewhere down the line [later in the conversation], we argue again. The cordless phone dies on me [runs out of batteries]. And I didn't have the number. We don't even have long-distance service here anyway.

I accepted my responsibility that I done made a screw up [by getting her pregnant]. But the night when she had called me up the second time, what I told her [about not planning on seeing her again after the sexual encounter], it was the truth. But I was trying so hard not to tell her. I was just going to suck it up and [provide for the baby] without having to tell her, "Well, I wasn't planning for this to happen. I wasn't planning on ever talking to you again." I guess she wasn't saying that all she wanted was to have sex. So we both really wasn't trying to tell each other how we feel, we was just gonna let this go. So really thinking about what happened after, I just really was trying not to tell her, 'cause I knew it would upset her.

Marcus originally intended for the sexual encounter to be a one-time event, with no further relationship. This is evident from his insistence that they had agreed before having sex that the encounter was not the beginning of a relationship and that they never expected to see each other again. Marcus was using the stunt frame when thinking of this girl. This does not seem to have been how the girl was thinking about him, however. She expected an ongoing sexual and romantic relationship with him, beyond just being a father to their child:

> I got this phone call that now she's around three months pregnant. She threw herself down the stairs, twice, on purpose.
>
> So I asked her, "Why did you do that?" She was like, "'Cause I didn't want to take care of the kid on my own." I said, "What did I tell you? That if it comes to anything having to do with the kid, whether it be money-wise or anything, my family and I will help you take care of that." And then she said something, and I was like, "Well then, from the get-go, we told you we would go half on the abortion. Why would you throw yourself down the stairs?" She couldn't answer me that question. So she was like, "Well, you wasn't man enough to take up your responsibilities." But I told her, "If the baby's sick, needs Pampers, needs outfit, we got that. My family and I have the money for that."
>
> So she was like still, "After you get me pregnant, you don't want to hang out with me." I was like, "I'm not gonna spend money on going to [your home], seeing a family that never met me before. And I'm supposed to sit in your house in front of your mother, your sisters and talk about a kid? And what else were we going to be able to talk about?" I was like, "That would have been a waste of my time, waste of my money."

As their conversation continued, it became even clearer to Marcus that the girl was interested in a romantic relationship, beyond their connection as parents of their child. This is not the lens through which he viewed their encounter. She viewed their sexual encounter and the resulting pregnancy as the start of that relationship, while he wanted nothing to do with her again unless it concerned the baby.

> I said, "Well, give me a topic on something we would have talked about that day." She said, "OK. I can't give you a topic, but we could have had sex that day." I said, "Well, that's not what I was looking for. I was not planning on sleeping with you a second time around. I don't know if I hurt your feelings, but I slept with you without a condom on. I'm not trying to make that same mistake again." And then she said, "Well, that's just an example." I was like, "No, that wasn't an example. That's what you wanted to do. So that's why I wasn't coming out there." And she couldn't say nothing to me after that. And so that's how I knew that she wanted, now that she thinks that I will be in a relationship with her now and that I will consider her boyfriend and girlfriend and leave everything else I was doing alone and now focus on her and that kid. And she started saying that she didn't want to have a relationship with me, but I know that's what she was pushing it towards. And she wanted to have a conversation in this and that. So thank God the phone died out again, and I haven't talked to her since.
>
> Pretty much I went out, smoked and drunk my brains out. It would be fair to say I was kind of relieved. But like I don't know. Like when they say you make a kid or something, like I was looking forward to it now. But she did whatever she did. I can't really say that I've gotta live with it for the rest of my life because I don't. She gots to live with it for the rest of her life, because she killed something that was inside of her.

In the end, Marcus felt at least a tinge of regret that the girl ended the pregnancy by throwing herself down the stairs, risking her own health and ending his chance to become a father. Yet he was still at a loss as to how these events might have been handled differently (other than not having sex without a condom), given the confusion and disagreement that surrounded their initial encounter and later interactions. Marcus's brush with teen fatherhood reveals how gender distrust and multiple relationship frames play out in boys' romantic relationships. Misunderstandings about the nature of a relationship, propelled by multiple relationship frames and fueled by gender distrust and biological urges, can lead to poor decision making regarding sex and contraception.

Teenage pregnancy also occurs in a second type of relationship context, one in which trust has been achieved within a long-term relationship. In this scenario, a couple who have been dating for a longer period of time, at least six months to a year, become complacent about effectively or consistently using contraception. For an adolescent boy in Franklin or Roxbury Crossing, a long-term relationship with a good girl featuring emotional intimacy and trust stands out in a world also populated by stunts and gold diggers. Compared to both his initial expectations for a relationship and the failed relationships he sees around him, a seemingly successful relationship looks very strong to a boy from Franklin or Roxbury Crossing. A couple in their late teens with this sort of relationship sees themselves as a partnership and as ready to become parents. This is another example of the importance of negative role models for calibrating expectations, discussed in chapter 2.

A long-term relationship also results in trust regarding STIs. After a period of time of sexual activity in which neither partner shows signs of an STI, the impetus to use condoms fades. Daniel, seventeen and from Roxbury Crossing, explains: "If you having sex for a long time, you staying with the same girl for like more than a year, you all are gonna be like, "Oh, let's not use condoms 'cause we know we both don't have nothing." And you both had that same mindset at the time."

An example of complacency about contraception in a long-term relationship comes from David, seventeen and a resident of Franklin. He and his girlfriend of eighteen months have gradually become complacent about using condoms when they have sex, using them when they have them, but relying on withdrawal when they do not have a condom on hand. At the beginning of their relationship, they always used condoms, but this changed over time. David believes he and his girlfriend are now prepared to be parents together because of the strength of their relationship. According to David, his girlfriend thinks about these issues in the same way. To understand David's perspective on contraception within the context of this relationship, we need to understand his past experiences and his larger perspectives with regard to girls and girlfriends.

Though David feels very confident with his current relationship, he is very distrustful of girls in general. He worries about some of the same things that the other boys described above, including girls tricking a boy into getting them pregnant.

DAVID: I have heard chicks talk. "Want to have a baby just like my friend." They will pop a condom while you ain't paying attention. I tell all my friends I would be careful about playing around with these chicks. If they want a kid, they find a way to get the kid.

INT: How often do you think something like that happens where it is the girl who wants to have the baby and she tricks the guy into having a baby?

DAVID: I think like 75 percent happens.

INT: Seventy-five percent of the time a young woman has a baby, she is doing something like that, is that what you are saying?

DAVID: Yeah . . . I heard [from] one of my friends a chick was so in love with him that the dude would be the one that she wanted to have a baby with, and she trapped him by saying she was pregnant [already] . . . And some chicks lie and some chicks tell the truth . . . I need evidence. I need to see papers.

David also worries about girls who are gold diggers, just after a man's money, or girls who will cheat on him. He worries about becoming infected with an STI. Before he began dating his current girlfriend exclusively, he would have himself and his partners tested for STIs regularly.

DAVID: We try to play it safe. Every time I sleep with somebody, I make an appointment to go to the clinic. I heard there is other ways people catch this stuff.

INT: So how many times have you been to the clinic?

DAVID: When I first dated my girl, I went to the clinic like three times a month while I was sleeping with her. I need a check up. She ain't giving me nothing. She got checked up. She is clean. I am clean. That is why sometimes I am not concerned we are not using a condom. Sometimes, I will.

It is in this context that David understands his contraceptive use with his long-term girlfriend. He and his girlfriend are in love and have established a long-term relationship that David believes is strong. One piece of evidence for him is that she has never given him an STI. He believes they could handle having a child together.

INT: So sometimes you guys didn't use a condom. Were you worried she might get pregnant?

DAVID: I was pulling out. I use [a condom] when we have it. I am older now. If I have a kid, I will just have a kid . . . Like once a week we might not use a condom but the rest of the week, we have a condom. If you don't have a condom, you have to go get one or I just pull out. If you are already in the mood.

INT: So you are not worried the pulling out is not really safe?

DAVID: No. If she get pregnant at seventeen, turn eighteen in a couple more months. I will just take care of my kid. It will be a shock to [my mother] but it won't matter . . . It would be okay. If it happened, it would be okay.

INT: And your girlfriend thinks the same way about it?

DAVID: She is like, if it happens, she will be okay . . . I love her. She loves me. If anything happens, I have the kid with her, and I won't have a second thought.

INT: But if it was someone like a girl you were just seeing for just a couple of months?

DAVID: No, it won't be okay because it would be too fast. I don't really get to know her because people change through the years. You need to know a person. If I go out with somebody that I want to be their friend first. I be their friend for like a good while.

INT: Why are you doing things differently with this girl?

DAVID: Because we feel deeply so I won't be wearing [condoms] like that no more. I will wear them but not like I used to when I first started meeting her. We love each other. So we don't really care. Well, I care if she get pregnant. Just like, if it happens, it happens . . .

INT: How have you guys been able to stay together for so long?

DAVID: We just trust each other. We argue a lot. We just trust each other and just try to make it work. Don't be all getting upset over corny stuff.

INT: What is an example of something where somebody else might have gotten upset about it but you guys were able to handle it?

DAVID: Like she get mad when I go to talk to another girl but then somebody will go tell her about it. I am like, "It is just my friend." She just be looking and then later on in the day she just upset. I am, "What are you upset for?" I was like, "You don't trust me?" I always say, "You don't trust me." She says, "I trust you."[7]

David's rather thin conception of what makes for a strong romantic relationship is an example of dilution. Multiple frames regarding relationships dilute his model of a long-term relationship, affecting how he thinks about contraception in the context of a relationship. David's perspectives on contraception can be compared to those of Coleman, also age seventeen and attending a Boston public high school. Coleman lives in Lower Mills with his grandmother because he does not get along well with his mother. He has been dating his girlfriend for about nine months, and he is very serious about their relationship. He described their plans together for the future and thinks they might someday get married. Like David and his girlfriend, Coleman and his girlfriend both want to go to college, though Coleman wants to serve in the military first. Similar to David, Coleman described how much he and his girlfriend trust one another.

INT: How long do you think this relationship will keep going on?

COLEMAN: I hope for a long time, 'cause she's not that type of person just to be like, "Oh well, I'm gonna cheat on you." Just say I would believe her more than others 'cause she's not that type of person. Girls can play that game, but she wouldn't show me her entire family and then expect to cheat on me.

INT: And what do you think she wants to do in the future? Like what kind of life?

COLEMAN: She told me all this. She wants to go to Georgia and go to college down there. Then she wants me to get out of the service after that and then go directly down there with her. She thinks I'm gonna stay in one spot. But I'm telling her like, I'm able to be down there and then go ship out. But she just pretty much wants like a condo to live in. She doesn't want to rent anywhere 'cause she doesn't feel like that's something that you own.

Yet Coleman and his girlfriend are far more careful than David and his girlfriend about contraception. He described how they use two forms of contraception. She takes birth control pills, and they also use condoms. For Coleman, the strength of his relationship with his girlfriend is not so out of the ordinary. While he is certainly aware that boyfriends and girlfriends cheat on one another, he is far less suspicious than David. He does not talk about girls who might give him an STI or are after his money or are going to trick him into getting them pregnant.

INT: What do you think girls are looking for when they are looking for a boyfriend?

COLEMAN: Not all of them want relationships, 'cause they're not able to handle them. Some of them just want fun and games. But in my opinion there are some out there that actually do want relationships and are ready for them. But it just takes a lot to get that out of them. Because like you could probably give and give and give all you want, but you might not give what they want. Now I'm not talking about material things, obviously.

INT: So do you think girls care about things like looks or money or personality?

COLEMAN: Oh, there are a lot of those, but there are a few that, "Whatever. If he gives me something, he gives me something." There's some out there that are very generous. If you give them something, they're shocked.

INT: And how many girls your age do you think would be faithful to their boyfriends?

COLEMAN: I don't know. These days with the cheating thing coming up and the player thing all around. It's not all that trustful these days. But if you feel like you're able to trust the person, then trust it.

INT: What do you mean by "the cheating thing that's coming up"?

COLEMAN: Like you see on TV, you see some of them are cheating. It's become more popular than it ever was before.

Coleman thinks that a major barrier to relationships involves some girls who are not serious about real romance, but he is much more optimistic than David about the prospects for true love. When it comes to cheating, Coleman refers to what he sees on television, not to the people he interacts with on a daily basis. The strength of his own relationship does not seem so unusual, and his contraceptive behavior is different as a result.

Heterogeneity of Fatherhood Frames

Duante, a seventeen-year-old from Roxbury Crossing, articulates a strong fatherhood frame:

> Can you step up to the challenge? It takes a real man to be a father early. Really, people see a young father, they'll ask, is he ready for this responsibility? Is he going to be able to step up to the challenge, and do what's best for his kid? . . . It's gonna be hard. And if you work under pressure, then you got it . . .
>
> You can talk negative about a young father, but you can't really know the real stuff until how he steps up to the challenge of having a child at a young age. You gotta judge by what he does then.

As Tamarr explained in chapter 5, having a child at a young age can cut short one's education and prove harmful to the baby, who will be raised by a father who is immature and inexperienced. This conventional or mainstream early-fatherhood frame can be contrasted with another, equally strong frame that views fatherhood as a form of status, though one that is highly contingent. This is the frame that Duante articulates above. Here fatherhood is a pathway to adulthood and the respect that comes with it. When a man has responsibilities—and fulfills them—he gains status in the eyes of others in the community. He has "stepped up" and met the challenges that he faces, even if those challenges are of his own making.

The dual nature of these frames regarding early fatherhood is succinctly summarized by Denzel, a fifteen-year-old resident of Franklin.

INT: How do you think young men who are teenagers who are fathers are treated in the community?

DENZEL: They're looked on in a negative way because they have a child at such a young age, but if they're taking care of their responsibilities, taking care of their kids, still finishing school, that's great. That's more respect to them.

According to this second frame, fatherhood involves an element of redemption, an opportunity to turn one's life around. Becoming a father means responsibilities, as a father must take into account not just his own well-being but that of his child. Fatherhood is a motivation to leave the streets behind and perhaps one of the only accepted reasons for spending less time with one's peer group on the street. It also means motivation to get a job or finish school. Fatherhood provides an opportunity to change, and the young man who makes that change is accorded a great deal of respect because it is the rare man who succeeds in doing so. Tyree, seventeen and from Roxbury Crossing, explained how he thinks becoming a father would change his life.

INT: How would you feel if you found out you were going to be a father? Say six months from now or something?

TYREE: I'm not saying I'd be looking forward to having a kid, but I would be happy because I'd be bringing a new life into this world. There's just something about having a kid; it's different. It makes you feel like a better person. You feel more responsible and there's more kids you have to take care of and there's no more running the streets and being wild because you got a kid now. So, I would say it's a good feeling.

INT: How do you think it would change your life?

TYREE: It wouldn't make me no different. Only thing, it would slow me down because I would have to take care of my responsibility. I can't hang out late. I would have to get a job and stay on my job. I would probably work two jobs if I had to.

INT: Do you think it would affect your plans in terms of your music [career] or going to barber school or anything like that?

TYREE: It would motivate me more to make a good living to take care of my family. I would want to go to school and get my trade as a barber so I could get a job and make good money so I could take care of them. I wouldn't be like, "Oh, I can't go to barber school now because I have a kid." That's what people use as an excuse so they don't have to do nothing.

Tyree struggled in his early teen years as he got involved in drug dealing and dropped out of school. But he is now in a relatively good position, at least compared to many of his peers in his Roxbury Crossing neighbor-hood. He spends his time at a program that is preparing him to take the GED exam and working on his music, and he recently started a job at a local fast-food restaurant. He plans to attend barber school once he earns his GED. Because early fatherhood carries multiple potential meanings in Franklin and Roxbury Crossing, it is easy to switch between a frame that views early fatherhood as negative to one, like the one Tyree articulates, that puts a more positive spin on it. Such frame switching is an example of model shifting and is made possible by heterogeneity of fatherhood frames.

In Lower Mills, by contrast, the conventional view that early fatherhood is a mistake and a hindrance is dominant and pervasive. Timothy, age fourteen, is clear on that point.

> INT: How are young men who are fathers viewed by this community?
> TIMOTHY: Irresponsible basically, no matter what.
> INT: How about by people your own age?
> TIMOTHY: Screwed. It's just like, "What are they gonna do?" Nowhere to go.
> INT: How would you feel if you found out you were going to be a father?
> TIMOTHY: I wouldn't be like, "Oh yeah! A kid!" All my plans in the future just been rearranged. It's still possible for them to happen, it's just gonna be twenty times more difficult.

In Lower Mills, this uniformly negative view of early fatherhood is not limited to younger teens. Jason, age eighteen, was equally insistent that having a child at this time in his life would create nothing but problems. Indeed, unlike Tyree, he could barely imagine what he would do if he became a father.

> INT: What are your plans in terms of having a family of your own in the future?
> JASON: Till I can actually afford to have all that, I don't plan on having any of that. Everybody wants it, but if you can't support it, no point in doing it. If I wanted to I couldn't support myself, so I can't support one other person.
> INT: So you're thinking about far in the future for that.
> JASON: As far in the future as possible [laughter]. You never know what happens really, but not any time soon, hopefully.
> INT: So what do you think it would be like to be a father?
> JASON: Weird. I just can't picture it right now. I can't picture anything what happens. I have a kid, like oh no . . .

INT: What about your friends, what would they say?

JASON: I'd probably get clowned. Some of my friends like [think] having babies [is] like having a disease, like you're stuck with it for life like an STD or something.

Conventional or traditional models of the family, with both parents and their children living together in the context of a marriage, abound in all three neighborhoods. The father is the main provider for the family, though the mother likely works as well. Dad is not just the provider, however. He is also heavily involved in the lives of his children.

Shaquille, eighteen and from Franklin, became a father to a baby girl several months before our interviews. Shaquille's "baby mother" was his girlfriend for three and a half years, and like David and his girlfriend, they became complacent about contraception after they had been together for three years. Shaquille and his "baby mother" broke up four months after she became pregnant when she suspected Shaquille of cheating on her. Shaquille currently lives with his own mother and sees his daughter almost every day, but he has a much different model in mind for what he would ideally like to do to be the best father he can.

SHAQUILLE: I want to be with my baby's mother and to be married and to have a house, but I really don't see myself there because we argue so much. But I can see myself getting there because we could take it one day at a time and not argue, and just have progress. Right now, I stay away from my baby's mother. If anything, when I call, I talk to her only about my daughter—if my daughter needs anything or just to bring my daughter by to come stay with me. I want to be able to have the little "happily ever after" family, but I don't know. Five years from now—it might be like that. It might be like that if I just take it one day at a time . . . I want to make sure my daughter gets the right education and everything. I wouldn't want to entrust anyone else. I would want to make sure myself that my daughter is doing everything she's suppose to do in her life . . .

INT: What do you think the chances are of you getting back together with your baby's mother?

SHAQUILLE: There's a good chance. I'm not patient enough for saying things. My thinking is it's either now or never. If it can't happen now, then why is it going to happen later on? . . . That could definitely happen 'cause we'll be older and more mature. Once you get older, and when money's involved and everything and everyone's financially stable, and they have a house—people look at situations differently. "I could live with him now instead of just being around him," or "he's able to take care of us, and just not take care of her [the baby]." So, it should be different.

Shaquille is struggling to keep this model of responsible fatherhood in sight, but it is slipping away from him. The life he pictured for himself, his girlfriend, and their daughter when he first found out that she was pregnant seems further from his reach. A high school graduate, Shaquille is currently unemployed, but expects to be rehired to his low-wage job in the cafeteria at a university when the fall semester comes around. Nevertheless, without a better job that provides "financial stability," he will not be able to create the model family he has in mind.

However, alternative models of responsible fatherhood are also available in his low-income neighborhood, and Shaquille may have to settle for one of these. Boys observe their relationships with their own fathers and draw conclusions. The lives of their friends, family members, and neighbors are themselves adaptations to less than ideal circumstances. One such alternative model emphasizes "being there" for one's child. Emotional involvement and spending time with one's child are paramount, while providing material resources is deemphasized.[8] Even if money is tight, one can be a good father by being involved in the child's life and by setting a good example. The best way to do this is to live with your child and the mother, even if marriage is not an option, as Duante explains.

> INT: So what do you think it takes to be a good father?
> DUANTE: Being there for your kid when he needs you. Set a positive example. If you split with your baby's mother, and [your son's] with you, make sure he sees you doing good, doing positive things, nothing negative 'cause that reflects back on him. It makes him like, "Okay, cool, I want to get a job, like get dressed up to go to interviews."
> INT: So what kinds of things is it important for a father to do?
> DUANTE: Have a job for one. I mean make sure your child sees that okay, working is a good thing. You need to work in order to get money. Have respect, home training, the whole nine . . . It's important to spend time with your kid and everything 'cause, if some kids think, "Okay, my pop don't want to spend no time, maybe he doesn't love me" . . . It's good to live with your child, so he can see you on a daily basis. You're having fun chillin' with dad. If you're not, then that's when all the questions is asked. Where's daddy, how come he doesn't stay here? How come you're not married? It's gonna keep coming up again, again again over the years, over the years.

When it is not possible to live with the child because the father and mother are no longer in a romantic relationship, the "being there" script stretches to focus on emotional involvement and time spent, rather than living with the child.[9] "It's hard to be a father," Tyree notes:

You can be a dad, but it takes a real man to be a father. A father is somebody who teaches their kid how to play basketball. Be there when they
need you to be at certain events. I asked my father plenty of times, "Oh,
I'm having a birthday party. I would like for you to come." He never show
up. Couple of weeks later, bring a present, and he think it's gonna be okay
because he brought something with him. It doesn't work like that. So, be
there and make sure your kid is happy because my father wasn't there for
me . . . I'm not saying you have to live with your baby's mother and your
child to make your child happy, but as long as you know you can come
and visit and be there, that's the important thing . . .

A father is not a person that spends a whole bunch of money on a kid.
A father is a person that's there in your life, and your kid knows you as
their father and not just as a person that comes 'cause he got money, and
who hasn't been here in three years but "I just came upon $30,000. I'm
gonna buy you the biggest and baddest bike there is." I might get him
a nice bike, but I'm not gonna try to win his or her love with money. I
would just say you can be a father without none of that stuff.

Implicit in Duante's statement and explicit in Tyree's is an experience
of noninvolvement with their own fathers when they were growing up.
Duante's father has been incarcerated for over a decade, and Duante has
never visited him in prison. Tyree's father is a drug addict who is constantly
in and out of jail. Though lack of father involvement is not universal, their
relationships—or lack thereof—with their fathers are typical of the boys
from Franklin and Roxbury Crossing. And it is a source of great emotional
pain. The loss of their fathers was experienced as outright rejection, even
when circumstances presumably outside the father's control, such as incarceration, were the cause. A father who really loved his children would
not put himself in a position to be removed from their lives. Even worse
was the father who had children by multiple women and focused on his
current family, ignoring his older children.

Few boys from Franklin and Roxbury Crossing knew men they would
consider to be good fathers, though they had plenty of *negative role models,*
those whose behavior was a model of how *not* to be a good father. In their
failures, these negative role models—their own fathers and the fathers
of their friends, neighbors, siblings, and cousins—informed their ideas
about what it takes to be a good father. If poor neighborhoods in areas
like Roxbury Crossing and Franklin had distinct subcultures, we might
expect that boys surrounded by failing fathers would reject fatherhood
as a valued role or minimize the importance of fathering for children's
well-being. Instead, their conceptions of fatherhood are also informed by

the importance attached to fatherhood in the larger culture and by their own experiences as the sons of "failed" fathers. Recall Tyree's focus on a father attending his son's birthday party as he recounted how his own father missed his parties. David, who above explained his complacency about contraceptive use, got a previous girlfriend pregnant when he was fourteen and a condom broke. She had an abortion, but he described how he reacted when he heard she was pregnant, comparing his plans for fatherhood with the behavior of his own father.

> DAVID: I was just like, it is going to be a little tougher than it already is. I have to deal with a kid for eighteen years. Then I was just a little bit happy because my father wasn't there—he was a backslider. So I was like, I can be different and show my father that I can take care of my kid, be there for my kid.
>
> INT: Why was it important to you to show your father?
>
> DAVID: Kids need a role model. Like [the father's] made a mistake. [The fathers] go live a different life. And when they get the money, they want to have kids. Some people try to step back into life and run the show. "I pay child support. That is taking care of them." But you don't see your kid. Everybody used to talk about their father. "Where is my father? Is he dead?" My father lives back and forth from New York and Jamaica. I just wish he was dead so I collect something. I just told them my father is dead. He's not alive in my life. He don't come to Boston. He work in the penitentiary out there in New York. I have seen him twice in my life. So I was like if he got all that money to buy a house, buy new cars for his wife and his [other] kids, he can't shoot down to Boston? It is a four-hour drive. That ain't no father.

Information about how not to be a father is as common, or more so, than instructions on how to be a good one. When the most important thing preventing one's own father from being a good example was that he simply was not there, then "being there" seems like the main requirement for the better version. Further complexities, such as competing obligations at work and at home, balancing firm discipline with emotional closeness, or teaching children moral values, are not evident to these boys. This is an example of dilution, when the presence of multiple cultural models dilutes the available information about any one model. The result is a set of rather "thin" models of fatherhood that underestimate the difficulties of parenthood. As Denzel put it when asked whether a teenage boy who was a father would have to drop out of high school, "No. He has to learn how to juggle things."

Lower Mills boys expressed more complicated views of what it meant to be a good father. Jason, age eighteen, talked not only about being there and providing materially, but also about the long-term and emotional responsibilities of being a parent.

INT: What do you think it takes to be a good father?

JASON: You have to have an idea where you want to go in life. If you have a set goal, you can kind of include everybody else in that goal too, trying to fit everything around each other so that way you're not going to clash . . . The father's the one that put the food on the table for the most part. That's supposed to be the person that holds the home together . . . You don't want a bunch of kids in life that just grow up and hate their father to death, they didn't feel like their father cared.

INT: So what kind of things shows that a father cares?

JASON: You have to say it every once in a while and let it roll with it. Some guys have too much pride to do that.

INT: And what sort of sacrifices are involved with being a father?

JASON: There's a lot of sacrifices when you're doing stuff that you can't do anymore. Sometimes you might not be able to hang out with your boys anymore or you can't go to the gym, or you saving up your money to go buy this new truck that came out with something, and now you can't do it.

Experiences outside the neighborhood, more common among Lower Mills boys, can also crystallize the consequences and responsibilities of fatherhood. Recall from chapter 4 that Esteban, seventeen and from Lower Mills, is particularly active in his church and his religious high school, and he plans to go to seminary and become a pastor. His church experiences in particular present a narrow but detailed model of fatherhood and marriage and when these should occur, a model that he does not see himself being able to fulfill in the near future. This model involves career, marriage, and the formation of a solid partnership with one's spouse before parenthood. This model was reinforced by his observations of a fellow church member who violated it:

[Early fatherhood] changes the course of your future. I'm not ready to be a father mentally, financially, in any way. The consequence would be that kid, he'd have a sucky father—a seventeen-year-old father. I can't make the decisions. Like I'd be the best father I could be, but it wouldn't be like the same as if I was twenty-seven. I don't know if I'd have to drop out. I might have to get a job to support this kid. It would not be a good circumstance in any way, shape, or form. And then ministry—what church wants a pastor that had a kid at eighteen, and who now doesn't really even have a degree?

People at church know that I want to go to seminary. They know that I want to be a pastor. And for me to have a kid at eighteen would be very embarrassing. Like the guy who was the leader over the junior high ministry, and he was the leader over the step team. He had to tell all the junior high parents what happened. He had to tell the bishop of our church what happened . . . Not just embarrassing, but shameful.

He doesn't do anything. He doesn't serve the ministry at our church anymore. At our church, once you get married, you take a year sabbatical, to spend the first year focused with your wife. So they married him so that they could say that the first year was spent with his wife, since that's what happens with everyone else.

Esteban's single, clearly defined model of fatherhood leaves little room for creative interpretation or modification and illuminates the consequences of failing to adhere to it.

The result of these more complete models of the good father is that fatherhood seems a much more daunting role for Lower Mills boys than for their counterparts in Roxbury Crossing and Franklin. Recall how David from Franklin felt "a little bit happy" when at fourteen his girlfriend became pregnant. Contrast this reaction with that of Marshall, now seventeen, who described how he felt at age fifteen when his girlfriend told him that she might be pregnant. Rather than happy, Marshall was panicked.

MARSHALL: At that point, I was just scared. I didn't really know what to think. I had trouble sleeping. It was on my mind just 24/7. Whatever I'll be doing, I'll still be thinking about that. I like to just be happy, but if there's something that's bothering me, that's on my mind, then I won't be at ease. And that's usually something I can control. Like if I have homework or something, I'll be like, okay, I'll get that done later or whatever, and that won't be on my mind anymore. But if it's something *that* serious, it's just constantly going to be on my mind.

INT: Would you feel that same way today if the same thing happened again, now that you're a couple years older?

MARSHALL: Yeah.

In comparison to the multiple models of a good father in Roxbury Crossing and Franklin, in all three neighborhoods there was only a single model of the good husband. The good husband must not only support his children but also his wife. He must provide for his family's basic needs, such as an apartment, food, and clothing, but a good husband also must provide a house in a good neighborhood, a car, and a wedding. The good husband comes home every day after work, rarely hangs out with his friends, and takes his family on vacation. While the boys in Roxbury Crossing and Franklin know many fathers, good and bad, they know few, if any husbands (good or bad). Their only model of the good husband is the conventional or traditional one. Media and other institutions such as religion, not interactions and direct observations, provide models of being a good husband. Boys are much more cautious about the idea of marriage, lest an expensive and messy divorce result. Better to forgo or postpone marriage than rush in and divorce, an all too common failure. This finding is consistent with those of Edin and Kefalas (2005), who find that poor women in Philadelphia and Camden value marriage so highly that they create very high standards for the type of relationship and type of man that are worthy of marriage and believe that financial security is a prerequisite for marriage, even though it is almost impossible to achieve.[10]

Problems of model shifting occur when a boy has multiple fatherhood frames. When faced with a situation in which being a good father as defined by one frame is difficult if not impossible, another model that is more conducive to one's situation is available. The requirements of fatherhood are easily redefined. We need only examine Marcus's situation to see how this can happen. Recall from above that Marcus got a girl pregnant when he had sex with her without a condom during a casual encounter. In another interview on a different day, Marcus described a second model of a good father, the model described above that defines a good father as a man who is involved in his son's life.

INT: What do you think it takes for someone to be a good father?
MARCUS: I mean, just spend time with your kid. I see a father as being responsible, just being there. That's about it.
INT: A lot of people say the main responsibility of a father is providing, but you wouldn't say that?
MARCUS: I wouldn't say that because, like with me, I could have cared less if my father brought me sneakers or a jersey, or gave me some money; like, all I really want from my parents is just love because, like love don't cost nothing, like all that trying to bribe me, that just don't cut it. All I want you to do is be there. Come to a couple of my basketball games, sit down and watch TV with me . . . Of course, you have to buy your kids Pampers and food for them . . . The basics. All that other stuff, if that kid wants it, he should go out and work and get it.

Marcus puts little emphasis on providing materially for a child when discussing fatherhood. Yet when he was actually about to become a father and the mother was someone he did not really want to see again, another definition of the good father was available. He offered to provide materially for the child, for example by buying Pampers, baby food, and baby clothes and helping the mother to pay her rent. He insisted that he was prepared to fulfill his responsibilities as the father of her child. When the girl accused Marcus of shirking his responsibilities by not wanting to see her when she was pregnant, he employs a bifurcated model: financial commitment to the child and emotional detachment from the mother:

> And she still was going on that I wasn't accepting my responsibilities and she wasn't getting it through her head. Maybe she didn't want to hear the truth. But I told her, "If the baby's sick, needs Pampers, needs outfit, we got that. My family and I have the money for that."

Marcus was prepared to defend himself to his child should the mother cut off all communication with him because he refused a relationship with her. Marcus does not know where the mother lives, does not know her last name, and does not have her phone number:

> She told me that if she did have the child she wouldn't have called me, if she was still gonna have the kid. So I told her, I said, "If you were gonna have that kid and not call me, that's your problem now." I said, "That's a problem that you and that child is gonna have to deal with on why I'm not there. Somewhere down the line you're gonna have to tell him that you never called me to let me know." And I said, "Eventually that kid is gonna want to know who his or her father is." I'd explain to that kid that "your father is not the type just to leave a kid somewhere. I was gonna take care of you. She just did not call me to let me know that you was born and she obviously took off, and you had your life and she never called me once to involve me in it 'cause I didn't have the number to that house."

Marcus simultaneously juggles multiple models of what a good father does. In one, the good father is "there" for his child: teaching him or her to play ball, and more generally spending time together. When the circumstances of the birth threaten to make that model difficult to implement because of conflict with the mother, another model is available, providing financially.

In contrast, Lower Mills boys described the father role as "the full package," as seventeen-year-old Nathan put it. Though Nathan himself grew up without a father, he sees little room for selecting some aspects of fatherhood and not others based on what is feasible. For him, the emotional and financial aspects of fatherhood are linked, and responsible fatherhood requires the father to live with his child.

NATHAN: The child needs to have their father there all the time, whenever he needs him. He needs to be attentive. If he's attached, he needs to attach himself to the situation.

INT: Do you think the father can be a good father if he does all the emotional and caretaking responsibilities but isn't good at doing the material providing?

NATHAN: No, because the child's still alive, he needs that from someone.

INT: What if the mother is able to that?

NATHAN: The father cares for someone on that level too. He needs to provide on all levels.

This richer, more detailed model of fatherhood was surprisingly common among Lower Mills boys. Even those who did not live with their own biological father saw neighbors and friend's fathers exemplifying these behaviors.

Boys and Teen Pregnancy in Poor Neighborhoods

How does the account of boys and teenage pregnancy in poor neighborhoods presented in this chapter compare with other sociological accounts? The most widely cited analysis of the role of boys in teenage pregnancy in poor neighborhoods is Elijah Anderson's ethnographic study of life in inner-city Philadelphia (presented in Anderson 1990, 1991, 1999, among other writings). Anderson divides youth into those from "decent" families, those who control and protect their children from neighborhood influences, and those enmeshed in "street" culture. For all young people in inner-city Philadelphia, prospects for employment that can sustain a middle-class or working-class lifestyle are slim, leading to an environment in which youth have less to lose. Among the boys embedded in the street culture, "the peer group places a high value on sex, especially what middle-class people called casual sex" (Anderson 1999, 150). Given that traditional pathways to masculinity such as employment are blocked, the peer group "emphasizes sexual prowess as proof of manhood, with babies as evidence" (147). Relations with females are viewed as a game—what Anderson calls "the Mating Game"—in which boys try to win control over the girl's body using their wit and promises of love, marriage, and family, and girls try to ensnare a man into a permanent relationship using sex and pregnancy. Among the boys, being caught in such a trap is looked down upon, and "long-term ties to a woman and children" are "a burden," given their poor economic prospects (156). Young people know little about contraception, so the result is often teenage pregnancy. In the context of persistent poverty, both males and females use sexual relationships to "extract maximum personal benefit" (176). "The basic factors at work here are youth, ignorance, the culture's receptiveness to babies, and the young man's attempt to prove his manhood through sexual conquests that often result in pregnancy. These factors are exacerbated by persistent urban poverty" (175–76).

There are some similarities between my account of Franklin and Roxbury Crossing and Anderson's account of a Philadelphia neighborhood. Both emphasize the role of concentrated poverty, not just the poverty of a boy's family, but the consequences of being surrounded by others who are also poor. Men and women turn to romantic and sexual relationships as a way to secure material resources and social status, and the absence of economic prospects makes risky behavior more appealing. Correspondingly, both accounts also include a strong element of gender distrust in which there is an expectation that members of the opposite sex will take advantage of a relationship for their own benefit. However, there are also important differences between the two accounts when it comes to how boys think about relationships and sex. I have emphasized the importance of mainstream or conventional cultural models regarding relationships and fatherhood as well as a competing set of local, alternative models, while Anderson's theory emphasizes a deviant subculture in which boys value casual sex exclusively and try to avoid the responsibilities of fatherhood. Those ideas are present in my data, and there are certainly some boys who behave in ways consistent with the subculture that Anderson describes. But these ideas are not dominant to the exclusion of the conventional model.

This is an important theoretical distinction, one between a culturally heterogeneous environment and a cohesive and bounded subculture within which behavior typically regarded as deviant by middle-class Americans is normative. The boys growing up in Boston's poor neighborhoods must sort out and juggle multiple competing and conflicting cultural models, while Anderson's account describes a coherent subculture that orients boys toward sexual conquest. While the boys in my study are certainly interested in casual sex without commitment and may use trickery to get it, they are also interested in long-term, emotionally intimate romantic relationships. In addition, they take the responsibilities of fatherhood seriously, even if they are not prepared to meet them. These differences have implications for understanding teenage pregnancy and the role of boys in such pregnancies. Teenage pregnancies occur not just as a result of casual sex but in long-term, committed relationships. Such pregnancies are not just the result of a girl trying to trap a man (though that is something that boys are wary of in casual encounters), but rather an assessment that the couple is ready to have a child together because the relationship is strong, at least in comparison to others in the local context.

How might we understand these different perspectives? There are several possibilities. First, this study was designed to include a diverse group of boys in each of three different neighborhoods, which may have resulted in a broader range of experiences and cultural models. Second, I gathered data in private interviews where adolescents are not performing for their peers or neighbors, perhaps allowing them to present themselves in ways that might not always be consistent with the public persona they display on the street. Third, I compare boys in poor neighborhoods to those in a working-class section of Boston, allowing me to more precisely define what is unique about high-poverty neighborhoods and what they share with working-class neighborhoods. More importantly, however, much time has passed and much has changed between the 1980s when Anderson began his Philadelphia fieldwork (his accounts of the Mating Game appear in his 1990 book *Streetwise*) and 2003–4 Boston when the fieldwork for this study was conducted. The boys who are the subjects of this study are the next generation of young people growing up in high-poverty inner-city neighborhoods. Public health and sex education messages regarding HIV/ AIDS and other sexually transmitted infections have increased the availability of information. The boys in this study seem to have much greater knowledge of contraception and STIs and are much more motivated to use condoms. The changes in gender roles that Anderson identified have continued, with girls even more likely to initiate relationships. Welfare reform, now fully implemented, has reduced alternative sources of support for single women with children that were more available in the 1980s. And finally, the boys I got to know in Boston are the sons of the contemporaries of Anderson's subjects, so they have felt the fallout from the behaviors that Anderson describes. The Boston boys' own experiences with father abandonment have influenced their views regarding the importance of responsible fatherhood. It is not possible to say from my data whether research design or the historical context or the geographic context accounts for these differences in findings, but given these important differences in historical context, I suspect that is the main source of the differences.

Conclusion

Cultural heterogeneity does not explain all aspects of boys' sexual and romantic behavior, but it does contribute to our understanding of neigh-

borhood differences. Among boys in poor neighborhoods, multiple conflicting cultural models are employed to understand their behavior and
that of others. Lower Mills boys are surrounded by a far more coherent
and homogeneous cultural environment. In Franklin and Roxbury Crossing, multiple frames capture boys' expectations about girls, romantic and
sexual relationships, the consequences of teenage fatherhood, and what it
takes to be a good father. Some of these frames and scripts can be found
in "mainstream" or middle-class culture, but alternative models that are
adaptations to the circumstances of poverty abound. The difference between these neighborhoods and Lower Mills is one of degree. While Lower
Mills youth are aware of the various cultural models with which their
counterparts in Franklin and Roxbury Crossing must contend, their expectations for their own behavior and that of others, including romantic
partners, are much more narrowly circumscribed and heavily weighted
toward conventional models. For sure, multiple models are everywhere,
as even middle-class adolescents are aware of the idea that there are "good
girls" and "loose women" as well as the idea that there are boys who are
looking for sexual conquest and boys who are interested in emotionally
involved relationships. Yet the mere knowledge of these models does not
in itself create problems. Cultural heterogeneity occurs only when there
is social support for both mainstream and alternative models and when
multiple models are taken seriously enough to influence expectations
and interpretations. This chapter shows that the poor neighborhoods in
Franklin and Roxbury Crossing do not contain a cohesive sexual subculture bounded by homogeneous social networks or peer groups. Rather,
they present adolescent boys with a heterogeneous cultural context when
it comes to romantic relationships and sexual behavior.

This chapter also argues that this cultural heterogeneity is not benign.
It has corrosive consequences, as the boys of Roxbury Crossing and Franklin juggle multiple competing and conflicting frames and scripts in their
efforts to understand and navigate sexual and romantic relationships.
Simultaneity—multiple frames for girls and for romantic relationships—
contributes to gender distrust among the boys in these neighborhoods.
Boys are wary of girls who might bring different expectations and different models of relationships to the interaction. From his perspective, the
boy who is looking for a good girl may actually be talking to a stunt, or
the boy who is looking for a stunt may actually be dating a gold digger.
This gender distrust, which happens on both sides, plays a role in teenage pregnancy by influencing the use of contraception. In casual sexual
encounters and in the beginnings of more serious relationships, gender

distrust makes negotiating contraceptive use more difficult, as condom use, for example, can carry messages of love and trust or of manipulation. In long-term relationships, the presence of multiple girlfriend frames dilutes the standard for a strong relationship, influencing how adolescents gauge their relationships. Relationships they see as particularly strong—strong enough to be worthy of being a parent and to be complacent about contraception—may be much weaker in the eyes of an outsider.

Boys' willingness to take these sorts of risks is influenced by the multiple frames for the consequences of fatherhood and multiple scripts for the good father. The dilution problem occurs when multiple scripts for the good father mean boys have thin conceptions of the challenges of responsible fatherhood. Model shifting occurs when boys, faced with a sexual encounter in which condoms are not available or faced with a relationship that seems strong enough for parenthood, can switch from a frame that defines early fatherhood as a hindrance to one that emphasizes the status of fatherhood or fatherhood as redemptive. A model-shifting problem also emerges when boys draw upon multiple scripts of responsible fatherhood when faced with a situation that might lead to irresponsible fatherhood by conventional definitions.

CHAPTER SEVEN

CULTURAL HETEROGENEITY AND EDUCATION

Fifteen-year-old Reed from Franklin knows that a college education is crucial for his future income and for the career he aspires to. Higher levels of education, he explained in chapter 5, result in higher salaries and open up occupations with more responsibility and opportunity for creativity. Yet when Reed describes the things he is doing in order to graduate from high school and go to college, an underlying confusion emerges. He mixes multiple models of educational advancement. He describes how playing sports will help him to make up for poor grades when it comes to graduating from high school:

> I'm going to try to keep myself situated so that when it's time for me to graduate from high school, I get extra points from basketball, football, or add-ons to me passing. So I can graduate and get my diploma . . . Like if you are on the team and you score, or just on the team in general, and you start winning. It just counts because you was on a football team and it gives you extra points . . . That's why I got in, and because I love football . . . Because I don't get straight As, so I'm looking for those extra points to help me graduate.

Boston public schools do not have a "point" system for high school graduation requirements. As with most school districts, there are course requirements for high school graduation. Reed seems to be confusing these requirements with the role of extracurricular activities in admission to elite colleges and universities. Yet he does not seem to have the grades to compete for these sought-after slots. If and when Reed goes to college, he will likely go to a local community college, where admission is open to anyone who has graduated from high school or earned a GED, or to a non-elite college where grades and test scores are the main admissions criteria and where he could perhaps get an athletic scholarship.

Reed's confusion comes from mixing ideas about admissions to elite colleges, the role of sports in college admissions and financial aid, and basic high school graduation requirements, ideas that are all present in his cultural world. Elite college admissions processes play a role in many mainstream movies, and Reed has also spent time with college students from elite colleges through an after-school program. Sports scholarships are routinely discussed in high school and college athletics, of which Reed and most of his peers are big fans, and during Reed's first week of high school, graduation requirements were discussed in school.

Reed's understanding of educational institutions exhibits the "simultaneity" problem that arises as a result of cultural heterogeneity. He juggles multiple scripts for getting to college. When multiple cultural models are adopted simultaneously and intermingled with one another, confusion results. In Reed's case, he has constructed a pathway to college for himself that pulls elements from different culturally provided models of educational advancement and has begun to put this mixture into practice in his educational behavior and decision making. Unfortunately, this mishmash will not guide him on a straight path to the higher education he seeks.[1]

Understanding High School Dropout

Though Reed is focused on college, for many young people in poor neighborhoods, graduating from high school is also a major hurdle. Many qualities predict dropping out of high school, including characteristics of students, their families, their schools, and their neighborhoods. Not surprisingly, students with lower grades and test scores, those with behavior problems, those who are male or members of minority groups, and those who have been held back a grade are more likely to drop out of high school. Students from families with lower incomes, those with parents with lower levels of education, those from families whose home language is not English, and those from single-parent families are also at greater risk of dropping out (Rumberger 1987, 1995; Cairns, Cairns, and Neckerman 1989; Ensminger and Slusarcick 1992). Family factors in particular are predictive of school dropout even when measured at very young ages (Garnier, Stein, and Jacobs 1997; Ensminger and Slusarcick 1992). Finally, those who attend larger schools and schools with lower teacher/student ratios (Rumberger 1995) or live in more disadvantaged or more violent neighborhoods are at greater risk of dropping out (Harding 2003, 2009a; Ensminger, Lamkin, and Jacobsen 1996).[2]

Knowing the predictors of dropping out of school does not help us understand why adolescents do so. When asked why they dropped out of school, dropouts gave reasons that included getting a job, becoming a parent, helping their family, and failing in school (Bridgeland, DiIulio, and Morison 2006). Yet mere knowledge of these objectives does not explain why adolescents believe they are valid reasons for dropping out and how they understand the range of options. Rather than conceptualizing high school dropout as a decision at a single point in time, we can think of it as a gradual process of disengagement from school, in which dropping out is only the last step.[3] Lack of effort in school and poor school attendance are both indicators and facilitators of this process, but by themselves they do not tell the whole story as it unfolds.

Among the boys in this study who dropped out, the typical pathway involved missing a significant amount of school (either from school suspensions, incarceration, or simple truancy), falling hopelessly behind in one's courses, failing courses, and being held back. Often the boys had been held back before (usually during elementary school), and repeating another grade would mean high school completion was even further away.[4] Repeating another grade would mean taking courses with students two years younger. Faced with these dismal prospects, they would stop going to school altogether. Marcus, age sixteen and from Roxbury Crossing, explained how he has seen many of his classmates fall victim to this downward spiral:

> So some kids would rather stay home all day than go to school. So that's mainly where they get in trouble at. Then their absences get racked up . . . You start failing classes. And then as soon as it gets to a point where you done got seventeen absences in a four-week grading term, you're like, "Damn, what other choice do I have [but] to drop out of high school." Because like, I've seen it's mostly the attendance that gets kids. It's not the kids can't do the work. It's that they feel that they're obligated to do something better with their time than show up for school . . . Now I'm dealing with that. Are they going to give me a grade because of my absences?

Add to this worry other competing demands, and dropout becomes a more attractive choice than repeating a whole year. For example, recall Ramon from Roxbury Crossing, whose experiences we will return to below. In chapter 2 he explained why working was more important than going to school: working provided the spending money he needed to resist the lure of easy money from selling drugs. Neighborhood context is not the only factor in school dropout, but conceiving of dropout as a process helps us understand the role it does play. It leads us to examine how that context influences adolescent decision making at various stages in the process. We will see below that because boys understand the value of college, postsecondary plans figure into decisions about high school as well.

Heterogeneity of Educational and Career Trajectories

Like Reed, the adolescent boys from Franklin and Roxbury Crossing drew upon multiple cultural scripts of educational and career trajectories when discussing their school experiences and plans for the future. In addition to the conventional script in which one graduates from high school, attends a four-year college, and then possibly continues in school to a professional or graduate degree program, many of the boys in Franklin and Roxbury Crossing also invoked the "star career."

The Star Career

According to the "star career" script, career success and economic well-being can be achieved through paths involving rare but highly paid professions, particularly musicians and professional athletes. Becoming a musician (usually a rapper) involves making a demo album and catching the attention of music executives or producers. For a small fee (several hundred to a thousand dollars), one can buy studio time to record an album. The process of attracting the attention of music producers is enhanced by building up a local following, generating "buzz" on the street. When the weather is warm in Boston, groups of young men can often be seen in the shopping district known as Downtown Crossing playing their demo albums on portable stereos, trying to sell copies to passersby. Connections to famous rappers and producers through friends and family members, however tenuous, can also provide hope for an avenue to get noticed or get heard. Chris, fourteen and from Franklin, explained his efforts to become a rapper.

> CHRIS: I want to be a rapper, but right now we got a studio already, we got a group. Five girls and five boys. It was called "Bean City." We working on this album called "Children of the Bean" . . . We got all the songs down in our heads or on paper. They ain't recorded. We should be done with our album in about a month. [My friend's] father got a studio.

INT: And then what happens? You record the CD, then you guys have money to make copies of the CD and all that?

CHRIS: My father's gonna do that. I know he'll do that . . . Just putting people on from the group, sitting out there selling CDs. Have a little stand out there selling. Pictures, we're trying to take group picture now so we can get the cover of the CD done. We got so many songs, they're just not recorded yet.

INT: So what do you think the chances are you guys will be good enough to make your living off this?

CHRIS: A hundred percent! We got hot! We got talent! We got these girls that can sing. We got some rappers too! We just be freestyling. We can make a whole album off our freestyling. It be HOT.

Chris has described the musician variant of the star career. In the athletics version, unique skills lead to the draft for professional basketball directly out of high school or in a scholarship to play football or basketball in college, followed by the call to a professional team. The boys understand, however, that what high school team they play for influences what college team they play for, which influences their chances of becoming a professional athlete. With daily practice and enough "heart," the athletic version of the star career is possible.

While it is of course not uncommon for adolescent boys to dream of being rap stars or professional athletes, what is striking about many of the boys of Franklin and Roxbury Crossing is that they strongly believe that their chances of success in a star career are high, not only in early adolescence but also later. While dreams of stardom are typical among middle-class youth as well, they tend to fade with time, as boys mature and develop more nuanced understandings of careers and the labor market. Plans involving star careers were common among the youngest boys—age thirteen and sometimes fourteen—in all three neighborhoods, but by the time they reached fifteen, the boys of Lower Mills had largely outgrown their star career aspirations. Yet the assessments of the older boys in the poor neighborhoods stood in stark contrast to those of their counterparts in Lower Mills. Why? Part of the reason is that the lure of the star career among the Roxbury Crossing and Franklin boys is reinforced by other cultural frames in their environment and by their observations of those who have succeeded. In other words, the star career has a great deal of what Schudson (1989) calls "cultural resonance" reinforcing its perceived viability.

Rap stars and professional athletes who the boys look up to are often from neighborhoods, schools, and families like theirs. The lore of the star career centers around a poor, minority youth from the inner city who rises above the challenges of the ghetto to become a star. Today's rappers and athletes stand as living proof of the viability of the star career script, and their paths to success are valorized in popular culture, such as the recent movies *Hustle and Flow* and *Get Rich or Die Tryin'*. Even when asked about the sheer numerical improbability of becoming a professional athlete, most boys insist that they—and all of their friends—will achieve the dream. Even the boys who were clearly too small to be professional football or basketball players insisted they would be able to "go pro" with enough practice.

A second frame with which the star career resonates strongly is one that emphasizes the role of hard work in achieving one's goals. Anything is possible with sufficient determination, as Daniel, seventeen and from Roxbury Crossing, explains.

> DANIEL: If you put your mind to something, you can complete it. Most people say you gotta have more realistic goals 'cause you don't want to get your high hopes up and you don't make it nowhere. But it's fifty-fifty really. You've got a 50 percent chance of getting it and then you have 50 percent chance of not getting it . . . My dad's told me that. People in school has told me that. And you just hear it from everybody, 'cause everybody is like, "Oh, I wanted to be this, but I couldn't be this 'cause my dreams is too high." It's like yeah, your dreams is too high, but you could have probably completed it if you kept on going.
>
> INT: And so we talked about your goals of being either a professional athlete or running your own restaurant. So you think of both of those as being fifty-fifty chances?
>
> DANIEL: Yeah.

As Daniel notes, American culture bombards youth with the idea that if one works hard enough, even the most improbable goal is achievable. Parents, teachers, and neighbors repeat this message as well, sometimes using it to motivate school effort. Teachers and parents promote the importance of reading and math by arguing that these skills are important to reading and understanding a recording or sports contract, implicitly endorsing the star career script as viable. While it is probably true that if every boy from a poor neighborhood worked hard to start his own business or to go to college, most could achieve those goals, it is simply impossible for all but a lucky few to become professional musicians or athletes.

Even in the face of clear barriers, the lore of the star career has powerful sway. Recall that Ramon, age seventeen and from Roxbury Crossing, has already dropped out of high school, unable to juggle his job at a grocery store, attending school, and caring for his elderly grandmother. He plans to go to night school to earn his high school diploma and then go to college. He still holds on to the dream of winning a football scholarship and becoming a professional athlete. Since he does not play on a high school football team, the chances of being spotted by a college recruiter are essentially zero, but he still holds out hope, explaining how it is possible:

> I really pray that I can get a sports scholarship in high school, which I really doubt I can even get because of where I'm at now . . . I know there's a Somerville Football League, semipro. I can join that, but I'd rather do it through, you know, high school and then from high school I would love to go to community college, no problem with that. And then, from a community college, go up to a four-year college, get my bachelor's degree, and then play football there and hopefully go to the pros.

In comparison, Lower Mills youth were more realistic about the probability of success in a star career. Jason, age eighteen and from Lower Mills, is more tentative about his chances in the music business, even though he has already had some success as a musician. He interprets the notion that you can do anything if you work hard enough differently than his counterparts in Franklin and Roxbury Crossing.

> JASON: I'll be performing on June 4th. It's like a party on a boat for a radio station. The DJ and me. It's like three floors. Doing two songs on a floor. And doing like a seven states tour . . . This guy I worked with from the talent show. And I won first place in the process, I did my first song with the dude. And then we kind of worked well together so he said, "I'll help you go on TV." And just started working together.
>
> I have one CD. That was practice. It came out good too, but when I listen to it, I was like, "Nah, I can do a lot better than that." So I'm almost done with another one. I did another CD with a group, which is like six other people.
>
> INT: That sounds pretty good so far.
>
> JASON: Yeah, I mean there's so many people trying to get there it's like, other people be getting picked. So the chances of that kind of [low].
>
> INT: So some people say that a young person can do anything they put their mind to. And others say it's more important to have realistic goals. What do you think about those two things?
>
> JASON: It depends on what unrealistic means. If you're like, "I want to be the first person that will get a flying car." It's like, whatever, OK. If somebody is like somebody who had a hard life and stuff and has a hard time

in school and wants to be a lawyer as quick as possible and works extra hard to do it, that seems realistic . . .

The NFL [National Football League], that's like music I suppose. Everybody wants to do that. They're gonna pick the best player they can find. You can be good but there's always somebody better.

For Jason, a star career is always fraught with uncertainty and the high possibility of failure, and so devoting all one's energies to becoming a musician is not sensible. Music is important to Jason, but at this point in his life, it is a hobby rather than a career.

Finally, the star career script carries a certain resonance with the structural circumstances of the boy growing up in a poor neighborhood. Reminded daily of the struggle not only of his own family's poverty, but that of many of his friends and neighbors, the star career provides a way to improve the lives of many others whom he cares about. The strength of social ties to the neighborhood itself, discussed in chapters 2 and 3, changes the calculation of risk and reward in pursuing the star career. For the boys of Roxbury Crossing and Franklin, success in a star career carries a different meaning. In addition to increasing his own well-being, wealth from a star career will enable the boy to help his family, friends, and neighbors. Daniel, seventeen and from Roxbury Crossing, and Simon, sixteen and from Franklin, explain what they plan to do for their communities when they "make it big."

> DANIEL: I do want to play professional in something 'cause I am pretty good and I think I can make it. Yeah. I'm trying to make my neighborhood a better place if I get enough money, if I ever make it big somewhere. Instead of having this crime where most people live at, like the projects and everything, apartment buildings. I'd own my own apartment buildings, make sure everything is up to date and stuff.

> SIMON: I want to be able to come back to my people, and try to get them in the direction to have what I have. I don't want to just sit on top of everybody. I want everybody to succeed like me. If I'm a big-time rapper or something—this is just an example. You just live right next door to me, and we've been friends for years. You've been rapping with me. All of a sudden I just become a big-time rapper, and I don't come back to the 'hood. I don't come back and put you on to how to become a star. How would you feel? That's how I think.

> If I make it, or whatever I do to become a successful person, my family and my friends, or even people I don't know, I'm going to try to help them do what they want to do because you only live one time. That's why I want to be rich, real quick.

Even after he is a star rapper, Simon cares about how his friends and neighbors view him. He measures his status through the eyes of this reference group, and so boosting his status using the wealth generated by a star career is an incentive.

The danger of the star career script is that it distracts boys from focusing on schooling as a pathway to future economic well-being, reducing school effort and attendance. The star career provides a competing alternative script in which education is unnecessary. This is particularly the case during middle school, when boys are most susceptible to the dream of the star career and when an important educational foundation is being laid for high school learning. As Chris explains, "You don't gotta go to college to be a rapper. I still pursue to be a rapper. I don't think you gotta go to college to be a basketball player either."

Sean, fourteen and from Franklin, is in the eighth grade at a Boston public middle school. He is by all accounts a bright young man, but his behavior problems have landed him in special education courses. He plays basketball almost every day after school and dreams of being a basketball player, the next Kobe Bryant (who was drafted to the National Basketball Association directly out of high school and did not attend college). While Sean sees the importance of college for future economic success, the availability of the star career script weakens his commitment to college. This was evident when we discussed whether he would take the placement exam for the city's exam (i.e., magnet) schools. Sean worried that going to an exam school would mean a lot more homework, though he also recognized it might improve his chances of going to college. He describes his reluctance to go to the exam school as "laziness," although this is merely what his family and teachers have called it. More homework will mean less time to play basketball after school.

> SEAN: My teachers be saying they want me to take the exam for Latin Academy. One of my teachers told me that. They said they get mad [a lot of] homework. And I only get a little bit of homework. I was like, "What??" So I don't really want to go there but I'm just gonna take the test and see what I can do.
>
> INT: And you said [during our last interview] that you probably weren't gonna try very hard on the test?
>
> SEAN: Nah, 'cause my Mom said if I make it, she's gonna make me go, even if I don't want to go. So I just don't want to do that 'cause I'm that lazy in school.
>
> INT: 'Cause you don't want to do all that homework basically?

SEAN: No, I don't want to do that. I want to go outside, or just go to my cousin's house. If I got homework every day, then I can't really do nothing.
INT: Do you think maybe if you went to Latin, you might get a better education?
SEAN: Yeah.
INT: But you don't think it's worth it.
SEAN: I think it's worth it, but I just don't want to do it.

Sean's responses are puzzling at first. He says he wants to go to college and recognizes the educational value of attending the exam school, but also thinks it is not worth it. Sean's responses begin to make sense only in light of the importance that he attaches to basketball and to the star career script. The star career provides an alternative career pathway that competes with conventional or mainstream frames regarding college, which Sean also subscribes to. This is an example of a simultaneity problem. Sean holds two competing ideas simultaneously, and allegiance to one means sacrificing the other.

Of course, dealing with multiple ideas is a common challenge for adolescents and not necessarily unique to those from poor neighborhoods, but comparing boys like Sean to their counterparts in Lower Mills reveals how seriously alternatives like the star career are taken in Roxbury Crossing and Franklin. Thirteen-year-old Jordan and fourteen-year-old Seth are neighbors in Lower Mills. As younger boys who spend all day after school at the local park playing football and basketball, as sons of single mothers who did not finish high school, and as boys living in poverty, they would seem to be especially susceptible to the lure of the star career. Yet neither mentioned being a professional athlete as one of their career goals. Instead, they both focused on college as the key part of their career plans. Sports scholarships did not even enter into their thinking.

INT: Tell me what your goals are for your life. What are you planning on accomplishing?
SETH: Graduating from college is first. Kids, my own house, I want to move out of Boston . . .
INT: If you for some reason had to choose between various goals, which of the goals you said is most important to you?
SETH: Graduating from college. So I can get a diploma. 'Cause people in my family, they didn't even go to college. They don't really have a job, a serious job. Like my cousin that didn't go to college works at Brighams [an ice cream shop]. That's really not a job to me. And my other cousin worked, at

food court in the mall. Those are really not serious. It's really not that interesting. Serving food would get boring to me, doing it all day every day.
INT: So in terms of college, have you started thinking about what it's going to take to get admitted to a college?
SETH: I guess they should be judging by your writing. I think you gotta have certain grades to get into certain schools. If you get good grades, you should be able to get into a good school.

For Seth, sports neither competes with his college plans nor figures into his understanding of college admissions. The star career script holds less salience for boys in Lower Mills.

Parenting and the Star Career

Simon is sixteen and from Franklin. His father was murdered when he was young, and he was raised by his mother, now thirty-one, living in a shelter, and recovering from stomach surgery. Sitting outside a relative's house early on a Saturday morning, she talked about where she sees Simon in the future. Though Simon has struggled in the past with school, fights, and run-ins with the police, she is optimistic, mostly because of his basketball skills.

INT: Thinking about Simon's future, what do you see as his strengths, and his weaknesses?
SIMON'S MOTHER: His weakness is his education, because Simon, if you talk to him, he can express it. But when it comes to pen and paper, he gets nervous. He doesn't want to express his feelings on paper. But other than that, I see him playing basketball, clear as day. But he doesn't want to play basketball any more. And I think basketball would be good, because no matter what he does, all he needs is a contract. And if he goes out there and breaks his leg, no matter what job he does, he will never make $12 million.
INT: Do you think if he really put his mind to it that he could end up in the NBA?
SIMON'S MOTHER: Yes, I do. Yes, I do. I know he can . . . He's going to college. Especially with his basketball, he would be the next Allen Iverson, and the neighborhood would pitch in for him to go to college because we know that basketball is for him.

Simon himself, however, has come to the realization that he is too short to have a basketball career, and he is now focused on being a rapper instead.

Though Simon's mother is somewhat unusual in her wholehearted endorsement of the star career, other parents also hold out the hope for an NBA or NFL career, as Joseph's mother explains:

> I expect that Joseph finish school. That he do something positive with his life, like basketball. Hopefully with that he can go to college. I think whatever he wants to do, he puts his mind to it. I just expect him to finish school and go to college. I think nowadays you need it, you have to, to get a good job.
>
> All kids have dreams of becoming basketball stars, and it just doesn't happen to everybody. So I think if he goes to college, that would be something that would be good for him. I don't know how the money is with it, but . . . Ummmm . . . [pause] Naaaahhh . . . He's short. [laughs]
>
> Being a professional, it's hard. You have to be really, really talented to get noticed. A lot of people around here say he's good, he has game. When he broke his arm, he played with his left hand. He learned to dribble with his left hand. A lot of people tell me he can play basketball, and he loves it. All he wants to do when he comes home, after he finishes his homework, "Can I go play basketball?" I just let him, because I know where he is and he's out of trouble.

While some Franklin and Roxbury Crossing parents, like Simon's mother, are caught up in the lore of the star career like their sons, most, like Joseph's mother, have a considerably more ambiguous take on their sons' plans for superstardom. On the one hand, a focus on basketball or music can distract a young man from school and other endeavors. On the other, most parents are hesitant to tell their sons that their dreams are unrealistic and distracting. A child's interest in sports or music can be leveraged in other ways, for motivating school work or, as Joseph's mother suggests, keeping young men away from the dangers of the streets.

James's mother illustrates the difficulties of sorting out these different points of view. She has seen how young men can get taken in and sidetracked by the lure of the basketball career, and so she encourages her son to pursue his interest in cooking and perhaps go to college for hotel and restaurant management:

> James got gifts in certain areas. Sometimes you got to really look at your kids and find out what kind of gifts they got. Sometimes they might not want to go to college. I'm not saying that he's not, because he definitely wants to go to college. He wants to play basketball for one thing. But I just don't see it. I'm looking at him, and I just don't think that he would be [tall enough].

James can cook really well. My father, he owned his own store and was a cook. But I feel that James has a gift in that area just like basketball. Certain kids his age can't make all the food that he can make. He's interested in how the ingredients work and stuff like that. I know basketball is you know—sometimes if parents kind of notice what their kids are about. I just wish—sometimes they say, oh, basketball, but when the kid goes to basketball what does he do if he want to be a cook. So I told him to take hotel management and restaurant management in school. So he can, like, get into hospitality or tourism, stuff like that.

James's interest in basketball keeps him out of trouble and away from the neighborhood's negative peers. Basketball practices and games keep him occupied, and he has made friends with other boys who are also interested in basketball and therefore do not spend their time hanging out on the street, as his mother remarks: "They're all basketball. He won't have friends that don't play basketball. He doesn't get too big into friends. You know, he's family-type kid. He'll bring a whole basketball team over here hungry. That's it, which is good."

Encouraging a child to focus on sports or music rather than neighborhood peers is one tool that parents have to limit the risks of growing up in a violent neighborhood. Yet managing that interest so that it does not become an all-consuming focus on unrealistic goals is particularly challenging for parents in a cultural environment in which the star career provides a strong alternative to conventional models of education and career trajectories.

In contrast, Lower Mills parents have an easier time shifting their sons away from the star career. Darnell's mother is realistic about her thirteen-year-old son's prospects for a star career as a rapper, so she pushes him into more reasonable careers in the entertainment industry, writing and sound production. Also, as discussed in chapter 2, Darnell's mother does not worry about keeping him away from a dangerous neighborhood or negative neighborhood peers. As a result, she can be more discouraging of his interests in being a rapper:

Right now he's very into writing and he's starting to get into music and rapping so I would like to see him doing something with that, like producing something . . . I hope he graduates high school, gets him some good scholarships. He wants to play football also, so hopefully he can get into that and just that keeps him focused . . . I think what he's doing he can go to any community college as long as he gets some kind of diploma that he graduated and took the courses and knows what he is doing. I don't want him to get sidetracked.

The biggest thing he talks about is his music, so rapping and stuff like that . . . It does keep him writing and reading and listening to things and interested in what is going on in the world so he can rap about it . . . Like I tell him all the time, "Darnell, you can't rap," but he can write. So I think he can, even if he's not the one on the microphone singing or rapping, I think he can still be in entertainment.

Darnell's mother tries to harness his interest in music and sports as a way to "keep him focused" and to motivate him to continue his education and to develop his skills. Indeed, when I talked to him about his career goals, Darnell mentioned becoming a lawyer, not a rapper.

Alternative Routes to College

The star career is merely one of many scripts for educational and career success, though most other scripts involve going to college in some way or another, even for high school dropouts. One alternative route to college is to go to night school to get one's high school diploma, attend a community college, and then transfer to a four-year college. Ramon explained how he could get to college via this route and continue to work at his job at a supermarket:

I'm about to go to this night school, by Madison. They say you can get your high school diploma, so I'm gonna start working in the morning, then I'm gonna go there at night. So it's only Tuesday and Thursday . . . I believe it's from 6:00 to 9:00 [p.m.]. There's no homework. Just got to sit back . . . But I think I just have to go there for two terms, or until I rack up enough points. When I rack up enough points and they feel that I'm ready to graduate, I just finish up whatever term and I guess I graduate after that . . . I want to get a high school diploma. I want to be able to go to a community college, then hopefully get into a big-time college somewhere.

Another alternative route to college is to drop out of high school, study for a GED, and then go to community college. The public schools that Boston youth attend are chaotic; maintaining order is necessarily the first priority. Faced with this challenging environment, other paths to success become appealing. Tyree, age seventeen and from Roxbury Crossing, dropped out of high school in the eleventh grade in favor of a GED.

TYREE: I would just say it was more nonfocused [at my high school]. There was a lot of other things going on. People were smoking inside the school, lighting fires in the school. There wasn't too many fights . . . Everybody was doing everything else except for school . . . Nobody cared about what you did, not even the teachers. They were still getting paid. Boston public schools is basically not the way to go because there is always going to be something to hold you back. Even though you already got a focus on school, but sometimes there is a lot of other things that catches your mind and you really are not able to focus. So I realize that [my school] was not the way for me, and that is when [a friend of my sister] referred me to [the GED program].

INT: At what point did you make that decision?

TYREE: When I stopped going to school for a while. 'Cause I really couldn't get with [my school] so I was just not going to school at all. Like a couple of months ago I stopped going to school weeks and weeks straight. But it was like I would go in and sign in so I was already marked in but I would leave school . . . I think [the GED program] is doing better for me now than what [my high school] would ever done. Because it was smaller classes [at the GED program], you get more attention by the teacher. And you learn a lot more because you are not worried about the kids making jokes behind you . . . I like to work and I know what it is about. You know what you got to do. You know what is getting done. And you know what you are going to get out of it.

[At my school], you go in there with your mind boggled up like what is going to go down today? Is there going to be a fire today? I am like, I can't do school like this and then that is when I started thinking like, this school thing is not working. I need to get into a GED program, Job Corps, something so I can get a trade . . . So then my sister talked to [her friend] and he told her about [the GED program] and he got me in here. I take my GED test the end of this month. I am going to try to get some college classes in the fall.

Unlike the star career, these alternative scripts for college are not by nature unrealistic or damaging, but the very presence of multiple scripts can cause problems. Tyree's account illustrates how the availability and social support for competing scripts can lead to model shifting, switching to an alternative, though socially acceptable, path when one's original path becomes challenging or unpleasant.[5] Tyree never felt in danger at his high school, nor did he describe the work as particularly difficult or the commute as particularly long. He simply felt that that school was unpleasant and not somewhere he wanted to be, and so when another socially supported option became available, he took it.

   Daniel, also age seventeen and from Roxbury Crossing, provides another example of the same process. Both Tyree and Daniel can employ multiple scripts for attaining a college degree, and when they encounter a difficulty or setback on the traditional route, another is available, in this case
dropping out, getting a GED, and going to community college. Daniel's
mother describes how he ended up dropping out of high school to attend
a GED program, with the hopes of continuing to community college:

> I was upset that he wasn't gonna pass. And it wasn't the teacher's fault
> or anything. It was mainly resting on him. I told him, "It is up to you. I
> have mine [my high school diploma]. I'm trying to make sure that you get
> yours and you goofing around. They're gonna keep on going to the next
> grade and you gonna be sitting back there or you gonna have to go to
> summer school. And when they see you next year, they gonna be making
> fun of you. So YOU make that choice."
>
> I have this problem right here because I'm sending him to school. He's
> leaving out of here every morning. But he's not in school. They're going
> downtown. And that devastated me for a while.
>
> I called up the school, me and his father, and try to find out what it
> is that we can do to salvage this. And then [my friend who works at the
> GED program], I told him what was going on and what happened. I said,
> "OK, if this doesn't work, he's going to Job Corps 'cause he's not gonna
> hang." 'Cause see he's at the age, he doesn't really have to go to school . . .
> He was out sixty-some times . . . And then wasn't doing his homework, his
> classwork, and handing it in half done and all that stuff. He would come
> to school, sign in, and leave out.
>
> He has to have structure because you can't be walking down them
> hallways at the Job Corps when you supposed to be in class. He needed
> more authority on it. 'Cause you come to school, your teacher marks you
> present. You go to one class. There's no real strong authority of making
> sure you get to your next class, 'cause they can't. It's his responsibility to
> go to school. Now while he's in the [GED] class, it's their responsibility to
> teach them. He can go get ready to take his GED . . . And then from there,
> he will go to college.

Daniel also explained why he decided to drop out of school and try the
GED program:

> I didn't like school that much. So I would go half the day but then certain
> classes I knew they all follow in a row. Like Spanish class, history class,
> and science. I really didn't like them because of the teachers mainly. I'm
> thinking, "I don't want to stay to the end of the day." You see about thirty
> other kids leave, and it's like I'm one of these thirty kids. . . .

So if I get my GED right now, after I take the test and I'm thinking like August and they send me back the paperwork, I can go to school in September, to college. And I be ahead of everybody else that was in the same grade as me last year. They still be in twelfth, I be a freshman in college. I'll probably graduate a year ahead like I did in high school and it will be pretty good. I'd rather do that instead of waiting a whole year, the teachers, to see faces I really don't like and don't want to see. Just finish it up.

I would try to go down south, to like Alabama or Georgia Tech or Georgia or maybe even Texas A&M, away from Boston and everything, so I can get out and see other people.

The notion that there are multiple viable pathways to educational and career success resonates with a particularly powerful narrative in Roxbury Crossing and Franklin, one of recovery and redemption. This "turnaround" narrative is a variant of the "rags-to-riches" story familiar to millions of Americans, in which someone from humble origins achieves success through ingenuity, hard work, and little bit of luck. This story is not just a widespread idea; it is also institutionalized in practices in many domains from education to religion to politics. The turnaround narrative involves recovery from a setback or personal failure. Success can be achieved by overcoming adversity. The key elements include the importance of failure for learning, personal growth, and perspective; recognizing the error of one's prior activities (such as addiction or street crime); separating oneself from people or places that contribute to past problems; securing resources though participation in mainstream institutions such as schools, churches, and community programs; and finally becoming economically independent through work, eventually able to support a family and even to help others do the same.

One way in which the boys from Franklin and Roxbury Crossing expressed support for this narrative was in their responses to a vignette about two men that a female cousin is considering dating. One man is a former drug addict who is now living with his mother and working a minimum-wage food-service job. The other is slightly older than the cousin, drives a fancy car, and has a lot of money, but is suspected of being a drug dealer. Boys from all three neighborhoods rejected the second man, both for his age and for the possibility of his involvement in crime. However, the boys from Franklin and Roxbury Crossing found the former drug addict acceptable because he had managed to make a change in his life. He fit the beginning stages of the turnaround narrative. Boys from Lower Mills, when forced to choose one or the other, would also choose the former drug addict, but they almost always said they would advise the cousin to stay away from both men.

Further evidence of the power of the turnaround narrative comes from the boys' discussions of their role models. Reed explained at first that his role models were Michael Jordan, Magic Johnson, and Bill Gates. When asked about people he considered role models whom he knew personally, he ignored my suggestions of his uncle who lives nearby or the local community outreach worker who runs Reed's youth group. Instead he chose his father, a former drug addict whom he rarely sees: "My father [is a role model], because he did bad things, but he changed . . . I think he's doing good because he's changed a lot . . . He's doing classes. He stopped smoking, he stopped drinking. He has a wife now." Similarly, Duante, age seventeen and from Roxbury Crossing, explained why he admired his grandfather, a bus driver.

> DUANTE: My grandfather, he's kind of successful. Because when he was in the projects, you know what I'm saying, he could be out there slinging drugs, but he turned his life around and started making money in legal ways. It was growing over the years. More money, more money, more money, more money . . . He is a provider . . . I know what type of person he is. He's not a stupid person. He likes to give.
>
> INT: So how was it that he became successful like that?
>
> DUANTE: Being shot, stabbed, jumped, the whole nine. Had kids? Seen the light. Started going to church. Really, trying to connect, not even connect with God, but be a decent person. Because he don't want that for his kids, seeing them out there, slinging. He wants to make sure they see something positive so they can do something positive. So they can provide for their family.

The turnaround narrative also applies directly to schooling. Manuel, of Franklin, is fourteen and is in the seventh grade at a Boston public middle school. He was held back once during elementary school, and is in danger of being held back again because he is failing two of his classes. He admits that he does not pay attention much in class and is easily distracted by conversations with his friends. If he does not bring these grades up, he will have to attend summer school or repeat the seventh grade. Yet he does not consider his situation a threat to his plans to go to college. Manuel believes he can wait until high school to bring his grades up, to make a turnaround.

> MANUEL: My mom got mad, said that "I don't want to see those Fs again." She said, "You got to do better so you won't have to go to summer school."

INT: What kind of things are you doing to do better?

MANUEL: Try to improve on my homework, do a lot of extracredit work, and just try to pass. The only two classes I have to pass this term is social studies and language arts. I pass those and I'm fine.

INT: We were talking about you going to college. Are you worried about having grades like that affecting whether you get to go to college?

MANUEL: When I go to high school, I'll try to just stay with good grades and I won't have to go through what I am doing like right now.

INT: So you'll get more serious when you're in high school?

MANUEL: Yeah, when I'm in high school, so I can get into like a real good college 'cause my cousins told me that the colleges, they really look at your high school stuff.

Absent from Manuel's account is any worry that the material (and study skills) he is learning in middle school might be important for success in high school. In contrast, boys from Lower Mills rarely include the turnaround narrative in their discussions about their future plans. Timothy, fourteen and from Lower Mills, described how important success at one stage in life is to success in the next stage, which stands in stark contrast to Manuel's view of the insignificance of middle school. Timothy contrasted his belief with the way that some of his classmates in middle school thought about school:

> Putting school before everything was the most important decision ever. 'Cause in sixth, seventh, and eighth grade all my peers used to say, "Why you getting the honor roll, high honors now when it doesn't count? 'Cause once you move to high school, everything is gone." The ones that said that, those are the ones that aren't doing so good now. And I said, "If you do good early, you'll do good on the future." So basically it's like I built my foundation in middle school, which leads to my good grades now [in high school].

With a much narrower range of scripts for educational and career success, the boys in Lower Mills are less susceptible to the model-shifting problems that affected the decision making of the boys in Franklin and Roxbury Crossing. Tyree and Daniel's decisions to drop out of high school in favor of the GED program can be contrasted with that of Nathan, who grew up in Lower Mills. Nathan has also been struggling with school attendance and school failure. Though a health issue is part of his problem, he admits that he was mostly using it as an excuse to miss school. When he was younger, he was an A and B student, but now he is earning some Ds and Fs, and only has a C average in high school. Though he is seventeen, he is only in the tenth grade because he has had to repeat that grade twice.

> NATHAN: I've used [my health problems] to my advantage, so I can miss school. So I've gotten into arguments about that [with my mother]. And also, staying up too late, missing school the next day, or getting to school late or just being pokey . . . My total absences were a hundred and twenty days [last year]. One hundred over the limit . . .
>
> I don't hate school. I like my school, when I get there, and I'm really into it. But like, there are certain classes like math, for instance, I can't wait for the bell to ring. But when I'm in English I'm participating or even when it's something that I'm interested. When it's something that's remedial or something that's dragging me down, then I'm not interested, that's when I get frustrated and I say I don't want to be there.
>
> INT: And so, why do you think you weren't going to school some of those days when maybe health reasons weren't the reason not to go?
>
> NATHAN: I don't even know. I'd fall asleep in my room. I'd say, "All right, I'm going to school today," but I'd go crash on my bed and fall asleep.

Despite these problems, Nathan says he has not given a thought to dropping out to get a GED, and even when pressed, says he would not even consider it. He sees no other option besides going to college through the traditional route. In his mind, he has no choice but to stick it out and finish high school.

Darnell, age thirteen and from Lower Mills, is also struggling in school, getting into fights in school that lead to suspensions. Since Darnell is still very young, dropping out is not an option, but he could change schools to one that will be easier for him. In contrast to Tyree and Daniel, Darnell's plans to go to college and then to law school keep him motivated to try to stay in his current school rather than pushing him toward transferring.

> INT: Are you worried about them saying, "You're expelled. You can't come back to [your school] at all?"
>
> DARNELL: Yeah. I think I would have to go to a different school that wasn't the same type of education, that had a worse education and not want to really help me. 'Cause they're not wanting to be able to get into a good college and then I probably won't get into law school.
>
> And then there's the problem that I don't really like this school, period. So sometimes I just get in trouble just 'cause I don't want to be there. That's what I can't figure out. Most of the time I want to leave the school and then I realize I gotta stay there in order to get ahead.

INT: What don't you like about the school that makes you want to leave so badly that you get in trouble?

DARNELL: I don't know. It's just this little place up in my head and things I do that make me just not like the school. I think most of the time probably it's just 'cause of the way I act, that the teachers get mad at me for things I don't do, or do do. And then I just start getting mad like, "Oh, I can't stand this school!" Then I want to leave. It built up to the point where I started just not liking the school, period.

The youth of Lower Mills see fewer viable pathways to educational and career success. Delbert, fourteen and a friend and neighbor of Darnell in Lower Mills, described how dropping out of high school would leave him with few viable options.

DELBERT: If I wasn't able to finish high school, my life would just be ruined. I wouldn't be able to do anything anymore. I would think of all that hard work in middle school and elementary school as just going down the drain.

INT: What about, some people go to like night school to finish up or they get a GED?

DELBERT: That's not the same as getting a high school diploma because you're not going to be able to get a good job if you do all those other things and dropping out of high school. And plus your life would go slow because you would have to go through different steps to get in, to go into night school, and it would take a long time because you're going to be an older person.

As Delbert's comments suggest, the alternative scripts for going to college that involve dropping out of high school carry a great deal of risk. If one does not both enroll in college and continue long enough to get a degree, one is left with a GED or alternative diploma rather than a traditional high school diploma. Economic research shows that the wage returns to a GED are less than the wage returns to a high school diploma (Cameron and Heckman 1993).[6] In the long term, if getting a GED is merely a route to college and a college degree is eventually earned, then boys like Tyree, Daniel, and Ramon may not suffer from having dropped out of high school. If they fail to pass the GED test or fail to earn a degree in college, however, their plan can backfire, and they will be left with only marginal educational credentials.[7] In his interview, Tyree acknowledged this potential problem, though only after some prodding.

TYREE: I would say the high school diploma and the GED is about the same thing, but they make it seem like it is harder. Like if you don't have a high school diploma, you are not as smart as the next person. To the system it is different. But as long as I am able to get my college degree, I would say it doesn't make me a different person. 'Cause if you have a high school diploma and I have a GED, and you have a college degree and I have a college degree, it doesn't make me different.

INT: For people who don't go to college, is there a difference between like having a GED and having a high school diploma?

TYREE: I would say there is, because you will be able to get a job, but there is not a lot of openings [for those with only a GED]. They look at a high school diploma like it is different, and it is only a piece of paper. But I would just say the system, it fools you to do what they want you to do. A GED and a high school diploma have nothing to do with your smartness. Just because I didn't do high school, it doesn't make me dumber than the next person. All that matters is what you learned from that twelve years of going to school . . . But the GED is not always twelve years 'cause you can get a GED at ninth grade. But the high school diploma they make it different because you did the whole four years of school of high school.

Tyree believes that the material he has learned over the last few months in preparation for the GED exam is the same as what he would have learned in his last two years of high school, but it is not clear that this is the case. In particular, mastering the material required for the GED is probably not adequate for preparing someone for success in college.[8] This is just one example of a larger problem that the boys in Franklin and Roxbury Crossing face: lack of information about what college requires and how to go about making the transition to college.

Navigating Educational Institutions

Whether or not one graduates from high school, enrolling in and graduating from college—particularly a four-year college—requires the student and his parents to successfully navigate complicated educational institutions, from application time lines and admissions requirements to financial-aid forms. Middle-class parents who have themselves been to college have the cultural capital to navigate such bureaucracies and institutions. However, sons of parents with low levels of education themselves, like the boys of Lower Mills, Roxbury Crossing, and Franklin, are at a particular disadvantage when it comes to navigating complex institutional rules and requirements. Lareau (2000) describes how parents with low levels of education are less likely and less able to intervene in their children's elementary schools. Parents who had not been successful in school were intimidated by teachers and staff and viewed school staff as entirely responsible for what happened at school. Similarly, low-education parents of boys in this study were also less able to help their sons navigate postsecondary educational institutions. In all three study areas, access to family members with knowledge of how to get a college education, usually parents but also aunts, uncles, cousins, or siblings, was a primary determinant of a boy's own knowledge of such matters.

Nevertheless, neighborhood matters for college enrollment as well. When parent education, occupation, and income are held constant, adolescents from disadvantaged neighborhoods are still less likely to enroll in college, and adolescents in culturally heterogeneous neighborhoods who want to attend college are less likely to enroll than their counterparts in more culturally homogeneous neighborhoods (Harding 2009b). How does neighborhood cultural heterogeneity have such effects? When there are multiple competing and conflicting scripts for getting to college or constructing a career, information about each of the scripts and about their consequences becomes diluted. As Reed's description of his educational plans at the beginning of the chapter illustrates, the result is that boys and their parents in Franklin and Roxbury Crossing have incomplete and at times inaccurate information about educational institutions and the process of transition to college.[9] Without this knowledge, they are often ill-equipped to make decisions about their secondary schooling that will prepare them for college.[10] The dilution effects of cultural heterogeneity produce ignorance about how to successfully navigate educational institutions.

The salience of the star career script means that much of the information about college among Franklin and Roxbury Crossing youth is filtered through institutions relating to college athletics, particularly media coverage of collegiate and professional sports. Joseph, fifteen and from Franklin, dreams of being a professional basketball player, and he practices every day after school at the court in his housing development. His thinking about his future educational and career trajectory is heavily influenced by his involvement in basketball, both on the court and on television. When it comes to a particular college, Joseph is thinking about the top basketball schools and about Harvard University, which he has visited a few times through a neighborhood summer camp and teen mentoring program.

INT: What goals have you set for yourself, or you're thinking about for the rest of your life?

JOSEPH: I want to play basketball. I want to make it to the high school team, I want to do good in the high school team, graduate from high school. If I don't get into the pros after high school, then I'll go to college. I want to go to college, and I want to do good there, in basketball and in education.

INT: So what sort of college do you want to go to? Have you thought about which colleges might be good?

JOSEPH: The colleges I want to go to are Harvard, Maryland, and Duke.

INT: Why did you pick those?

JOSEPH: I like Harvard. I like Maryland's and Duke's basketball team.

Like Joseph, when boys talked about college, they typically mentioned colleges with nationally ranked football or basketball programs or the most well-known local colleges such as Northeastern University, Boston College, Roxbury Community College, and Harvard University. Colleges with nationally known sports programs, such as the University of Miami, Duke University, and University of Maryland, are regularly featured in television coverage of their own games and of professional sports in which their alumni play. Local colleges that might more readily meet their academic needs and financial resources or have admissions standards more in line with their academic backgrounds, such as Bay State College, Simmons College, and Massachusetts Bay Community College, were generally not known. When they discussed what it takes to go to college, they focused more on athletic scholarships or athletically based admissions criteria rather than on test scores or grades.

Though James, fourteen and from Roxbury Crossing, no longer believes he can make it to the NBA, he thinks about college admissions and financial aid in terms of basketball. After college, he wants to open his own business, such as a restaurant.

INT: What are your goals for yourself for the future?

JAMES: To play basketball. Not even necessarily in the NBA or on a high level. To compete with other people overseas, wherever it takes me. But I really want to own my own business, restaurant . . . I want to go to college on a full basketball scholarship so I won't have to pay. But no particular college. Usually D-1 basketball would be lovely, be great.

INT: What do you think the chances are of getting that?

JAMES: Good chance. In Boston, there's a lot of schools Division 1. Lot of schools . . .

INT: And these goals, have they changed over time?

JAMES: They've changed over time, especially basketball-wise. I'm not the tallest person in the world, not the best basketball player in the world either. So most of the time if I don't make it in basketball, I can always make it owning my own business . . .

INT: What made you realize that maybe being an NBA star wasn't realistic?

JAMES: I learned about college, how many different colleges there is. And some guy came to our school and talked to us. And the chance of someone making it as an NBA player is chance of getting struck by lightning.

Boys in Lower Mills also come into contact with more people who have been to college, either in their own extended families or in their neighborhoods, and they have a better sense of how the conventional script for college enrollment works. Though no one in Jordan's (age thirteen, Lower Mills) family has been to college, an older boy from the neighborhood attends college and told him about his experiences when he returned during the holidays. Cyril (sixteen, Lower Mills) also met neighbors who had been to college, who told him a little about the challenges they experienced in college.

INT: So, everybody worries about the future sometimes. When you worry about the future, what kind of things do you worry about?

CYRIL: Money. And school and stuff. Like, if something happens in school. Those are the only two things I worry about.

INT: And when you say you worry about school, what kind of things do you worry about?

CYRIL: College, the time schedules and stuff. I don't know how that is. So, I worry about that. If I don't know the times, or I'm not used to waking up at a certain time, then, it's going to be strange to adapt to that . . . People told me it's like hard.

INT: And who's telling you about this kind of stuff?

CYRIL: My mother, my parents, and people I know who went to college, my friends and stuff.

The concrete experiences of these individuals may reinforce the salience of conventional routes to college at the expense of otherwise abstract alternatives, like the star career. William, who is sixteen and currently lives in Lower Mills (though he has also lived in suburban communities around Boston), knows much more about college admissions, the role of athletics, and his own (poor) chances of receiving an athletic scholarship. Instead, he was focused on improving his academic record and planned to attend a college prep program after high school graduation and before applying to colleges.

WILLIAM: I'm planning on going to prep school and probably going to college I guess. Like I'll probably go to like Maine Central [Institute] after

I graduate, before I go to college. Or I might go senior year . . . It's like a boarding school. It's a good school. There's a good football and basketball program 'cause you get to play like Division 1 teams, the junior varsity teams . . . That's good for experience. And academics is good and good teachers . . . I know one person up there 'cause he just moved there, he went to my school.

INT: And so why not just go right from graduating from high school to college?

WILLIAM: 'Cause if I go to Maine, I can get a little extra boost that will look better when they look at my transcripts, like the schools I went to. Academically too it would just be better.

INT: Have you thought about where you want to go to college?

WILLIAM: I might want to go to college up here, but I doubt it. I want to go to college like Florida State, Florida University, somewhere down south where it's not cold . . . Plus Florida State, I like their sports program and they have a good school I heard. I went on their Web site. It's like academics. But I want to meet new people and it's farther away.

INT: So are you thinking about the possibility of getting a basketball scholarship?

WILLIAM: Well, I don't know. I'd try to but depending on the class of school you go to, too. Like if you go to [my school], the odds of you getting a basketball scholarship, it's like not high but it's not really low. But they don't really go there to look. Like you know the O'Bryant [School of Mathematics and Science, a Boston exam school]? Like that school is known for basketball players. The kids that come out of there, there's like fifteen that go straight to college right after high school. Play there for scholarships. A lot of people went to Duke and if you went to Northeastern, you would be better off, you could go to the NBA from Duke than Northeastern because they have better program.

INT: So what does it take to get into a good college that you would want to go to?

WILLIAM: Good grades. PSAT. I think they're like in a week or something. I forget when they are. But those and good grades.

William still holds out the hope of playing college basketball and leveraging his basketball skills to help him with college, but in his actual planning, he is thinking more about academics, as evidenced by his desire to go to the college prep school and his plans to take the PSAT.

Heterogeneity of cultural models about careers and education also results in the dilution of what the word "college" means. As discussed in chapter 5, boys and their parents in poor neighborhoods have received the conventional cultural messages about the importance of college for economic success, but what exactly constitutes a college education has expanded along with the options for postsecondary education. Technical education programs for which graduates typically receive training certificates were often confused with colleges that offer associate's and bachelor's degrees. This is perhaps unsurprising, as trade schools increasingly market themselves in ways similar to colleges, and as colleges increasingly market themselves in ways similar to trade schools—even offering more "certificate" programs in addition to conventional academic degrees. Institutions as different as Harvard University's summer and continuing education programs and the Benjamin Franklin Institute of Technology's technical education programs advertise in similar ways in the trains and buses that the boys ride to and from school every day. Without other sources of reliable information, some degree of confusion is inevitable. For some youth and parents, college has come to mean any postsecondary education or training. Andrew is fifteen and has been living in a Franklin housing development almost his entire life. He explained his plans for the future.

ANDREW: I'm just pretty much an average student. I pretty much want to stay with like Cs and Ds. It's like one time I did have an F this year [in math], so that's why I worked in that particular subject real hard and try to improve it . . .

INT: Can you tell me a little bit about what are the goals you want to accomplish in your life?

ANDREW: I want to be a computer technician . . . 'Cause I have a big interest in computers and like technical stuff.

INT: So if that didn't work out, what else do you think you might do?

ANDREW: I don't really know. I still am deciding about that. But for now, probably be like an electrician . . . 'Cause I'm a lot interested in electrical technology.

INT: What about when it comes to your education? What type of goals do you have?

ANDREW: I just want to finish high school, go to college and finish college.

INT: Have you thought about what colleges you would be interested in going to?

ANDREW: Harvard . . . 'Cause I visited it before and I got interested in looking around, seeing the view and talking to people there . . . Used to be every Tuesday, because there was a little tutoring program in there. And so they would just come by and pick us up and drive with us and help us out with like problems with the school.

INT: So what do you think it takes to go to college?

ANDREW: It's pretty much what you know up here that will take you to college . . . It's sort of like how much knowledge you have.

INT: What do you think it takes to get into like a school whether it's Harvard, or Northeastern University or Boston University?

ANDREW: Well that I don't really know. It could be like I heard that some colleges just choose people by random, or they just check by their standards.

Andrew is mixing two different types of postsecondary education, trade schools where he might learn to be a computer technician or electrician and traditional colleges like Harvard that offer a general liberal arts education. While C and D grades might be fine for admission to a trade school that will likely accept anyone who meets a minimum standard, they will not meet the admissions standards of Harvard College, Northeastern University, or Boston University. Though Andrew wants to be on a pathway to college, he is unknowingly on the pathway to trade school.

Even among parents there is confusion over what it means to go to college, as parents are at times affected by cultural heterogeneity as well. Miguel is sixteen and from Roxbury Crossing. His mother is herself enrolled in college, studying toward a bachelor's degree, and works at a clerical job at a local college, and she talks about how important it is for Miguel to go to college. However, when we talked about her goals for Miguel, she also confused automotive trade school with college.

INT: So what goals do you have for him for the future? What would you like to see him doing?

MIGUEL'S MOTHER: I would like to see him do whatever he wants. I want him to go to college. He's not sure yet. He says that for what he wants to be, he doesn't need college. That's not the way it works. You'll need college no matter what. He wants to be a fireman. I really wasn't happy about it but that's what he wants. Fireman and policeman, that's a no-no for me. Those are very dangerous professions.

INT: When you say, go to college, what sort of college would you like to see him go to?

MIGUEL'S MOTHER: Well, he's talking about mechanics, you know. That's up to him. Northeastern, I would like him to take something like paramedics. That would help him for what he wants to be. You know, fireman, paramedic. He sure needs to go to the academy for that, I think.

The process of applying to and enrolling in college is a source of endless confusion for the boys. Information about application time lines and requirements as well as financial aid was often incomplete or incorrect.

Few high school students in Roxbury Crossing and Franklin knew about applying for college admission or financial aid during their senior year of high school or about taking the SAT or ACT exams. Even older youth such as Daniel, age seventeen and from Roxbury Crossing, who was about to take his GED test and then, if he passed, enroll in college, often did not understand the institutional time lines of college application and enrollment. He talked about taking his GED exam during the summer and then enrolling in a large state four-year university for the fall term, as if he could just sign up for classes a few days before the beginning of the semester.

A similar misconception is that moving from high school to college is the same as moving from middle school to high school, where one just continues on into the next grade. Fernando, (age fifteen and from Franklin) and Deon (age thirteen and from Roxbury Crossing) are in the dark about the differences.

> INT: What does it take to go to college?
> FERNANDO: Staying in school. That's about it; staying in school. Staying in school, and trying to work as hard as you can, and you hit college. Anybody can go to college.
> INT: How about someone who doesn't have a lot of money to pay for college, though?
> FERNANDO: If he study hard, he can get a thing that they have free. You get good grades for the whole high school, or you can get your GED.

> INT: How much of a challenge do you think it will be to finish high school?
> DEON: Not a challenge. College is gonna be a challenge, but not high school. High school I would say, I haven't been to high school but I already know what high school is gonna be like . . . All you have to do in high school is come to school every day, not skipping school, do all your homework, turn in all your homework completely and that's easy. Go to college.
> INT: How do you know that about high school?
> DEON: I have people that's in high school that wants to go to college, and has been in the basketball game, that does all his homework, never skips school, might have skipped a class or two, but not skipping school.

These sorts of misunderstandings were considerably less common among boys from Lower Mills. For example, Charles, age fifteen and from Lower Mills, has been struggling at his Boston public high school. Like many of his peers, he cannot relate to the teachers and has trouble focusing in the chaotic school environment. But unlike his peers from more disadvantaged neighborhoods, he does not see an alternative path to his career goal—being a veterinarian—other than through college, specifically a four-year college. He understands that going to a four-year college will require him to compete with other potential students, and his current troubles in high school have him worried. He and his mother are strategizing about getting him out of that school and into another, but Charles is stressed because he sees few other pathways to his goals beyond success in high school.

> INT: And so what does it take to be a veterinarian?
>
> CHARLES: A college education. You have to know what you are doing because animals can't tell you what's wrong with them. You have to have a degree because people are not gonna want to work for you or respect your idea if you don't have a degree.
>
> INT: What do you think your chances are of going to college and graduating from college?
>
> CHARLES: If you want it bad enough, you can do it, but the odds aren't good . . . Because there's so much people, and the colleges don't accept everybody.
>
> INT: But there are some colleges that do pretty much accept everyone. Like Roxbury Community College, for example.
>
> CHARLES: I don't want to go to a community college.
>
> INT: You want to go to a four-year college?
>
> CHARLES: Yeah . . .
>
> INT: So, when you think about your future, what kind of things do you worry about?
>
> CHARLES: Am I gonna make it? And what do I have to do to make it? Like these two schools that I might go to. The one, that's okay. And the other one, I don't know, will that be better for me?

The comparison between Lower Mills youth and their counterparts from Roxbury Crossing and Franklin reveals that lack of knowledge about the institutions that lead to college is not just a function of youth and inexperience in Franklin and Roxbury Crossing. Indeed, in other domains, including the music industry and professional athletics, Roxbury Crossing and Franklin boys displayed considerably detailed knowledge.[11]

The power of multiple cultural models to dilute knowledge about how to get to college depends critically on whether the multiple models are contradictory or can be integrated. In other words, the content of the models matters as much as the number of models. When the prominence of the star career script competes with more traditional pathways to college or career success, it only dilutes knowledge about those traditional pathways because the steps involved differ. One of the secondary career pathways discussed by three of the Lower Mills boys was enlisting in the military. (None of the Roxbury Crossing or Franklin boys planned to enlist in the military.) Rather than conflicting with traditional pathways to college, enlisting in the military is a complementary pathway. Both involve graduating from high school, and the military will help its members pay for college once their enlistment ends. Understanding the military route to a college education actually helps a boy understand other routes as well. Coleman, seventeen and from Lower Mills, does not have anyone in his family who has been to college, but he explains how enlisting in the marines leaves the college option open while providing him a clear career path after high school.

COLEMAN: I'm actually thinking about going into the military. Specific branch would probably be the marines. They just offer a little bit more than the army and I'm not really an air force person, or a navy person. I did all the research I can do possibly. I even talked to recruiters and got what they had to say. The whole thing is to get you in there, but I just talked to them to see what they had to say . . . I'm going exactly after high school, in the summertime. And from there on I'll be in boot camp I guess.

INT: And do you want to make that a career or do you want to do that for a couple of years?

COLEMAN: Couple of years. By then I'll have some stableness because I'm sure about my life. I'll have a lot of thinking done during that time.

INT: Are you interested at all in college or anything like that?

COLEMAN: I have thoughts about it. I'm not so sure. I'm not like, "I'm definitely going to college." Actually, to tell you the truth, if like it could be a fifty-fifty. 'Cause after that I may not be sure if the military was something right for me. I'd be like, "What did I waste my time for?" But I get benefits.

Unsure whether he wants to go to college, enlisting in the military provides Coleman with a career pathway that will still leave him prepared for college—perhaps even more so, given the training he will receive in the military and the education benefits the military offers—should he decide to go. These alternative pathways are not contradictory but complementary.

Parents and College Knowledge

Though there is significant confusion, particularly among parents with the least education, typical parents in Franklin and Roxbury Crossing are considerably better informed about college than their sons, at least with regard to requirements for admission, the importance of grades and test scores, and the availability of financial aid. Among the parents in all three neighborhoods, the knowledge that does exist is a product of their own experiences and those of family members, friends, and in some cases co-workers, rather than of the neighborhood environment. Not surprisingly, parents who had attended at least some college themselves had the most information about college, but family members were also another important source of information. When the parents' siblings had been to college or when they had guided their own children to college, information on how to do that moved through family social networks. Another important source of experiential knowledge for parents was their older children, the older brothers and sisters of the sons included in this study. As chapter 4 discusses, many of the boys had social networks that centered on neighborhood peers. This was less the case for their parents, whose social lives tended to be more family-based.

Most parents in Franklin and Roxbury Crossing knew that grades were the most important determinant of both admission to college and merit-based college scholarships. Many described the importance of earning mostly A and B grades. Many Franklin and Roxbury Crossing parents were also familiar with the local community college options, including Massachusetts Bay Community College, Bunker Hill Community College, and Roxbury Community College (RCC), which is located in the Roxbury Crossing area. They saw community college as an important option for transitioning their sons from high school to college. RCC's simple and flexible admissions procedures, relatively low prices, and nearby location provided a way to "try out" college, and perhaps earn an associate's degree before transferring to another institution to continue one's studies and earn a bachelor's degree.

An area in which Lower Mills parents did seem to have more information than Roxbury Crossing and Franklin parents was in the role of standardized tests such as the SAT and ACT and in understanding admissions procedures at more competitive colleges and universities, such as UMass-Boston. Such test scores are generally not required for community college admissions, but are important in determining admission to more competitive four-year colleges and universities. Generally, high school students wishing to attend more competitive colleges and universities must begin the admissions process in the fall of their senior year of high school. If one does not know this and waits until after high school graduation to make plans for college, this option is foreclosed, at least for another year.

Differences between parents and sons in knowledge about college underscore the importance of neighborhood context in these educational processes. Recall Andrew from Franklin, who above revealed his confusions about the differences between trade schools and traditional colleges and universities such as Harvard. Andrew's mother actually has considerable information about college admissions and financial aid. Though his mother only graduated from high school and earned a training certificate, Andrew's older sister and four older step-siblings all graduated from college. Despite having talked to Andrew about college, his mother cannot seem to impart this accumulated family knowledge to him. He remains confused about the difference between trade school and a liberal arts college, a problem that does not beset his mother. Boys whose networks are focused in these culturally heterogeneous neighborhoods are exposed to a wide array of models regarding educational and career trajectories. Even when parents have information about college, their ability to effectively communicate that information to their sons is hindered by the alternative models that are available in the neighborhood. These models can dilute rather than reinforce the messages that parents are trying to communicate regarding preparing for college. All parents of course have difficulties communicating with their adolescents, but when parents are not just competing with teenage rebelliousness but also with alternative cultural models, effective communication is all the more difficult. (This is but one example of a more general phenomenon. Recall from chapter 3 how Chris's mother lamented her inability to compete with alternative messages Chris was receiving from older peers regarding sexual behavior.)

Focusing on Passing

Though many parents in Franklin and Roxbury Crossing had considerable knowledge about college, there was also a sizable subset who were as uninformed as their sons. These parents had not been to college themselves and did not have the benefit of relationships with family members, coworkers, or neighbors who had. Unlike their counterparts in Lower Mills, their neighbors were much less likely to have had college experiences. These parents lacked the same information that the neighborhood boys did, about the difference between college and trade schools or certificate programs, timing and requirements for application to college, and the importance of grades and test scores for admission to competitive-admission institutions. This lack of information influenced not just their ability to guide their sons through the college process, but more importantly how they thought about the relationship between high school and college.

When information about admissions standards and procedures is lacking, parents set their expectations for their sons' school performance according to more local comparisons and standards. This is another example of the leveling of expectations that occurs in poor neighborhoods (see chapter 2). When it comes to education, this means a focus on passing or graduating. Aspects of educational performance having more to do with learning the material and acquiring the skills for college are not emphasized, though these parents would certainly agree they are important. As one Franklin parent put it, "All my kids got promoted to the next grade. All five of them. So that's telling you they're doing all right."

Duante's mother provides another example of this leveling of expectations. She herself dropped out of high school and eventually earned a GED. She is particularly interested in whether Duante and his younger brother are passing their classes so that they do not have to take summer school and are not at risk of being held back.

> INT: What sort of expectations do you have for Duante in terms of his grades and attendance and homework and things like that?
> DUANTE'S MOTHER: I expect him to go to school; I expect him to do his homework. I expect him to graduate. I don't want him to go get a GED. But if you have that opportunity to walk across that stage and have that diploma placed in your hand, do it. And then from there, I would like for him to go to college, but I told him that's his decision. It's a good idea for you. I think it's the best thing for you; but ultimately, that's your choice. *I want that diploma.* After that, you go on and do what you want.

For Duante's mother, the path to high school graduation involves passing each grade and advancing to the next until twelfth grade is complete. While this is of course correct, it will not necessarily leave Duante prepared for college, which is also one of her priorities. What it will do, however, is put him ahead of his many of his peers in the neighborhood.

Conclusion

This chapter describes some of the ways in which neighborhood cultural heterogeneity influences the schooling decisions of the boys of Franklin and Roxbury Crossing as compared to their counterparts in Lower Mills, particularly with regard to dropping out of high school and the availability and content of information regarding college. As college has become the normative educational goal among all sectors of society, decisions about secondary education have come to be intertwined with prospects and plans for college. In culturally heterogeneous neighborhoods such as Roxbury Crossing and Franklin, young people are presented with a wide array of competing and conflicting frames and scripts regarding educational and career trajectories. The star career and a set of alternative pathways to college that do not require completion of a traditional high school program are front and center alongside a conventional path to a high school diploma and college enrollment. They are not only present but socially supported. While these models are available to young people from all walks of life, they are particularly salient and powerful for the young people from poor areas like Roxbury Crossing and Franklin because they resonate with other cultural ideas present in those environments and with the structural circumstances that the boys experience.

This heterogeneity of cultural models has implications for boys' decision making regarding their educational careers. Simultaneity, model shifting, and dilution result from exposure to an array of competing and conflicting frames and scripts. Young people can construct pathways for themselves that mix elements of multiple frames or scripts, creating plans or making decisions that are actually inconsistent or insufficient for achieving their goals (simultaneity), as when Reed plans to use sports participation to help him graduate from high school or when Andrew confuses trade schools and traditional colleges. With alternative cultural models available and socially supported, boys may also shift from model to model when the challenges of one model become unpleasant or overwhelming (model shifting), such as when Sean chooses to emphasize the star career script and attempts to leverage his basketball skills rather than studying more, or when Daniel and Tyree elect to drop out of high school and take an alternative and riskier route to college that involves getting a GED. With exposure to multiple career and educational trajectories, information about potential pathways becomes diluted and information gaps result (dilution), as when Deon and Fernando assume that going to college is as simple as going from middle school to high school.

CHAPTER EIGHT **CONCLUSION**

In the introduction, I argued that understanding the role of neighbor-hoods in the lives of adolescent boys—the mechanisms by which neighbor-hood context affects their daily lives, their cultural models, their decision making, and their behavior—comes down to two linked questions. First, what are the social and cultural characteristics of poor neighborhoods that distinguish them from working- and middle-class neighborhoods? And second, how do these characteristics affect the boys growing up in poor neighborhoods? The first question is a neighborhood-level question: it connects the structural characteristics of an area, meaning the economic and social positions of the individuals who live in it, to the neighborhood's social and cultural characteristics, meaning the organization of social re-lations and the content of the cultural milieu. The second question is a truly *contextual* question in that it connects the neighborhood's social and cultural characteristics to the behavior of individual boys.

When neighborhood effects are conceptualized in this way, it becomes clear that although we have plausible answers to the first question, we understand considerably less about the second. The two dominant theo-ries of neighborhood effects on youth—social isolation theory and social organization theory—clearly specify how poor neighborhoods may differ from others. According to social isolation theory, poor urban neighbor-hoods, particularly those that are racially segregated, are isolated from mainstream institutions and social networks, leading to cultural isolation in which alternative cultural repertoires develop in response to blocked opportunities. Yet even if we accept this account of the cultural context of poor neighborhoods (which I do not), how this particular social and cultural environment is experienced by the youth who grow up in poor neighborhoods is significantly undertheorized. We are left with the rather vague explanation that youth make decisions regarding education and romantic and sexual relationships under the influence of the deviant local cultural milieu of their neighborhood peers. This explanation leaves almost no room for heterogeneity of outcomes or individual agency, although we know that most teens in poor neighborhoods don't get pregnant or drop out of school (though they do so in higher proportions than do teens in middle-class neighborhoods). According to social organization theory, poor neighborhoods lack the economic and institutional resources and strong social ties needed to exert social control over residents and to enforce commonly held norms. The result is that alternative forms of behavior, particularly deviant behavior like crime and violence, are free to emerge. Yet again, how this social and cultural environment is experienced by adolescents and leads to negative consequences—particularly in domains other than crime and violence—is undertheorized.

This book has argued that two characteristics of poor neighborhoods illuminate the mechanisms underlying neighborhood effects on adolescent boys: neighborhood violence and cultural heterogeneity. Beyond distinguishing poor neighborhoods from others, these neighborhood characteristics also affect the ways that boys and their parents evaluate and understand opportunities, consequences, potential pitfalls, and pathways to success. Living in a violent neighborhood colors the lens through which residents view their social worlds. Where the threat of violent victimization is omnipresent, it structures social relations, reinforces neighborhood identities, organizes local status hierarchies, and influences boys' use of space. I emphasize the role of cultural heterogeneity because it is a more accurate way to characterize the cultural context of poor neighborhoods and because of the theoretical importance of culture in decision making.

Though neighborhood differences in rates of violence and other crime have been the subject of much social science research, the social and cultural implications of living in a violent environment, where the threat of victimization is significant, have received less attention. Thus I have focused in this volume on the second of the two neighborhood questions discussed above: How does this particular neighborhood characteristic, violence, structure decision making and behavior? The role played by neighborhood violence in the daily lives of adolescent boys is a product of both its frequency and the way in which it is socially organized. In Boston much of the most serious violence results from cross-neighborhood rivalries, long-standing "beefs" that ebb and flow in intensity and bloodshed. These rivalries both structure and are structured by neighborhood identities—the strong emotional attachments to place and the people who live there that serve to demarcate insiders and outsiders, potential friends, and potential enemies. Though only a small minority of boys who live in these areas participate in the cycles of retribution and revenge that fuel neighborhood conflicts, all face the potential for victimization when they venture into rival neighborhoods and neutral territories. As a result, the neighborhood becomes a critical physical and social space, intensifying same-age friendships and facilitating cross-age interactions and cross-cohort socialization.

Because the neighborhoods in question are quite small and school attendance in Boston is not based on neighborhoods, boys must often leave the relative safety of their own neighborhoods, and they develop strategies to provide themselves with a measure of protection. The older boys and young men who sit atop the neighborhood social hierarchy because of their ability to navigate dangerous streets are potential sources of protection, both through direct intervention and—more importantly—through the status their association confers. In addition to their effect on physical safety, these interactions are also a key source of cross-cohort socialization, through which younger boys are introduced to local cultural models. Same-age peer groups also provide some protection through safety in numbers, and common experiences with danger and confrontation serve to strengthen bonds to neighborhood friends. These peer relations are also important in the transmission of local cultural ideas. More generally, these findings illustrate how adolescent social relations in poor neighborhoods are in part a product of the conditions of daily life in such neighborhoods—beyond individual and family circumstances. Moreover, adolescent social relations also reflect individuals' strategies for coping with the problems created by the conditions of daily life.

Violent neighborhoods provide plenty of negative role models—peers and young men involved in crime and violence—whose cultural power on the streets exceeds their actual numbers. These negative role models serve to level the expectations of parents and boys alike by redefining success. Parents focus on keeping boys away from prison, danger, violent behavior, and the underground economy, leaving less energy for parenting in other domains like schooling and romantic relationships. Greater violence in the neighborhood also exposes boys to greater contact with elements of the criminal justice system, particularly the police. For many, this is one of their first experiences of sustained contact with a major social institution other than school, and it is overwhelmingly negative. Being stopped and questioned by police leaves them feeling disrespected and mistreated.

At the same time, the failure of the police to actually make their neighborhoods safe—despite their power—leaves adolescents questioning (perhaps
correctly) whether society really cares about people like them. The result
is the development and reinforcement of a frame of institutional distrust,
a lens they bring to their interactions with authority figures in other institutions such as schools.

The canonical account of the cultural context of poor neighborhoods,
social isolation theory, holds that socially isolated neighborhoods develop
a separate subculture that leads to negative outcomes among youth. I have
argued that this description of the cultural context of poor neighborhoods
is inaccurate. Rather, adolescents in poor neighborhoods are exposed to
and grapple with both "mainstream" and "alternative" cultural models.
Each model receives social support in their neighborhoods. A weakness
of past qualitative research is that the definition of "mainstream" culture
was left vague or undefined. In this study, the inclusion of the Lower Mills
comparison neighborhood reveals that poor neighborhoods are distinguished by cultural heterogeneity, by a wide array of competing and conflicting cultural models.

Why are poor neighborhoods especially heterogeneous when it comes
to frames and scripts regarding schooling, work, and romantic and sexual
behavior? These neighborhoods contain a wider variety of lifestyles and
behaviors, many of which are visible in public space. As social organization theory predicts, residents of poor neighborhoods have less capacity
to regulate public behavior. However, local and nonlocal institutions such
as churches, schools, and the media transmit mainstream messages, and
these are taken seriously in poor neighborhoods. Though media by themselves may seem like a thin form of cultural exposure to mainstream life,
they are part of a set of institutions, both local and nonlocal, that produce
largely mutually reinforcing cultural messages.

Residents of poor neighborhoods experience the negative effects of heterogeneity through three processes: model shifting, dilution, and simultaneity. Model shifting occurs when adolescents switch among various competing cultural models because alternative models are readily available
and socially supported. Dilution occurs when information about any particular cultural model is diluted by the presence of many models. Simultaneity occurs when multiple competing models are mixed unsuccessfully.

Cultural heterogeneity helps us understand some of the ways in which
neighborhoods affect romantic and sexual behavior. Boys in culturally heterogeneous neighborhoods have at their disposal a wide array of frames
and scripts regarding girls, relationships, and responsible fatherhood.

Multiple frames for girls and relationships lead to a high degree of gender distrust, as boys may expect girls to act like "stunts" or "gold diggers" who will try to take advantage of them. In this cultural context, condom use becomes fraught with meaning, and social support for these alternative frames influences how boys understand their own relationships and contraceptive behavior. In initial encounters, condom use can signal lack of trust or interest in a long-term relationship. In longer-term relationships, boys may view their relationships as strong in light of their cultural context, and thus do not protect against the possibility of sexually transmitted infections or even pregnancy, believing that their relationships are ready for parenthood. Though boys take the responsibilities of fatherhood seriously, multiple frames for responsible fatherhood make the role easy to redefine and reinterpret, and this multiplicity dilutes information about what it actually takes to be a father.

Boys in culturally heterogeneous neighborhoods can also draw upon a wide array of frames and scripts regarding schooling and careers. Though they believe college is the key to future labor-market success, multiple scripts make it difficult for them to construct feasible pathways to their educational and career goals. They mix and match pieces of different scripts without realizing their incompatibility, and the availability of alternative pathways makes it easy to jump from one to another when barriers or challenges are encountered, often without understanding the long-term consequences and risks. Multiple models for educational and career success also dilute information about each, making it more difficult for boys to navigate access to complex postsecondary institutions.

Though for analytical purposes I have, up to this point, discussed neighborhood violence and cultural heterogeneity separately, they are theoretically linked as mechanisms underlying neighborhood effects. The cultural heterogeneity perspective evokes two key questions: How are adolescents exposed to alternative or "ghetto-specific" cultural models? And why do those models effectively compete with more mainstream models? Neighborhood violence helps us answer these questions. The cross-cohort socialization that violence encourages is an important source of such alternative models, as the older boys and young men who provide protection and sit atop neighborhood hierarchies have considerable cultural power. They model alternative behaviors and decisions and introduce and reinforce certain alternative cultural ideas, even while reinforcing more conventional ideas. Alternative models also resonate with the experiences of boys in violent neighborhoods, as violence leads to the development of institutional distrust and the leveling of mainstream expectations.

These arguments have implications for both social isolation and social organization theories of neighborhood effects. The findings in chapter 4 regarding the importance of neighborhood friends and neighborhood organizations for adolescents generally support the underlying premise of both theories—that neighborhood is an important context for adolescent social interaction. However, my argument calls into question one of the fundamental ideas of social isolation theory—that disadvantaged neighborhoods are isolated from mainstream or middle-class culture. Instead, I posit that disadvantaged neighborhoods contain a mix of mainstream and alternative cultural models. Social isolation theory may apply in the poorest, most segregated neighborhoods of former industrial cities like Chicago, but its predictions do not seem to hold in Boston's poor neighborhoods or—as my analysis of national survey data shows—in the typical poor neighborhoods in U.S. urban areas.

Rather, the findings in this study are generally supportive of neighborhood effects models based on social organization theory and move us toward understanding the mechanisms underlying these models. Social organization theory highlights the limited capacity of residents in disadvantaged communities to regulate the behaviors of their neighbors, particularly young people. Heterogeneity in cultural lifestyles or orientations can be understood as the failure of more middle-class or mainstream-oriented residents of disadvantaged neighborhoods to control behavior in their communities. The result of this failure is that neither "oppositional" nor "mainstream" behavior is dominant in disadvantaged communities. The importance of violence in structuring social relations and in contributing to the development of alternative cultural models also extends social organization theory by showing how a poor community's diminished capacity for regulation of behavior can have collateral consequences in other domains.

Toward a Culturally Informed Theory of Neighborhood Effects on Adolescents

In this volume I have endeavored to identify the main weaknesses in our understanding of the mechanisms that create neighborhood effects and to put forward theoretical and empirical arguments that develop a more complete picture of the key social and cultural processes implicated in such effects. In this section, I take a step back from the particulars of the data analyzed here and draw upon these arguments, as well as previous research, to propose a theory of the effects of poor neighborhoods on individual outcomes. To be successful, such a theory must (1) link structural differences in neighborhood characteristics to differences in outcomes across neighborhoods, (2) allow for heterogeneity of outcomes within neighborhoods, (3) allow for some degree of individual agency by considering individual decision making, (4) ensure that the theory presents an empirically accurate view of the cultural context of urban neighborhoods, and (5) explain how cultural and structural factors relate to one another.

To begin, I consider the neighborhood-level consequences of concentrated poverty. Social organization theory argues that neighborhoods with a large number of poor families will have weak capacity for collective action and the regulation of public behavior, due to low levels of collective efficacy, a product of weak social ties and institutional neglect. A long line of ethnographic research on poor communities also documents how poor individuals, when faced with discrimination and few opportunities, adapt to these circumstances by developing alternative lifestyles, status systems, and survival strategies. Youth growing up in such an environment come into contact with a different set of individuals and institutions than their counterparts in more advantaged neighborhoods. In the process of constructing their own identities and mapping out their futures, adolescents in these poor neighborhoods are exposed to a diversity of behaviors, cultural models, and lifestyles and to an environment in which violence and crime are commonplace.

Yet mere physical proximity to these problems does not by itself change individual behavior. Between structure and behavior lie culture and individual agency. Furthermore, competing influences, such as parents, religious institutions, schools, and the media, present youth with middle-class or mainstream cultural ideals that compete with the alternatives that are developed locally. Mainstream values continue to have strength, even as young people are presented with a heterogeneous array of frames, scripts, and other cultural models that make decision making difficult. The result is a cultural repertoire among youth in poor neighborhoods that is far more complex, conflicting, and confusing than that of their counterparts from more advantaged neighborhoods. In other words, neighborhood context plays an important role in structuring adolescents' cultural repertoires; a heterogeneous cultural environment leads to a heterogeneous cultural repertoire. The examples presented in chapters 6 and 7 illustrate how individual boys in Franklin and Roxbury Crossing struggle with the multiple cultural models in their repertoires. In turn, a heterogeneous repertoire leads to the dilution, model-shifting, and simultaneity problems that characterize decision making and behavior, as discussed above.

These problems are of course exacerbated by the other barriers that many youth from poor neighborhoods face, including those related to family background and racial discrimination.

Such a theory emphasizes the cognitive view of culture that has gained prominence in cultural sociology over the last two decades by drawing on concepts such as frames, scripts, and repertoires. A key theoretical advantage of this view of culture is that it allows for considerable individual agency. Individuals evaluate and employ various elements of their cultural repertoires in strategizing and decision making. Thus structural and cultural factors can constrain behavior without directly determining it. This also allows room for heterogeneity of outcomes among those who face the same or similar structural circumstances and cultural environment. Individuals facing the same structural circumstances and cultural environment will not necessarily have the same repertoires, as individual experiences and interpretations also influence repertoire construction. A second source of heterogeneity in outcomes is differential exposure to the cultural context of the neighborhood. Not all youth who live in a particular neighborhood have a great deal of social interaction with their neighbors, and therefore different boys in the same neighborhood can have different cultural repertoires.

This theory also provides an account of how neighborhood structural and cultural factors interact. Neighborhood structural characteristics affect the degree of heterogeneity in the neighborhood's cultural environment by shaping the lifestyle, behavior, and views of the older peers and adults who serve as models (both positive and negative) to local adolescents. Joblessness has long been cited as a critical structural characteristic of poor neighborhoods (Wilson 1996), and it plays a role in my account as well. High rates of joblessness, especially among younger adult males, mean that alternative lifestyles and behaviors are readily available for adolescent boys to observe and experience on the streets of poor neighborhoods. Cross-cohort socialization is possible only in neighborhoods where older adolescents and young adults are regularly present on the streets and available for social interaction rather than at work or in school.

Moreover, structural circumstances may also affect how individuals evaluate and deploy the elements of their cultural repertoires. Certain cultural frames and scripts will resonate more with youth from neighborhoods with particular structural characteristics. For example, as discussed in chapter 6, the "gold-digger" frame regarding girls resonates with the experiences of boys in poor neighborhoods, who see friends, family members, and neighbors struggling to provide basic necessities for their families. As discussed in chapter 7, the "star career" script also resonates with boys from poor neighborhoods because it promises remuneration sufficient to lift many others out of poverty as well. In other words, objective conditions of life in poor neighborhoods, such as limited labor-market and schooling opportunities and high levels of violence, and the daily experiences they engender, form the basis on which individuals evaluate and deploy cultural frames and scripts.

Such a theory suggests novel avenues for future theoretical and empirical research. A critical component linking cultural repertoires, decision making, and behavior is which of the cultural models from their repertoire adolescents choose to apply in any given circumstance. Yet beyond the notion of cultural resonance, how individuals choose to deploy some models and not others remains undertheorized, making this area ripe for future investigation. A second issue concerns the relationship between different domains. Although here I considered the domains of education and romantic and sexual relationship separately, I see considerable room for conflict across these domains in available frames and scripts. For example, the demands of a romantic partner may compete for time and attention with schooling. When and how individuals are able to resolve these contradictions and their consequences also warrant investigation. Third, to the extent that social relationships provide key conduits for the transmission of cultural models, it is critical to understand the social networks and time use of adolescents and how those differ across neighborhoods and individuals. This knowledge may help us understand heterogeneity of outcomes within neighborhoods, as adolescents who are differentially socially attached to a neighborhood will be differentially affected by it. Chapter 4 provides one example of an analysis of neighborhood social attachment, but it is necessarily incomplete, focusing largely on violence and neighborhood identity and limited to the sixty boys in this study. Fourth, I have focused primarily on comparisons across neighborhoods, but we also need to better understand variation of outcomes within neighborhoods. While concepts such as cultural heterogeneity and cultural resonance provide a potential framework for theorizing the sources of this variation, further empirical investigation is required.

Implications for Policy and Practice

A book about social problems like neighborhood poverty, school dropout, and early childbearing would seem incomplete without some discussion of the policy implications of its findings. In other words, given what we've

learned, what should be done? Before discussing this question, it is important to note that the research that forms the foundation of this book is not
policy research. That is, this research evaluates neither policies nor the
implementation of programs—either of which would be expected to lead
to specific policy recommendations. Rather, this book is about understanding the problems and challenges that adolescent boys growing up in poor
neighborhoods face as a result of the conditions of their neighborhoods.
Often the link between understanding the social and cultural processes
that create social problems and successful social policies to ameliorate
those problems is a loose one. Political will, the complexities of implementation, unintended consequences, and human agency all stand between
social science and effective social policy. As a result, the proverbial "policy
chapter" that often concludes books like this one typically overreaches
and underwhelms. My goal in this section is more modest. Rather than rec-
ommending specific programs or policies, I will focus on what the findings
of this study say about how policy makers should approach social policies
designed to improve the lives of adolescent boys like those of Roxbury
Crossing, Franklin, and—to some degree—Lower Mills.

The role that violence plays in structuring social networks and cultural
frameworks means that successful efforts to permanently reduce violence
in disadvantaged neighborhoods will produce benefits not just for safety,
emotional well-being, and health, but also likely for other domains such
as schooling and early childbearing. In evaluating the costs and benefits
of violence-reduction programs, the collateral consequences of violence
on school dropout and teenage pregnancy should be taken into account,
which may make antiviolence programs even more cost effective. Also,
efforts to reduce violence in poor neighborhoods must take into account
the ways violence is organized. For example, Boston's inner-city violence
is not just the product of interpersonal disputes or large highly organized
gangs. It is also driven by neighborhood rivalries, often sustained by small
numbers of individuals. The "Boston Miracle," a large drop in youth homicides during the late 1990s, was engineered by religious leaders, law
enforcement, street workers, and social service providers who recognized
the way youth violence is organized in Boston and targeted (with both
sanctions and services) the "impact players" who maintained the rivalries,
intervening when they appeared ready to turn bloody.

A key finding of this research is that violence is embedded in a system
of social relations and not just the result of individual decision making. As
such, it is not necessarily easily manipulated by changing costs and benefits for individuals, such as get-tough policies that increase prison time.

It is not at all clear that increased penalties for violent behavior make the "marginal" adolescent significantly less likely to engage in violence, as he must consider many other factors, not the least of which is his own physical safety should he fail to maintain loyalty to his peer group or fail to stand up for himself when tested. Moreover, for those "hard core" youth who drive neighborhood rivalries and ignore the long-term consequences of violent behavior, more severe sanctions may simply serve to disadvantage them further, as extended incarceration exacerbates their already tenuous connection to the labor market and produces a stigma that will disadvantage them for years to come. Although tougher legal sanctions by themselves may reduce violence at the margins, they are unlikely to be effective on a larger scale, given other exigencies, and any benefits they may yield are likely to be swamped by the long-term costs incurred by those harshly punished, not to mention the increased costs to taxpayers of prison and jails.[1] Instead we need more creative approaches to violence reduction that draw on an understanding of the social organization of youth violence to intervene in conflicts at key points, with key individuals, and with an appropriate combination of sanctions and services.

For those concerned with preventing early childbearing, an important lesson of this and other research is that contraceptive decisions are embedded in relationships and that early childbearing is not just the result of inexperience, lack of maturity, and one-night stands. We know from prior research that the longer a relationship between adolescents or young adults continues, the less consistently condoms are used (Fortenberry et al. 2002; Ku, Sonenstein, and Pleck 1994). Yet for too long, the public image of the role of males in teenage pregnancy in poor communities has been one in which boys are predators who trick girls into sexual activity without contraception and then abandon the children that result. While this sequence undoubtedly occurs, such "bad behavior" is not the typical story. Moreover, when relationships end in this way, such a pattern is not what boys intend at the beginning. The evidence presented in chapter 6 indicates that boys often see themselves as following conventional scripts for relationships and fatherhood (though delaying marriage), and that they see themselves and their partners as ready for childbearing when they judge the relationship to be strong by local standards. The problem is that conventional scripts are muddied and modified by the range of mixed messages and the context of gender distrust in poor neighborhoods. The message about the importance of condoms for the prevention of sexually transmitted infections has gotten through to the boys in this study—since such diseases are universally considered negative—but it does not necessarily extend to pregnancy. In poor neighborhoods, messages about pregnancy get distorted by the range of alternative ways of framing early fatherhood. Policies or programs that seek to change boys' intentions misunderstand the problem, and policies that seek to clarify the risks of early childbearing must help adolescents sort through the competing messages to which they are exposed. Policy makers and practitioners must also understand that contraceptive decisions are often made in the context of long-term relationships.

With regard to education, my findings indicate the importance of helping poor adolescents from poor neighborhoods to understand and navigate the complexities of educational institutions from an early age (middle school or earlier), when boys and their parents begin to make decisions, often unknowingly, with long-term ramifications for schooling. The problem is not that the benefits of high school graduation and a college education are undervalued. On the contrary, as chapter 7 discusses, postsecondary education was a goal of almost every boy, and they understood the labor-market consequences of failing to finish high school. Their troubles often lay instead in constructing realistic and informed pathways for achieving their educational goals. Immersed in a cultural environment that presents multiple competing educational and career options, from earning a GED and enrolling in community college to sports scholarships to big-name colleges to Job Corps, the ins and outs of these various pathways and the risks and opportunities associated with each were challenging to discern, particularly when others in the family had little experience with them. Though these pathways all lead toward postsecondary schooling or training, they are linked to decisions about high school. For example, since their goal was often enrollment in college, boys saw dropping out of high school and taking the GED exam as a viable option, without understanding the requirements of the GED exam or the risk of failing to pass it. With better access to the information that adolescents in middle-class schools or social networks take for granted, boys growing up in poor neighborhoods could make better schooling decisions. A simple lack of information is of course not the whole story of high school dropout or other educational disadvantages. Carter (2005) and Dance (2002), for example, have shown how middle-class teachers and school staff often misinterpret adolescent cultural practices or strategies to deal with street violence as oppositional behavior and create a school environment that is inhospitable and unwelcoming to such youth. Such cultural mismatch is important, but lack of information is another key piece of the puzzle.

Three patterns emerged from this research that have particular relevance for those running social programs for youth in poor, violent neighborhoods. First, social programs in poor neighborhoods are often overwhelmed, and as a result the most disadvantaged youth in such neighborhoods are the least likely to gain access to services. Resources will be quickly secured by the parents who are most adept at doing so, leaving little for youth who might benefit the most. These youth, often called "hard core" or "street" by social service providers, do not walk in the door on their own. If social programs are to reach out to these boys, they must go where these boys are: the corners, basketball courts, and porches where they hang out. These boys will put on a hard face and resist. Having been failed before by adults, they will test those who claim good intentions, but more often than not, persistence will be rewarded.

Second, service providers must also understand the organization of neighborhood violence and the way it structures where boys will go and with whom they will socialize. Social agencies may have a hard time providing safe, welcoming environments if they ignore these realities of neighborhood life. Third, a social services gap often exists for teens between the ages of thirteen and fifteen. At thirteen, youth are too old for most summer camps and after-school programs, but they are unable to work until age sixteen. During the key developmental period of early adolescence, when independent social identities are being formed, peer pressures are strongly felt, and experimentation is the norm, youth are most disconnected from mainstream institutions other than school and most susceptible to the cross-cohort socialization I have described.

Finally and most generally, my research and this book can help reorient how we think about the cultural context of poor neighborhoods and, by extension, of poverty. I have argued that rather than being characterized by a subculture distinct from mainstream society, poor neighborhoods are more accurately described as culturally heterogeneous. In particular, the goals and values that most Americans subscribe to—education, hard work, marriage, and family—are also dominant in poor neighborhoods. Poor neighborhoods are distinguished by the presence of competing cultural models that vie for the loyalties of youth. Yet many of our social policies seem to assume that the poor have different values and that strong incentives are needed to encourage behavior that accords with mainstream values of work, schooling, and marriage. While not denying the conflicting incentives sometimes created by social policies like welfare, I argue that the challenge in poor neighborhoods is not a lack of mainstream values and goals: it is a lack of access to the tools and resources needed to realize them, as well as lack of the knowledge and information necessary to take advantage of such tools and resources. In other words, by misdiagnosing the problem, social policies that assume that the poor are somehow culturally "defective" waste precious resources on issues like compliance with requirements that could be put to better use helping the poor realize the goals we all share.

APPENDIX: FIELDWORK METHODOLOGY

My fieldwork involved in-depth, unstructured interviews with sixty adolescent boys ages thirteen to eighteen living in three predominantly African American areas of Boston, with twenty boys per area. The areas were selected to allow for explicit comparisons between similar youth who live in neighborhoods that vary on a key structural characteristic: the poverty rate. Two of the areas ("Roxbury Crossing" and "Franklin") have high rates of family poverty (between 35 and 40 percent in the 2000 census). The third area ("Lower Mills") has a low poverty rate (below 10 percent). Each area consists of two contiguous census tracts. Selected characteristics from the 2000 census are provided in table A.1. Franklin and Roxbury Crossing have many of the social and economic characteristics associated with high-poverty neighborhoods, including lower proportions of workers in professional and managerial occupations, fewer affluent families, greater receipt of public assistance, lower levels of education, more female-headed families, and greater unemployment. In contrast, Lower Mills exhibits the characteristics of relatively more advantaged areas, such as more owner-occupied housing, low unemployment, higher levels of education, less receipt of public assistance, and more affluent families. As I have defined them, Roxbury Crossing, Franklin, and Lower Mills are geographic areas of the city rather than social neighborhoods. Each area encompasses multiple locales that more closely approximate neighborhoods that residents recognize as such. Yet the neighborhoods within each area share broadly parallel histories, demographic and structural characteristics, and relations to the larger Boston metropolitan region.

The interviews investigated how the subjects think about their neighborhoods as geographic and social spaces and how that overlaps with their social networks, daily travel, and contact with institutions (see chapter 4). It is important to note that when the boys and their parents describe their neighborhoods, they are referring to very small spaces, often only a few blocks in any direction. The boundaries of these limited spaces are to some degree reinforced by the geographic patterning of violence described in

TABLE A.1. Selected characteristics of study fieldwork areas

	Franklin (tracts 924 & 1001)	Roxbury Crossing (tracts 805 & 806)	Lower Mills (tracts 1004 & 1009)	City of Boston
Demographics				
Black	75%	56%	64%	25%
Hispanic	25%	33%	6%	14%
Female	55%	54%	55%	52%
Children (age 0–17)	38%	33%	27%	20%
Foreign born	27%	23%	26%	26%
Socioeconomic status				
Family poverty	36%	38%	10%	15%
Median household income in 1999	$23,157	$15,371	$43,973	$39,629
Managerial/professional occupation	30%	44%	55%	70%
Affluent families (1999 income > $75K)	8%	4%	27%	26%
Households with public-assistance income, 1999	15%	9%	3%	4%
College education (age >25)	7%	10%	22%	36%
Less than high school education (age >25)	38%	35%	20%	21%
Female-headed families (with children)	65%	69%	41%	40%
Male joblessness (age 16–59)	45%	51%	35%	31%
Male unemployment (age 16–59)	15%	14%	6%	8%
Residential stability				
Owner-occupied housing	22%	6%	51%	32%
Same residence 5 years ago	59%	55%	61%	48%
Density (people/square mile)	22,750	17,314	17,253	12,172
Total population	11,900	6,166	9,567	589,141

SOURCE: Author's calculations from 2000 census data.
NOTE: Male joblessness is number of working-age (age 16–59) employed males divided by population of working-age males. Male unemployment is number of working-age (age 16–59) employed males divided by working-age males in labor force (working or actively searching for work).

chapter 2. The terms "Roxbury Crossing," "Franklin," and "Lower Mills" serve as shorthand to delineate the three study areas and to provide anonymity for the research subjects by broadening the geographic scope of reference. I use the term "neighborhood" to refer to the geographic and social spaces defined by the subjects, and the term "area" to distinguish the three larger study areas. As in previous research (e.g., Furstenberg et al.

1999; Furstenberg and Hughes 1997), there was great variation in subjects' conceptions of their neighborhoods (even among neighbors) and the degree to which their neighborhoods overlapped with their social networks. For this reason, and because long-form census data are not generally available at such small levels of aggregation, I do not attempt to report characteristics for subject-defined neighborhoods.

The adolescent male interview subjects were black, Latino, or mixed race, with Latinos being primarily of Puerto Rican or Dominican descent. Each boy was interviewed multiple times, with at least two sessions per subject and sometimes as many as four. Multiple interview sessions were required to cover all the material in detail, but they also provided the benefit of repeated interactions between the interviewer and subject, which can serve to build trust and rapport (Eder and Fingerson 2003). For 80 percent of the subjects, a single interview was conducted with a family member, almost always the mother, to understand a caretaker's perspective on the neighborhood and on the young man's experiences. The adult interviews also provided a check on the accounts and experiences offered by the adolescent boys.

Each interview session lasted from sixty to ninety minutes. Most interviews took place in the subject's home, but some were conducted in community centers and occasionally in a park or coffee shop. Each youth or parent was paid $20 per interview session. While some scholars question the practice of compensating research subjects on the grounds that it may result in an unrepresentative sample or influence answers or even subsequent behavior, doing so is becoming the norm in social science and medical research. In this study, subjects were asked to spend up to several hours of their time doing the interviews, so it was important for them to know in advance they would get something out of the study as well. I believe that not paying subjects for their time would have been interpreted as taking advantage of them, especially given the sensitive nature of some of the interview topics, and would have been interpreted as disrespectful of the subjects and their communities. Subject payments were also an important recruitment tool, though I do not believe they influenced the content of the interviews once a subject agreed to participate, nor were the payments large enough to appreciably affect their behavior or life circumstances.

The interviews with the boys and their family members were conducted in two stages. Fourteen pilot subjects were first interviewed in September, October, or November 2003. The remainder of the interviews were conducted between May and August 2004. Subjects were promised individual anonymity but were informed that the general locations of their neighborhoods would be disclosed. All names used in this book are pseudonyms. Table A.2 displays demographic characteristics for each adolescent male subject.

In summer 2003, prior to the pilot interviews, I interviewed fifty community leaders, religious leaders, youth workers, social workers, and school officials who were knowledgeable about particular neighborhoods or about youth in the city in general. These "neighborhood informants" included parish priests, African American ministers, administrators of social service agencies and community centers, school principals and teachers, tenant leaders, business leaders, public housing managers, and—most importantly—street workers or youth workers from community centers, health centers, nonprofits, and city government who worked with Boston youth on a daily basis. Neighborhood informant interviews provided background information on the fieldwork neighborhoods, youth issues in Boston, and entrée into the fieldwork neighborhoods. Many neighborhood informants assisted with contacting boys and their parents. The neighborhood informants also provided an additional check on the boys' accounts and descriptions of their neighborhoods. Two research assistants and I conducted a total of 233 interview sessions (188, or 81 percent, of which were conducted by me). During the fieldwork period, I also attended weekly community meetings and other events in which youth issues, particularly youth violence, were discussed by community members, police, ministers, social workers, street workers, and the youth themselves. These meetings provided important background and context for preparing for and understanding the interviews with individual youth.

The youth interviews centered on three general topics. First was the relationship between the young man's geographic neighborhood and "social" neighborhood, including peer networks, use of neighborhood and nonneighborhood institutions and organizations, time use, and local and extended family. Second was the young man's experience with school and work, including plans for the future. Third was the young man's experience with girls, romantic and sexual relationships, contraception, and fatherhood, including plans for the future and views toward marriage and child rearing. The emphasis on violence in the first half of this book emerged from the initial round of pilot interviews. At the start of the research, violence was not specifically included in the interview protocol. This was also the case for the age of friends and other peers. Yet both themes, and the connection between them, were clearly important differences across neighborhoods even from the small set of pilot interviews, so more specific questions were included in the final protocol used during the main period of fieldwork.

For forty-eight (80 percent) of the adolescent boys, a family member who was one of the boys' primary caretakers was also interviewed. These family members included thirty-nine mothers, four fathers, three grandmothers, one stepmother, and one adult brother. The family-member interview included a brief life history, a discussion of the neighborhood, a discussion of parenting attitudes and strategies, and a discussion of the subject's views of the boy's educational, work, and relationship experiences as well as prospects for the future in those areas. The goals of the family-member interview were (1) securing an alternative, adult account of the boys' experiences; (2) securing an alternative, adult account of the social and cultural neighborhood environment; and (3) understanding parenting practices, particularly, though not exclusively, as they related to neighborhood context.

With a qualitative research design and a small sample size, representativeness of recruited subjects is not possible. Rather, the goal was to interview a broad cross section of boys in each neighborhood, rather than just those adolescents most visible on the street who are often the focus of research on youth in disadvantaged neighborhoods. In particular, a key goal was to interview boys from various family socioeconomic backgrounds in each study area to allow for cross-neighborhood contrasts of comparable adolescent boys. In other words, efforts were made to recruit boys from more disadvantaged family backgrounds in the low-poverty area (Lower Mills) and boys from more advantaged family backgrounds in the high-poverty areas (Franklin and Roxbury Crossing). The final sample was by no means balanced across study areas in terms of family background. For example, 10 percent of the boys in both Franklin and Roxbury Crossing lived with married or cohabiting biological parents, whereas 30 percent of those in Lower Mills did so. However, there was enough diversity within each area to allow for reasonable cross-neighborhood comparisons of boys with similar family backgrounds. In other words, although the mean characteristics of the three groups of boys were not identical, there was sufficient overlap across the areas to allow for meaningful individual-level comparisons of boys in low-poverty with boys in high-poverty areas.

The ability to make comparisons across neighborhoods is a key aspect of this study's research design. By asking similar questions and discussing the same topics with individuals in different types of neighborhoods, key differences in the daily lives of adolescent boys in those neighborhoods can be revealed. For example, it was only through these explicit

TABLE A.2. Demographic characteristics of adolescent male research subjects

Pseudonym	Study area	Age	Race/ ethnicity	Family structure	School enrollment
Andrew	Franklin	15	Latino	Single mother	Public middle school
Chris	Franklin	14	Black	Single mother	Public alternative school
Dalton	Franklin	15	Black	Single mother	Charter school
David	Franklin	17	Black	Single mother	Public high school
Denzel	Franklin	15	Black	Single mother	Suburban high school
Fernando	Franklin	15	Latino	Father + stepmother	Charter school
Jared	Franklin	18	Black	Single mother	High school graduate
Joseph	Franklin	15	Latino/ white	Parents cohabiting	Public high school
Junior	Franklin	15	Black	Single mother	Public high school
Manuel	Franklin	14	Latino	Single mother	Public middle school
Montel	Franklin	15	Black	Single mother	Public alternative school
Paul	Franklin	14	Black	Single mother	Public middle school
Ramiro	Franklin	16	Latino	Mother + stepfather	Public high school
Reed	Franklin	15	Black	Single mother	Public high school
Rico	Franklin	16	Latino	Mother + stepfather	Dropout
Sean	Franklin	14	Black	Aunt	Public middle school
Shaquille	Franklin	18	Black	Mother + stepfather	High school graduate
Simon	Franklin	16	Black	Single mother	Dropout
Tamarr	Franklin	14	Black	Single father	Public middle school
Terrell	Franklin	16	Black	Parents married	Public high school
Aaron	Roxbury Crossing	13	Black	Single mother	Suburban middle school
Daniel	Roxbury Crossing	17	Black	Single mother	Dropout
Deon	Roxbury Crossing	13	Black	Grandmother	Charter school
Dillan	Roxbury Crossing	14	Black	Single mother	Public middle school
Duante	Roxbury Crossing	17	Black	Single mother	Public high school
Dustin	Roxbury Crossing	15	Black/ Latino	Single mother	Charter school
Eduardo	Roxbury Crossing	17	Latino	Single mother	Dropout
Edwin	Roxbury Crossing	15	Black	Single mother	Charter school
Elijah	Roxbury Crossing	13	Black	Parents married	Public middle school
Emilio	Roxbury Crossing	13	Black/ Latino	Single mother	Public middle school
Ivan	Roxbury Crossing	15	Latino	Single mother	Public high school

TABLE A.2. (*continued*)

Pseudonym	Study area	Age	Race/ ethnicity	Family structure	School enrollment
Jamar	Roxbury Crossing	14	Black	Aunt	Public middle school
James	Roxbury Crossing	14	Black	Single mother	Charter school
Jerome	Roxbury Crossing	13	Black	Single mother	Public middle school
Malcolm	Roxbury Crossing	13	Latino	Grandparents	Public middle school
Marcus	Roxbury Crossing	16	Black	Grandmother	Public high school
Miguel	Roxbury Crossing	16	Latino	Parents married	Public high school
Ramon	Roxbury Crossing	17	Latino	Grandmother	Dropout
Tyree	Roxbury Crossing	17	Black	Single mother	Dropout
Zach	Roxbury Crossing	14	Black	Single mother	Public middle school
Bradley	Lower Mills	13	Black	Grandmother	Charter school
Charles	Lower Mills	15	Black	Single mother	Public high school
Coleman	Lower Mills	17	Black	Grandmother	Public high school
Cyril	Lower Mills	16	Black	Father + stepmother	Public high school
Dante	Lower Mills	16	Black	Parents married	Public high school
Darnell	Lower Mills	13	Black	Single mother	Suburban high school
Delbert	Lower Mills	14	Black	Single mother	Suburban high school
Elton	Lower Mills	17	Black	Parents married	Home schooled
Esteban	Lower Mills	17	Black/ Latino	Parents married	Religious school
Isaac	Lower Mills	13	Black	Foster mother	Public middle school
Jason	Lower Mills	18	Black	Parents married	Private school
Jordan	Lower Mills	13	Black	Mother + grandmother	Public middle school
Kevin	Lower Mills	13	Black	Mother + aunt	Public middle school
Marshall	Lower Mills	17	Black	Parents married	Public high school
Nathan	Lower Mills	17	Black	Single mother	Charter school
Reynard	Lower Mills	13	Black	Single mother	Public middle school
Seth	Lower Mills	14	Black	Single mother	Public middle school
Tavon	Lower Mills	18	Black	Single mother	Dropout
Timothy	Lower Mills	14	Black	Parents married	Public high school
William	Lower Mills	16	Black	Single mother	Suburban high school

NOTE: "School enrollment" refers to school last attended if interviewed in summer between middle school and high school. "Public schools" are Boston public schools. "Alternative" schools are for students removed from a regular public school for behavioral problems.

comparisons that differences across neighborhoods were revealed in boys' experiences of violence and threat of victimization, in the role of older males in social networks, and in gender distrust.

I used a variety of procedures to recruit the research subjects. First, subjects were recruited through the social networks of the neighborhood informants. Since this was a diverse group, ranging from ministers to street workers to ex-convicts, the young people recruited in this way were also a diverse group. Second, I posted flyers around the neighborhoods that read,

> Young Men (13–18) Needed to Participate in Study of Boston Neighborhoods; Harvard Researcher seeks families with teenage sons or grandsons for interviews about Boston Neighborhoods and Boston Schools; Compensation Provided; Everyone interviewed will be paid $20 per interview; All Interviews Confidential and Anonymous; Time and Location are Flexible—We'll come to you when it is convenient for you.

The flyers included my name, cell-phone number, and e-mail address. The flyers also generated a diverse set of subjects. It was primarily parents and other guardians who responded to these flyers, but they varied considerably. On one extreme were parents who regularly grabbed any opportunity for their son and saw the chance to talk to a university researcher as yet another potentially positive experience. On the other extreme were parents who were at the end of their wits in controlling their sons' behavior and were hoping the interview experience would serve as a positive shock. Finally, I recruited fourteen subjects through snowball sampling, recruiting the friends of other subjects. Neighborhood informants were recruited for participation through letters to heads of key institutions and organizations and at community meetings and events. Because there was a greater density of community centers and youth services in the two high-poverty areas, recruitment of youth subjects through neighborhood informants was more successful there. In contrast, flyers were relied upon more frequently in Lower Mills, where they were delivered door to door in areas not already represented among the subjects. Snowball sampling was responsible for similar numbers of subjects in each neighborhood. In Franklin, fourteen subjects were recruited through neighborhood informants, four through snowball sampling, and two through flyers. In Roxbury Crossing, ten subjects were recruited through neighborhood informants, four through snowball sampling, and six through flyers. In Lower Mills, five subjects were recruited through neighborhood informants, six through snowball sampling, eight through flyers, and one through a meeting on the street.

Within the domain of qualitative studies of neighborhoods, there are multiple possible research methodologies, each with its own strengths and weaknesses. Qualitative neighborhood studies are typically single-neighborhood ethnographies (recent examples include Patillo-McCoy 1998; Small 2004; and Kefalas 2003). However, I chose to pursue in-depth unstructured interviews rather than ethnography, focus groups, or other methodologies. First, interviews allow for an efficient research design when the research question is already theoretically well-defined, when comparison across contexts is necessary, when diversity of individuals within neighborhoods is required, and when only certain content domains are included in the scope of the project. Interview topics and subject recruitment can be tailored to specific research goals. Second, interviews provide subjects the opportunity to reflect on and discuss their experiences and views privately, which is particularly important when what subjects think is a key part of the study (Young 2004). Particularly with issues like sexual behavior and romantic relationships, adolescents tend to discuss them in joking or playful terms when doing so in a group, so interview-based studies are common when these topics are involved (Eder and Fingerson 2003). Interviews remove the need for subjects to perform for peers or others with whom they will have future interactions or with whom they need be concerned about the repercussions of their statements. This, of course, is a weakness as well as a strength. As Goffman (1959) has argued, all social interaction is to some degree performance, and research interviews are no exception. Subjects may also perform for the researcher, particularly when the researcher is not a fixture in the natural setting of the subject's daily life and therefore is less able to check the veracity of subjects' statements. Gathering data from multiple sources—boys, parents, neighborhood informants—as I have done here, can provide only a partial check. Using friendship networks to recruit subjects, as was done for some of the subjects in this study, provides another source of information, as friends were asked to describe one another and their interactions and activities together.

Yet even when boys tell somewhat exaggerated stories of their experiences or act to impress an outside interviewer, the way they construct their narratives—the identification of key actors, the categories they use to describe individuals, groups, or events, and the cause-and-effect interpretations they attach to events—reveal as much about their understandings of their social worlds as the "facts" of their stories. Given that a primary goal of this research is to comprehend how the subjects interpret and understand their social interactions, neighborhood contexts, and prospects for the future, how the subjects construct and relate their narratives is as important as the details of the actual events. That said, however, aside from the hyperbole that is regularly a part of adolescent male discourse, I uncovered only a few outright falsehoods and report only results based on consistent patterns across multiple subjects.

Challenges of Interviewing Adolescent Boys

Interviewing the youngest boys, those ages thirteen and fourteen, proved to be one of the main fieldwork challenges in this research. It should come as no surprise that young adolescent boys vary widely in their ability and willingness to articulate their thoughts. In addition, their lack of experiences with some topics of conversation, such as sexual and romantic relationships, made it difficult for them to elaborate their opinions and views with concrete examples. There was considerable variation, however, in the degree to which this was an issue, and it was not a concern at all for most of the boys. The challenge was selecting specific topics around which to have a conversation without leading the boys too much by introducing issues that they did not regularly think about already. In order to keep the discussions concrete and grounded, the interviews focused on the boys' own experiences and their understandings of those experiences.

When it became necessary to abstract away from the subjects' own daily experiences to understand their expectations for the future or their strategies for dealing with potential problems, interview techniques were used that would at least allow the conversation to be grounded in concrete ideas. For example, one technique was using vignettes to allow for discussion of a particular situation, dilemma, or decision. The vignettes were paragraph-long stories about different problems or decisions that adolescent boys might confront. They included (1) fights between groups of boys, (2) competing priorities for school effort, particularly girlfriends, (3) choosing which school to go to, (4) being judged by one's clothing and appearance, (5) a girlfriend who does not want to have sex, (6) deciding what to do after a girlfriend becomes pregnant, (7) resolving a conflict between mother and girlfriend, and (8) deciding whether to marry the mother of one's baby. Each vignette was presented and then followed by a set of debriefing questions designed to elicit the subject's opinions about how to react to the situation and what the consequences of various reactions would be. These questions also included a variety of additional details or contingencies for the vignette to probe the range of responses. An initial set of vignettes was constructed and then revised after testing during the pilot interviews. The challenge in constructing the vignettes was to create a story that presented the subject with a difficult decision (one in which social desirability did not immediately suggest a particular response) and that led to variation in responses across subjects. Swidler 2001 contains another example of vignettes.

A second technique was to introduce into the interview a few paper survey questions that asked for subjects' attitudes and opinions. They covered the subject's own and the subject's parents' aspirations and expectations for schooling; expectations regarding marriage, fatherhood, income, and safety; and consequences of getting someone pregnant. At various points in the conversation, the minisurveys were administered, and then the subject's responses were debriefed. They proved especially useful in requiring subjects to be more specific in their responses and in opening up topics of conversation that were potentially embarrassing for adolescent boys to talk about. The questions were taken from the Wave 1 In-home questionnaire of Add Health (which improved interpretation of survey questions used in subsequent analyses of these survey data). An initial set of questions was tested in the pilot interviews and then pared down based on subject responses. Both vignettes and minisurveys were used after more open-ended questions so as not to affect subjects' responses to open-ended questions.

The third technique, also borrowed from the Add Health questionnaire, was to administer a set of "relationship script" questions. This required the subject to think about his ideal relationship and then sort a set of relationship events into the order he would like them to occur, removing unwanted events. The same task was repeated for one actual romantic relationship. Following each sorting, the relationship script was debriefed. The subject was asked to explain how and why he ordered the events in a particular way, how a particular ordering came about in the actual relationship, what the experiences were like, and any differences between the ideal and actual relationship scripts. This also proved useful in eliciting additional detail regarding romantic and sexual relationships.

Another challenge of the interviews was the "social distance" between the interviewer and the subjects. The author (a white male from a middle-class background in his late twenties at the time of the interviews) conducted the vast majority of the interviews. A number of techniques were used to bridge the social distance between interviewer and subject.

First, because I spent a year living and working in inner-city Boston as a community organizer and was already at least somewhat familiar with the study neighborhoods, I could subtly signal my "insider" knowledge of the places and institutions (and sometimes people) discussed in the interviews. For example, asking whether the basketball hoop had been fixed yet in the local park favored by the subject or noting some new store in a commercial strip could indicate a more long-term presence in the community and establish common reference points for the discussion. Second, the interviews always started with the least invasive topics, beginning with sports, movies, music, and video games, progressing to neighborhood, friends and family, school, and finally romantic and sexual relationships and fatherhood. This allowed rapport and trust to build over time during the interview and across interview sessions before more sensitive topics were discussed. Very quickly in the first interview, almost all subjects became enthusiastic about participation and required little extra pushing to articulate their ideas (and sometimes offered even more detail than was really necessary, particularly on romantic and sexual behavior). No subject refused to participate in a second or third interview after experiencing the initial interview.

Third, the interviews were framed for the subjects as being their chance to play the "expert" on the local neighborhood and to tell the interviewer about what living in the neighborhood is really like. Most subjects seemed to enjoy being the expert on their neighborhoods and their experiences in the context of the interview. This framing quickly upended their expectations about the interviewer based on prior experiences, and reduced the power dynamics that are particularly at play in interviews with youth (Eder and Fingerson 2003). Most of their prior interactions with adult men, particular white men, were in institutional settings such as schools, health care clinics, or criminal justice institutions where the subjects had little or no power or authority and were not allowed to express their opinions or views. Once it became clear that the purpose of the interview was to allow them to tell their stories from their perspective, they became engaged.

Fourth, outsider status, while certainly a disadvantage in some of the ways discussed above, can also be an advantage. Because an outside interviewer is removed from the subjects' social networks, there are fewer ramifications to information disclosure in the interview setting. There is little chance that information, attitudes, and displays of emotion or distress conveyed in the interview will reach others in a subject's social network. Subjects displayed many behaviors in the interviews that might lead to "loss of face" on the street, including the pain of feeling abandoned by their fathers, their desire to separate from their neighborhood peer group out of fear for physical safety, and their desire to eventually marry their girlfriend.

Fifth, as a partial check on the importance of social distance between interviewer and subject, two African American male students (one a graduate student and one an advanced undergraduate) also conducted interviews with some of the subjects. Both of these interviewers had either prior personal or professional experience with the subject population. The analysis detected no differences between interviewers in the boys' willingness to share their experiences and views or in the types of experiences or views they recounted.

Finally, given Boston's history of racial strife, it is important to understand how race did—and did not—play a role in the fieldwork. Race and ethnicity was far more salient in the parent interviews than in the interviews with the adolescent boys. Black parents discussed, and lamented, racial changes in the neighborhood as Latinos moved into Boston's public housing, and Latino parents often blamed blacks for violence and other neighborhood problems. Some black parents also expressed considerable distrust of whites—particularly the working-class whites associated with South Boston and past conflicts over busing—and white-controlled institutions such as city hall and the police. Yet, as has been reported elsewhere (e.g., Carter 2005), race was far less salient to adolescents. Many reported having friends of other racial or ethnic groups, and because large-scale Latino immigration is relatively new in Boston, there is less history of conflict between black and Latino gangs than in other cities such as Chicago or Los Angeles (Sullivan 1989 also reports little interethnic gang conflict in the three New York neighborhoods he studied). Boston is a relatively small city, and racial isolation is less severe than in larger cities. In contrast to what one might expect from neighborhoods on the south side of Chicago, for example, most residents of the study areas regularly see whites in their neighborhoods and interact with whites in stores, schools, or other institutional settings. Other than the "social distance" issues discussed above, I experienced no racial hostility. This may have been in part due to my affiliation with Harvard University, which clearly distinguished me from the white working class of South Boston and which has a positive reputation in many of Boston's poor communities as a result of the community service projects (summer camps, after-school programs, mentoring programs) that Harvard undergraduates run with university and community support.

Analysis

With the permission of the subjects, interviews were recorded and transcribed for analysis. As the fieldwork progressed, I wrote a series of memos on emerging patterns, a strategy suggested by Lofland and Lofland (1995). These memos then informed revisions to the interview protocols after the pilot interviews. The importance of older peers was not hypothesized in advance but rather emerged from the neighborhood informant interviews and the initial set of pilot interviews in Roxbury Crossing and Franklin. It was not until the revised protocol that explicit probes about age of friends and acquaintances were incorporated into the interviews, which was critical for examining differences across neighborhoods. Similarly, neighborhood violence was not a focal topic in the fieldwork until after the pilot interviews, when it became clear that violence and fear of victimization structured much of the boys' use of space and social networks in Roxbury Crossing and Franklin, and that this was a key difference between neighborhoods in these two areas and those in Lower Mills.

After all interviews were complete, transcripts were coded into categories using Atlas.ti, based on codes generated in two ways. One type of code included a priori theoretical perspectives derived from prior research and theory. The second type included codes generated from preliminary findings described in the memos. (A full list of codes and their descriptions, too long to include here, is available from me.) The final set of coded transcripts allowed two complementary modes of analysis. Person-centered analysis was conducted by considering each subject individually to understand the relevance of various theoretical concepts to his perspectives and daily experiences, for example, reading through coded transcripts one by one and noticing the connection between the "peers-age" code and the "neighborhood rivalries" code among Franklin and Roxbury Crossing subjects. Once key themes emerged (or having already emerged from the memos, were confirmed in the systematically coded data), a neighborhood-centered analysis was conducted by comparing interview data in theoretical categories across neighborhoods. Using Atlas, I generated queries based on codes and compared coded quotes systematically across neighborhoods to understand the key differences across neighborhoods. These sets of quotes then became the basis for the initial book draft, as they indicated which interviews contained the clearest and most complete examples. As this evidence was introduced into the book, however, I returned to reading the whole transcript for each interview to understand the larger context of the quotes extracted using the Atlas software.

Fieldwork Neighborhoods

The objective in selecting fieldwork areas was to allow explicit comparisons between similar youth in structurally different neighborhoods, in other words to compare youth in advantaged neighborhoods with youth in disadvantaged neighborhoods. I selected two high-poverty areas and one low-poverty area. In Boston, high-poverty neighborhoods vary depending on their geographic position within the city, with some neighborhoods geographically isolated from mainstream institutions and some proximate to mainstream institutions. I selected one geographically isolated high-poverty neighborhood and one nonisolated high-poverty neighborhood. This allowed me to focus on neighborhood processes that are common to both types of high-poverty neighborhoods.[1]

Based on data from the 2000 U.S. census and my own initial investigations and observations of six high-poverty and five low-poverty African American areas in the Boston area, I selected three fieldwork areas, each consisting of two adjacent census tracts. Roxbury Crossing and Franklin are high-poverty areas, while Lower Mills is a low-poverty area. They are indicated on figure A.1, a map of census-tract poverty in Boston based on the 2000 census (darker is higher poverty). Selected characteristics from the 2000 census are listed in table A.1, and each area is described in chapter 1 and its notes. Neighborhood-specific maps are displayed in figures A.2 through A.4.

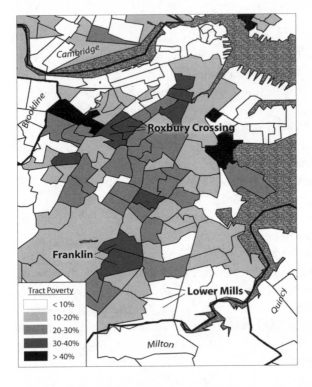

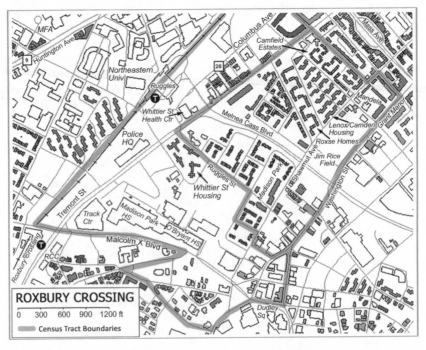

Figure A.1. (left) Neighborhood poverty in Boston (2000 census tracts)

Figure A.2. (below) Map of Roxbury Crossing

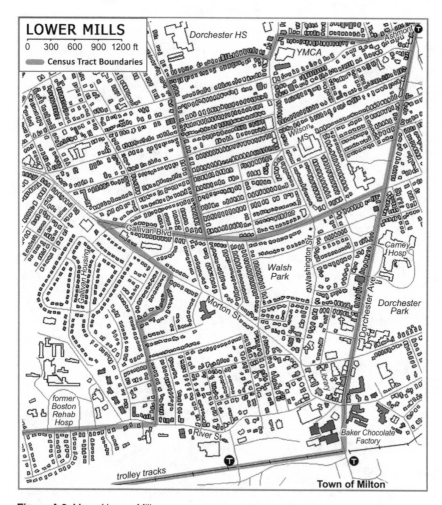

Figure A.3. Map of Lower Mills

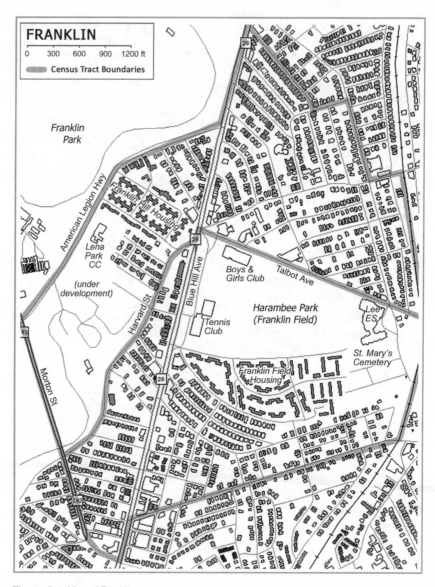

Figure A.4. Map of Franklin

NOTES

Chapter one

1. This image covered almost a third of the front page of the *Boston Globe*'s "City and Region" section on June 24, 2004.
2. The Orchard Park development was renamed Orchard Gardens after the start of its renovation through HUD's HOPE VI program.
3. Suzanne Smalley, "Raid hits '24-hour' drug ring; 15 in Roxbury arrested," *Boston Globe*, June 24, 2004, B1, B4.
4. Ralph Ranalli, "Teen died as he lived—helping others: Sullivan fatally stabbed aiding friend in fight," *Boston Globe*, July 9, 2004, B1, B4.
5. Three explanations have been offered for the higher rates of teenage childbearing among the urban poor (Small and Newman 2001). The peer-culture hypothesis holds that among poor urban women early childbearing is a source of status among peers (Anderson 1999). The weathering hypothesis holds that early childbearing is a rational response to the deteriorating health of urban poor women as they age, making the teen years the optimal period for healthy childbearing. Finally, the poverty-of-relationships hypothesis holds that teenage girls have children to compensate for a lack of other meaningful social relationships and for lack of prospects for finding rewarding work.
6. Wilson's account of the creation of concentrated poverty neighborhoods has not gone unchallenged. Massey and Denton (1993) criticize Wilson for ignoring the continued importance of racial discrimination, especially in the housing market (see Yinger 1995). They argue that blacks of all classes experience similar levels of racial segregation. Middle-class blacks could not escape the ghetto, as new ghettos formed when whites moved out and blacks moved in. Massey and Denton claim that racial segregation is behind the concentration of poverty. As the black poverty rate rose, the concentration of blacks, created by continued high levels of residential segregation, caused black-neighborhood poverty rates to rise as well. However, while residential segregation by race clearly accounts for the historical persistence of high levels of neighborhood poverty among blacks, as Jargowsky (1997; Jargowsky and Bane 1991) and Quillian (1999) point out, residential segregation by race has been declining, so it cannot account for an increasing concentration of poverty among blacks over time.

   The first aspect of Wilson's thesis, regarding the decline in manufacturing, has also met with considerable challenge, mostly from critics who contend that it applies only to Chicago and perhaps other northern industrial cities. Jargowsky (1997) notes that manufacturing employment never paid very well outside the North and that the decline in manufacturing employment is not correlated with increasing concentrations of poverty. Orfield and Ashkinaze (1991) argue that in Atlanta blacks fared poorly during the 1970s and 1980s despite a strong economy and political control of the city. Waldinger (1996) shows that blacks were never well integrated into the manufacturing sector in New York City and that manufacturing in New York is not a high-wage sector. He develops an alternative model that views the labor market as a group labor queue with ethnic groups in conflict over employment niches. Blacks fared poorly because they were kept out of white ethnic niches by discrimination and social networks. After the civil rights movement, middle-class blacks took over the public-sector employment niche, but because this niche required higher education, it could employ only more fortunate blacks.

7. Jargowsky (1997) attributes this rise to both population growth in already poor neighborhoods and increases in neighborhood poverty rates.

8. Among Latinos, the concentration of poverty (defined as the proportion of the poor living in high-poverty census tracts) changed little between 1970 and 1990, remaining around 20 percent. But large increases in the Latino population led to an increase in the number of Latinos living in high-poverty tracts (Jargowsky 1997).

9. The number of high-poverty neighborhoods declined by more than a quarter in the 1990s, and the number of people living in such neighborhoods fell by 24 percent, even though the overall poverty rate fell only slightly, from 13.1 percent to 12.4 percent. The number of African American residents of high-poverty neighborhoods fell by 36 percent while the number of Latino residents of such neighborhoods increased slightly, by 1.6 percent, driven largely by population growth and immigration from poor countries (Jargowsky 2003).

10. There are undoubtedly differences between poor neighborhoods depending on racial/ethnic and immigrant composition. See Wilson 1996 for a discussion. The present study focuses on majority black neighborhoods.

11. See, e.g., Crane 1991; Brooks-Gunn et al. 1993; Brooks-Gunn, Duncan, and Aber 1997; South and Crowder 1999; Aaronson 1998; Ginther, Haveman, and Wolfe 2000; Rubinowitz and Rosenbaum 2000; Ludwig, Duncan, and Hirschfield 2001; Harding 2003.

12. Harding (2003) uses propensity score matching on geocoded data from the Panel Study of Income Dynamics to compare groups of adolescents matched on individual, family, and metro-area characteristics during childhood who experience different neighborhood contexts (defined by the census-tract poverty rate) during adolescence. A sensitivity analysis, which varies the association between a hypothetical confounder and neighborhood context and the association between the confounder and the outcome, shows that the confounder would need to have strong associations with both in order to reduce neighborhood effects to zero. An example of a similar sensitivity analysis that is based on regression models can be found in Harding 2009a.

13. For further information on Moving to Opportunity and a repository of research on MTO, see www.mtoresearch.org.

14. The early results from MTO seemed to be consistent with the neighborhood effects hypothesis, showing that families in the first treatment group moved to better-off neighborhoods and began to experience better outcomes than control families in a number of domains (Goering and Feins 2003). The interim results were interpreted by readers as indicating small or nonexistent effects of neighborhoods, since the randomization in the experiment had created groups that were comparable on individual and family characteristics (though the studies' authors correctly pointed out that many of the null findings were due to lack of statistical significance rather than precisely estimated

zero effects [Ludwig et al. 2008]). We are now waiting for results from the final evaluation, which will examine differences in outcomes over a decade after the experiment
began.

15. For example, though experimental families who used the vouchers initially went to
low-poverty neighborhoods, many soon moved back to high-poverty neighborhoods.
While the average control-group family ended up in neighborhood that was 45 percent poor (and 87 percent of families ended up in neighborhoods that were at least
30 percent poor), the average experimental-group family ended up in a neighborhood
that was 33 percent poor (and 53 percent of these families ended up in neighborhoods
that were at least 30 percent poor; Kling, Liebman, and Katz 2007, table 1). While these
differences were statistically significant, a neighborhood that is 30 percent poor still
has a very high poverty rate, and would be considered a high-poverty neighborhood
by many standards. In previous nonexperimental studies, researchers had compared
families living in neighborhoods that were less than 10 percent poor with those living
in neighborhoods that were greater than 20 percent poor (e.g., Harding 2003). Clampet-
Lundquist and Massey (2008) and Sampson (2008) also note that both MTO experimental and control-group families ended up in racially segregated black neighborhoods,
where resources, institutions, and schools are typically weaker, which are more often
located adjacent to poor neighborhoods, and which experienced socioeconomic decline
over time.

16. Other criticisms of the MTO design may also be relevant. Though MTO randomized
participants to treatment and control groups, it could only randomize those families
that agreed to participate in the program. Nonparticipants look similar to participants
on observed variables, but it is precisely the unobserved variables that motivated the
need for a randomized experiment in the first place. If families who elected to participate and agreed to be randomized into treatment and control groups were somehow
better off than nonparticipants in unobserved ways, they might be the families we
would least expect to be harmed by poor neighborhoods, since they are likely best at
shielding their children from the dangers of such neighborhoods. Furthermore, the
MTO design inherently confounds neighborhood context and residential mobility, as
participants had to move in order to experience better neighborhoods (Sampson 2008).
Since residential mobility itself is suspected of being harmful to children, such effects
could have offset any benefits of living in lower-poverty neighborhoods. For additional
discussion of the ability of MTO to assess neighborhood effects, see Clampet-Lundquist
and Massey 2008; Ludwig et al. 2008; Sampson 2008.

17. From a counterfactual perspective, we can conceptualize this question as potentially
involving two different types of comparisons. First, we might imagine how the same
individual would fare if he or she were moved to a more affluent neighborhood. This is
the question that the MTO experiment attempts to answer. Second, we might imagine
how the same individual would fare if key social or cultural aspects of the neighborhood were improved. See Sampson 2008.

18. For a discussion of methodological considerations relating to within- and between-
neighborhood heterogeneity in quantitative analyses of neighborhood effects, see Cook
et al. 1997.

19. These figures for individuals and households in high-poverty neighborhoods are of
course lower than national averages for the entire U.S. population in 1990. Nationwide, 75 percent of those age twenty-five or older had graduated from high school, and

27 percent had an associate's degree or higher. Among men age sixteen or over, 70 percent were employed or in the armed forces, and among women, 53 percent were employed or in the armed forces. Twenty-six percent of workers worked in managerial or professional occupations, 91 percent of households nationwide received some income from work, and 80 percent of families with children were headed by men (these calculations are based on 1990 Census STF-3 files). The key point, however, is that although residents of high-poverty neighborhoods are worse off than their counterparts elsewhere, poor neighborhoods are not devoid of individuals and families engaged in lifestyles and behaviors typical of the larger U.S. population.

20. The names I have selected for the three fieldwork neighborhoods are not official city designations nor are they names that denote areas with clear or consistent boundaries in the eyes of local residents. However, these names are recognizable to local residents as referring to the general areas of the city where the fieldwork neighborhoods are.

21. Sullivan (1989) also reports little interethnic gang conflict in the three New York neighborhoods he studied.

22. Harvard's reputation in the community is far less positive in neighborhoods of Allston and Cambridge, where university growth threatens existing neighborhoods.

23. This area is bordered to the west by Northeastern University and the Orange Line/commuter rail tracks, on the east by Washington Street, and on the north by Massachusetts Avenue. Dudley Square, long a center of commerce for Boston's African American community, is to the south. The surrounding neighborhoods have moderate poverty levels, in the range of 15 to 25 percent poor.

This area of Roxbury is central to the history of blacks, and the growth of black churches, in Boston. In 1910 approximately 7,000 blacks lived in the area enclosed by Tremont, Ruggles, Washington, and Northampton streets, the largest of three small black neighborhoods in the city (the others being just to the north in the South End and on Beacon Hill). From there, Boston's "black belt" spread south into Roxbury and north into the South End, driven during the first half of the twentieth century by a mix of Southern migrants, black immigrants from the Caribbean, and native New England blacks. This population drove the growth in black churches, many of which opened in Roxbury Crossing and surrounding neighborhoods (McRoberts 2003). Today the area has a high concentration of black churches and is home to many of the historically black churches that have been pillars of Boston's black community for decades.

24. A 1958 Boston Redevelopment Authority report described the northernmost sections of Roxbury near Dudley Square, Madison Park, and Roxbury Crossing as having some of the worst housing in the city, with 40 percent of the housing stock classified as dilapidated in 1950 and with conditions worsening during the ensuing decade. Boston Redevelopment Authority Report 2425, "Building a Better Boston: Renewal for Roxbury," City Planning Board Boston, March 6, 1958.

25. These developments include Madison Park, Roxse Homes, Camfield Estates, Mandela Homes, and Grant Manor.

26. According to Boston Housing Authority residency statistics, between 1993 and 2003, Camden changed from 69 percent black and 29 percent Hispanic to 35 percent black and 60 percent Hispanic, Lenox from 62 percent black and 33 percent Hispanic to 30 percent black and 62 percent Hispanic, and Whittier Street from 71 percent black and 38 percent Hispanic to 27 percent black and 56 percent Hispanic.

27. The Neponset River flows by Lower Mills and out to the bay, making it an ideal loca-

tion for industry early in its history. Between 1660 and 1830 many mills and factories were constructed here, including those producing or processing woolens, grains, paper, lumber, tobacco, and gunpowder. Because of the success of local industry, Lower Mills was at first a strong residential community that was distinct from Boston and the surrounding rural and agricultural villages in Milton and Meeting House Hill. Lower Mills was the most densely developed section in Dorchester by the 1830s. Chocolate was produced in Lower Mills beginning in 1765 in what would eventually become the Walter Baker Chocolate Company, purchased by General Foods in 1927 and closed in 1965. A 1979 report by the Boston Redevelopment Authority describes Lower Mills as having "a proud past, strong social and ethnic ties, active neighborhood groups, distinctive industrial and residential architecture, and a superb natural setting." "Dorchester Lower Mills: An Urban Village in the 1980s: A Revitalization Strategy," August 1979, Boston Redevelopment Authority.

The social history of Lower Mills is in many ways the history of St. Gregory's parish, which today includes the section of Lower Mills included in this study and the predominantly white area east of Dorchester Avenue. Lower Mills began as a middle-class suburb of Boston and was designated part of St. Gregory's when the parish was created by the archdiocese in 1862. As density increased, the territory covered by St. Gregory's parish shrank to its current geography. Lower Mills, remote from black sections of Boston, remained a largely white ethnic neighborhood of middle- and upper-middle-class families until the 1980s, when blacks gradually moved in from other neighborhoods in Dorchester and from Mattapan (Gamm 1999).

28. In 2000 that census tract was about 20 percent black.

29. The Franklin area began its life as a streetcar suburb and was annexed to Boston in 1870 along with the rest of Dorchester. Development took off in 1906 when a streetcar line running down Blue Hill Avenue was extended south to Mattapan Square. By 1920 Blue Hill Avenue housed a variety of businesses to serve the mixed-class Jewish community that inhabited the area. However, as middle-class and professional Jews moved to the upscale suburbs of Brookline and Newton during the 1940s, the area became primarily a working-class Jewish neighborhood. The initial occupants of Franklin's two main housing developments were largely Jewish and, though often poor, generally lived in two-parent households with at least one worker. The developments were well integrated into the surrounding Jewish neighborhoods, and Blue Hill Avenue continued to bustle with commercial activity. During the 1960s, as Jews continued to leave Boston for the suburbs, blacks moved south into Dorchester from Roxbury, and by the end of the decade the area had become majority black. Blockbusting by real estate agents, aided by racial fears and concerns over riots, pushed this transformation along, as it did in countless American urban neighborhoods during this period (Vale 2002; Massey and Denton 1993). Also during the 1960s, Franklin was an area of heavy loan activity by the Boston Banks Urban Renewal Group (BBURG), an organization of local banks set up to encourage home ownership in parts of Dorchester, Roxbury, and Mattapan. Though intended to encourage home ownership and housing rehabilitation, the long-term consequence of BBURG lending was to concentrate black home ownership in particular areas of the city and to accelerate the decline of the housing stock. The negative effects of these practices are still visible today in Franklin's abandoned houses and vacant lots. Today's residents were shocked to hear that Blue Hill Avenue was once a bustling commercial district with its own trolley line running south to Mattapan Square.

30. Community members and city officials speculated that the Boston Housing Authority was denied by HUD because the BHA had already been a frequent recipient of such funds or because it insisted on a high number of housing units for low-income individuals (rather than the mixed-income plan favored by HUD) due to the severe shortage of low-income housing in Boston.

31. Between 1993 and 2003, for example, the Franklin Field development shifted from 70 percent black and 24 percent Hispanic to 46.6 percent black and 49 percent Hispanic, and Franklin Hill shifted from 68 percent black and 30 percent Hispanic to 39 percent black and 57 percent Hispanic (according to BHA residency statistics).

Chapter two

1. Nicole Fuller, "Dorchester man fatally shot in hallway," *Boston Globe*, June 20, 2003, B2.
2. Boston Police Department spokesman, community meeting.
3. Boston is divided into twelve police districts. The two police districts in which Roxbury Crossing and Franklin are located (B2 and B3) accounted for 38 percent of all homicides and 34 percent of all aggravated assaults in 2003 and 61 percent of all Boston homicides and 34 percent of all aggravated assaults in 2004. FBI Uniform Crime Reports as tabulated by Boston Police Department, http://www.ci.boston.ma.us/police/crimeStats .asp.
4. As reflected in the robbery and aggravated-assault figures, the three homicides in Lower Mills are something of an anomaly and may reflect the spillover of violence from nearby neighborhoods. Lower Mills subjects were surprised by these homicides and did not know the victims, suggesting they were not from the area. For example, after a body was found in Walsh Park, sixteen-year-old Cyril was surprised: "Like all the stuff you hear on the news, it's not really around here except for that recent thing that was at the park . . . I didn't know what to think of it. Like how did that happen because that usually don't happen at that park. 'Cause that park's like everybody's friends over there. We all get along. We might have arguments and stuff; we don't like do something like that. I don't know who that guy is."
5. Table N.1 presents the proportion of adolescents who say they feel safe in their neighborhood by urbanicity, gender, and census-tract poverty rate.
6. The role of age-segmented peer groups in structuring violence is discussed in Thrasher 1927; Suttles 1968; and Horowitz 1983.
7. As part of the interviews, I asked many of the young men to discuss their understandings of terms that are regularly used to categorize people, particularly teenage boys and girls.
8. See also Hunter 1974, 180, on the transmission of "symbolic definitions of local areas" over time.
9. As Suttles (1972) notes, neighborhood definitions are informed as much by relations with outsiders as by social processes internal to the neighborhood, a variant on the classic sociological notion that group boundaries are informed by who is deemed an outsider as well as by the characteristics of the group's members.
10. A survey of Boston high school students found that about one-third felt unsafe riding the T. "T begins to address students' safety fears," *Boston Metro*, September 3, 2003, 12. During the 2003–4 school year, MBTA and school police and administrators patrolled T stations to prevent violence as part of Operation Stopwatch.

TABLE N.1. Proportion of adolescents who say they feel safe in their neighborhood

Tract poverty	Urban Males	Urban Females	Suburban Males	Suburban Females	Rural Males	Rural Females
0–10%	0.93	0.91	0.94	0.93	0.94	0.96
	(0.01)	(0.01)	(0.01)	(0.01)	(0.02)	(0.01)
	1,131	1,264	3,732	3,700	725	686
10–20%	0.86	0.85	0.91	0.87	0.96	0.93
	(0.02)	(0.02)	(0.02)	(0.02)	(0.01)	(0.02)
	714	757	639	679	349	371
20–30%	0.77	0.72	0.81	0.83	0.90	0.87
	(0.03)	(0.03)	(0.03)	(0.02)	(0.03)	(0.02)
	445	480	334	386	330	311
30–40%	0.73	0.74	0.85	0.83	0.93	0.87
	(0.05)	(0.04)	(0.05)	(0.08)	(0.03)	(0.05)
	217	227	154	157	111	133
40%+	0.67	0.61	0.87	0.71	0.93	0.86
	(0.08)	(0.07)	(0.05)	(0.06)	(0.03)	(0.08)
	122	125	122	174	21	27

SOURCE: Author's calculations based on data from National Longitudinal Study of Adolescent Health, Wave 1 In-home survey.
NOTE: Within each cell, the top number is the mean, the number in parentheses is the standard error of the mean, and the bottom number is the raw number of cases in the cell. Because the focus of this chapter is descriptive, these estimates are calculated using Add Health Wave 1 In-home weights, sampling strata identifiers, and primary sampling unit identifiers with Stata's "svy" commands for complex sample designs to produce nationally representative estimates.

11. Two occasional exceptions are classmates from school or youth they come into contact with through family members.

12. The effect of gangs on levels of crime and violence in inner-city neighborhoods has recently come into question by Katz and Jackson-Jacobs (2003). They argue that criminologists have produced no real evidence of an association between gangs and crime rates and note that there is no relationship between the rising and falling crime rates over time in cities and gang problems in those cities. They suggest that violence may cause gangs rather than gangs causing violence, and they discuss a number of methodological problems hampering gang research. Yet few dispute that gangs influence the character of violence in poor communities. Thrasher (1927), working in the Chicago school tradition, views gangs "as a symptom of community disorganization." The play groups of young boys evolve into gangs because other institutions that might meet their needs are ineffectual or nonexistent. The notion that gang involvement is the product of blocked opportunities is a recurring theme in gang research (e.g., Cloward and Ohlin 1960; Hagedorn 1988; Venkatesh 2000).

Researchers have frequently turned to two theoretical concepts to understand the organization of gang conflict: status contestation and age segmentation. According to Thrasher (1927), conflict with other gangs is a central element in gang life, and "gang warfare" erupts over status as well as over economic assets, territory, and the safety of members. Short and Strodtbeck (1965) argue that gang conflict is also a part of status management within the gang, as gang members and leaders use violence among gang members and between rival gangs to establish and maintain leadership roles.

13. In recent years the nature of the gang itself has come into question. While Thrasher (1927) and most subsequent researchers (e.g., Short and Strodtbeck 1965; Suttles 1968; Horowitz 1983; Hagedorn 1988) have viewed gangs as loosely knit groups of young people who engage in delinquency and crime and frequently fight with other groups, the rise of the organized and underground drug economy has led to the development of so-called supergangs or corporate gangs in some larger cities such as Chicago and Los Angeles. It is this notion of a gang that has largely taken over popular conceptions of the gang and of gang violence, perhaps due to the popularity of films and music in the late 1980s and 1990s that presented the "gangsta lifestyle" to the general public.

Venkatesh (2000) argues that in Chicago, gangs transitioned from "classic" gangs to corporate gangs as they began to take over the underground economy in Chicago public housing projects. With this transformation came clearer boundaries between members and nonmembers, more formal leadership hierarchies and roles, increases in the magnitude and geographic scope of gang activity, and the separation of gangs from particular home turfs (see also Padilla 1992). Such gangs may now more closely resemble organized crime syndicates than street-corner groups. In his study of gangs in New York, Los Angeles, and Boston, for example, Sánchez-Jankowski (1991, 28–29) defines a street gang as an organization having the following characteristics: quasi-private, quasi-secretive, possessing a leadership structure with assigned roles and codes of behavior for those roles, and providing both social and economic services for its members and for its own maintenance as an organization.

In his study of Milwaukee gangs, Hagedorn (1988) finds that gangs that maintained a more classic form lost their close association with particular neighborhoods due to school busing for desegregation. I find no evidence in Boston that busing led to a decrease in the significance of neighborhoods.

14. It is possible that for some ongoing beefs the initial contests, now long in the past, were indeed contests over drug turf that have since evolved into the types of conflicts described here, but my data cannot speak to that question.

15. Whether the neighborhood groups described in this chapter are classic gangs or corporate gangs is not relevant to this chapter's larger point about the role of the neighborhood organization of violence in structuring the social lives of adolescents. In addition, most research on gangs and gang violence focuses on the gang members themselves or the gang as an organization. Here I focus on the consequences of neighborhood conflict on other aspects of adolescent life. As the following chapters show, the social dynamics of neighborhood violence in Boston have consequences beyond crime, safety, and victimization, and they have consequences both for those who are directly involved and for their neighbors who sit on the sidelines.

16. See also Newman (1999), who describes a similar role played by family members on welfare.

17. On the effects of incarceration on labor-market outcomes, see Western 2006.

18. Marcus's grandmother is referring to restrictions on public housing and other benefits that come with a criminal conviction.

19. Since the early Chicago school studies of city and community, neighborhoods characterized by poverty and population instability have been thought to cause crime, vio-

lence, and delinquency. Lack of resources, ethnic and racial heterogeneity, and population turnover lead to fewer social ties and therefore diminished social control (Park
and Burgess 1925; Shaw 1929). Today, local formal and informal institutions are also
thought to affect the ability of neighbors to maintain social control (Bursik and Grasmick 1993). These institutions influence norms and expectations and provide contexts
within which social ties are created and maintained. External institutions, such as police, city government, and markets, affect the resources available for both formal and
informal methods of social control. At the individual level, violence among young people, especially remunerative crime, has long been understood to result from a blocked
opportunity structure (Cloward and Ohlin 1960).

Sampson and colleagues extend the social control perspective with the concept of
collective efficacy, or "social cohesion among neighbors combined with their willingness to intervene on behalf of the common good" (Sampson, Raudenbush, and Earls
1997; Sampson, Morenoff, and Earls 1999; Sampson and Raudenbush 1999; Morenoff,
Sampson, and Raudenbush 2001). Neighborhoods with high collective efficacy are organized to maintain social control. Collective efficacy is not merely social capital from
a tight-knit neighborhood social structure. It is a collective and subjective belief in the
ability and willingness of neighborhood residents to harness social capital for collective action, both in informally maintaining order and in securing resources for formal
social control from external institutions. Collective efficacy helps explain the relationship between neighborhood disadvantage and crime in Chicago (Sampson, Raudenbush, and Earls 1997).

20. Suttles (1968) sees youth gangs as one of many groups composed of individuals of similar age, gender, ethnicity, and territory that make up the "ordered segmentation" of
inner-city communities. Conflict between these age-segmented groups is structured by
a hierarchy of the organizing principles of gender, age, ethnicity, and territory. While
fights among male groups of the same age and ethnicity are common, different age
groups will also join forces to combat groups of other ethnicities, and groups of different ethnicities will collaborate in conflicts with other territories. While Horowitz (1983)
also observed gender- and age-segregated groups, she argues that such segmentation
has cultural rather than structural roots, particularly the "code of honor" that governs
respect and retribution.

Anderson (1999) describes how young men in Philadelphia "campaign for respect"
on the streets. In an environment in which victimization is common, young people see
a reputation for toughness or violence as a source of protection. Such a reputation is
created and maintained by posturing and fighting. Running away from confrontation
or failing to put in a respectable performance in a fight means grave damage to one's
reputation, and more importantly, increases the chances of being challenged for one's
pocket money, shoes, or potato chips, the next time one goes outside. In the absence
of access to other forms of status, campaigning for respect becomes campaigning for
status.

Dance (2002) describes a similar dynamic among Boston youth. Survival in the
streets requires putting on a performance for others that projects an image of being
"hard" or "hardcore." Most important is a "gangsterlike demeanor" involving an icy
stare and a willingness to engage in violence to defend oneself, but speech, mannerisms, and clothing are also important. The opposite of being hard is being a "punk." If
someone takes another youth's jacket or even his soda, or verbally or physically disre-

spects him or his friends or family without a response, he has "punked" him. A punk is someone who is a coward or a weakling, and a reputation as a punk means a young man will not put up a fight if challenged. While only a small minority of youth are actually gangsters, Dance argues, all must perform as such in order to survive the streets. The result is often difficulty dealing with teachers and other adults who do not understand daily life in the streets.

21. With my data it is impossible to say whether neighborhood-based violence is important in other cities, but some other evidence is suggestive. Anderson (1999) briefly mentions beefs between youth from other neighborhoods and the importance of "representing" one's neighborhood, though he does not develop an account of the dynamics or the consequences. The "Boston Miracle" model of youth violence intervention is based on an understanding of neighborhood rivalries, and it has been expanded to other cities.

Chapter three

1. Jessica Bennett and Jack Hagel, "Boy, 15, fatally stabbed outside Dudley station," *Boston Globe*, February 15, 2004, B1; John Ellement and Brian MacQuarrie, "Jacket may have spurred fatal stabbing," *Boston Globe*, February 24, 2004, B2.
2. Mac Daniel and Michael Rosenwald, "Arrests made in Dudley stabbing," *Boston Globe*, February 24, 2004, B1; Ellement and MacQuarrie, "Jacket may have spurred fatal stabbing," B2.
3. One exception is Brody et al. (2001), who find that ten-to-twelve-year-olds in disadvantaged neighborhoods are more likely to describe their friends as engaging in deviant behaviors such as skipping school, graffiti, and using drugs or alcohol.
4. There are also other reasons that neighborhood violence may be important for adolescent outcomes or development.

Community social organization: As discussed above, the violence that is endemic to disadvantaged neighborhoods can be understood as a direct consequence of the lack of social organization in these neighborhoods, which limits the capacity of local residents to maintain order. However, violence itself may also affect the social organization of local communities, as individuals respond to fears of victimization and engage in adaptive behaviors necessary for survival (Skogan 1992; Venkatesh 2000). For example, in a violent neighborhood, individuals are often cautious about intervening in conflicts or monitoring other people's children for fear of retribution. Residents keep to themselves rather than interacting with neighbors, resulting in more sparse social networks and weaker capacity for cooperative behavior. Violence engulfs public spaces such as sidewalks, parks, and commercial areas, depriving adult residents of the opportunity to socialize with neighbors and thereby build the networks needed to marshal resources in support of a common goal or public good (Anderson 1999; Venkatesh 2000). As a result, adult residents find it increasingly hard to monitor and control the behavior of community members, especially young people. Community norms regarding school attendance or sexual behavior may weaken, and parents may be less likely to help one another monitor youth behavior, leading to greater likelihood of school dropout and teenage pregnancy among adolescents.

Biosocial pathways: A second theoretical perspective emphasizes the developmental or psychological consequences of neighborhood violence. Such violence has been linked to post-traumatic stress disorder, anxiety, depression, and aggressive behavior, and is thought to disrupt the developmental trajectories of children (Margolin and Gordis 2000; Garbarino, Kostelny, and Dubrow 1991; Aneshensel and Sucoff 1996; Bingenheimer, Brennan, and Earls 2005). Ongoing community violence and recurring episodes of violence lead to heightened arousal or hypervigilance, as well as a perception by the child or adolescent that he or she is not worthy of being kept safe (Margolin and Gordis 2000). The results of such exposure to violence may be slowed cognitive development, poor academic achievement, and trouble forming relationships with peers and others (Margolin and Gordis 2000), all risk factors for high school dropout.

Massey (2004) draws upon this physiological research on biological responses to stressors such as neighborhood violence to develop a biosocial model of racial stratification. Socioeconomic inequality combined with residential segregation leads to geographically concentrated poverty, which in turn leads to the concentration of other social problems, particularly crime and violence. Long-term experience of chronic stress created by exposure to violence and threat of victimization can have physiological consequences, one of which is "allostatic load," persistently high levels of production of adrenaline and cortisol. In addition to long-term physical health effects, allostatic load can influence cognitive functioning by inhibiting the formation of connections between neurons in the brain and by impairing memory. Allostatic load can also lead to greater aggressiveness, impulsivity, anger, and susceptibility to substance use (see Massey 2004 for a review). The stresses associated with growing up in a violent neighborhood can extend beyond the immediate threat of victimization, as negative experiences of family members also cause further stress (Charles, Dinwiddie, and Massey 2004; Massey and Fischer 2006). These biosocial consequences of violence—poor cognitive development, risk taking, and substance use—may in turn increase the risk of school dropout or teenage pregnancy.

Rational choice: A violent environment may directly affect adolescent decision making by changing the perceived costs and benefits of schooling or sexual activity. A rational-choice perspective suggests that when individuals feel their lives may be cut short at any moment, they are less likely to invest time and effort in schooling and are more likely to engage in risky behaviors such as unprotected sex.

5. Note that I am not arguing that adolescents from violent neighborhoods have more friends or closer friendships than their counterparts in more advantaged neighborhoods. Harding (2008) shows that, controlling for individual and family characteristics, adolescents in violent neighborhoods have the same number of friends and the same degree of friendship closeness (as measured by joint activities) as adolescents in less-violent neighborhoods, based on nationally representative data from Add Health. Rather, youth in more violent neighborhoods have stronger obligations and stronger loyalties to one another, which, among other things, should increase their susceptibility to peer effects.

6. Two occasional exceptions are classmates from school or youth they come into contact with through family members.

7. Due to high rates of incarceration in the 1990s, Boston's poor communities are now experiencing an influx of former prisoners (Winship 2004), making the available older role models an even more disadvantaged group.

8. These figures are averages of the two census tracts making up each of the study areas. Additional area characteristics from the census are available in the appendix in table A.1. Although the citywide and Lower Mills male joblessness rates may seem high

given its poverty rate, note that all males ages sixteen to fifty-nine are included in this figure whether or not they are in the labor force, including those who are in school, disabled, or retired, or otherwise choose not to work because they have other sources of income.

9. Schudson (1989) outlines five "dimensions of cultural power": retrievability, rhetorical force, resonance, institutional retention, and resolution.

10. Such a conclusion is possible only because of the explicitly comparative research design used in this study, illustrating the value of comparing the lives of adolescents in different neighborhoods for understanding neighborhood social processes and neighborhood effects.

Chapter four

1. One exception is spatial mismatch theory, which seeks to explain higher unemployment by the distance between residential neighborhoods and places of employment (see Jencks and Mayer 1990a for a review).

2. Previous research on neighborhood effects rests on an assumption of correspondence between what Tienda (1991, 259) calls "geographic neighborhoods" and "social neighborhoods, defined by the boundaries of social networks and the density or interaction patterns."

3. One exception is Turley (2001), who interviewed twenty children living in neighborhoods of varying socioeconomic status in New Mexico, Arizona, and Nogales (Mexico). She finds that children's interaction with neighbors is structured by density, demographics, and time use.

4. Though proposals were floated to return to neighborhood schools, Boston public schools at the time of the fieldwork were not neighborhood-based. High schools all had citywide attendance areas, and elementary and middle schools were divided into three attendance zones. One merely had to attend a school in one's zone, though a proportion of spots in most schools were reserved for students within walking distance.

5. Existing research examining the relationship between neighborhood environment and social isolation focuses on adults and examines whether neighborhood poverty is related to network ties to employed or college-educated individuals or to organizational participation, controlling for individual characteristics. Tigges, Browne, and Green (1998) report that adults in higher-poverty neighborhoods in Atlanta have smaller "discussion networks" (people they talk to about important matters) and discussion networks with fewer employed or college-educated individuals. Rankin and Quane (2000) find that neighborhood poverty predicts lower organization participation and fewer ties to employed individuals and to the college-educated and more ties to welfare recipients among adults surveyed in Chicago in 1991. Fernandez and Harris (1992) report similar findings from Chicago adults surveyed in 1986 and 1987.

We know somewhat more about the social support networks of urban and minority adults, though some of the findings are contradictory and few speak directly to social isolation. Ethnographic research on urban poverty emphasizes the role of kin and "fictive kin" networks in spreading the risks associated with poverty (Stack 1974). Newman (1999) finds that some seemingly separate households are actually closely linked socially, emotionally, and materially, and that the workplace also provides important social ties for low-wage workers. However, survey research suggests that blacks have smaller and less supportive networks than whites, both in terms of kin and nonkin, and that urban dwellers in general have networks with more nonkin and fewer kin (Fischer 1982; Marsden 1987; Lee and Campbell 1999). These differences may be due to the inability of survey instruments to correctly assess nontraditional social networks. Another possibility is that ethnographers are studying single neighborhoods that are unrepresentative. A third is that, without a middle-class comparison, ethnographic work has no benchmark with which to compare networks in poor communities to networks in more advantaged communities. The immigration literature emphasizes the importance of ethnic enclaves, spatially clustered networks of coethnic business owners that provide easier access to capital, labor, and local product markets (Portes and Zhou 1993; Portes 1995, 1996).

Fischer (1982) and Wellman (1999) examine the social networks of urban adults (see also Kadushin and Jones 1992; Greenbaum and Greenbaum 1985). Fischer (1982) finds that urban dwellers do not lack social support or social ties, but that their ties take on different forms. Urban dwellers have fewer kin ties and more nonkin ties. They have fewer "multistranded" ties, less dense networks, and more spatially dispersed networks. Fischer concludes that urbanism matters less than other individual characteristics, especially education. Blacks and Mexicans have smaller, less supportive networks (as measured by individuals they can turn to for help), and more culturally homogeneous networks. Based on a longitudinal study of the social networks of Toronto residents, Wellman (1999) concludes that community ties are narrow, specialized relationships, not broadly supportive ties; that most people have sparse, loosely bounded, frequently changing networks (suggesting that individual network ties may matter more for support than the structure of the network within which one is embedded); and that communities are now spatially dispersed and not focused on physical neighborhoods. There is still a relationship between physical distance and strength of tie, but the primary distinction is not at the neighborhood but at the city level. This last conclusion is at odds with the importance attached to neighborhoods in the urban-poverty literature, though Wellman is concerned with the general urban population. Finally, Gans's classic research on neighboring in *Levittowners* (1967) finds that neighborly interaction in early suburbia was based in small areas.

6. During the interviews, I asked the boys to discuss their perceptions of the neighborhood and its boundaries, their social networks and romantic and sexual relationships, their local and extended families, their daily activities and time use, their contact and relationships with nonfamily adults, and their use of places and spaces throughout the city, including forms of transportation. These data form the basis for an analysis of the relationships between neighborhoods, daily activities, time use, social networks, and institutional participation. By tracing in detail how, where, and with whom adolescents spend their time, we can understand the importance of neighborhood in their social lives.

7. Turley (2001) reports results from interviews with twenty children age nine to seventeen. Consistent with the results in this chapter, she finds that both physical and social features affect how children conceptualize their neighborhoods and that social interaction with neighbors is influenced by physical features, neighborhood demographics, and children's time use.

8. Hunter (1974) finds that those at the ends of the age distribution perceive smaller neighborhoods, as do those who are poor and those who are wealthy, with middle-

class individuals identifying larger areas as neighborhoods. Those who have lived in a neighborhood longer and those who are more involved in the community have more consistent definitions of neighborhood boundaries, and homogeneous neighborhoods tend to have smaller neighborhood definitions.

9. Clearly many physical features of cities are themselves socially constructed, but from the perspective of an adolescent, these features are relatively fixed and taken as given.

10. Grannis (1998) defines a tertiary street community as a set of residential (tertiary) streets bound by major roads or other obstacles such as railroad tracks, parks, and shopping centers for which all streets are accessible to all others using only tertiary streets. He shows that networks of tertiary street communities, rather than spatial distance, define residential racial segregation in San Francisco and Los Angeles.

11. See Furstenberg et al. 1999; Furstenberg and Hughes 1997; Suttles 1972.

12. Even the boundaries between these areas are sometimes contested. For example, the exact line between Dorchester and Roxbury in the Grove Hall area remains in dispute among area residents.

13. Also consistent, Fischer (1982) finds that adults with more opportunities for forming nonneighborhood ties (such as through the workplace or other nonneighborhood organizations) are less likely to be enmeshed in neighborhood-based social networks.

14. I have not shown the subjects' actual residences because of confidentiality.

15. Although it is conventional wisdom that poor neighborhoods have fewer institutions and organizations, there is little evidence that this is the case, even if the organizations and institutions they do have may be smaller or of lower quality. Small and McDermott (2006) find that poor neighborhoods have no fewer commercial establishments than more advantaged neighborhoods, and Small and Stark (2005) find that poor neighborhoods in New York have fewer privately funded child-care centers but more publicly funded centers than more advantaged neighborhoods.

16. These figures include only male friends, as few boys reported any female friends. The exact definition of friendship was left largely to the boys themselves, though we did talk about friends as those they spent free time with or those they talked with regularly.

17. As Laumann et al. (2004, 19–20) argue, "The more firmly embedded individuals are in a network, the more likely other network members are to influence their sex-market choices . . . We also expect networks to affect the nature or quality of sexual partnerships."

18. Briggs (1997) also reports lack of nonfamily adult contact among a sample of youth living in Yonkers, NY.

19. Furstenberg et al. (1999) describe parents as structuring the links between communities and children because parents select social contexts for their children.

20. Jarrett (1997a, 1997b) also discusses parenting strategies, though these strategies are more general in that they include more than those that limit neighborhood influences. Jarrett's strategies include (1) family protection, or limiting the child's social and physical world; (2) child monitoring, or confining the child to the home; (3) resource seeking, or actively seeking resources inside and outside the neighborhood and working to extract more benefit from these resources; and (4) in-home learning, or making up for poor school quality by providing supplementary learning at home and by creating congruence between home and school.

21. Future research on neighborhood effects should take these findings into account. First, as others have noted, an individual's conception of the neighborhood rarely cor-

responds to official neighborhood designations used in quantitative research, such as census tract or block-group boundaries. The perspective on daily activity patterns, developed in this chapter, offers one way to construct more sensible neighborhood measures in future survey research. Neighborhood definitions can be tailored to the geographic and social spaces that individuals actually find themselves in on a daily basis. Social scientists have already developed multiple methods to track the time use of both adults and children (e.g., Larson 1989; Juster and Stafford 1985; Robinson 1977), but none of these studies measure where people spend time in relation to their neighborhoods. Activity patterns and social networks can also be used to measure the neighborhood attachment and the interactions within neighborhoods needed to further understand and account for the contingent nature of neighborhood social attachment. Second, differences in neighborhood social attachment imply that there is considerable heterogeneity within neighborhoods in the effect of neighborhood processes on individuals. Failing to model this heterogeneity would likely lead to downward bias in neighborhood effects estimates for those who are affected.

Chapter five

1. Young (2004) also reports support for ideals of hard work and education among a sample of impoverished African American men in their twenties living in the near west side of Chicago.
2. The importance of conventional views on these issues in poor neighborhoods has been documented by others as well. Edin and Kefalas (2005) have documented the high value that poor women place on marriage and the high standards that they hold themselves and their romantic partners to in considering marriage. The adolescent boys of Franklin and Roxbury Crossing (and Lower Mills) are of the same mind.
3. Shaw and McKay (1969) argued that socially disorganized slum neighborhoods present youth with a wide array of "competing and conflicting moral values," both conventional and unconventional, creating a breakdown of social control, which leads to higher rates of delinquency in such neighborhoods. "In the areas of low rates of delinquents there is more or less uniformity, consistency, and universality of conventional values and attitudes with respect to child care, conformity to law, and related matters; whereas in the high-rate areas, systems of competing and conflicting moral values have developed. Even though in the latter situation conventional traditions and institutions are dominant, delinquency has developed as a powerful competing way of life" (170). Heterogeneity of values underlies social disorganization theories, including both Shaw and McKay's social control theory and Mertonian strain theory (Kornhauser 1978).
4. There are undoubtedly cultural dimensions on which middle-class neighborhoods have comparable or greater heterogeneity than poor neighborhoods, such as political views, fashion preferences, and religious beliefs. The focus of this analysis is on cultural dimensions related to individual outcomes typically studied by poverty and inequality researchers, such as schooling, employment, and early childbearing.
5. Indeed, in a paradoxical twist on social isolation theory, Young (2004) finds that those young men who are most isolated within their poor neighborhood on Chicago's near west side are the most optimistic with regard to racism, opportunity, and social barriers to mobility.
6. This classic Chicago school approach has been criticized for overemphasizing the im-

portance of structural factors, for failure to differentiate black neighborhoods from other ethnic neighborhoods, and for reliance on the oversimplified concentric-zone model of the city (Sampson and Morenoff 1997).

7. Exceptions include Browning, Leventhal, and Brooks-Gunn (2004, 2005), who show the importance of neighborhood collective efficacy for neighborhood differences in early sexual initiation.

8. Recent work at the nexus of inequality and cultural sociology has focused on the analysis of class. Symbolic boundaries have been used to understand how groups create and maintain their separation from and dominance over other groups (e.g., Lamont 1992, 2000; Kefalas 2003; for a review see Lamont and Molnar 2002). Cultural capital theory has been used to understand how the upper class employs signals, credentials, and knowledge to exclude others and to pass on advantages to children (Bourdieu and Passeron 1977; Bourdieu 1984; Lamont and Lareau 1988; DiMaggio 1982; Erickson 1996; Bryson 1996). Lareau (2000, 2003) has shown class differences in parenting practices and their role in educational outcomes. Increasingly, poverty scholars have also employed cultural analysis, particularly in documenting the cultural world of the urban poor, describing how they understand their options and make decisions with regard to work, welfare, schooling, parenthood, and marriage (Newman 1999; Anderson 1990, 1999; Waller 2002; Hays 2003; Young 2004; Carter 2005; Edin and Kefalas 2005). Yet culture has been less explicitly incorporated into the recent literature on the role of neighborhood context in the intergenerational transmission of poverty.

9. One exception is Young (2004) who reports that, among a sample of impoverished African American men in their twenties from Chicago's near west side, those whose social networks are most confined to their own neighborhoods and had the least contact with whites and with mainstream institutions were the least pessimistic about racism and economic opportunity and saw the fewest social barriers to mobility. This is the opposite of what an oppositional culture version of social isolation theory would predict.

10. See also Willis 1977 and MacLeod 1995 for more class-based versions of this type of argument.

11. Fordham and Ogbu (1986) are often interpreted as arguing that academic success itself comes to be defined as "acting white" within an oppositional culture, but in a recent paper, Ogbu (2004) clarifies that their argument was that behaviors that lead to academic achievement are what are defined as "acting white" by poor black adolescents.

12. Fischer (1995, 544) defines a subculture as "a large set of people who share a defining trait, associate with one another, are members of institutions associated with their defining trait, adhere to a distinct set of values, share a set of cultural tools, and take part in a common way of life." Fischer himself is concerned not with poor neighborhoods or subcultures among the poor but with the effect of city size on the number of distinct subcultures. For an application of this notion of subculture to poor neighborhoods, see Sánchez-Jankowski 2008.

13. It is difficult to discern in Anderson's work whether he views his "decent" and "street" typology to indicate separate groups within the community or merely different "orientations" that are available to everyone in the community. For example, in *Code of the Street* (1999, 35), he begins with the latter conception: "The decent family and the street family in a real sense represent two poles of value orientation, two contrasting con-

ceptual categories . . . There is also quite a bit of circumstantial behavior—that is, one person may at different times exhibit both decent and street orientations, depending on the circumstances." This quote suggests that Anderson views "decent" and "street" as ideal types. It is also consistent with the notion of cultural repertoire or tool kit if "decent" and "street" orientations are viewed as elements of one's tool kit when one lives in a poor neighborhood. On the other hand, when discussing adolescent sexual behavior later in the book, Anderson seems to employ the separate-groups version of his typology. Adolescents' peer-group norms explain their behaviors, and whether one is "street" or "decent" indicates one's peer group. This is more consistent with subcultural models. "In self-defense the young men often choose to deny fatherhood; few are willing to own up to a pregnancy they can reasonably question. *Among their street-oriented peers*, the young men gain ready support for this position; a man who is 'tagged' with fatherhood has been caught in the 'trick bag'" (157; emphasis added).

14. For example, Burton has argued that African American adolescents living in poverty experience an accelerated life course and inconsistencies in role expectations between families and other institutions as a result of poverty and other structural disadvantages (Burton, Obeidallah, and Allison 1996).

15. A conception of culture as heterogeneous and contradictory appears elsewhere as well. For example, Sewell (1992, 17) notes that "social actors are capable of applying a wide range of different and even incompatible schemes." He also describes cultures as contradictory, loosely integrated, contested, subject to constant change, and weakly bounded (Sewell 1999).

16. Hybrid models are also possible. For example, Fischer (1995) suggests that a subculture may provide its members with a particular repertoire.

17. Tilly (1978) is also credited with the development of the concept of repertoire in his work on "repertoires of collective action."

18. Swidler's tool-kit metaphor has been criticized for failing to specify how individuals choose which elements of their tool kit to employ in different situations (Lamont 1992; Lamont and Thévenot 2000). Lamont (1992) suggests that both proximate and remote structural conditions influence such selections. For a comparison of repertoires across cultural groups, see Lamont and Thévenot 2000.

19. This view of culture can be seen in Shaw's earlier analyses of deviance and social control. For Shaw (1929), culture is the customs, traditions, folkways, and mores of a group, which are the results of its previous experiences. Social standards and attitudes are embodied in institutions and groupings within the community. Conflict between the home culture of immigrants and the social environment of the city leads to breakdown of social control within the group.

20. A key difference between the aims of Sánchez-Jankowski (2008) and this book's aims is that Sánchez-Jankowski is not concerned with processes of social mobility or the intergenerational transmission of poverty, but rather with how people living in poverty make a life for themselves from day to day, particularly as it relates to the interaction between culture and institutions in poor neighborhoods.

21. Lamont (1992) suggests that both proximate and remote structural conditions influence which elements of their tool kit individuals employ in different situations. For an example of comparison of repertoires across cultural groups, see Lamont and Thévenot 2000.

22. See chapter 1, which discusses results from Jargowsky 1997.

23. There are of course many factors that determine the capacity of culture to influence behavior. Schudson (1989) outlines five "dimensions of cultural power": retrievability, rhetorical force, resonance, institutional retention, and resolution. Here I emphasize retrievability, the availability or accessibility of a cultural model or cultural object. Schudson suggests that retrievability is highest when a cultural model or object is physically present, institutionalized in common practice or public memory, or more salient because it is more recent or more dramatic.

24. I follow Quinn and Holland (1987, 4) in my use of the term "cultural models," which they define as "presupposed, taken-for-granted models of the world that are widely shared (although not necessarily to the exclusion of other, alternative models) by the members of a society and that play an enormous role in their understanding of that world and their behavior in it." I consider frames, scripts, and goals to be three types of cultural models.

25. Similar themes are present in ethnographic research on crime and delinquency in urban neighborhoods. Sullivan (1989) shows how wider meanings about work and economic success change in the context of structural disadvantage, so that crime becomes defined as work for economic gain ("getting paid"). What is deviant or criminal is constructed and reconstructed through social interaction. Bourgois (1995) documents the culture of El Barrio drug dealers. The "inner-city street culture" is a complex and conflicting web of beliefs, symbols, modes of interaction, values, and ideologies, all understood in the context of exclusion from mainstream society. The Puerto Ricans of El Barrio draw upon "oppositional mentality" imported from their homeland, the result of long-term colonial rule. The drug dealers explicitly understand their own behavior as oppositional to that of mainstream society because they feel rejected by it. Crack dealers are motivated as much by the search for dignity and respect as by economic gain, and the paths to respect and dignity are culturally constructed. At the same time, however, these men do not completely reject mainstream culture, as evidenced by the value they place on the work ethic in their drug-dealing business and their periodic attempts to secure legal employment.

26. To the extent that those espousing or modeling alternative cultural models have strong ties to one another and exert their own social control, alternative models may hold even greater sway. On the strong ties among peer groups and the connection to neighborhood violence, see chapter 3. This is another example of the "negative" side of social capital (see Portes 1998; Portes and Landolt 1996).

27. While ethnographers such as Suttles (1968) and Hannerz (1969) have described the strong divisions along ethnic and lifestyle lines that occur when groups in physical proximity define themselves as fundamentally different or better than one another, today's young people may be more forgiving of racial and ethnic differences than those of the 1960s (see, e.g., Carter 2005). In addition, Hannerz's neighborhood hierarchies are created and maintained largely by adults, not adolescents. Indeed, he describes how "mainstream" parents go to great pains to keep their children away from "street families," efforts that were paralleled by those of the parents in Roxbury Crossing and Franklin (see chapter 4; see also Furstenberg et al. 1999).

28. Unfortunately there are no parallel measures of education scripts in these data. For education scripts we must rely on the analysis of the interview data in chapter 7.

29. This issue is the source of one of Wacquant's (2002) critiques of Anderson's *Code of the Street* (1999). Wacquant correctly notes that Anderson uses the decent-street dichotomy developed by his research subjects to understand their social worlds as his analytical categories in explaining their behavior. This led Anderson directly to a subcultural explanation of sexual behavior based on peer-group norms despite its theoretical incompatibility with the notion that "street" and "decent" are merely ideal types (see note 13 above).

30. As cultural models, frames, scripts, and goals can be thought of as somewhat similar to Bourdieu's concept of habitus (1998), inasmuch as both habitus and cultural models are dispositions toward action, without being determinative. However, an important difference is that frames, scripts, and goals are usually conscious rather than unconscious and specifically allow for heterogeneity.

31. For instance, one's frame about the advantages and disadvantages of early parenthood may face frequent challenge from others with different frames.

32. In the case of education, these processes can also be thought of in terms of Bourdieu and Passeron's notion of cultural exclusion by "relegation" (1979), ending up in disadvantageous positions due to poorly informed decisions. The information problems that I am attributing to cultural heterogeneity can result in decisions that lead adolescents toward educational ends, such as a GED, that are markers of low educational achievement in the labor market (see also Lamont and Lareau 1988).

33. Space limitations prevent a full discussion of these analyses here, but see Harding 2007 and 2009b for results and details.

34. Whether adolescents are more affected by culturally heterogeneous neighborhoods than adults or children cannot be evaluated with my data. An examination of this hypothesis awaits further data collection.

Chapter six

1. The gold-digger frame provides an example of the concept of cultural resonance that was discussed in chapter 5. The legitimacy of a frame or other type of cultural model is reinforced when it accords with other cultural models, one's personal experiences, or one's structural circumstances.

2. This is not to suggest that girls have the same latitude in categorizing boys as the boys do in categorizing girls. Such categorizations must also conform to gender regimes in the wider society.

3. The notion that boys care about the emotional aspects of romantic and sexual relationships, while counter to conventional wisdom, appears elsewhere as well. See Giordano, Longmore, and Manning 2006.

4. On gender distrust more generally in African American communities, see Patterson 1998; Franklin 1982.

5. Chris's mother tells a different account of his conception. She says she became pregnant despite being on the pill.

6. One Franklin boy reported even going so far as to ask girls or potential girlfriends for recent test results proving that they are currently disease-free.

7. Noticeably absent from David's discussion of his relationship is the prospect of marriage either in the future or if his girlfriend were to become pregnant. When David

described his views on marriage later, he echoed the sentiments that are common to boys from poor neighborhoods: one does not need to get married if a pregnancy occurs, and marriage is something for much later in life, when the couple is more financially secure. These issues are discussed further below.

8. See Liebow 1967 on how poor men create adaptations to circumstances in which achieving mainstream goals is extremely unlikely.

9. See also Rodman 1963 on the "lower-class value stretch."

10. Lack of alternative models for successfully fulfilling one's role as a husband may help to illuminate lower marriage rates in poor communities. When there is only a single way to be a good husband, fewer men will see themselves as ready to be one. Of course, unlike becoming a father, one must make an active and deliberate decision to become a husband, so there is less need to negotiate alternative conceptions of the good husband.

Chapter seven

1. The analysis in this chapter employs a very different perspective than that of MacLeod (1995), who implicitly uses a subculture approach to understand educational outcomes among two groups of adolescent boys in a housing project. MacLeod argues that one group of boys, a mostly white group he calls the "Hallway Hangers," develops an oppositional subculture based on family experiences and peer effects. The Hallway Hangers develop alternative, group-specific criteria for success, such as fighting ability and group loyalty. The second group of boys, black youth he calls the "Brothers," develops an achievement ideology consistent with dominant culture. While the Hallway Hangers see the opportunity structure as basically closed, the Brothers view it as open, attributing their own families' poverty to legacies of racism. The educational aspirations of the two groups are structured by these achievement ideologies. While the Brothers do better in school on average, in the end the labor-market outcomes of both groups are more structured by their lack of cultural capital (understanding how to navigate educational institutions to derive the most benefit) and social capital (access to job networks). The black and Latino boys in this study have an achievement ideology similar to that of MacLeod's Brothers. See chapter 5 on the theoretical differences between the subculture approach and cultural heterogeneity perspective used here.

2. For a review of perspectives on high school dropout, see Rumberger 2004.

3. Rumberger (2004, 133) describes dropping out of high school as "the final stage in a dynamic and cumulative process of disengagement from school." He suggests that there are two types of engagement, academic and social. Social engagement includes attendance, behavior, and involvement in school activities.

4. Scholars of high school dropout have identified the transition to high school as a key point of vulnerability, as students who fail to be promoted from the ninth to the tenth grade are very likely to drop out of high school (Orfield 2004).

5. This is consistent with research reviewed by Tyler (2003), who argues that the availability of the GED option may cause some students to drop out of high school.

6. Whether there are any economic returns at all to earning a GED among high school dropouts is an open question in the research literature. Some researchers find that

there are no economic benefits of the GED (Heckman and LaFontaine 2006; Cao, Stroms-dorfer, and Weeks 1996), while others find benefits only for those with low cognitive skills (Tyler, Murnane, and Willet 2003; Murnane, Willet, and Boudett 1999), or only for whites (Tyler, Murnane, and Willet 2000). There is also some evidence that the GED increases the likelihood of employment but does not increase wages (Tyler 2004) and that it increases the rate of wage growth over time (Murnane, Willet, and Boudett 1995).

7. There is some evidence that the GED sends a mixed signal to employers, signaling greater cognitive skills but low internalization of institutional norms and therefore the potential for trouble getting along with coworkers and supervisors (see Smith 2003 for a review). In addition, among GED holders there are very low rates of postsecondary education and job training (Tyler 2003), suggesting that many young people do not successfully make the transition to further schooling after earning a GED.

8. Cameron and Heckman (1993) report that while those who earn a GED are more likely to enroll in further education or training, they are less likely than those with traditional high school degrees to complete postsecondary schooling. Murnane, Willet, and Boudett (1997) find that participation in postsecondary education and job training was greater among high school dropouts who received a GED. These findings suggest that the GED is a route to further education for high school dropouts, but that GED holders are less likely to successfully complete such postsecondary schooling or training.

9. Based on data gathered from high school students in California, Venezia and Kirst (2005) report that lower socioeconomic status students have less information about the academic requirements of college.

10. While we know quite a bit about the role of individual, family, and school characteristics in predicting college enrollment and performance, there has been relatively little research to date on the role of neighborhoods in college enrollment. Family income, wealth, parental education, family structure, academic performance in high school, failure to advance a grade, high school dropout, and attending a Catholic school all predict college enrollment (DeLuca and Bozick 2005; Eccles, Vida, and Barber 2004; Cabrera and La Nasa 2001; Conley 2001; Sandefur, Meier, and Campbell 2006; Kane 2004). Social capital, as measured by parental expectations, parent-child discussions, parent-school contact, and parent involvement in school activities, predicts college attendance above and beyond SES and demographic characteristics (Sandefur, Meier, and Campbell 2006). With regard to neighborhoods, Smith (1972) finds that neighborhood characteristics are strong predictors of plans for college among a sample of Milwaukee high school seniors from the late 1950s. Massey and Fischer (2006) show that among minorities enrolled at elite colleges and universities, growing up in segregated neighborhoods and violent and disorderly neighborhoods is a predictor of academic performance in college.

11. A further example of institutional knowledge, in yet another domain, comes from Paul, age fourteen and from Franklin, who described how a young woman who was pregnant could move up the waiting list for a coveted Section 8 housing voucher, with which she could rent her own apartment in the private market and have the rent subsidized by the government. By leaving her family's home and moving into a shelter, she and her new baby would be classified as homeless and given priority for a Section 8 voucher. Paul explained how staying in a shelter for six to nine months would pay off in the long run through a subsidized apartment.

Chapter eight

1. On stigma and the role of incarceration in inequality, see Pager 2003; Western 2006.

Appendix

1. A third potential axis on which neighborhoods might vary is their relationship to public schools. In Boston, however, all public high schools are open to students anywhere in the city. For assignment of students to middle schools, the city is divided into three zones, and students can attend any school in their zone. Those who do not explicitly request a school are assigned to the nearest school with an open spot.

REFERENCES

Aaronson, Daniel. 1998. "Using Sibling Data to Estimate the Impact of Neighborhoods on Children's Economic Outcomes." *Journal of Human Resources* 33:915–46.

Ainsworth-Darnell, James, and Douglas Downey. 1998. "Assessing the Oppositional Culture Explanation for Racial/Ethnic Differences in School Performance." *American Sociological Review* 63:536–53.

Anderson, Elijah. 1978. *A Place on the Corner*. Chicago: University of Chicago Press.

———. 1990. *Streetwise: Race, Class, and Change in an Urban Community*. Chicago: University of Chicago Press.

———. 1991. "Neighborhood Effects on Teenage Pregnancy." In *The Urban Underclass*, ed. Christopher Jencks and Paul E. Peterson, 375–98. Washington, DC: Brookings Institution Press.

———. 1999. *Code of the Street: Decency, Violence, and the Moral Life of the Inner City*. New York: W. W. Norton.

Aneshensel, Carol S., and Clea A. Sucoff. 1996. "The Neighborhood Context of Adolescent Mental Health." *Journal of Health and Social Behavior* 37:293–310.

Bayer, Patrick, Randi Hjalmarsson, and David Pozen. 2007. "Building Criminal Capital behind Bars: Peer Effects in Juvenile Corrections." National Bureau of Economic Research Working Paper 12932.

Bearman, Peter, and Hannah Bruckner. 1999. *Power in Numbers: Peer Effects on Adolescent Girls' Sexual Debut and Pregnancy*. Washington, DC: National Campaign to Prevent Teen Pregnancy.

Benford, Robert D., and David A. Snow. 2000. "Framing Processes and Social Movements: An Overview and Assessment." *Annual Review of Sociology* 26:611–39.

Berrien, Jenny, and Christopher Winship. 2002. "An Umbrella of Legitimacy: Boston's Police Department–Ten Point Coalition Collaboration." In *Securing Our Children's Future: New Approaches to Juvenile Justice and Youth Violence*, ed. Gary S. Katzmann, 200–228. Washington, DC: Brookings Institution Press.

Bingenheimer, Jeffrey B., Robert T. Brennan, and Felton J. Earls. 2005. "Firearm Violence Exposure and Serious Violent Behavior." *Science* 308:1323–26.

Bourdieu, Pierre. 1984. *Distinction: A Social Critique of the Judgment of Taste*. Cambridge, MA: Harvard University Press.

———.1998. *Practical Reason*. Stanford, CA: Stanford University Press.

Bourdieu, Pierre, and Jean-Claude Passeron. 1977. *Reproduction in Education, Society and Culture*. Beverly Hills, CA: Sage.

———. 1979. *The Inheritors: French Students and Their Relations to Culture*. Chicago: University of Chicago Press.

Bourgois, Philippe. 1995. *In Search of Respect: Selling Crack in El Barrio.* Cambridge: Cambridge University Press.

Braga, Anthony A., and David M. Kennedy. 2002. "Reducing Gang Violence in Boston." In *Responding to Gangs: Evaluation and Research,* ed. Winifred L. Reed and Scott H. Decker, 264–88. Washington, DC: National Institute of Justice.

Bridgeland, John M., John J. DiIulio, Jr., and Karen B. Morison. 2006. *The Silent Epidemic: Perspectives of High School Dropouts.* Report by Civic Enterprises in association with Peter D. Hart Research Associates, and the Bill and Melinda Gates Foundation. Washington, DC: Civic Enterprises.

Briggs, Xavier de Souza. 1997. "Moving Up versus Moving Out: Neighborhood Effects in Housing Mobility Programs." *Housing Policy Debate* 8:195–234.

Brody, Gen H., Xiaojia Ge, Rand Conger, Frederick X. Gibbons, Velma McBride Murray, Meg Gerrard, and Ronald L. Simons. 2001. "The Influence of Neighborhood Disadvantage, Collective Socialization, and Parenting on African-American Children's Affiliation with Deviant Peers." *Child Development* 72:1231–46.

Brooks-Gunn, Jeanne, Greg J. Duncan, and J. Lawrence Aber. 1997. *Neighborhood Poverty.* 2 vols. New York: Russell Sage.

Brooks-Gunn, Jeanne, Greg J. Duncan, Pamela K. Klebanov, and Naomi Sealand. 1993. "Do Neighborhoods Influence Child and Adolescent Development?" *American Journal of Sociology* 99:353–95.

Browning, Christopher R., Tama Leventhal, and Jeanne Brooks-Gunn. 2004. "Neighborhood Context and Racial Differences in Early Adolescent Sexual Activity." *Demography* 41:697–720.

———. 2005. "Sexual Initiation in Early Adolescence: The Nexus of Parental and Community Control." *American Sociological Review* 70:758–78.

Bryson, Bethany. 1996. "Anything but Heavy Metal: Symbolic Exclusion and Musical Dislikes." *American Sociological Review* 61:884–99.

Bursik, Robert J., Jr., and Harold G. Grasmick. 1993. *Neighborhoods and Crime: The Dimensions of Effective Community Control.* New York: Lexington Books.

Burton, Linda M., Dawn Obeidallah, and Kevin Allison. 1996. "Ethnographic Insights on Social Context and Adolescent Development among Inner-City African-American Teens." In *Ethnography and Human Development: Context and Meaning in Social Inquiry,* ed. Richard Jessor, Ann Colby, and Richard A. Shweder, 395–418. Chicago: University of Chicago Press.

Cabrera, Alberto F., and Steven M. La Nasa. 2001. "On the Path to College: Three Critical Tasks Facing America's Disadvantaged." *Research in Higher Education* 42:119–50.

Cairns, Robert B., Beverly D. Cairns, and Holly J. Neckerman. 1989. "Early School Dropout: Configurations and Determinants." *Child Development* 60:1437–52.

Cameron, Stephen V., and James J. Heckman. 1993. "The Nonequivalence of High School Equivalents." *Journal of Labor Economics* 11:1–47.

Cao, Jian, Ernst W. Stromsdorfer, and Gregory Weeks. 1996. "The Human Capital Effect of General Education Development Certificates on Low Income Women." *Journal of Human Resources* 31:206–28.

Carrell, Scott E., Richard L. Fullerton, and James E. West. 2008. "Does Your Cohort Matter? Measuring Peer Effects in College Achievement." National Bureau of Economic Research Working Paper 14032.

Carter, Prudence L. 2005. *Keepin' It Real: School Success beyond Black and White.* New York: Oxford University Press.

Charles, Camille Z., Gniesha Dinwiddie, and Douglas S. Massey. 2004. "The Continuing Consequences of Segregation: Family Stress and College Academic Performance." *Social Science Quarterly* 85:1353–73.

Clampet-Lundquist, Susan, and Douglas S. Massey. 2008. "Neighborhood Effects on Economic Self-Sufficiency: A Reconsideration of the Moving to Opportunity Experiment." *American Journal of Sociology* 114:107–43.

Cloward, Richard A., and Lloyd E. Ohlin. 1960. *Delinquency and Opportunity: A Theory of Delinquent Gangs.* New York: Free Press.

Comey, Jennifer, Xavier de Souza Briggs, and Gretchen Weismann. 2008. "Struggling to Stay out of High-Poverty Neighborhoods: Lessons from the Moving to Opportunity Experiment." Three-City Study of Moving to Opportunity Brief 6. Urban Institute Metropolitan Housing and Communities Center, March.

Conley, Dalton. 2001. "Capital for College: Parental Assets and Postsecondary Schooling." *Sociology of Education* 74:59–72.

Cook, Phillip, and Jens Ludwig. 1998. "The Burden of 'Acting White': Do Black Adolescents Disparage Academic Achievement?" In *The Black-White Test Score Gap,* ed. Christopher Jencks and Meredith Phillips, 375–401. Washington, DC: Brookings Institution Press.

Cook, Thomas D., Shobha C. Shagle, and Serdar M. Degirmencioglu. 1997. "Capturing Social Process for Testing Mediational Models of Neighborhood Effects." In *Neighborhood Poverty,* vol. 2, *Policy Implications in Studying Neighborhoods,* ed. Jeanne Brooks-Gunn, Greg J. Duncan, and J. Lawrence Aber, 94–119. New York: Russell Sage.

Coulton, Claudia J., Jill Korbin, Tsui Chan, and Marilyn Su. 2001. "Mapping Residents' Perceptions of Neighborhood Boundaries: A Methodological Note." *American Journal of Community Psychology* 29:371–83.

Cove, Elizabeth, Xavier de Souza Briggs, Margery Austin Turner, and Cynthia Duarte. 2008. "Can Escaping from Poor Neighborhoods Increase Employment and Earnings?" Three-City Study of Moving to Opportunity Brief 4. Urban Institute Metropolitan Housing and Communities Center, March.

Crane, Jonathan. 1991. "The Epidemic Theory of Ghettos and Neighborhood Effects on Dropping Out and Teenage Childbearing." *American Journal of Sociology* 96:1226–59.

Dance, L. Janelle. 2002. *Tough Fronts: The Impact of Street Culture on Schooling.* New York: RoutledgeFalmer Press.

DeLuca, Stephanie, and Robert Bozick. 2005. "Better Late than Never? Delayed Enrollment in the High School to College Transition." *Social Forces* 84:531–54.

DiMaggio, Paul. 1982. "Cultural Capital and School Success: The Impact of Status Culture Participation of the Grades of U.S. High School Students." *American Sociological Review* 47:189–201.

———. 1997. "Culture and Cognition." *Annual Review of Sociology* 23:263–87.

Dohan, Daniel. 2003. *The Price of Poverty: Money, Work, and Culture in the Mexican American Barrio.* Berkeley: University of California Press.

Du Bois, W. E. B. 1899. *The Philadelphia Negro: A Social Study.* Reprint. Philadelphia: University of Pennsylvania Press, 1996.

Duneier, Mitchell. 1992. *Slim's Table: Race, Respectability, and Masculinity.* Chicago: University of Chicago Press.

Eccles, Jacquelynne S., M. N. Vida, and Bonnie Barber. 2004. "The Relation of Early Adolescents' College Plans and Both Academic Ability and Task-Value Beliefs to Subsequent College Enrollment." *Journal of Early Adolescence* 24:63–77.

Edelman, Peter, Harry Holzer, and Paul Offner. 2005. *Reconnecting Disadvantaged Young Men.* Washington, DC: Urban Institute Press.

Eder, Donna, and Laura Fingerson. 2003. "Interviewing Children and Adolescents." In *Inside Interviewing: New Lenses, New Concerns,* ed. James A. Holstein and Jaber F. Gubrium, 33–54. New York: Sage Publications.

Edin, Kathryn, and Maria Kefalas. 2005. *Promises I Can Keep: Why Poor Women Put Motherhood before Marriage.* Berkeley: University of California Press.

Ensminger, Margaret E., Rebecca P. Lamkin, and Nora Jacobsen. 1996. "School Leaving: A Longitudinal Perspective Including Neighborhood Effects." *Child Development* 67:2400–2416.

Ensminger, Margaret E., and Anita L. Slusarcick. 1992. "Paths to High School Graduation or Dropout: A Longitudinal Study of a First-Grade Cohort." *Sociology of Education* 65:95–113.

Erickson, Bonnie. 1996. "Culture, Class and Connections." *American Journal of Sociology* 102:217–51.

Fernandez, Roberto M., and David Harris. 1992. "Social Isolation and the Underclass." In *Drugs, Crime, and Social Isolation: Barriers to Urban Opportunity,* ed. Adele V. Harrell and George E. Peterson, 257–93. Washington, DC: Urban Institute Press.

Ferryman, Kadija, Xavier de Souza Briggs, Susan J. Popkin, and Maria Rendon. 2008. "Do Better Neighborhoods for MTO Families Mean Better Schools?" Three-City Study of Moving to Opportunity Brief 3. Urban Institute Metropolitan Housing and Communities Center, March.

Fischer, Claude S. 1975. "Toward a Subcultural Theory of Urbanism." *American Journal of Sociology* 80:1319–41.

———. 1982. *To Dwell among Friends: Personal Networks in Town and City.* Chicago: University of Chicago Press.

———. 1995. "The Subcultural Theory of Urbanism: A Twentieth-Year Assessment," *American Journal of Sociology* 101:543–77.

Fordham, Signithia, and John Ogbu. 1986. "Black Students' School Success: Coping with the Burden of 'Acting White.'" *Urban Review* 18:176–206.

Fortenberry, J. Dennis, Wanzhu Tu, Jaroslaw Harezlak, Barry P. Katz, and Donald P. Orr. 2002. "Condom Use as a Function of Time in New and Established Adolescent Sexual Relationships." *American Journal of Public Health* 92:211–13.

Franklin, Clyde W. 1982. "Black Male–Black Female Conflict: Individually Cursed and Culturally Nurtured." *Journal of Black Studies* 15:139–54.

Fuller, Bruce, Susan D. Holloway, Marylee F. Rambaud, and Constanza Eggers-Pierola. 1996. "How Do Mothers Choose Child Care? Alternative Cultural Models in Poor Neighborhoods." *Sociology of Education* 69:83–104.

Furstenberg, Frank, Jr. 1993. "How Families Manage Risk and Opportunity in Dangerous Neighborhoods." In *Sociology and the Public Agenda,* ed. William Julius Wilson, 231–58. Newbury Park, CA: Sage.

Furstenberg, Frank, Jr., and Mary Elizabeth Hughes. 1997. "The Influence of Neighborhoods on Children's Development: A Theoretical Perspective and Research Agenda." In *Neighborhood Poverty,* vol. 2, *Policy Implications in Studying Neighborhoods,* ed. Jeanne Brooks-Gunn, Greg J. Duncan, and J. Lawrence Aber, 23–47. New York: Russell Sage.

Furstenberg, Frank F., Jr., Thomas D. Cook, Jacquelynne Eccles, Glen H. Elder, Jr., and Arnold

Sameroff, eds. 1999. *Managing to Make It: Urban Families and Adolescent Success.* Chicago: University of Chicago Press.

Gamm, Gerald. 1999. *Urban Exodus: Why the Jews Left Boston and the Catholics Stayed.* Cambridge, MA: Harvard University Press.

Gans, Herbert. 1962. *Urban Villagers.* New York: Free Press.

——. 1967. *The Levittowners: Ways of Life and Politics in a New Suburban Community.* New York: Columbia University Press.

Garbarino, James, Kathleen Kostelny, and Nancy Dubrow. 1991. "What Children Can Tell Us about Living in Danger." *American Psychologist* 46:376–83.

Garnier, Helen E., Judith A. Stein, and Jennifer K. Jacobs. 1997. "The Process of Dropping Out of High School: A 19-Year Perspective." *American Educational Research Journal* 34:395–419.

Gaviria, Alejandro, and Steven Raphael. 2001. "School-Based Peer Effects and Juvenile Behavior." *Review of Economics and Statistics* 83:257–68.

Geronimus, Arline T. 1996. "Black/White Differences in the Relationship of Maternal Age to Birthweight: A Population-Based Test of the Weathering Hypothesis." *Social Science and Medicine* 42:589–97.

Ginther, Donna, Robert Haveman, and Barbara Wolfe. 2000. "Neighborhood Attributes as Determinants of Children's Outcomes: How Robust Are the Relationships?" *Journal of Human Resources* 35:603–42.

Giordano, Peggy C., Monica A. Longmore, and Wendy D. Manning. 2006. "Gender and the Meaning of Adolescent Romantic Relationships." *American Sociological Review* 71:260–87.

Goering, John, and Judith D. Feins. 2003. *Choosing a Better Life: Evaluating the Moving to Opportunity Experiment.* Washington, DC: Urban Institute Press.

Goffman, Erving. 1959. *The Presentation of Self in Everyday Life.* Garden City, NY: Doubleday.

——. 1974. *Frame Analysis.* Cambridge, MA: Harvard University Press.

Goldenberg, Claude, Ronald Gallimore, Leslie Reese, and Helen Garnier. 2001. "Cause or Effect? A Longitudinal Study of Immigrant Latino Parents' Aspirations and Expectations, and Their Children's School Performance." *American Educational Research Journal* 38:547–82.

Grannis, Rick. 1998. "The Importance of Trivial Streets: Residential Streets and Residential Segregation." *American Journal of Sociology* 103:1530–64.

Greenbaum, Susan D., and Paul E. Greenbaum. 1985. "The Ecology of Social Networks in Four Urban Neighborhoods." *Social Networks* 7:47–76.

Hagedorn, John M. 1988. *People and Folks: Gangs, Crime, and the Underclass in a Rustbelt City.* Chicago: Lake View Press.

Hannerz, Ulf. 1969. *Soulside: Inquiries into Ghetto Culture and Community.* New York: Columbia University Press.

Hanushek, Eric A., John F. Kain, Jacob M. Markman, and Steven Rivkin. 2003. "Does Peer Ability Affect Student Achievement?" *Journal of Applied Econometrics* 18:527–44.

Harding, David J. 2003. "Counterfactual Models of Neighborhood Effects: The Effect of Neighborhood Poverty on Dropping Out and Teenage Pregnancy." *American Journal of Sociology* 109:676–719.

——. 2007. "Cultural Context, Sexual Behavior, and Romantic Relationships in Disadvantaged Neighborhoods." *American Sociological Review* 72:341–64.

———. 2008. "Neighborhood Violence and Adolescent Friendships." *International Journal of Conflict and Violence* 2:28–55.

———. 2009a. "Collateral Consequences of Violence in Disadvantaged Neighborhoods." *Social Forces* 88 (2).

———. 2009b. "Neighborhood Cultural Heterogeneity, College Goals, and College Enrollment." Research Report 09-682, Population Studies Center, University of Michigan.

———. 2009c. "Violence, Older Peers, and the Socialization of Adolescent Boys in Disadvantaged Neighborhoods." *American Sociological Review* 74:445–64.

Harris, Kathleen Mullan, Francesca Florey, Joyce Tabor, Peter S. Bearman, Jo Jones, and J. Richard Udry. 2003. "The National Longitudinal Study of Adolescent Health: Research Design." Carolina Population Center, University of North Carolina. http://www.cpc.unc.edu/projects/addhealth/design.

Hayes, Sharon. 2003. *Flat Broke with Children: Women in the Age of Welfare Reform.* New York: Oxford University Press.

Haynie, Dana L. 2001. "Delinquent Peers Revisited: Does Network Structure Matter?" *American Journal of Sociology* 106:1013–57.

Haynie, Dana L., and Wayne D. Osgood. 2005. "Reconsidering Peers and Delinquency: How Do Peers Matter?" *Social Forces* 84:1109–30.

Heckman, James J., and Paul A. LaFontaine. 2006. "Bias-Corrected Estimates of GED Returns." *Journal of Labor Economics* 24:661–700.

Hochschild, Jennifer L. 1995. *Facing Up to the American Dream: Race, Class, and the Soul of the Nation.* Princeton, NJ: Princeton University Press.

Holloway, Susan D., Bruce Fuller, Marylee F. Rambaud, and Constanza Eggers-Pierola. 1997. *Through My Own Eyes: Single Mothers and the Cultures of Poverty.* Cambridge, MA: Harvard University Press.

Horowitz, Ruth. 1983. *Honor and the American Dream: Culture and Identity in a Chicano Community.* New Brunswick, NJ: Rutgers University Press.

Hunter, Albert. 1974. *The Image of the City: The Persistence and Change of Chicago's Local Communities.* Chicago: University of Chicago Press.

Jackson, John L. 2001. *Harlemworld: Doing Race and Class in Contemporary Black America.* Chicago: University of Chicago Press.

Jargowsky, Paul A. 1997. *Poverty and Place: Ghettos, Barrios, and the American City.* New York: Russell Sage.

———. 2003. *Stunning Progress, Hidden Problems: The Dramatic Decline of Concentrated Poverty in the 1990s.* Living Cities Census Series, Center on Urban and Metropolitan Studies. Washington, DC: Brookings Institution Press.

Jargowsky, Paul A., and Mary Jo Bane. 1991. "Ghetto Poverty in the United States, 1970–1980." In *The Urban Underclass,* ed. Christopher Jencks and Paul E. Peterson, 235–73. Washington, DC: Brookings Institution Press.

Jarrett, Robin L. 1997a. "African American Family and Parenting Strategies in Impoverished Neighborhoods." *Qualitative Sociology* 20:275–88.

———. 1997b. "Bringing Families Back In: Neighborhood Effects on Child Development." In *Neighborhood Poverty,* vol. 2, *Policy Implications in Studying Neighborhoods,* ed. Jeanne Brooks-Gunn, Greg J. Duncan, and J. Lawrence Aber, 48–64. New York: Russell Sage.

Jencks, Christopher, and Susan E. Mayer. 1990a. "Residential Segregation, Job Proximity, and Black Job Opportunities: The Empirical Status of the Spatial Mismatch Hypothesis." In *Inner-City Poverty in the United States,* ed. Lawrence E. Lynn, Jr., and Michael G. H. McGreary, 187–222. Washington, DC: National Academy Press.

——. 1990b. "The Social Consequences of Growing Up in a Poor Neighborhood." In *Inner-City Poverty in the United States,* ed. Lawrence E. Lynn, Jr., and Michael G. H. McGreary, 111–86. Washington, DC: National Academy Press.

Juster, F. Thomas, and Frank P. Stafford, eds. 1985. *Time, Goods, and Well-Being.* Ann Arbor: Institute for Social Research, University of Michigan.

Kadushin, Charles, and Delmos J. Jones. 1992. "Social Networks and Urban Neighborhoods in New York City." *City and Society* 6:58–75.

Kane, Thomas J. 2004. "College Going and Inequality." In *Social Inequality,* ed. Kathryn M. Neckerman, 319–54. New York: Russell Sage.

Katz, Jack, and Curtis Jackson-Jacobs. 2003. "The Criminologists' Gang." In *Blackwell Companion to Criminology,* ed. Colin Sumner, 91–124. Malden, MA: Blackwell Publishers.

Kefalas, Maria. 2003. *Working-Class Heroes: Protecting Home, Community, and Nation in a Chicago Neighborhood.* Berkeley: University of California Press.

Keller, Suzanne. 1968. *The Urban Neighborhood: A Sociological Perspective.* New York: Random House.

Kling, Jeffrey R., Jeffrey B. Liebman, and Lawrence Katz. 2007. "Experimental Analysis of Neighborhood Effects." *Econometrica* 75:83–119.

Kling, Jeffrey R., Jens Ludwig, and Lawrence Katz. 2005. "Neighborhood Effects on Crime for Male and Female Youth: Evidence from a Randomized Housing Voucher Experiment." *Quarterly Journal of Economics* 120:87–130.

Kornhauser, Ruth R. 1978. *Social Sources of Delinquency.* Chicago: University of Chicago Press.

Ku, Leighton, Freya L. Sonenstein, and Joseph H. Pleck. 1994. "The Dynamics of Young Men's Condom Use during and across Relationships." *Family Planning Perspectives* 26:246–51.

Lamont, Michèle. 1992. *Money, Morals, and Manners: The Culture of the French and the American Upper-Middle Class.* Chicago: University of Chicago Press.

——. 2000. *The Dignity of Working Men: Morality and the Boundaries of Race, Class, and Immigration.* Cambridge, MA: Harvard University Press.

Lamont, Michèle, and Annette Lareau. 1988. "Cultural Capital: Allusions, Gaps, and Glissandos in Recent Theoretical Developments." *Sociological Theory* 6:153–68.

Lamont, Michèle, and Viràg Molnár. 2002. "The Study of Boundaries across the Social Sciences." *Annual Review of Sociology* 28:167–95.

Lamont, Michèle, and Laurent Thévenot. 2000. *Rethinking Comparative Cultural Sociology: Repertoires of Evaluation in France and the United States.* Cambridge: Cambridge University Press.

Lareau, Annette. 2000. *Home Advantage: Social Class and Parental Intervention in Elementary Education.* Second edition. Lanham, MD: Rowan and Littlefield.

——. 2003. *Unequal Childhoods: Class, Race, and Family Life.* Berkeley: University of California Press.

Larson, Reed. 1989. "Beeping Children and Adolescents: A Method for Studying Time Use and Daily Experience." *Journal of Youth and Adolescence* 18:511–30.

Laumann, Edward O., Stephen Ellingson, Jenna Mahay, Anthony Paik, and Yoosik Youm, eds. 2004. *The Sexual Organization of the City.* Chicago: University of Chicago Press.

Lee, Barret A., and Karen E. Campbell. 1999. "Neighbor Networks of Black and White Americans." In *Networks in the Global Village: Life in Contemporary Communities,* ed. Barry Wellman, 119–46. Boulder, CO: Westview Press.

Lewis, Oscar. 1966. *La Vida: A Puerto Rican Family in the Culture of Poverty—San Juan and New York.* New York: Random House.

———. 1969. "The Culture of Poverty." In *On Understanding Poverty: Perspectives from the Social Sciences,* ed. Daniel Patrick Moynihan, 187–200. New York: Basic Books.

Liebow, Elliot. 1967. *Tally's Corner: A Study of Negro Streetcorner Men.* Boston: Little, Brown.

Lofland, John, and Lyn Lofland. 1995. *Analyzing Social Settings: A Guide to Qualitative Observation and Analysis.* Belmont, CA: Wadsworth.

Ludwig, Jens, Greg J. Duncan, and Paul Hirschfield. 2001. "Urban Poverty and Juvenile Crime: Evidence from a Randomized Housing Mobility Experiment." *Quarterly Journal of Economics* 116:655–80.

Ludwig, Jens, Jeffrey B. Liebman, Jeffrey R. Kling, Greg J. Duncan, Lawrence F. Katz, Ronald C. Kessler, and Lisa Sanbonmatsu. 2008. "What Can We Learn about Neighborhood Effects from the Moving to Opportunity Experiment?" *American Journal of Sociology* 114:144–88.

Lynch, Kevin. 1960. *The Image of the City.* Cambridge, MA: MIT Press.

MacLeod, Jay. 1995. *Ain't No Makin' It: Aspirations and Attainment in a Low-Income Neighborhood.* Boulder, CO: Westview Press.

Margolin, Gayla, and Elana B. Gordis. 2000. "The Effects of Family and Community Violence on Children." *Annual Review of Psychology* 51:445–79.

Marsden, Peter V. 1987. "Core Discussion Networks of Americans." *American Sociological Review* 52:122–31.

Massey, Douglas S. 2004. "Segregation and Stratification: A Biosocial Perspective." *Du Bois Review* 1:7–25.

Massey, Douglas S., and Nancy Denton. 1993. *American Apartheid: Segregation and the Making of an Underclass.* Cambridge, MA: Harvard University Press.

Massey, Douglas S., and Mary J. Fischer. 2006. "The Effect of Childhood Segregation on Minority Academic Performance at Selective Colleges." *Ethnic and Racial Studies* 29:1–26.

Matsueda, Ross L., and Kathleen Anderson. 1998. "The Dynamics of Delinquent Peers and Delinquent Behavior." *Criminology* 26:269–308.

Maxwell, Kimberly A. 2002. "Friends: The Role of Peer Influence across Adolescent Risk Behaviors." *Journal of Youth and Adolescence* 13:267–77.

McRoberts, Omar M. 2003. *Streets of Glory: Church and Community in a Black Urban Neighborhood.* Chicago: University of Chicago Press.

Morenoff, Jeffrey D., Robert J. Sampson, and Stephen W. Raudenbush. 2001. "Neighborhood Inequality, Collective Efficacy, and the Spatial Dynamics of Urban Violence." *Criminology* 39:517–59.

Murnane, Richard J., John B. Willet, and Kevin P. Boudett. 1995. "Do High-School Dropouts Benefit from Obtaining a GED?" *Educational Evaluation and Policy Analysis* 17:133–47.

———. 1997. "Does a GED Lead to More Training, Post-secondary Education, and Military Service for High School Dropouts?" *Industrial and Labor Relations Review* 51:100–116.

———. 1999. "Do Male Dropouts Benefit from Obtaining a GED, Post-secondary Education, and Training?" *Evaluation Review* 23:475–503.

Newman, Katherine S. 1992. "Culture and Structure in *The Truly Disadvantaged.*" *City and Society* 6:3–25.

———. 1999. *No Shame in My Game: The Working Poor in the Inner City.* New York: Vintage and Russell Sage.

Ogbu, John U. 2004. "Collective Identity and the Burden of 'Acting White' in Black History, Community, and Education." *Urban Review* 36:1–35.

Orfield, Gary, ed. 2004. *Dropouts in America: Confronting the Graduation Rate Crisis*. Cambridge, MA: Harvard Education Press.

Orfield, Gary, and Carol Ashkinaze. 1991. *The Closing Door: Conservative Policy and Black Opportunity*. Chicago: University of Chicago Press.

Padilla, Felix M. 1992. *The Gang as an American Enterprise*. New Brunswick, NJ: Rutgers University Press.

Pager, Devah. 2003. "The Mark of a Criminal Record." *American Journal of Sociology* 108:937–75.

Park, Robert E., and Ernest W. Burgess. 1925. *The City*. Chicago: University of Chicago Press.

Patillo-McCoy, Mary. 1998. "Church Culture as a Strategy of Action in the Black Community." *American Sociological Review* 63:767–84.

———. 1999. *Black Picket Fences: Privilege and Peril among the Black Middle Class*. Chicago: University of Chicago Press.

Patterson, Orlando. 1998. *The Ordeal of Integration*. New York: Basic Civitas.

Popkin, Susan J., Tama Leventhal, and Gretchen Weismann. 2008. "Girls in the 'Hood: The Importance of Feeling Safe." Three-City Study of Moving to Opportunity Brief 1. Urban Institute Metropolitan Housing and Communities Center, March.

Portes, Alejandro, ed. 1995. *The Economic Sociology of Immigration: Essays on Networks, Ethnicity, and Entrepreneurship*. New York: Russell Sage.

———, ed. 1996. *The New Second Generation*. New York: Russell Sage.

———. 1998. "Social Capital: Its Origins and Applications in Modern Sociology." *Annual Review of Sociology* 24:1–24.

Portes, Alejandro, and Patricia Landolt. 1996. "The Downside of Social Capital." *American Prospect* 26 (May–June): 18–22.

Portes, Alejandro, and Min Zhou. 1993. "The New Second Generation: Segmented Assimilation and Its Variants." *Annals of the American Academy of Political and Social Science* 530:74–96.

Quillian, Lincoln. 1999. "Migration Patterns and the Growth of High-Poverty Neighborhoods, 1970–1990." *American Journal of Sociology* 105:1–37.

Quinn, Naomi, and Dorothy Holland. 1987. "Culture and Cognition." In *Cultural Models in Language and Thought*, ed. Dorothy Holland and Naomi Quinn, 3–40. Cambridge: Cambridge University Press.

Rainwater, Lee. 1970. *Behind Ghetto Walls: Black Families in a Federal Slum*. Chicago: Aldine.

Rankin, Bruce H., and James M. Quane. 2000. "Neighborhood Poverty and the Social Isolation of Inner-City African American Families." *Social Forces* 79:139–64.

Raudenbush, Stephen W., Chris Johnson, and Robert J. Sampson. 2003. "A Multivariate, Multilevel Rasch Model with Application to Self-Reported Criminal Behavior." *Sociological Methodology* 33:169–211.

Robinson, John P. 1977. *How Americans Used Time in 1965*. Ann Arbor, MI: Institute for Social Research.

Rodman, Hyman. 1963. "The Lower-Class Value Stretch." *Social Forces* 42:205–15.

Rubinowitz, Leonard S., and James E. Rosenbaum. 2000. *Crossing the Class and Color Lines: From Public Housing to White Suburbia*. Chicago: University of Chicago Press.

Rumberger, Russell W. 1987. "High School Dropouts: A Review of Issues and Evidence." *Review of Educational Research* 57:101–21.

——. 1995. "Dropping Out of Middle School: A Multi-level Analysis of Students and Schools." *American Educational Research Journal* 32:583–625.

——. 2004. "Why Students Drop Out of High School." In *Dropouts in America: Confronting the Graduation Rate Crisis*, ed. Gary Orfield, 131–56. Cambridge, MA: Harvard Education Press.

Sacerdote, Bruce. 2001. "Peer Effects with Random Assignment: Results for Dartmouth Roommates." *Quarterly Journal of Economics* 116:681–704.

Sampson, Robert J. 2008. "Moving to Inequality: Neighborhood Effects and Experiments Meet Social Structure." *American Journal of Sociology* 114:189–231.

Sampson, Robert J., and Jeffrey D. Morenoff. 1997. "Ecological Perspectives on the Neighborhood Context of Urban Poverty: Past and Present." In *Neighborhood Poverty*, vol. 2, *Policy Implications in Studying Neighborhoods*, ed. Jeanne Brooks-Gunn, Greg J. Duncan, and J. Lawrence Aber, 1–22. New York: Russell Sage.

Sampson, Robert J., Jeffrey D. Morenoff, and Felton Earls. 1999. "Beyond Social Capital: Spatial Dynamics and Collective Efficacy for Children." *American Sociological Review* 64:633–60.

Sampson, Robert J., and Stephen Raudenbush. 1999. "Systematic Social Observation of Public Spaces: A New Look at Disorder in Urban Neighborhoods." *American Journal of Sociology* 105:603–51.

Sampson, Robert J., Stephen Raudenbush, and Felton Earls. 1997. "Neighborhoods and Violent Crime: A Multilevel Study of Collective Efficacy." *Science* 227:918–24.

Sampson, Robert J., and William Julius Wilson. 1995. "Toward a Theory of Race, Crime, and Urban Inequality." In *Crime and Inequality*, ed. John Hagan and Ruth Peterson, 37–56. Stanford, CA: Stanford University Press.

Sanbonmatsu, Lisa, Jeffrey R. Kling, Greg J. Duncan, and Jeanne Brooks-Gunn. 2006. "Neighborhoods and Academic Achievement: Results from the Moving to Opportunity Experiment." *Journal of Human Resources* 41:649–91.

Sánchez-Jankowski, Martín. 1991. *Islands in the Street: Gangs and American Urban Society.* Berkeley: University of California Press.

——. 2008. *Cracks in the Pavement: Social Change and Resilience in Poor Neighborhoods.* Berkeley: University of California Press.

Sandefur, Gary D., Ann Meier, and Mary Campbell. 2006. "Family Resources, Social Capital, and College Attendance." *Social Science Research* 35:525–53.

Schudson, Michael. 1989. "How Culture Works: Perspectives from Media Studies on the Efficacy of Symbols." *Theory and Society* 18:153–80.

Sewell, William. 1992. "A Theory of Structure: Duality, Agency, and Transformation." *American Journal of Sociology* 98:1–29.

——. 1999. "The Concept(s) of Culture." In *Beyond the Cultural Turn*, ed. Victoria E. Bonnell and Lynn Hunt, 35–61. Berkeley: University of California Press.

Shaw, Clifford R. 1929. *Delinquency Areas.* Chicago: University of Chicago Press.

Shaw, Clifford R., and Henry D. McKay. 1969. *Juvenile Delinquency and Urban Areas.* Revised edition. Chicago: University of Chicago Press.

Short, James F., Jr., and Fred L. Strodtbeck. 1965. *Group Process and Gang Delinquency.* Chicago: University of Chicago Press.

Skogan, Wesley G. 1992. *Disorder and Decline.* Berkeley: University of California Press.

Small, Mario L. 2002. "Culture, Cohorts, and Social Organization Theory: Understanding Local Participation in a Latino Housing Project." *American Journal of Sociology* 108:1–54.

———. 2004. *Villa Victoria: The Transformation of Social Capital in a Boston Barrio.* Chicago: University of Chicago Press.

Small, Mario L., and Monica McDermott. 2006. "The Presence of Organizational Resources in Poor Urban Neighborhoods: An Analysis of Average and Contextual Effects." *Social Forces* 84:1697–1724.

Small, Mario L., and Katherine S. Newman. 2001. "Urban Poverty after the Truly Disadvantaged: The Rediscovery of the Family, the Neighborhood, and Culture." *Annual Review of Sociology* 27:23–45.

Small, Mario L., and Laura Stark. 2005. "Are Poor Neighborhoods Resource-Deprived? A Case Study of Childcare Centers in New York." *Social Science Quarterly* 86:1013–36.

Smith, Robert B. 1972. "Neighborhood Context and College Plans: An Ordinal Path Analysis." *Social Forces* 51:199–217.

Smith, Thomas M. 2003. "Who Values the GED? An Examination of the Paradox Underlying the Demand for the General Educational Development Credential." *Teachers College Record* 105:375–415.

Sobo, Elisa J. 1995. *Choosing Unsafe Sex: AIDS-Risk Denial among Disadvantaged Women.* Philadelphia: University of Pennsylvania Press.

Solorzano, Daniel G. 1992. "An Exploratory Analysis of the Effects of Race, Class and Gender on Student and Parent Mobility Aspirations." *Journal of Negro Education* 61:30–44.

South, Scott J., and Eric P. Baumer. 2000. "Deciphering Community and Race Effects on Adolescent Premarital Childbearing." *Social Forces* 78:1379–1407.

South, Scott J., and Kyle D. Crowder. 1999. "Neighborhood Effects on Family Formation: Concentrated Poverty and Beyond." *American Sociological Review* 64:113–32.

Stack, Carol. 1974. *All Our Kin.* New York: Basic Books.

Sugrue, Thomas J. 1996. *The Origins of the Urban Crisis: Race and Inequality in Post-war Detroit.* Princeton, NJ: Princeton University Press.

Sullivan, Mercer. 1989. *Getting Paid: Youth, Crime, and Work in the Inner City.* Ithaca, NY: Cornell University Press.

Suttles, Gerald. 1968. *The Social Order of the Slum: Ethnicity and Territory in the Inner City.* Chicago: University of Chicago Press.

———. 1972. *The Social Construction of Communities.* Chicago: University of Chicago Press.

Swaroop, Sapna, and Jeffrey D. Morenoff. 2006. "Building Community: The Neighborhood Context of Social Organization." *Social Forces* 84:1665–95.

Swidler, Ann. 1986. "Culture in Action: Symbols and Strategies." *American Sociological Review* 51:273–86.

———. 2001. *Talk of Love.* Chicago: University of Chicago Press.

Thrasher, Frederic M. 1927. *The Gang: A Study of 1313 Gangs in Chicago.* Chicago: University of Chicago Press.

Tienda, Marta. 1991. "Poor People and Poor Places: Deciphering Neighborhood Effects on Poverty Outcomes." In *Macro-Micro Linkages in Sociology,* ed. J. Haber, 244–62. New York: Sage.

Tigges, Leann M., Irene Browne, and Gary P. Green. 1998. "Social Isolation of the Urban Poor: Race, Class, and Neighborhood Effects in Social Resources." *Sociological Quarterly* 39:53–77.

Tilly, Charles. 1978. *From Mobilization to Revolution.* Reading, MA: Addison Wesley.

Timberlake, Jeffrey M. 2007. "Racial and Ethnic Inequality in the Duration of Children's Exposure to Neighborhood Poverty and Affluence." *Social Problems* 54:319–42.

Turley, Ruth N. Lopez. 2001. *Neighborhood Effects on Children: Mechanisms, Interactions, and Relative Deprivation.* Ph.D. dissertation, Department of Sociology, Harvard University.

———. 2003. "When Do Neighborhoods Matter? The Role of Race and Neighborhood Peers." *Social Science Research* 32:61–79.

Tyler, John H. 2003. "The Economic Benefits of the GED: Lessons from Recent Research." *Review of Educational Research* 73:369–403.

———. 2004. "Does the GED Improve Earnings? Estimates from a Sample of Both Successful and Unsuccessful GED Candidates." *Industrial and Labor Relations Review* 57:579–98.

Tyler, John H., Richard J. Murnane, and John B. Willet. 2000. "Estimating the Labor Market Signaling Value of the GED." *Quarterly Journal of Economics* 115:431–68.

———. 2003. "Who Benefits from a GED? Evidence for Females from High School and Beyond." *Economics of Education Review* 22:237–47.

Vale, Lawrence J. 2002. *Reclaiming Public Housing: A Half Century of Struggle in Three Public Neighborhoods.* Cambridge, MA: Harvard University Press.

Valentine, Charles A. 1968. *Culture and Poverty: Critique and Counter-proposals.* Chicago: University of Chicago Press.

Venezia, Andrea, and Michael W. Kirst. 2005. "Inequitable Opportunities: How Current Education Systems and Policies Undermine the Chances for Student Persistence and Success in College." *Educational Policy* 19:283–307.

Venkatesh, Sudhir A. 2000. *American Project.* Chicago: University of Chicago Press.

Wacquant, Loic. 2002. "Scrutinizing the Street: Poverty, Morality, and the Pitfalls of Urban Ethnography." *American Journal of Sociology* 107:1468–1532.

Waldinger, Roger. 1996. *Still the Promised City? African Americans and New Immigrants in Postindustrial New York.* Cambridge, MA: Harvard University Press.

Waller, Maureen R. 2002. *My Baby's Father: Unmarried Parents and Paternal Responsibility.* Ithaca, NY: Cornell University Press.

Wellman, Barry, ed. 1999. *Networks in the Global Village: Life in Contemporary Communities.* Boulder, CO: Westview Press.

Western, Bruce. 2006. *Punishment and Inequality in America.* New York: Russell Sage.

Whyte, William. 1943. *Streetcorner Society.* Chicago: University of Chicago Press.

Willis, Paul. 1977. *Learning to Labor.* New York: Columbia University Press.

Wilson, William Julius. 1987. *The Truly Disadvantaged: The Inner-City, the Underclass, and Public Policy.* Chicago: University of Chicago Press.

———. 1996. *When Work Disappears: The World of the New Urban Poor.* New York: Knopf.

Winship, Christopher. 2004. "The End of a Miracle? Crime, Faith, and Partnership in Boston in the 1990's." In *Long March Ahead: The Public Influences of African American Churches,* ed. R. Drew Smith, 171–92. Durham, NC: Duke University Press.

Yinger, John 1995. *Closed Doors, Opportunities Lost: The Continuing Costs of Housing Discrimination.* New York: Russell Sage.

Young, Alford A., Jr. 2004. *The Minds of Marginalized Black Men: Making Sense of Mobility, Opportunity, and Life Chances.* Princeton, NJ: Princeton University Press.

Zimmerman, David J. 2003. "Peer Effects in Academic Outcomes: Evidence from a Natural Experiment." *Review of Economics and Statistics* 85:9–23.

INDEX

Crowder, K. D., 272n11
cultural authority, of the old head, 105
cultural capital theory, 286n8, 290n1
cultural context (cultural milieu), 239–40;
and adolescent decision making, 134;
of poor neighborhoods, 5, 18–19, 26,
139, 141, 155, 239–40, 242, 251; of
urban neighborhoods, 245–46
cultural heterogeneity, 140–44, 146, 148–
49, 152–56, 158–61, 164, 172, 176,
200–202, 205, 226, 229, 236–38, 240,
242–47, 251, 289n32, 290n1; effect on
parents, 231; in educational decision
making by adolescent boys, 6, 237–38;
negative effects, 5; of poor neighborhoods, xi, 3, 19, 26, 134–35, 138
cultural models, 141, 143–50, 154–60,
194, 201–2, 239, 247, 289n30; about
careers and education, 229; alternative,
5–6, 19, 135–36, 150–51, 236, 238,
243–44, 288n26; mainstream or conventional, 200; multiple, 134, 147–49,
158, 194, 205, 233, 245
cultural power, five dimensions, 288n23
culture, 12, 136–44; as frame or script,
142–47, 154–60; as repertoire, 142,
144, 146, 148–49, 155, 245–47; effect
on behavior, 140; ghetto-specific, 5–6,
109, 134–39, 150, 243; in scholarship
on urban poverty, x, 5, 134; mainstream, 135, 242; traditional view in
urban sociology literature, 145

Dance, L. J., 250, 279n20
death, 56–57, 64
Degirmencioglu, S. M., 11
delinquency, 3, 71
Denton, N., x, 271n6, 134
desegregation, 12
Detroit, 43
dilution, as a negative effect of cultural
heterogeneity, 5, 157–59, 161, 186, 194,
203, 226, 229, 233–34, 236, 238, 242,
245
discrimination, 17, 138, 141, 245, 272n6.
See also racial discrimination

diversity, 76, 140, 148–49, 154–55, 159,
261
Drake, St. Clair, ix
drama, as system of neighborhood-based
rivalries and conflict, 18–19, 30–31,
34, 41, 85
drugs, 55, 59
drug abuse, 71
drug addicts, 60–61, 99, 127, 193, 220–21;
not negative role models, 60–61
drug dealers, 1–2, 24, 33, 43–45, 56, 147,
220, 288n25; as negative role models,
60–61, 105–6
drug dealing, 1, 53–54, 60–61, 65, 77, 88,
125, 153
drug economy, underground, 278n13, 149
drug turf, 278n14, 54
Du Bois, W. E. B., ix
Duke University, 227, 229
Duncan, G. J., 272n11
Duneier, M., 150

Earls, F., 11, 150
economy, underground, x, 3, 91, 106
Edin, K., 147, 197, 285n1
education, 139, 141, 145, 147, 151, 247,
250–51; choices and issues, 5, 43, 72;
postsecondary, 35, 207, 226, 230–31,
243, 250
educational models, frames, and scripts,
153, 204, 216, 238; multiple, 204, 233,
243
educational performance, racial differences, 138
educational programs, 116
employment, 3, 8–9, 199
English, standard, 138
ethnicity, 16–17, 265
ethnography: neighborhood, 14, 29, 261;
urban, 150
expectations, leveled, 4, 7, 18, 25, 54–55,
57–58; on the part of parents, 61

faithfulness, in relationships, 169–70
family, conventional or traditional models,
191, 251

father absence, and influence of older
peers, 96–98, 104
fatherhood, 14, 160, 193–94, 203, 287n13;
and status, 152, 188; as opportunity,
189; avoiding, 42, 59, 65; being tricked
into it, 173–74, 184, 187, 199–200; conventional scripts, 249; early (teenage),
106, 147, 153, 183, 190, 195, 202, 250;
frames for, 188, 190, 197, 202; models
of, 194–96, 198–200; responsible, 6, 19,
192, 201, 242–43
fathers, lack of involvement, 193, 201
fears, of violence, 70
feminism, 146
Fernandez, R. M., 282n5
fertility, 18
fieldwork: challenges, 13–14; methodology, 253–70
fieldwork neighborhoods, 20–25, 254,
274n20; level of violence in, 28 (*see
also* Franklin, Lower Mills, Roxbury
Crossing)
fighting/fights, 28, 30–38, 45–47, 51–53,
73–76; for a friend, 77, 80
financial aid, for college, 153, 157, 205,
225, 227, 231–32, 235–36
Fischer, C. S., 139, 283n5, 284n13, 287n16,
291n10
Fordham, S., 138
frames and scripts: cultural, 5–6, 101,
107, 142–46, 154, 156, 160, 246–47;
for girls, 178 (*see also* stunt, gold digger,
good girl, wifey, shorty); teenage pregnancy, 154, 159
Franklin: boundaries, 112; description,
23–25, 253–54, 267; father absence
rate, 96–97; history, 275n29; map, 270;
police response, 99, 101; rate of male
joblessness, 88
Franklin Field public housing development, 23–25, 33–34, 40, 44, 46, 49, 74,
84, 112–13, 173
Franklin Hill public housing development,
23–25, 27, 30, 32–34, 39–40, 44, 46, 49,
74, 84, 112–13, 173
Franklin Park Zoo, 23

Franklin, C. W., 289n4
friendship: intensity affected by neighborhood violence, 72–81; same-age, 104,
241; same-sex, 4, 26, 130. *See also* peer
relationships, same-sex
friendship ties, 6, 117; at school, 119;
outside neighborhoods, 118; within
neighborhoods, 117, 119, 121
Fullerton, R. L., 71
Furstenberg, F., 284n11, 284n19

Gallivan Housing Development, 44–45
gangs, 36–37, 53–54, 278n15, 73; and
crime rates, 277n12; classic or street
versus corporate, 53, 278n13; nature
of, 278n13
gang conflict, 16, 274n21, 278n12
gang violence, 278n15; in Boston's inner
city, 1
gangbangers, 53, 55–56, 61, 68, 106
gangstas (gangsters), 36, 44–45, 53,
278n13, 55, 58, 280n20
Gans, Herbert, ix, 11, 14, 145, 283n5
Gates, Bill, 221
GED, 25, 116, 153, 157, 160, 190, 204, 217–
19, 222–25, 232, 237–38, 250, 289n32,
291n7, 291n8; economic returns,
290n6
gender, conventional view, 170
gender distrust, 173, 176, 178–88, 200,
202–3, 243, 249, 289n4
gender regimes, 289n2
gender roles: changes in, 201; traditional,
165
gentrification, 22
ghetto-related behaviors, 151
Ginther, D., 272n11
Giordano, P. C., 289n3
Goffman, E., 261
gold digger, 165–69, 171, 173, 176, 178,
184–85, 202, 243, 246
good girl, 166–69, 171–72, 176–78, 184
grades, 58–59, 71, 126, 159, 204–5, 227,
231, 235, 237
graffiti, 53
Grannis, R., 111